THE HI
OF TH

THE HIDDEN POWER OF THE GOSPELS

Four Questions, Four Paths, One Journey

. . .

Alexander J. Shaia

with Michelle Gaugy

HarperOne

An Imprint of HarperCollinsPublishers

THE HIDDEN POWER OF THE GOSPELS: *Four Questions, Four Paths, One Journey.* Copyright © 2010 by Alexander J. Shaia and Michelle L. Gaugy. All rights reserved. Printed in the United States of America. No part of this book may be used or reproduced in any manner whatsoever without written permission except in the case of brief quotations embodied in critical articles and reviews. For information address HarperCollins Publishers, 10 East 53rd Street, New York, NY 10022.

HarperCollins books may be purchased for educational, business, or sales promotional use. For information please write: Special Markets Department, HarperCollins Publishers, 10 East 53rd Street, New York, NY 10022.

HarperCollins Web site: http://www.harpercollins.com

HarperCollins®, 📖®, and HarperOne™ are trademarks of HarperCollins Publishers

FIRST EDITION

Library of Congress Cataloging-in-Publication Data is available upon request.
ISBN 978–0–06–189801–3

10 11 12 13 14 RRD (H) 10 9 8 7 6 5 4 3 2 1

To the many anonymous women and
men who millennia ago
heard the words, chanted the gospels,
and walked the journey

and

in memory of my Sitto Butrus and Jiddo Shaia

From this it is clear that the Word, the artificer of all things, being manifested to [all] gave us the gospel, fourfold in form but held together by one Spirit

Bishop Irenaeus of Lyons, 180 CE

Your pattern is perfection
It quiets the soul that knows it
And its eloquent expression
Makes everything clear
So that even the simple are wise

Psalm 19, translation by Norman Fischer

Contents

Preface

I INVITE YOU TO JOIN in a fresh, inspiring, and pragmatic exploration of the traditional Christian gospels. I believe this new perspective on these ancient, beautiful, and frequently contentious words has
been long awaited. It is my belief that this reawakened journey holds the
key to unlock what has too long been closed, fearful, and rigid within ourselves and our faith.

If you choose to come along, you will discover that the four traditional
gospels provide a complete spiritual and psychological map that stretches
across time, place, and culture. This view, though it may seem revolutionary, is actually a restoration of the full process of spiritual transformation
laid out by early Christians, now validated through current understandings
of psychology, anthropology, sociology, and science. Since the journey is
sequential, encompasses all four gospels, and cannot be shortened, I have
named it *quadratos.* I will use that concise and intuitive way to refer to the
process throughout.

In this inspiring picture of the gospels, you will find practices that give
purpose and meaning to life, transform anxiety into equanimity, resentment into compassion, and loneliness into community and joy. This book
will provide new and vital ways for you, your family, and your community

to respond to unexpected dilemmas—and will do so without forsaking Christianity's sacred history and traditions.

We will begin by examining how we came to have four gospels. After all, during the first and second centuries, at least fifty gospels were written. Why did we end up with four? Why not one? Or three, or fifty? And why were *these* four selected? And why were they put into a Sunday reading cycle in the sequence of Matthew, Mark, John each Lent and Easter, then Luke (which is not the order in the Bible), a cycle that took three years to recite and that most churches used until the seventh century? Why was that cycle then abandoned? Then restored in Roman Catholicism and mainline Christian churches in the 1970s?

It turns out that this particular sequence had a very important purpose. Each of the four gospels was written for a specific early Christian community undergoing a spiritual dilemma. Each writer composed an account of the life, death, and resurrection of Jesus the Christ to be used as a living reality for the succor of that group. The gospel became their prayer and practice—in effect, it answered their spiritual dilemma. Matthew is the gospel of beginning, and addresses the question, "How do we face change?" As we cross into the second stage, a time of deep difficulty, Mark answers the question, "How do we move through suffering?" Understanding does arrive, yet we may not be ready, so John speaks to the question, "How do we receive joy?" Finally, completing the transformational process, Luke responds to the challenges of "How do we mature in service?"

This Sunday reading sequence, the simple recitation of four gospels so apparently similar, yet so profoundly different, that was established two millennia ago is now revealed as an extraordinary primer—for Christians and for any serious student of spiritual transformation. The four questions constitute precisely the steps needed to reach psychological and spiritual maturity. Furthermore, if we simplify the questions to "beginning, struggle, expansion, and application," we behold the same essential pattern revealed everywhere in both the human and natural worlds. Therefore, for believing Christians who want certainty in the gospels as revelation of divine truth, what could possibly be truer than the reflection of a pattern we see every single place we look?

Christians also want these sacred texts to live in a faith that unites hearts *and* minds today, a time much more complex than village life millennia ago. Many have left Christianity and gone to Eastern religions, or have become unchurched, because pastoral leaders are unable to provide a mature course that satisfies a hunger for wholeness. This book shows us the mysticism, the intellectual content, and the pragmatism in the gospels and explains how to use them on an everyday basis. For the non-Christian, this book offers a refreshing viewpoint on Christianity and a practical guide to personal growth that transcends faith.

Quadratos welcomes you as we begin our journey across a vast terrain.

THIS IS NOT intended to be a textbook, but if you want to get some real value out of the concept of quadratos, this is no overnight read; it is, rather, a *journey*. For some, the ground will be entirely new. For others—those who have studied the gospels before—many of the steps may feel familiar, yet they will take you deeper, or to a different place altogether. We will begin with two introductory chapters, one dealing with the personal odyssey that led to the discovery of quadratos, and the second laying out the general historical, sociological, and scientific principles in which this gospel journey is embedded. As you read, you may find yourself saying, "Of course!"

Four gospel chapters follow, in the sequence of the ancient reading cycle, and of quadratos: Matthew, Mark, John, then Luke. Each chapter opens with a poem, allowing us to begin with imagery rather than jumping straight into linear words. Each of these four gospels, which we designate as *paths,* is discussed in terms of its function in the transformational journey. We give the historical background of the gospel and then move through the gospel itself, from opening to resurrection accounts. Excerpts are quoted and ancient and contemporary insights provided. Differences among the gospels are noted and explained. Each gospel chapter closes with a prayer, a summary, and "exercises"—recommendations for study and practice that build sequentially from each gospel path to the next. At the end of Luke's gospel, we have provided a separate chapter with extensive recommended practices for continuing study for individuals and groups. The final chapter holds thoughts and conclusions.

You may choose to read all the way through the book, or you may observe that a gospel calls out to you at a particular moment as you read. If it does, please stop and study that part. Be present with your heart and your soul. Heed the inner voice of Mystery, and allow all those extra pages to wait their turn. There is time.

The gospels are, to me, *the* sacred texts of my Christian faith, because they hold the living experience of the Christ and the answers to the four deepest questions we will ever face as humans—and we will face them over and over and over again as we move through life. Quadratos puts the four together in a universal sequence that brings those questions into a process of emotional, psychological, and spiritual transformation. Whether we read the gospels, or pray them aloud, or listen to them in church, they lessen our loneliness, increase our compassion, support our community, and enliven our faith. No single gospel can accomplish all these things. This is why the vitality of the four is unequaled and critically important. The gospels teach us that we belong to each other and that we belong to God.

Alexander J. Shaia
Santa Fe, New Mexico

The Hidden Power
of the Gospels

1

. . .

The Story of Quadratos

WHEN I WAS SEVEN years old, racists burned my grandmother's house to the ground. They waited until nightfall so they could slip through the shadows. Then they scoured her house, dug in her closets, opened her wooden chest, stripped the mantels of her beloved mementos, and put everything into a big pile in the living room. All the Catholic artifacts, statues, and family pictures from her tiny home were added to the stack. Placing the crucifixes atop the heap, they poured on kerosene, lit matches, and fled.

Fire engulfed the structure in minutes. Summoned from my bed, I rushed to her house with my family and watched the conflagration, despairing, certain that my grandmother was inside, perishing in agony. We all called her "Sitto," which is Arabic for grandmother, and she was especially beloved to me. Since she walked with a crutch, I was sure there was no way she could have escaped the terrible fire. However, hours later she appeared, having fortuitously been taken to church by a friend that evening. Her restoration to us was joyful, but I will never, ever forget the smell of the charred wood, nor my fear, nor the palpable experience of hate that surrounded me that night. Indelibly imprinted on my seven-year-old heart was the clear understanding that being "outside" meant the risk of pain and terror, and perhaps even the loss of life itself.

Why was Sitto's home burned? Because in that 1950s southern community, all of us in the Shaia family were outsiders. My grandparents had emigrated from Lebanon, and we were Maronite Catholics. At that time, Birmingham, Alabama, was less than one-half of one percent Catholic, and Maronites were a tiny, obscure minority even among those Catholics. I was truly a minority of a minority within an immigrant minority in a city that was, in those days, not kind to minorities.

Step by Step

When it came time to write this book, I felt that the fire of my past was the perfect image for the beginning of my spiritual journey. You may share some of these feelings if you think of the terrible pain of the last unforgiven argument you had with a loved one and then try to imagine it magnified by dozens, by hundreds, and by thousands outward—into your family, your community, your country, and your world. As simplistic as it sounds, aren't most of the conflicts in the world unforgiven arguments at their core? The beginnings of change often come from the charred embers of loss or the hard, rocky ground of necessity. Mine did. I vowed to commit myself to: "No more, and never again."

To provide an image for the work of transformation for which we are striving, I'd like to tell you about my family's Sunday dinner five days after the fire. We always met on Sundays at Sitto's house—everyone: parents, brothers, aunts, uncles, cousins, the whole extended crowd—and usually we sat around the big, old mahogany table, which was covered for the occasion with embroidered linen and china. My recollection isn't clear whose house we went to that week, but I do remember that the tables were planks on sawhorses, the chairs were folding metal, and the tablecloths were paper.

The grown-ups sat in the middle, the kids around the edges. Sitto, as always, was at the head of the table, and when the room hushed, she led us in saying grace. Afterward, there was silence, and then her eyes, clear and direct above the glasses perched midway down her nose, slowly moved to meet the eyes of every person in the room—even ours, the children. We all waited patiently in the silence. Finally she spoke. Her voice was soft, and she said only two words, though she repeated them until she was sure we understood and accepted them: "No hate. No hate. . . ." And I felt the burden lift from the heart of my family.

So, despite the intolerance and misunderstanding that pervaded Birmingham in those days, within the circle of my large Semitic family I had a childhood filled with beauty, mystery, and love. "Semitic" describes the culture shared by the settled village people of Israel, Jordan, and Lebanon, as distinguished from the nomadic Bedouin and Arab traditions. Even transplanted to America, our culture had changed little from that lived by my ancestors. My grandparents, aunts, and uncles were as familiar to me as my parents, and my cousins felt like my brothers and sisters. Family and faith made up the cornerstones of our "village." We spent every Sunday together—usually at my grandmother's, as I said—and the rhythms of that day never changed: morning mass, shared breakfast, an elaborately prepared lunch, all followed by an afternoon of leisurely conversations, cards, and sports. At nightfall, each family made its way home, knowing that the next Sunday, and the next and the next, would be the same.

My mother's mother, my "sitto," and my father's father, my "jiddo," were the beacons of my childhood. They were also the heart of our entire family, and they lived until I was in my late twenties. Sitto was the anchor of compassion for us all, and I never heard her speak an unkind word of another human being. Jiddo, well known in our community, was a peddler and folk healer. Tradition forbade him from healing his own family, but there was a constant stream of friends knocking on his back door. He smelled of the earth and mystery, and though he could neither read nor write, he was certainly the first mystic I knew.

These elders immersed me in the richness of their Middle Eastern heritage, which was in many ways still their primary world. The stories and word pictures painted by Arabic idioms, beautiful words drawn from the language and traditions of centuries, filled our daily life and instilled in me a poetic heart. I learned to be comfortable with ambiguity, for when I requested the English translation of an Arabic phrase, Sitto's patient reply was: "Oh, honey, Arabic is poetry. It won't come out in English."

I left this closeness and entered the University of Notre Dame, intending to eventually go on to seminary. In shifting to that academic environment,

I felt I had fallen from a high cliff. Nothing made sense to me. I was engulfed by a maze of intellectual, philosophical discourse. Students stayed up all night talking about whether God was dead. This wasn't even remotely credible. I was part of God. How could God be dead? *I* would be dead. Immense words and theories swirled around me, but no one was cooking spicy Sunday dinner and holding hands in prayer. My fellow students were good people, even friends. They were smart, knowledgeable, and articulate, but they weren't speaking of the God I knew. The God I understood was founded in poetic mystery, not reason. Worship was an experience I could feel in my body, not an ideology. Confused and lonely, again I felt I was standing outside.

I floundered in this new, complicated environment, and neither my Semitic understandings nor the academic concepts I was studying addressed the challenges I faced. I often went to the Grotto, which sits behind Notre Dame's Basilica and is a replica of Lourdes. It has a bank of a thousand vigil candles flickering with the light of individual hopes. I would add my own and pray for guidance. I found it to be a place of quiet solace and reflection. Eventually, I was led to switch my major from theology to cultural anthropology with a focus on indigenous peoples and their rites of initiation. These traditions were closer to my own early culture, and I found them beautiful. They also seemed more flexible, more adaptable to change than the Western systems of thought that seemed so frustrating to me.

The indigenous cultures also described a consistent journey of spirit, even though each people had their own cosmology and stories and their own vocabulary and worldview. In every society there was a multistage process that was deemed necessary in order to make the transition from childhood to adulthood. The first stage always called for "entering"; it involved ignorance and loneliness. The second always held pitfalls or trickery. The third brought dawning understanding, even ecstasy. The fourth held the final keys to maturation, which were carried back into the community in some way. Although I wasn't sure why, I found that these simple, yet arduous steps held an emotional logic that "made sense" to me.

Feeling much more grounded by my anthropology studies, I was then able to find professors at Notre Dame who helped me synthesize the richly embroidered past of my heart with the intellectual abundance of Western and Christian thought. In particular, Henri Nouwen and Morton Kelsey validated my mystical sense of God and the gospels at a time when many considered such a point of view irrational. John Dunne opened a bridge for me between Western and Eastern theologies and led me to discover the mysticism in many Western religious perspectives that I had believed devoid of it. Joseph Campbell lectured on the gospels as a mythic journey, and his words opened new ideas in me that connected with my anthropology studies. The writings of C. G. Jung, which I discovered through my coursework, helped me find a way to join the mythic (though unreflective) Semitic tradition in which I had been raised with the postmodern Western world in which I now lived.

My time at Notre Dame set me on a path of seeking how to balance critical thought and deep feeling, as well as how to bring soaring vision to ordinary and practical life. Then, in my senior year, I took a class on liturgy from Mark Searle. I learned about the ancient four-gospel reading cycle that had been rediscovered by the scholars of the church and just restored to use in Sunday worship. I was so taken by the idea that the early church had had a beautiful and systematic design for all four gospels that I determined to pray them that way myself on a weekly basis. And I have done so, from that day forward.

After my graduation from Notre Dame, full of confidence—and following a custom in existence for every Alexander in my family (save three) since the year 1300!—I entered seminary to become a priest. But this long-anticipated plan did not work at all. The spiritual home in which I found myself failed to nurture my spirit as expected. I sought expansiveness and joy, yet found instead an institution training people to become narrow and lifeless, threatening to lose the deep resonance of centuries. However, becoming a priest was the rock on which I had invested the entire vision of my future life—not to mention all the expectations of my huge extended family. I felt that there was no way I could turn my back on it. Not only would I be shamed and bereft, but I would have to start over again—somehow rediscover a way to accomplish the things that mattered to me. That seemed a prodigious task, yet I was gradually becoming aware that a larger life awaited me outside those walls. So, after much prayer and great soul-searching, I left and began my own journey. As I drove away, in grief for the loss of my dreams, I stopped, turned back, and remembered Sitto's little house in flames. I thought, "This time, my own home is burning, and *I* set the fire." Then I faced forward again and settled in for my long drive.

Still wanting to serve my faith in some way, I soon found a position on the staff of a Catholic parish. At that time, the Roman Church was in the midst of dramatic changes. Among them was the restoration of the ancient rite of Christian baptism, a much more extensive and lengthy process than the simple pouring of water. I was asked to help implement this change, and my parish duties became focused on this practice and the spiritual renewal it promised. My anthropology studies allowed me to immediately see its profound links to other wisdom traditions I had studied. This high Catholic ritual was a fourfold rite of initiation and maturation! Here, in Western language and culture, was the same grace, deep truth, and power that I had found when I studied the practices of indigenous peoples.

The Catholic Church has ornate names for the four steps of the full baptism process: inquiry, catechumenate, purification/enlightenment, and mystagogia. But these complicated words define the same basic stages I had seen so often in indigenous cultures. The candidate for baptism enters the process, goes through a time of prayer to achieve spiritual/personal growth, gains illumination or understanding, and then deepens the understanding and carries it back to the community in some way. Whether people underwent the ritual in the lengthier manner of ancient times that required extensive study, or in the shortened version we were restoring, it was clear that, just as in the native cultures, they were undergoing a journey of spirit.

The church began a formal effort to teach all dioceses how to reincorporate the ancient baptism process. I was appointed a teacher of the rite and spent a decade facilitating this renewal all across America. As I did so, I became more and more convinced of the ritual's wisdom and broad efficacy. I even wished its stages could somehow be incorporated into "regular," ongoing church ritual, not just the initiatory sequence of baptism. I started to wonder if the four-stage, or four-step, or four-path structure itself, which I had found in these apparently diverse transformative journeys, might be significant and, perhaps, hold its own truth.

Then, ten years after I graduated from Notre Dame, I entered a doctoral program in clinical psychology. I was still trying to meld critical thought and deep feeling—more specifically, to meld my spiritual inclinations with what I had learned about human behavior. I met and trained with Dora Kalff, a Swiss Jungian analyst, devout Christian, and practitioner of Tibetan

Buddhist meditation. She had combined a therapeutic technique known as "Sandtray" with the principles of Jungian psychology and the meditational practices of Buddhism. Frau Kalff called her synthesis "Sandplay."

In Sandplay, a therapeutic client creates a scene or picture in a tray of sand by shaping the sand and (or) placing figures and objects in it. Over the course of making a series of these scenes, the client reveals a personal narrative that unfolds on a level beneath conscious awareness. Healing comes through the subconscious process of creating and "telling" the story.

When I began my clinical practice, I chose to use Sandplay as my primary therapeutic method and became a practitioner and certified teacher. I consulted on myriad cases throughout North America, as well as in Europe and Asia. Over and over, I saw an identical fourfold pattern sequentially disclosing itself. Sandplay psychotherapists often identify one of the earliest scenes made by clients as a "Numinous Tray"—one that holds images indicating the intent to submit to an inner journey. This tray is followed by a series of scenes describing increasing tension, polarization, and conflict. In the next phase, a scene will appear that is called a "Self Tray," which reflects an experience of union. Eventually, a series of trays will show a return to everyday life, but with a larger sense of consciousness that includes obligations beyond those of the personal self.

As a practitioner, I have seen hundreds upon hundreds of Numinous Trays and Self Trays and the trays that followed them. It didn't matter if the clients were children or women or men. It didn't matter if the figures they chose were icons from current culture, mythical figures, or phantasmagorical creatures, nor did it matter if twigs or seashells or bright, glittery stones surrounded them. In every single instance, the outer story told by the images matched the inner story experienced by the client, and the pattern was invariably fourfold and sequential. This happened with or without the conscious intention, or even awareness, of the individual. To me, the conclusion seemed inescapable. Here was the same journey, containing the same four paths—this time in the practice of psychology, and in a totally contemporary and cross-cultural setting.

Wondering if anyone else had noticed the pattern, I began investigating. I learned that storytellers identify four parts in the great myths and epics of ancient literature—parts known as hearing the summons, enduring the obstacles, receiving the boon, and returning to community. In *The Different Drum: Community-Making and Peace,* psychiatrist M. Scott Peck describes four stages of community formation: pseudocommunity, chaos, emptiness, and genuine community. Then I read *Original Blessing,* by the then Catholic and now Episcopal priest Matthew Fox. *Original Blessing* announces four paths of religious progression, which Fox names Via Positiva, Via Negativa, Via Creativa, and Via Transformativa. Next, I turned back to the classics of Western spirituality, and in Teresa of Avila's *The Interior Castle* I found the same spiritual journey—although she made more divisions, breaking the pattern into seven parts or castles, rather than four.

Looking beyond Christianity, I found the cycle in Judaism's preeminent story: escaping slavery in Egypt, wandering in the wilderness, arriving in the Promised Land, and finally creating a fruitful home there. And, though the vocabulary is quite different, the same journey can be discovered in the Four Noble Truths of Buddhism and Hinduism's epic accounts of Shiva, Parvati, and Ganesha. At that point, I became absolutely certain that this fourfold inner pilgrimage is a universal spiritual truth whose imprint can be found across time, geography, culture, and religious tradition. Every single pattern asks the journeyer to begin and start some form of inquiry. Next comes a time of trial, often involving pitfalls, and sometimes trickery, but always bringing new and hard-won understanding. The gift of enlarged comprehension, wholeness, and greater perspective is third, sometimes coming suddenly, often with the sense of outside assistance. The fourth step requires actual practice of the wisdom gained, with some component of bringing that knowledge back to the community or those who follow after the journeyer.

Epiphany

I continued to practice and teach, still on my own spiritual journey, never dreaming that what I was observing and learning would become this book. Then suddenly, a decade later, in the year 2000, on a cold, star-filled night in northern New Mexico, my entire world changed. I was on sabbatical and had chosen New Mexico as an appropriately peaceful place to study and meditate. On the night of November 1, I found myself reading *The*

Four Witnesses, authored by Robin Griffith-Jones, an Anglican priest and Oxford University scholar.

It was through Jones's book that I learned how deeply and empathetically the gospels of Matthew, Mark, John, and Luke had been directed to specific communities of early Christians. I read the story of each long-ago audience, noting their distinct historical, geographical, and cultural differences. Each community had wrestled with a unique and critical spiritual question. As I read, I felt a rising sense of familiarity. I *knew* these questions. In fact, I knew them very well.

The fourfold spiritual journey appeared in my mind. I saw the procession of indigenous peoples growing into their communal lives. I saw initiates moving into the mature practice of their various faiths. I saw troubled men, women, and children shifting objects in sand as they worked through trauma. Invariably, each person moved through four paths, and each path mirrored one of the emotional and spiritual challenges faced by a specific early Christian community to whom one of the four gospels responded. Suddenly, my enjoyment of the still night on the high plateau disappeared. My thoughts became a frenzy of swirling progressions. The pattern of four seemed to be everywhere. It was clear—and amazing.

I grabbed my Bible, turned to the Gospel of Matthew, and started to read. I read for most of the night, the passages illuminated by my new perspective. The familiar words—the import of the passages—that I had read hundreds of times before were transformed before my tired eyes. Suddenly, I realized that each gospel was organized around a different metaphorical landscape. Matthew, writing after the Great Temple of Jerusalem had fallen, uses the metaphors of mountain and rock and stone. Mark, directing his gospel to Christians under the sentence of death, uses the metaphor of wilderness and Jewish historical equivalents for wilderness—deserts and bodies of water. John's gospel, likely written as a study for baptism, uses the metaphor of garden, often explicitly the Garden of Eden. The Gospel of Luke, written to burgeoning communities of new Christians throughout the Mediterranean, has a core metaphor that is less apparent—the road: everything in Luke happens *between* places.

As I read, I realized that even the writing style of each author seemed to synchronize with the message held by that particular gospel. The Gospel of Matthew is a bit flowery and has a lot of reassuring adjectives. Mark has absolutely no extra words at all: it is short, almost hard, and completely to the point. John is glorious metaphysical poetry, while Luke is practical, matter-of-fact, almost chatty. These discoveries awed and excited me. But a deeper revelation was still to come.

I thought of the many times I had puzzled over the ancient Sunday reading cycle. I had prayed the cycle for many years; I found it deeply meaningful and loved it profoundly. But I had often asked, *Why* was it read Matthew, then Mark, then John (at Lent and Easter), then Luke? I always thought there must have been some good reason, yet no one had ever been able to give me one, and though I had searched, I had never found any explanation. Now my old questions kept intruding: Who had created it originally, and why? Did that sequence hold some special truth? My already overloaded brain added these further queries to the cerebral stew.

For a long time afterward, I thought of what happened next as my "discovery." I now realize that, in fact, I discovered nothing. The deeper wisdom of the gospels found *me*. All of my upbringing and prayer and education and life experience had been preparation for the moment that came that night under the limitless stars. To me it seemed as though thunder sounded and a door flew open, though there wasn't a cloud in sight. I believe I know how Archimedes felt when he discovered the displacement of water and shouted, "Eureka!"

Suddenly and with perfect certainty, I comprehended the original reading cycle in a completely new way. I trembled in the dark as I saw revealed the landscapes of faith, the ancient journey that the early mothers and fathers had walked—but which had been long forgotten. I saw the four gospels as Christianity's great teaching of the universal journey.

Four early communities wrestled with *four* distinct sets of challenges when faced with *four* distinct sets of historical circumstances that prompted *four* deep questions requiring answers. There are *four* universal paths to spiritual maturity. There are *four* necessary levels to reach psychological maturity. Early Christians commonly placed the *four* gospels into a specific sequence and read them that way in most communities until the seventh century. Without psychology, without all the self-knowledge we have gained in the last two millennia, clearly inspired by a much greater wisdom, those early fathers and mothers of Christianity managed to grasp and set out the universal progression in a clear and workable fashion. *The four gospels in ancient sequence disclose the full internal/eternal journey, the great and immutable design, the heart of God that moves all creation.*

And oh, yes! They were so clearly the same four paths that had led me to this extraordinary moment. On that November night, as I reviewed the history of the early Christians, I also retraced my own. I realized that the deep counsel of Matthew's gospel had first reached me in college. So many customs, expectations, and beliefs had gone with me to Notre Dame. That matriculation was the repository of unreal hopes—mine and the frozen dreams of the entire extended Shaia family. And just as surely as the Great Temple of Jerusalem, that repository crumbled when confronted with the powerful forces of my real life. Using my new perspective, I could see that the first path of my spiritual journey was strewn with the boulders of disappointment and confusion.

I realized that my departure from the Gospel of Matthew and my entrance into the bleak despair of the second path of Mark had been precipitated by my decision to leave seminary and not enter the priesthood. The next years I was in the wilderness and desert of hard learning—wandering from one experience to another, staying in prayer, trying to turn each new effort into a sincere time of humility and obedience to Spirit. Mostly it was my hope that I would find a place with enough resonance and meaning to hold me. I searched for purpose while I prayed.

Epiphany finally arrived in that wonderful instant when I comprehended the purpose of the gospel cycle. The sonorous poetry of John's gospel echoed in my ears and coursed in my blood, raced through the bones and muscles of my body, filling my soul as I knew the deepest joy imaginable. After that night, I spent a long while resting in the wonderful complexities of this glorious garden, allowing my heart and my mind and all of myself to be immersed in the new truth.

Since that November moment in 2000, and after my immersion time, I have been walking, most of the time, on Luke's road in the fourth path. I have been learning more about my own maturity, and taking the message of the ancient gospel journey into larger reality. I coined the word *quadratos* to provide a concise and intuitive way to express an understanding of the fourfold process. My own comprehension of the Journey of Quadratos grows daily. Through my studies, and my own life, I have come to realize and appreciate with gratitude how solidly the model for that journey has been there for us, all this time, leading us. In these, our most needful hours, it has reappeared so that we might make it conscious and find a renewal of spirit by our fresh acceptance and practice.

2

. . .

Preparing for the Journey of Quadratos

THERE IS AN IMMENSE dilemma in most spiritual traditions today—Judaism, Islam, Buddhism, Hinduism, and Christianity. Many would use even stronger vocabulary and speak of a crisis. Statistics show that increased percentages of people consider themselves "nonbelievers." Are they opting out because they are choosing some form of secular humanism instead? Or because no belief system they have considered is providing what they seek? Or because they are disgusted by what they perceive as issuing forth from the "God industry"? Memberships in traditional churches have declined dramatically over the last half-century, while those in churches, temples, synagogues, and mosques that preach clear, unequivocal messages and provide strong community have skyrocketed. Several major denominations have undergone schism, and others threaten to. Single issues dominate convocations, no matter the denomination—or even the religion—and problems surrounding questions of authority, patriarchy, sexism, extremism, sexual abuse, political involvement, and just plain boredom proliferate.

What is the real dilemma here? What is the core issue underlying all the tumult? We think the problem is the question of why religion exists at all.

Religion is supposed to be an organization through which we can understand God's intention for our lives and transform ourselves so that we may
have lives filled with meaning and greater purpose. Religious leaders are
supposed to be trustworthy stewards who help us through these changes.
In this immensely complicated time—a time when people and things and
countless decisions are pulling at us ceaselessly, stressfully—how is this actually accomplished? And precisely who are the specific people we should
trust to help us with this daunting task?

Who Holds the Truth?

When most of us talk about meaning and greater purpose, we generally
mean an inner feeling that keeps us steady and grounded, provides a sense
of equanimity, allows us to feel vigorous, sensual, and joyful, and tells us that
our lives are worthwhile. We are also usually referring to our experiences
in spirit and our contributions to community, rather than our acquisition of
"stuff." So our very specific question becomes, Can we trust our communal
and religious leaders? Are they doing the job we need them to do for us?
Are they shepherding us through the journey of spiritual transformation?
And if not, why not—and what should we do in response? Whom *can* we
trust to help us with our spiritual lives? So many questions have been raised
that we are left asking, Can we trust even our sacred books, on which we
have relied for centuries? Quadratos has answers to these questions. And
though we believe many of these problems pervade *all* religions, we will
speak only for the religion we know well—for Christianity.

Quadratos addresses the large group of Christian believers who want
to find the meaning for their spiritual lives in the sacred texts and rituals
of Christianity. We include ourselves in this group. We want to be led by
enthusiastic, knowledgeable shepherds who will help us in a lifelong journey of spiritual transformation. We cherish our traditions and yearn for
them to grow beyond their current illogic and lack of charity, flexibility,
and passion—to become more mature, more like the embodiment of the
great teachings that guide us. We go to church, some of us regularly, yet are
often not nourished by what we hear. We leave hungry. Some of us eventually stop going at all.

We recognize the challenges. We know that Christianity is wonderfully diverse, even in its troubles. We are well aware of those who have closed their minds and hearts to all forms of religion because they have been so injured or angered by the illogical or uncharitable practices of our faith. We also know that there are people sitting in the pews who *are* content— who believe that the specific words in the sacred texts are both literal and inerrant. We understand the many among us who have embraced Eastern faiths, even though those religions are grounded in foreign and inaccessible languages and cultures—mysticism and wholeness are not very available in the way Christianity is presented and practiced. We know others who are forging new ways and using new vocabularies, and we salute them.

These observations about the state of Christianity today reflect a tragic, but redeemable, quandary. Large numbers of people believe that the solution to the question of meaning will be found in discovering the precisely "true" words of Jesus the Christ, or perhaps those of his closest disciples. Since all of the gospels we have were composed some time after Jesus's death, and largely from oral accounts, there are inevitably questions about accuracy. Our attitude seems to be that if we could only find a few sentences we could completely trust, sentences we *knew* we could be absolutely *certain* were really Jesus's own words—well, then we might possibly be willing to accept all the other words. The subtext is that *if* we could extend our trust this far, *if* we could really believe that those words were real, we would know exactly how to live our lives, and—most importantly—then we wouldn't feel overcome by our fears. Conversely, when an archaeologist finds something that casts doubt on a couple of sentences, our intellects (bolstered by our fearful egos) positively race to question the veracity of the entire document. Doubting Thomas had nothing on us!

Therefore, in Christianity, particularly over the past three decades, a huge industry has developed around the analysis of biblical texts and archaeological discoveries. Eminent scholars and pastors have dissected the traditional texts, analyzing them, retranslating their words, and searching out the history of Jesus in an ostensible attempt to quell our fears and answer the question of "truth," and therefore get to the question of meaning. Others have pored over newly unearthed documents and additional gospels in the hope of providing some lost message of Jesus, a revelation that would end all confusion. In the end, though, all of this just feeds our insecurities and our hopes that the next fragment of papyrus or the next, more precise etymological deconstruction will reveal something to enliven our faith. But this scriptural research does not stop us from avidly following the assertions of writers—even in fiction!—as they offer us findings they believe the early church suppressed for a malign purpose.

Not only have the differing answers we have received been confusing; they have effectively disqualified the traditional Gospels of Matthew, Mark, John, and Luke. We find ourselves trapped between head and heart. Are the four gospels in the Christian Bible really there because they are genuinely more holy—spiritually truer or somehow more significant? That is what most of us want to believe. Or are they merely the four that survived for now-obscure reasons of power or privilege? In the many writings that have disappeared through chance or design, are there equal, or maybe even greater, truths?

With every new analysis, our hungry hearts war with our minds, pleading, "Why do I keep analyzing all of this? What is the point? Where is the Great Design for my life—useful Christian practices that fully engage my head *and* my heart. Where are they?" Well, as it turns out, the answers we seek are right where we started—in the traditional four gospels. The early church fathers and mothers walked to the rhythm of a universal cycle— but until the present, no one was aware of its cadence, nor understood its source. Now a rediscovery has been made, unlocking a perspective on the Gospels of Matthew, Mark, John, and Luke that has been sealed within them for over a millennium. To reinforce that perspective, we have added our modern knowledge about psychology, sociology, anthropology, and science. This is the map of Christian practice based on the heart of our greatest teachings. It is the Journey of Quadratos, and it completely frees us from our preoccupation with finding the "true" words of Jesus and his disciples.

The Gospel Inconsistencies

Now we're going to discuss a bit about differing theories of the gospels so that you can see where quadratos fits in. We begin with the question of authorship. Throughout this book, we will refer to Matthew, Mark, John, and

Luke as though they personally wrote down every word of the gospels that bear their names. Actually, many scholars now think it more likely that the gospels began as an oral tradition, and that each "author" represents words originally developed and taught aloud for many years

In the case of each gospel, sometime during the first century CE someone, or maybe a group—with full inspiration and deep compassion—crafted an entire body of teachings into a written document that was specifically refined to meet the needs of a particular community at a particular point in history. Perhaps this was indeed the "author." But maybe it was a scribe, or even a group of students. In early tradition, the Greek word *kata,* "according to," was attached to each of the four gospels. It may have signified a kind of warranty that the gospels were "according to" the named author (regardless of who actually recorded the words) and thus the material in them was faithful to his accounts; alternatively, it may have meant that the author actually transcribed the account himself.

What most people find more confusing than the question of actual authorship is the presence of significant discrepancies in the life of Jesus as recounted in the four traditional gospels. Careful readers know, for example, that the story of Jesus's birth varies dramatically in each account, and even disappears entirely in the Gospel of Mark. The arrest, trial, crucifixion, and resurrection accounts are equally disparate, as are many other details. Each gospel uses very different language, selectively highlights parts of Jesus's life and teachings, and employs a distinct metaphorical "landscape," as we discussed in the previous chapter.

The traditional belief has been that these discrepancies are nothing more than to-be-expected variations between eyewitnesses. This argument appeals to our hearts and is acceptable to the felt sense of mystery in these texts that goes beyond pure logic. However, in the face of more recent scholarship, this view falters. In the last several decades, other scholars have presented new theories and evidence, which largely fall into three categories. One, promulgated by Marcus Borg and John Dominic Crossan, contends that the existence of the discrepancies proves that the four gospels are inaccurate historical accounts and therefore the texts cannot be relied on as records of the life and words of Jesus. Their work has shown that the gospels are not literal transcripts and, thus, forces us to find a new view of them.

Another, posited by the religious expert Elaine Pagels and others, contends that the many writings from early Christianity are theological accounts with little historical accuracy that were composed by competing factions as the early Christians sought to define their beliefs. This theory gives a pragmatic sense of how religion and social systems develop and adds critical dimensions to theological study.

The third perspective is the most recent and comes from Bart Ehrman, who describes himself as a former believer, now an agnostic. Ehrman contends that two millennia of apocrypha and mistranslations have created a totally unknowable Jesus. Going further than the view of Borg and Crossan, this theory would remove the gospels from a useful role as either historical *or* faith documents.

All four beliefs—even the traditional one—are essential contributions to the religious conversation. The limitation of the four, with respect to the problem of scriptural discrepancies, is that none of them really helps our questing hearts *and* minds. None of them is sufficient to resolve our sense of uncertainty, or our spiritual need for meaning. While they do not completely defeat the gospels, neither do they bring the gospel words—or the words of any other early writings—into manifest reality in our daily lives, emotionally, intellectually, and spiritually.

The Journey of Quadratos offers a starkly different answer—one that speaks to both head and heart. It is based on ancient truth. Through it, we will come to understand that the discrepancies are not only correct; they are purposeful and useful. They derive from the way each gospel was composed. In the hundred years after Jesus's death, each of the four traditional gospels was written during unique historical circumstances for a specific group of early Christians in a distinct geographical location. In each case, the writer reframed the core story of Jesus's life, death, and resurrection, emphasizing and even altering its elements to give that particular gospel clear relevance and guidance for the singular historical realities and dilemmas of its audience.

For example, Mark was the first gospel composed. It combined elements derived from the apostle Paul's writings with stories of Jesus shared by groups of desperate Messianic Jews condemned to death by Emperor Nero in first-century Rome. Those courageous believers would meet as they could in homes or cells and try to allay each other's fears and bolster their slim hopes through the ancient tradition of storytelling. As they did, their extreme emotional realities—their agony and their ecstasy—became folded into their recounting of the life and inspiration of Jesus the Christ. This way of storytelling combined present-moment realities with prophetic and practical lessons. The accounts were instructive, interesting— even exciting—and completely distinct from previous Jewish scriptures or Greco-Roman prose. This new form of narrative, which became known as a gospel (meaning "good news"), profoundly helped the desperate community experience the Christ's continuing and living presence in their struggles.

Mark then put this form into writing; he made the gospel form official. His written story of Jesus the Christ was different from a lecture or a formal sermon. Just as the oral form had done, Mark's words enabled people to see themselves in the accounts that were written down. When the stories were read aloud—or chanted as prayer, which was their usual use in those early times—people listening could discern patterns and then understand that Jesus was not simply a historical figure, but was an ongoing experience within each person, a doorway to the compassion and strength and sense of purpose they needed to maintain their faith. This gospel form quickly found a home in Messianic hearts and took root. Later, Matthew, John, and Luke all followed Mark's pattern of mixing stories of the historical Jesus with their communities' living participation with the Christ.

In the first century, there was already a long Jewish tradition of determination in the face of suffering. That tradition may have been a significant factor in keeping the early believers from abandoning their young faith. However, fortitude alone cannot possibly account for the rapid spread of belief in the Christ, particularly in the face of great opposition.

At the time, throughout the Mediterranean region, fewer tribes were roaming around in solitary groups. More had moved into urban areas in search of work, although the environments they discovered there were often very crowded, polluted, and oppressive. As these tribes encountered each other, their cultures inevitably clashed, often dramatically. Then as now, diversity brought challenges. Perhaps the gospel form was the egalitarian and engaging agent of communication capable of attracting disparate people and carrying them onward through their dilemmas. It is likely that this new form of sacred story, which is so much closer to a conversation than a lecture or a recounting of history, played an important role in swelling the number of believers.

When Mark chose language and metaphors to hearten the Romans, and when Matthew and John and Luke shaped many of the "facts" of the story so that their account would be meaningful to their audience, they did not betray the truth of the message of Jesus the Christ. On the contrary. Their inspired changes made that message real, alive, and useful to the people who needed it. The changes, and specifically the "discrepancies," made it possible for a particular early Christian community to live their daily lives with the sure knowledge that God was with them in their time of trial. And later, in the fourth century, those same discrepancies made it possible for the four gospels to serve the quadratos sequence, an even greater purpose. Today, those same inconsistencies reopen the ancient journey once again, this time for us.

The Ancient Mystery of the Gospel Sequence

In 315 CE, Emperor Constantine legalized Christianity. As Roman oppression lifted, easy communication began to be established between the various Christian communities, which had coalesced around five major centers of influence: Milan, Gaul (now France), Spain, Rome, and the Byzantine churches (what we think of today as the Orthodox churches). Christians realized that wide differences in belief existed. Theological arguments erupted. In the fourth century, twenty organizing councils were held, beliefs were standardized, and practices were developed, refined, and formalized. Gospels were one of the many things systematized. At the time, there were at least fifty gospels! A number of historians have suggested that sexism, power, and privilege had a great hand in the winnowing. If we look at the process logically, it certainly does seem surprising that *multiple* gospels were selected. After all, if the point was to tell the story of Jesus's life, death, and resurrection, you would need only *one* account—right? However, the *four* Gospels of Matthew, Mark, John, and Luke were affirmed as "true." Why were *four* gospel accounts chosen, and why *these* four? There are no written documents that definitively answer these questions, but there are abundant theories and some significant clues.

We know that Irenaeus, the bishop of Lyons, attached divine and universal significance to the number four in 180 CE, saying that "The Gospels could not possibly be either more or less in number than they are. Since there are four zones of the world in which we live, and four principal winds . . . it is clear that the Word . . . gave us the gospel, fourfold in form but held together by one Spirit." The four gospels together were entitled *Euaggelion,* which means "the good news of the kingdom." Eusebius, bishop of Caesarea and a church historian, labeled Matthew, Mark, John, and Luke "the holy quaternion of the gospels" in about 300 CE.

Most importantly, in those early centuries, as disciples walked from village to village, it seems that these four gospels (of all the accounts then available) were the ones most often read to open new hearts. Believers chose to pray and pass *these* words on to others. The early communities appear to have found a power in these four gospels that was not present in other texts and therefore disseminated them more widely. It is my belief that their efficacy in the transformation of people's lives, transmitted through the gospel form, went hand in hand with the rapid and powerful spread of the Christian faith.

Subsequent to the organizing councils, the five Christian regions each adopted a Sunday reading cycle (a lectionary). We have few details about them, and each region likely had variations from Sunday to Sunday, but it appears that there was broad consistency. From the fourth through the seventh centuries, in Sunday services throughout the Christian world, all four gospels were read aloud over a three-year cycle. This maintained the custom derived from Judaism (called the Palestinian Cycle) that called for reciting the entire Torah over three years of Shabbat.

The first year was dedicated to the Gospel of Matthew, the second to Mark, and the third to Luke. These "synoptic" gospels tend to have clear story lines. John's gospel—less a story and more a series of thematic meditations—had a special purpose. Used during the seasons of Lent and Easter since the second century, John was interspersed in each year's readings to illuminate, deepen, and complete the message of the other three gospels, though it maintained its primary Lenten/Easter role. Despite regional variations, the widespread use of this reading progression meant that hearing the four gospels *in a sequence* formed a significant element of the bedrock of early Christian faith.

Exactly how and why did the idea of combining a general belief in "four-ness" with the selection of specific gospels in a clear sequence occur? Were the Christians aware of some ancient universal pattern—perhaps from an earlier, indigenous tradition—and did they see it reflected in the four gospels? Was this perhaps a customary way the four were already read? Were lots drawn? We do not pretend to know. It may have been happenstance or calculation, the work of an individual or a committee. Our belief is that people who were charged with discernment and decision-making converged with a sequence of spiritual practices already known to work well in human lives. The pressures, realities, and needs of the society at that particular point in history played their part, as they always do. Then a large helping of grace stirred the pot, and the pattern was set. Over time, it was discovered that the pattern functioned successfully and seemed "right." It is highly unlikely that we will ever be objectively sure. What is undeniable is that the fourfold reading cycle held a great design that went far beyond the stories and lessons told by the individual gospels. It seemingly worked very well for hundreds of years. Then, abruptly, it was gone.

Sometime in the early 600s, the Christian church apparently decided that it needed a simpler story. Christendom had been under attack for two centuries from northern warlords, and its cities were crumbling wrecks. Weakened churches were largely the only remaining centers for education, food distribution, and often law and order. We don't know which of the several popes (Sabinian, Boniface III, St. Boniface IV, St. Adeodatus I, or Boniface V) who ruled very briefly and followed the long reign of Gregory the Great actually changed the reading cycle, but one of them did. We suspect that the impulse came from Gregory's influence, which derived from his reliance on the views of the great monk Benedict of Nursia, the founder of the Benedictine Order. Benedict believed in and taught "nothing too harsh and nothing too burdensome." It is easy to see that, in a time when few people could read and when the church was totally overcome with demands and focused on survival, a short, straightforward gospel message would seem very appealing.

Regardless of the precise history and the exact theological reasons, which we will never know for certain, the beautiful, complex, three-year, four-gospel reading cycle was abandoned. To replace it, the first uniform lectionary for Western Christendom was issued: fifty-two Sunday lessons selected from all four gospels that, in combination, told a succinct sacred biography of Jesus's life and teachings. This change removed the sequence (plus about seventy percent of all the gospel texts) from Sunday worship. It may have been inevitable, even necessary, that this change happen for historical reasons (interestingly, Judaism went to the Babylonian Cycle, a one-year cycle, during the same period), but the change had significant, even tragic, consequences for the Christian faith.

Although the four-stage progression was still present in the ritual structure of Sunday worship, when the three-year cycle disappeared, churchgoing Christians lost their opportunity to naturally and regularly discover and internalize an exalted journey. What had been the sounding of a great and resonant bell in the hearts of believers dwindled to a barely heard whisper. The ancient pattern, though not totally absent, became indistinct and dim. Gradually, understandably, and unfortunately, Christianity became concentrated on the details of Jesus's life, a focus that remains today.

Subsequent centuries saw the rise of education, the invention of the printing press, the wide dissemination of books, and the Protestant Reformation. The public began reading the scriptures, fresh translations appeared, and many Reformation congregations returned to reading the entirety of the four gospels at Sunday services, although none of them followed the ancient sequence except inadvertently. Sadly, these traditions seemed unaware of the ancient three-year reading sequence. The great design had been lost.

More centuries passed. Suddenly, in the 1940s, the Roman Catholic Church, after locking scholars out of the Vatican libraries for hundreds of years, reversed course and opened its immense collection for research. The ancient three-year cycle was rediscovered. After much study, but without grasping its deeper significance, the Roman Catholic Church reinstated the three-year cycle in 1969, seeing it as a way to have all four gospels read, communicated, and used for worship—and also as a way to increase membership. Within ten years, the Episcopal, Anglican, Lutheran, Presbyterian, United Church of Christ, Disciples of Christ, and Methodist churches followed suit. Today, every Sunday, these Christian churches, with minor exceptions, all read the same gospel passage. Despite the reinstatement, however, there is no general knowledge of the original purpose of the sequence. The passages are simply read aloud with no connection to their real intention or transforming potential—much as we often overlook complexities concealed within our well-worn patterns and long-accustomed ways of thinking.

When scholars hunt for new papyri, posit deeper truth in the beautiful words of the Gospel of Thomas, or claim more substance in the Gnostic texts than in the four gospels, we can only guess that they are searching for something different than we are. Transcendent understandings or intellectually rapturous ideas are beside the point to us, whether they're gathered in a single book or fill an entire library. What we are interested in is human lives filled with meaning and the awareness of greater purpose each and every day—and this requires spiritual transformation. And transformation is a journey, which cannot be accomplished by a single gospel. However, we are absolutely certain that in their ancient sequence, the Gospels of Matthew, Mark, John, and Luke—and *only these four*—hold the internal and eternal map of transformation. This is the living treasure of the Christian faith, and it is the only ancient mystery that really matters.

The Great Map of Transformation

Whatever your vocabulary, whatever need you feel in your heart, whatever religious or philosophical question you have in your mind, a vital answer can be found in an understanding of the ancient gospel sequence. Because the design is universal, it holds relevance for each and every one of us in the world today, no matter what our faith is—or even if we claim no faith at all. A summary follows of the gospels, their core metaphors in the ancient reading cycle, and how they are reflected in quadratos and its life questions:

The Gospel of Matthew: Climbing the Great Mountain
How Do We Face Change? The First Path

Matthew's gospel was written to the Messianic Jews of Antioch two to five years after the destruction of the Great Temple of Jerusalem and the massacre of all its priests. The Jewish community was being torn apart by intense grief and tremendous struggles. The Temple had represented the center of their lives, and they were certain that God had abandoned them. They felt alone and frightened.

Matthew used the image of a mountain as a deeply poignant and evocative metaphor throughout his gospel, because Mount Moriah, the site of the Temple, had been the holiest place in Judaism for millennia. He knew the power of this image for his fearful and faltering readers, and he used it to bring them to a new truth. Through it, he revealed a revolutionary teaching of Jesus the Christ to the Jews: they no longer needed a bleating lamb, a particular place, a physical temple, or even the mediation of priests as a condition of faith. In Matthew's account, Jesus taught of a new temple that was found within each individual. And this new temple mandated full personal responsibility for the condition of one's heart and behavior.

Matthew understood times of confusion and trial well. In this gospel Joseph and Mary were engaged to be married, when Joseph suddenly discovered that Mary was with child, and not by him. Hurt and confused, but wanting to avoid disgrace, he planned to dismiss her quietly. "But just when he had resolved to do this, an angel of the Lord appeared to him in a dream and said, 'Joseph, son of David, do not be afraid to take Mary as your wife, for the child conceived in her is from the Holy Spirit. She will bear a son, and you are to name him Jesus'" (1:20–22). Joseph did as the angel commanded—and we know the rest of the story. But the point is that the angel came to Joseph in stillness, in the midst of his confusion, and Joseph was willing to honor the message he received, even though it contradicted family practice and tradition. Change often requires this kind of attentive listening, as well as new resources of courage.

In the first path of our own spiritual journey, we ask, *How do we face change?* We find ourselves in much the same place as the Messianic Jews. We have been going about our lives in an unreflective way. Suddenly, we are brought up short by the crumbling of a part of our life we have taken for granted. Maybe a loved one dies, or our finances fail, or we are betrayed. None of the habits and assumptions we've built up helps us. We don't know what to do. We feel lost—lonely and estranged. Attempting to find a solution, we whirl around in desperation, trying this, avoiding that. Finally, we take a small step out of our confused and self-involved spin and begin the journey. But we are immature and ignorant, and when we enter the unknown, inevitably we fall short. We begin again.

The Gospel of Mark: Crossing the Stormy Sea

How Do We Move Through Suffering? The Second Path

The City of Rome at the time of Mark's gospel was a terrible place for Messianic Jews. Made scapegoats by Nero and held responsible for an immense seven-day fire that had burned much of Rome, they found themselves at the mercy of the centurions, who went through the city knocking on doors in search of followers of Jesus. Once found, these believers and their entire families were taken away, horrifically tortured, and murdered before crowds in the Circus Maximus. The entire Jewish community was in chaos, bitterness, and despair; and believers in Jesus as the Messiah were asking themselves if their belief was true, and whether it was worth the sacrifice of their lives and their children's lives. Mark's stark language and metaphorical images of wilderness and trackless sea reflected the bleakness of their terrible dilemma.

Each of the messages Mark offered held both despair and hope. His account of Jesus's life and teachings assured his readers that their suffering—or even death—fulfilled a plan greater than their individual lives. He helped the Messianic Jews believe they could trust that God had not abandoned and would not abandon them. He assured them that their time of suffering would eventually end. Even the lives lost, he told them, held value and meaning and would benefit future generations.

Mark's gospel included many vivid images of endurance through faith, but the best known are probably those of Jesus and his disciples making multiple nighttime crossings of the Sea of Galilee during violent storms. The disciples quaked with terror, while Jesus the Christ peacefully slept, eventually waking to quell the tempest. On the final crossing, Jesus completely lost patience with the fearful disciples, saying, "Do you still not perceive or understand? Are your hearts hardened? Do you have eyes, and fail to see? Do you have ears, and fail to hear? And do you not remember?" (8:17–18). The second path can be very bleak and frightening, and we often long for an all-powerful person or substance to remove our pain and terror. The disciples had seen Jesus stop the storm, and they wanted him to do it again; but he refused. The inner strength we find in faith will carry us through all adversities if we trust it—if we "remember," as Jesus instructed.

The second path requires great endurance. Our question is, How do we move through suffering? While most of us are probably not facing imminent physical death, we still quake at the strangeness of the new reality we have entered at this stage of our journey. It feels alien and filled with fear, but we can't turn around and go back, because we know the old ways won't work. Our ego-self, author of all our well-worn patterns of behavior and thinking, finds itself under assault. It desperately tries to reestablish control. Persistent, it sets up deceptions, which we must unmask and ignore if we are to continue on. Competing voices and values tear at us. We feel lost and are even afraid we might die. Somehow, though, we remain on a course to a distant future, a place we cannot yet discern. The glimmers of hope and faith that we remember and find in prayer and meditation sustain us. We clutch them with grim determination.

The Gospel of John: Resting in the Glorious Garden

How Do We Receive Joy? The Third Path

The Gospel of John stands apart from the other gospels in many ways. Rather than employing a story line of Jesus's life to accomplish his objectives, John used long, philosophical narratives, with a primary metaphor of garden—specifically, the Garden of Eden. It is likely that these discourses were used as prayer—part of believers' preparations for the early Christian baptism ritual in the city of Ephesus. By the time this gospel was written at the end of the first century, followers of Jesus called themselves Christians, and they came from many backgrounds, not just Judaism. The new faith spread rapidly in this thriving port city and spirits were high—but the euphoria of those high spirits threatened to slip into self-righteousness and division. John sought to establish a common and deeper grounding for the followers of the young Christian faith and warned them of the dangers presented by their immaturity.

The mysticism of the third path is literally "not of this world," as John well knew (and made reference to throughout his gospel). But he also knew that once we each experience the epiphany of wholeness and eternal love, we will never forget it. "And I will ask the Father, and he will give you another

Advocate, to be with you forever. This is the Spirit of truth, whom the world cannot receive, because it neither sees him nor knows him. You know him, because he abides with you, and he will be in you" (14:16–17). This inner knowledge of union is the joy of John's garden—and the template for our further practice.

When the Gospel of John was placed in the reading sequence, it was broken into parts and put in the midst of the recitation of each of the other three gospels. This placement tells us that if the Christians of the third and fourth centuries did in fact establish the reading cycle with conscious intention, they knew the rigors of the spiritual journey well—and also had a terrific grounding in practical psychology. They knew that if the journey could be sustained, a moment of revelation would arrive, but that the wonderful moment was simultaneously glorious and perilous. The seeker would receive an epiphany, but there was grave danger that he or she could quickly "lose it" or significantly misconstrue it. With the gospel incorporated into the cycle in this fragmentary way, John's words were there throughout the journey—sounding a recurring and carefully calculated call of joy and wholeness and caution.

However, there are times in our lives, precisely as those early Christians anticipated, when the separated sections of John's meditations cohere into a revelatory whole—a complete, complex, and glorious garden, an ecstatic, poetic song of the soul. After the trials represented by the Gospels of Matthew and Mark, the things that have seemed separate—the pieces of ourselves, the pieces of our lives, and the pieces of the gospel—suddenly, and usually unexpectedly, come together. Almost miraculously, everything makes sense. We want only to open ourselves to this wondrous and radiant experience. In us, all around us, the mystery of union unfolds, and we feel—deeply—the truth of oneness with Spirit. We are filled with ecstasy, or perhaps the deepest calm we have ever known. At these times, the full Gospel of John is nothing less than a life-giving oasis in what had seemed an endless, trackless sea of sand. Hence, the deep meditation of the third path is, *How do we receive joy?*

We learn that we need to stay awhile. We must hold to an inner stillness and reflection, allowing the parts of us still mired in shame and unworthiness to come forward and join the divine embrace. Everything we see wears the face of love, as gratitude awakens and grows. Gradually, questions of obligation arise, and we realize that our new truth has further responsibilities; we also realize that if we do not meet those responsibilities, our revelation will sour into pain and division. Then, when the time comes (recognizing that we are still immature, that we have more to learn), we make the choice to leave this still-unfinished—though blissful—state. We continue the internal/eternal journey.

The Gospel of Luke: Walking the Road of Riches

How Do We Mature in Service? The Fourth Path

The Gospel of Luke was written as a two-volume document in the last part of the first century to assist and instruct various communities of Christians throughout the Mediterranean region. Although growing and thriving in their faith, many Christians carried new pain, as they were formally cast out from Judaism, their mother faith. Penalties and legal sanctions against the practice of Christianity that had existed only in Rome spread outward after the schism with Judaism in the mid-80s, and the Roman Empire became a much more active oppressor. These two historical events presented significant obstacles to the emerging Christian communities. How were they to respond to hurt? To injustice? Part of Luke's answer was contained in his primary metaphor. Everything happened "on the road," or while traveling. The destination was secondary.

Luke called the early Christians to practice. He asked them to change their previous ways of responding to difficulty and crisis, telling them to model their lives on the example set by Jesus and the apostles. He encouraged them to offer compassion when faced with oppression and to thereby demonstrate the values of Christianity. He instructed them to trust in their spiritual practice, and have faith that the changes they sought would ultimately arrive. Luke asked Christians to forsake any bitterness over their separation from Judaism, and to avoid direct combat with the Romans. His narrative reiterated, over and over, that the only proper course for Christians was to "be" the change they desired.

Luke filled his gospel with stories of compassion and service to an extent not found in any other gospel, and his Beatitudes were revelatory. But the simplest instruction came in response to the lawyer's question, when he "stood up to test Jesus. 'Teacher,' he said, 'what must I do to inherit eternal life?' He said to him, 'What is written in the law? What do you read there?' He answered, 'You shall love the Lord your God with all your heart, and with all your soul, and with all your strength, and with all your mind; and your neighbor as yourself.' And he said to him, 'You have given the right answer; do this, and you will live'" (Luke 10:25–28). Jesus went on to illustrate the principle further with the story of the Good Samaritan. But the entire truth was complete already: when we love our neighbor as we love ourselves, we are compelled to live our lives in service. This is how our transformation truly occurs, allowing the meaning and purpose of our lives to unfold.

In the fourth path, we ask, *How do we mature in service?* We are much like those early Christians. Our ego-selves need to become grounded. We have to learn the behavior—not just the theory—of a new way. Our inner guidance continues to grow so that we may reduce, even eliminate, the old ego-self's protective and controlling reactions to events. This path of full psychological and spiritual transformation takes time. As it becomes familiar, we discover that the new way is more fluid and less predictable than the ways we have known. Our daily practice becomes a faithful and ongoing study of joy, compassion, and integrity, and our sense of equanimity strengthens. We comprehend that our journey will never end. The fourth path leads back to a new first path, filled with promise. As we reflect back and peer ahead, we welcome this perpetual cycle of new beginnings and the fresh opportunities we will have to learn and deepen in a conscious way.

The Universal Design

Four stages, four gospels. We surrender, we struggle and endure, comprehension finally dawns, and then we gradually learn the practices that make our understanding or our discovery repeatable, consistent, and real—and then we bring our works and our words to each other. We believe that this is the identical fourfold sequence that describes the process an artist uses to create—and a scientist to discover. We think that it is the core pattern of all social, political, and institutional change, as well as that of our civil discourse. We find it both humbling and inspiring to know that we walk to the same ebb and flow we hear in Mozart, read in Shakespeare, and see in Michelangelo.

We have mentioned finding the progression of four in indigenous cultures, in other religions, in various psychological and philosophical writings, and in clinical Sandplay practice. But those are certainly not the only places. In literature from worldwide cultures, the Hero's Journey invariably follows the same arc. As they developed, classic structures for opera, symphony, and theater all demonstrated this same pattern (though modern times have created changes). And though the divisions into four are not quite as crisp and clear, the same process and trajectory can readily be discovered in a wide range of contemporary programs, such as the "twelve steps" of recovery, sequential plans for increasing creativity, and programs for developing community. These are among the many places we find versions of the fourfold Journey of Quadratos, in its wholeness and its universality.

When we examine the underpinning of the process, which is the structure of four-ness itself, we find still more mirrors, and they are at a much more fundamental level. As Bishop Irenaeus of Lyons stated in defense of four gospels, "the natural activity of the Lord is fourfold." He based his premise on the great amount of "four-ness" readily observable in the world around him. He wrote of "four zones of the world . . . four principal winds" and, in another text, "quadriform animals." In 2004, almost two millennia later, distinguished scientists Geoffrey West and James Brown published research in *Physics Today* that continues to support the importance of four-ness. West and Brown investigated the laws governing the "scaling" of the following systems for humans, animals, and plants: metabolic rate, life span, growth rate, heart rate, DNA nucleotide substitution rate, length of aortas and genomes, tree height, mass of cerebral gray matter, density of mitochondria, and concentration of RNA. (Scaling is the relationship between different internal systems and the whole as plants/animals change size.) Remarkably, the researchers found that *all* these systems change with size *on a ratio of one to four.*[*] Coincidentally, the article is entitled, "Life's *Universal* Scaling Laws" (italics mine). At an earlier lecture for the 2001 Stanislaw Ulam Memorial series, Dr. West stated, "It appears that nature's magic

---

* Geoffrey B. West and James H. Brown, "Life's Universal Scaling Laws," *Physics Today*, Sept. 2004, 36–42.

number is four." It is probably only a bit of an overstatement to say that we, and our world, are both built on and "nested in" units of four-ness.

The pattern of quadratos is universal, and the thread of four clearly runs through every aspect of existence. Whether we accept or decline the invitation to make it *conscious,* every one of us will be—indeed, already is—in submission to the monumental sequence. However, this does not in any way mean that quadratos is precise, or smooth, or simple, or linear. It is cyclical. In fact it is *multi*-cyclical. Questions arise in one path and begin to find resolution in the subsequent path just as they simultaneously yield to myriad new questions in another. We have traveled and will travel each of the paths many times.

We will grow from the dependence of childhood to the autonomy of adulthood, sometimes alone and sometimes with company. We will be healthy and we will be sick. Life's seasons will constantly change and call out to us with their individual necessities. Different aspects of our life will consistently appear at varying points of the sequence. For instance, our personal life may be occupied with the challenges of one path, our professional life with another, while our communal life is on yet a different path altogether, and the resultant tumult can be very difficult to discern—and to negotiate. Life, and the grace available to it, is rarely linear and well defined.

The journey is as complex as we are. While most of us use our voice to speak, we also understand that the endless variations of tone and pitch make each of our voices unique. In the same way, our spiritual walk is both constant and infinitely variable, shared but at the same time singular. Nonetheless, throughout our journey the underlying pattern persists, and for all of us, the rhythm beats in a measure of four.

The Great Sequence—Always Present

The fourfold progression contained in the reading cycle not only predates and even transcends most of the fixed structures of Christianity; it is also the foundation for many of Christianity's established rituals. For example, we have talked about how the sequence can be found in the design of the full baptism ritual—one of the most enduring celebrations of Christianity. The four elements of entering, prayer/growth, illumination, and commitment to service perfectly echo the lessons taught in the gospel order of Matthew, Mark, John, and Luke. Scholars tell us that the full four-step process leading to baptism had formally appeared by 300 CE. The four-step process for baptism and the gospel sequence so perfectly mirror each other that we surmise the two grew together and likely became common practice in the same time period, sometime between 180 and 300 CE.

We also find the sequence in other aspects of Christian practice as it developed. Beginning in the fourth century, faithful believers thought it their solemn duty to make a pilgrimage to Jerusalem once in their lifetime. However, by the twelfth century, that journey had become unsafe, and coincidentally the labyrinth had entered Christianity, seemingly as its symbolic replacement. Both pilgrimage and labyrinth display a fourfold progression. First: the pilgrim makes the decision to set out on his journey, or to cross the labyrinth's threshold. Second: the pilgrim embarks on the journey, following a circuitous path while paying careful attention and praying fervently. Third: upon arrival in the holy place, or center, the pilgrim spends time there in reflection. Fourth, and last: the pilgrim returns home, back out through the pattern, with his or her prayers focused on the integration of revelations gained back into everyday life. This is precisely the Journey of Quadratos.

The high Christian ritual known today as the mass (called "the Breaking" and "the Eucharist" in earlier Western tradition) also reflects the sequence of four. First, the believer forms an intention and enters the sacred place (church) for mass, opening her heart to inspiration and challenges. Second, the words of scripture and sermon charge her with stringent self-examination. Third, she experiences the oneness of being All with God, called "communion." Lastly, the believer receives the final blessing, the *missa* (which means "to be sent"), mandating her to go out into the world in service.

Though often not set in any formal sequence, all four paths can also be intuitively grasped in a variety of mystical and spiritual Christian texts by authors as diverse and venerable as the Desert Fathers and Mothers, St. Benedict, and St. Francis of Assisi. In the twelfth century, Hildegard of Bingen, in her *Book of Divine Works*, wrote about "progress" in terms of a specific cycle of four, which she also called "the very pulse of life." She wrote that progress begins with a time of "purging and purification," followed by "confrontation with temptuous impulses," then moves into "vigorous life and enchanting fragrance," and finally reaches "the ripeness of nature and the perspicacity of the increasingly alert and mature human being."

The "Spiritual Exercises" developed by St. Ignatius of Loyola in the sixteenth century constitute a four-week series of meditations that closely matches the quadratos sequence and has gained immense popularity in recent years, even outside Christianity. Designed to be led by a spiritual director over a thirty-day retreat, it is a series of exercises, meditations, and prayers. The retreatant is supposed to focus on Ignatius's exercises, although the gospels are also used in the process. The first week is spent in deep contemplation of God's love and in praying to be purified and rid of "disordered attachments"—anything that stands in the way of doing God's will. In the second week, the life of Jesus the Christ is contemplated, with the objective of moving beyond mere history into a sense of Jesus's life as a present, participatory reality. The third week is devoted to a complex understanding of union through an empathetic joining with Jesus's death—combining prayers for suffering with pondering the intensity of God's unconditional love. The final week shares in the joy of resurrection and synthesizes the experience so that a whole vision may be achieved. The objective is a daily life that glorifies God and extends love to others.

St. Teresa of Avila, in the same century, described the identical spiritual journey in her work *The Interior Castle,* although she divided it into seven steps, or "castles," instead of four. From the twentieth century, we previously mentioned the stages of four in the books of Matthew Fox and M. Scott Peck. Henri Nouwen wrote extensively on matters of faith and discovery, as did Thomas Merton, and many of their books—particularly some of the more autobiographical ones, such as Merton's *The Seven Storey Mountain* and Nouwen's *The Inner Voice of Love: A Journey through Anguish to Freedom*—are filled with their personal progression through the four paths, though they do not explicitly name them so. And throughout their lives, both men were committed to using their spiritual maturity in witness to issues and needs in the larger human community.

So we may see that the four paths have endured in Christianity, which is to be expected, since they are universal patterns. But for centuries they have remained under our awareness. We have walked them, often randomly, without conscious intention. Now the time has come for us to reconstitute and consciously welcome the full four-path design. Why? Because it is genuinely needed.

The Unconscious Tragedy of Three

For far too long, Western religions—and, more recently, psychology—have been centered on a three-step pattern. Although there are many different vocabularies, generally mainline Christian theology and spiritual direction describe a progression of purgation, illumination, and union. Psychology uses surrender (or commitment), testing (or trial), and illumination (or resolution). Regardless of what words are used, the implication in all three-step designs is that once you have found "it"—union or illumination or resolution—all you have to do is maintain "it." Not only is this mistaken; in our present world, it is a dangerous and damaging misconception.

Three-step processes produce electrifying conversion stories and seemingly instantaneous changes, which look great and warm our hearts. Quadratos shows what happens after the dramatic change, however. Sadly and almost inevitably, the old habits, attitudes, or behaviors return—usually with a vengeance. Alternatively, elaborate fantasy worlds in which everything remains "nice" on the surface are constructed and maintained. Sometimes, whole groups can participate in these fantasies. In either form of regression, nothing approaching authentic behavior is possible, because pain, anger, and disappointment underlie every single action. Overall, individuals are generally in worse condition than before they began their journey, primarily because now they carry a heavier burden of disappointment and shame, and are therefore arguably a greater detriment to society. Genuine community is completely out of the question. By the time we reach the end of John's gospel, we will understand why it is only by the completion of the third *and* fourth paths that we ensure our journey engages the responsibilities of spiritual maturity and reaps true benefit for others as well as for ourselves.

The normal reaction when this allegation is made is—not in *my* church, or *my* practice. *We* practice service in *our* church; *we* do charity; *I* do follow-up with *my* clients. And that may well be true. But does your church spend as much time and depth and attention *on an ongoing basis* on its worship and educational practices devoted to an actual and complete fourth path as it does to other topics? Our guess is your answer would be no. It is unlikely that your therapist spends as much time and energy with you on how you are living your life *after* you have figured out your problems. And that is a significant dilemma, as we will see.

Which churches are we referring to when we make such a charge? Sadly, we have to say that we believe almost every denomination suffers from this malady. Gladly, we also have to say that there are, here and there, joyous exceptions, and they are likewise found in every denomination. But why should this be surprising? There is no fault to be found here. No one knew about the real reasons behind the quadratos sequence until now, so how could anyone use it? A few years ago, there was a television program that interviewed Nobel laureates, and one laureate was asked how he felt about his astounding discovery. He shrugged and said, "Look, the information was there, and it was just the right time for it to be found. If it hadn't been me, it would have been someone else." Quadratos is exactly like that.

It is almost certain that as curious scholars continue to research the first century, discovering more about where and how the four gospels were composed, some of the historical information in this book will expand, change, or even be overturned. Should that concern us or disqualify this thesis? Not at all. The basis for quadratos is its pattern, and the consistency and universality of that pattern, not historical detail. Changes in historical details as they arise will be fascinating minutiae that will and should interest our intellect, but not engage our souls. The selection and ordering of the traditional four gospels in the reading cycle contain a universal physical, psychological, spiritual, and emotional logic we find irrefutable. Quadratos is also a proven tool for transformation, and transformation is the bedrock that guarantees the spiritual truth of the gospels.

This great map has finally found its way back to us. If we are able to spread its word, then no longer will readers and listeners in our churches have to strain from exhaustion—struggling from their mutual efforts to eke out the nurture of real meaning from the great book of the gospels sitting on the lectern. It has been like searching for something in a dark room by the light of a flickering candle. Every week that Sunday services persist in focusing on the gospels as four different versions of a biography, the souls of huge numbers of church leaders and parishioners will continue to go hungry and congregations will suffer. Quadratos can provide the light we need on the ancient, great, and sacred book—so that we may see it illuminated as the fully integrated and inspired blueprint for our faith. And when the sequence is preached with full understanding, everything will change. Pews will fill again, and faces will be upturned with joy and enthusiasm. Lives on both sides of the lectern will be inspired, because we will be engaged in our proper purpose—transformation.

A Significant Note

It is almost time for us to move forward into our study of the gospels. Before we do, however, we must restore another piece of early Christian belief that has been tragically flattened and left by the wayside over the centuries. We don't know exactly how it happened, but it was likely a natural outgrowth of the abandonment of the four-gospel reading cycle and the ensuing focus on Jesus's human life and the crucifixion.

Today, in much of Christian conversation, there seems to be an underlying assumption that Jesus was born, lived, died, was resurrected—and then somehow died again. There is an overwhelming emphasis on the crucifixion and on "Jesus died for our sins." Both of these treat Jesus as though he were still dead. But if we are Christians, our fundamental witness is that Jesus the Christ *lives.* Early Christians never made this mistake, in part because they never used the name Jesus. They *always* used the full sacred name Jesus the Christ, and they lived the truth of this name in their spiritual practices.

The apostle Paul is the earliest known Christian writer. In about 45 to 60 CE, Paul wrote extensively and translated many concepts from their original Aramaic, spoken in Palestine, into Greek, the language of commerce most widely understood in the Mediterranean region. It is generally believed that Paul's writings predate the first of the four gospels by at least five years. When he wrote, Paul chose the classic Greek word "Christos," which meant "the anointed one" to replace the Aramaic word "Messiah," which had a corresponding definition.

Paul genuinely understood the full import of Jesus's words and life. He knew that the names "Messiah" and "Christos" were both inadequate—indeed, that *no* words could express the full truth of the divine. Although the meaning of "Christos" was important, and would carry a strong part of Hebrew history forward, Paul knew he had to do more in order to faithfully transmit Jesus's message. Paul therefore tried to build an understanding through everything he wrote that expanded the concept of "the anointed one." He knew he had the responsibility to carry the greatest of messages, not just to Jews, but to all people. Paul's example and precepts were a great influence on gospel writing in general and on all four of the gospel writers, although we will see his direct impact most powerfully in the Gospel of John.

In 1 Corinthians, thought by some scholars to be the only letter solely composed by the apostle himself, Paul made it clear that he knew the Christ as preexisting the world. He wrote that the Christ was "the spiritual rock" from which Moses drank (1 Cor. 10:4). Also, "Yet for us there is one God, the Father, from whom are all things and for whom we exist, and one Lord, Jesus Christ, through whom are all things and through whom we exist" (1 Cor. 8:6). Other letters say that Moses "suffered abuse for the Christ" (Heb. 11:26). And in Colossians, we find written that the Christ was "the image of the invisible God, the firstborn of all creation; for in him all things in heaven and on earth were created, things visible and invisible, whether thrones or dominions or ruler or powers—all things have been created through him and for him. He himself is before all things, and in him all things hold together" (Col. 1:15–17).

These and many other of Paul's writings make it clear that he understood the Christ as an overarching, eternal, holy power without individual characteristics of any kind, existing in all dimensions, simultaneously within time and completely outside of time. For example, the Christ was present with Moses, long before Jesus's physical arrival on earth. Paul knew and wrote of the Christ as an *eternal reality,* and he comprehended Jesus as an individuated embodiment of that reality.

Although Paul had frequent disagreements with the other apostles, who initially saw things in a more limited way, eventually Paul's views prevailed. By the time the four gospels were written, and throughout the early centuries of Christianity, the formal name used by all believers was the full three words long: Jesus the Christ. If anyone were to have used a shortened version, it would still have held the unlimited and immutable reality of the full name. The power of Paul's persuasion is undeniably clear, because the new religion ultimately derived its name from the sacred title he devised, becoming "Christian," instead of what might have been more likely—Jesusian.

The deep understanding with which Paul imbued this prodigious name is also a significant factor in the revolutionary story form of the "gospel." We have noted that the form itself was new and powerful because it was spread by believers who met in homes and talked in story form to bolster each other's hopes and spread "the good news." By the time the first gospel was written, in those horrendous days in Rome, Mark was really not telling the biography of Jesus at all. In fact, Mark was recounting Jesus the Christ as a living, present-moment reality to his community, as the great name, in effect, *mandated* he do—even though it was some thirty years after Jesus's death and resurrection. And so were the gospel writers who came after him. In general, scholars of the period have failed to note the fact that readers in those early days knew and accepted and acknowledged the resurrection without hesitation. Therefore, the words "Jesus *the* Christ" in the four gospels automatically meant that those accounts were heard (or read) as present-moment realities and not at all as historical biographies.

In the second, third, and fourth centuries, this experience of Christ as a living reality was continued in the ritual of baptism. Individuals joining the Christian community after having completed their full course of study emerged from the waters to hear the entire assembly cry out their name followed either by "a Christ" or "in Christ." Imagine what that felt like—coming up from full immersion to hear everyone assembled calling your name—"Rachel a Christ!" "Michael a Christ!" It must have been an extraordinary experience. Christians knew that the Christ lived—and lived *in them.* A thousand years later, this understanding had been lost, along with the beautiful four-step process for baptism.

Early believers in Jesus the Christ were called "Followers of the Way." They knew that walking a Christian life was not a static reality; it was a continually unfolding process. Recommitment to the great name and our unceasing transformation is essential today if we are to follow the ancient gospel path—the Journey of Quadratos. This new consciousness invites us—each and all—into a new and ever-changing eternal reality. Our spiritual vision becomes attuned to the dynamic, ongoing process of creation, of the universal design in all things, and we find that many of our old, rigid concepts begin to fall away.

When we look at the four gospels we find, not one Jesus who lived briefly, two millennia ago, but a universal Jesus, a presence of the eternal Christ, who shows us a different face of wisdom and compassion in each gospel, in each path of our journey. The prophets and saints of the past walk at our sides as we, too, become Followers of the Way. The Christ did not die but lives still, guiding us in wisdom and compassion. When we recover this understanding, on a personal and communal level, we have calm assurance to meet today's unexpected dilemmas with sound discernment. We have the courage to hear the text of the gospels in new ways, neither slavishly tied to a literal history nor at the beck and call of personal whim and desire.

If we truly understand the heart of this book, our conversations with each other change. The rhythms of quadratos open to us, and in response, our own hearts and lives flower. We engage in prayer and conversation with each other that focus on our spiritual practice rather than on theological ideas. Our ability to be intentional as we make our life journey increases—as does our ability to honor all other great faiths and ways of making the journey. Our eyes meet in respectful gaze. It is possible for us to live in peace.

This is necessary now, today, as we find ourselves in a world of increasing complexity and genuine danger. We need the maturity of a fully formed spiritual journey, and the wisdom of true elders who hold us and help us to live through anxiety and challenges. We need to pray that our faith leaders will take up this challenge; but more importantly, we need to take it up ourselves and become the people we need now, and our children will need soon.

The Journey of Quadratos awaits. Enter it with us now, and begin its first path—Climbing the Great Mountain of the Gospel of Matthew.

3

. . .

Climbing the Great Mountain of Matthew

WARNING
Before you enter this terrain
there are a few things
you should know.

There is no entry fee,
but it will cost you plenty
to make this journey.

Pack a lunch. Lose your map.
Travel lightly. The weather
is unpredictable.

I am prone to sudden washouts,
to the startling crumbling of earth.
It's good to watch your step,
but what is underneath is strong
and you are welcome to settle there
to rest for the night
or stay for a season.

Be careful at dusk.
It's when the beasts come to the water,

and it's not that they would devour you,
but they are protective of their terrain
and will not easily yield.
I can tell you
they will never be utterly tamed,
but with choice morsels
and soothing words,
you may have them
eating from your hands.

If these warnings sound harsh, good;
this terrain is not
for the faint of heart
or for those who would travel
its contours crudely,
littering its landscape
and stripping its soil.

But I think you are made
of stronger stuff
and more tender,
that you already know
the lay of this land;
how its treasures will yield
to your searching fingers,
how its wellsprings will ease
your traveler's thirst,
how its brambles and thorns
will give way
to the waiting hidden garden
where grows the sweetest,
most exquisite fruit
waiting to be consumed.

Jan L. Richardson

The First Path: How Do We Face Change?

We begin our journey with Matthew, the gospel that answers the question, How do we face change? As we set out, what can we expect? To begin with, we can anticipate a certain internal sequence to this first path. And though each person's walk may vary in its chronology, every single aspect of that sequence must be experienced, regardless of how we make our way through the process. No ignoring, evading, or avoiding will be possible. The good news is that you have accomplished the first phase already—and probably the second also—without even realizing it!

That is because we ourselves, just as we are today, comprise the first part of the path. This concept is fundamental and very important, but it frequently gets ignored. We each begin this walk with the unique elements of our own individual nature and a life that has been lived and experienced. Each of our personal stories, even if unreflective until now, is integral to the process. It is the matrix from which our new lives will be formed. Our singular selves and histories, in this very moment, press the first footprint onto the path.

Feelings mark the second phase. A sense of estrangement, or loneliness, or discomfort arises. The specific feelings and timing may differ, but discomfort will be universal. And though we are aware of these inner tremors, we may not clearly understand that they signal the opening of an inner rift. Their rocking, gentle at first, but then increasing, alerts us to a disconnection between our interior and exterior lives—often extreme, and sometimes total. Our first and completely natural instinct is to push these feelings away. We have busy lives and no desire to disrupt them. We dismiss the feelings as minor, and related "only" to a specific outward event—a disappointment or a loss. We attempt to ignore them. In the short term, this may be a successful strategy for us, especially if they are indeed minor.

However, if the underlying dislocation is genuine and more extreme, our feelings become much more difficult to set aside. We find ourselves in a great dilemma. The small self we have been, spiritually and psychologically, is just not up to dealing with the life we have. Increasingly, as challenges mount, so does our inclination to blame them on things outside ourselves. Victimhood looms and our future dims. The quandary in our hearts and souls calls out for relief. Some of us are more attuned to the inner call, but many of us may be aware consciously only of the ways the dilemma manifests *outwardly*—broken relationships, abuse, depression, and fear. Yet as awful as we feel, it is the terrible pain we undergo that provides our impetus for change. We begin to be willing.

Willingness is the seed from which change can sprout, and once it has been planted, our journey of spirit will genuinely begin. Even though we feel as though our beginning goes in fits and starts, and that it is a struggle that lasts for quite some time—as we change partners or substances, read the latest self-help book, withdraw from the world—eventually we will be called firmly onward. At some point, we will discover that the time and effort we spent skirmishing amongst temporary "solutions" were experiences we needed to open us further.

Once we are sufficiently receptive, the invitation arrives, as the third part of this path. It comes in myriad ways, differently for each of us. Our spouse says, "I need to talk with you," and our plummeting stomach is accompanied by a heart that leaps at the hope for a renewed relationship. The doctor pronounces, "I'm afraid I have to tell you . . . ," and we struggle for the hope of healing as a new stage in life. Financial reverses become opportunities to examine and adjust how we are living out our value system, and a call from the school principal can beckon us to improved communications with our child. Within grief and confusion, we are able to also discern a greater and more productive possibility for our lives.

Nonetheless, we still have to deal with the shock we felt when the invitation first arrived—and it can throw us into the kind of despair that makes our shoulders slump way down and our chin drop to our chest. Yet even this despair has a good purpose. It can lead us to further willingness—this time to make a reluctant, yet vital, admission: we are unable to "go it alone."

Our pain joins our sadness and our humility and our faint hopes, and an amazing spiritual alchemy transpires. An internal decision mysteriously forms. Our personal history bends with reluctant compliance and becomes perfumed with the extra-special component I identify as grace. From the deepest part of our being, like the sounding of the bell that calls us to worship, "I will" is pronounced to the invitation for journey. A far vista appears on the horizon, and its beauty beckons our soul.

So we set forth, holding a kernel of belief that we can actually manage to reach that distant, beautiful place that has called to us, though we do not yet understand how. Almost immediately, the fourth phase steps right into our path: increased challenges. That shouldn't be a surprise. We're new at this, after all, so immaturity and ignorance are naturally going to lead us into missteps and, sometimes, greater difficulties. But it is a troubling time. Our initial resolve begins to weaken. We are filled with powerful longings to return to our old emotional home, no matter how cracked and crumbled it is. We try all of our usual logic and solutions on the dilemma, but they don't work. They never did work too well, and now they are ineffective with our new problems. Confused and squirming, in one way or another we inevitably betray the intention of the journey—yet even this betrayal is a necessary step.

In our floundering we start to soften a bit and discover a new, often awkward self-compassion. Employing it, we begin to identify the inner sources of our errors and slowly correct their influence on our actions. Each self-correction merits self-congratulation and gives us greater inner confidence. Our increasing self-knowledge enables us to continue despite frustration, and to do so with conviction instead of resignation. This is the fifth and concluding part of the first path: the ability to restore our course when we fail. It is also the most vital.

For some people, the initial self-aware time on the first path may last for a very long time. Whether long or short, it has substantial trial and error within it. Over the course of our lives, we will come to know the first path well, as we cycle over and over again through the quadratos process; we will grow to recognize the signs of its arrival. Although the stumbling struggle of beginning sometimes goes more smoothly for us than at other times, when we are in deep crisis it can still have the full awkwardness and pain of our first experience.

Within the Gospel of Matthew, we will uncover a profound guide who will awaken us to all of the hope and challenge of quadratos's first path. Our exploration of the gospel will begin with a study of its historical context, which starts long ago with Jerusalem's Great Temple and its importance to the Jewish people of the first century. Then we will move on—to Matthew's words and counsel.

Before we enter these ancient times, let us prepare some "common ground." Although our outer lives could not be more different from those of people in the first century, we still have "temples" today. Each of us has beliefs, aspects of our lives we regard as fundamental, on which we rely for our interior stability. These may be health or body or love, family or fortune. We derive joy and meaning from these interior beliefs. We think, we hope, that they will never change. When we look back on them, or tell their stories, our mental editings are charitable—simplicity and satisfaction reign. Sometimes our "temples" are inherited; they can easily become family traditions. Sometimes we build them. We count on them. No matter what they are, we consider them central, solid, and sacred. We yearn to make them secure and expend great effort in attempts to make them so. They have genuine roles in our lives—but we are sometimes forced to discover that they have no real permanence.

Across time and culture, people have felt a desire for permanence. In reflections of their desire, they have imbued physical landscapes—particularly high mountains and standing rocks—with meaning. Mountains connote the eternal; they represent basic and unchanging security. Governments and companies regularly use them as iconic images to instill confidence and faith—think of insurance companies, banks, and the Rock of Gibraltar. Spiritual traditions have built pyramids and stone circles, raised altars on cliffs, put their temples on rock, and incorporated the metaphor into their foundational theologies.

Nonetheless, at some point, even rocks crumble. All of us come to the experience of enormous loss. Whatever it is that we believed would stand forever, trembles and falls. Dark chasms and precipices appear with the suddenness and drama of a volcanic eruption. It is precisely at this point that we find ourselves standing on the first path, barefoot and covered in ashes. This is where the millennia disappear and we are on "common ground." Our hearts could as well be in first-century Jerusalem.

Earliest Days: The Great Temple of Jerusalem

In the first century CE, the Temple of the Jewish people was in Jerusalem, high atop the pinnacle of Mount Moriah. This had been its sacred location for a thousand years, and a place of Jewish destiny for two thousand. The

Temple was the religious, political, and financial heart of the Jewish faith and of all its traditions. It was deemed central to life itself.

The high altar of the Temple was believed to stand on the precise place where Abraham, the father figure from whom all Jews (and Muslims and Christians) count their lineage, built the altar on which to sacrifice his precious son Isaac. Abraham's willingness to make that horrific offering—though his hand was stilled from completing it—had secured the covenant between Yahweh (the Hebrew name for God) and the Jewish people. And by that covenant, they had come to understand themselves as "chosen."

A thousand years later, King David was led to that same mountain. There he built a great city that he named Jeru-Shalom, place of peace, now Jerusalem. The site of Abraham's surrender to Yahweh's will—Moriah's peak—was designated as the location for the sole, monumental temple of the Jewish people. Although David never built the edifice, his son Solomon fulfilled his father's dream, completing the immense structure that became known as the First Temple (or Solomon's Temple) about 900 BCE.

Over the centuries that followed, the Jewish people came to believe that Solomon's Temple and the sacrifices offered there were, quite literally, the things that guaranteed God's relationship with them. In the hour before dawn each day, the high priest prayed and solemnly poured the blood of a fresh-killed lamb over the high altar. His actions reaffirmed and resecured Abraham's covenant, providing assurance that the sun would rise that morning. The whole Jewish order of creation depended on that prayer of that high priest, standing at that altar, in the still hour before dawn of that day—and of each and every day. It was a deeply accepted belief that when the Messiah came, in accordance with the prophecies, he would come to this exact spot: to the holy place of Abraham's and the high priest's sacrifice. And he would come as a direct result of the perfection and fidelity of the religious practices of the priests and the chosen people they led.

Then, in the sixth century BCE, the Babylonians overran Jerusalem, destroying large portions of the First Temple, capturing the priestly class, and removing them into exile. Undaunted, their beliefs and traditions secure, the Jews laid the stones anew and rebuilt the Temple a mere hundred years later. This building, erected on Solomon's foundation, was called the Second Temple.

Late in the fourth century BCE, when Alexander the Great conquered the region, a new and more hopeful reality began for the Jews. Alexander allowed much greater freedom of religious practice. Indeed, his relationship with the people of Abraham was so benevolent that in the first year of his reign, the Jews named all of their first-born sons Alexander, introducing that foreign name into the Semitic world.

Unfortunately, the harmonious years were brief. Alexander died only seven years after conquering Palestine, and his entire empire was quickly divided among regional kings. Palestine's new rulers, who came from the Greco-Syrian region, continued Alexander's benevolence through their early reigns. However, as time passed, matters began to change. Successors imposed increasingly harsh restrictions on Jewish life and worship, and attitudes toward the Jews shifted dramatically.

Eventually, there was desecration. The Greco-Syrian kings raised statues to their own gods on the high altar of the Second Temple and held athletic competitions in its heretofore sacred courtyards. Nonetheless, the Jewish people and their priests held fast to their pride and faith. They knew that the Temple's basic foundation had survived for a thousand years, despite all trials. They were certain it would continue to stand and would forever provide the security and promise of Abraham's covenant. As a great and chosen people, they were confident they would prevail against every onslaught. Their sense of security could not be shaken.

In the mid-second century BCE, the Maccabean brothers led a Jewish revolt and resecured the Temple. Subsequently, it was ritually cleansed, and an eight-day Feast of Rededication (which Jews now celebrate as Chanukah) was held in 164 BCE. Within twenty years of the Temple's reclaiming, an independent Jewish state was completely in place, and the chosen people were once more free to follow their traditions. But this surcease was to be brief.

In 63 BCE Syria and Palestine were absorbed into the Roman Empire and a brutal occupation began. People throughout the expanded empire were heavily taxed, nearly to starvation. Rome ignored, even mocked, the independence of the Jewish people and installed a single Roman to serve as both high priest and ethnarch (provincial king) over the region. Although the Jewish resistance and outcry against this step caused the positions of priest and ethnarch to be separated back into two, Rome persisted in its unceasing political pressure. The critical roles of both king and high priest became virtual puppet positions of the Roman Empire, filled only by those who accepted and followed Roman directives.

The Jewish people remained undaunted. Though small in number and resources, they firmly continued to believe that they could throw off the Roman emperor as their forebears had thrown off Pharaoh more than a thousand years before. Their high estimation of their own power and destiny was unambiguous and frequently claimed. The Roman governor watched the community with a wary eye, and at each Passover—the spring-time remembrance of the Jewish liberation from Egypt—the governor became very, very nervous. As a huge and fervent throng came to make their annual sacrifice at the Temple, tensions inevitably rose.

Approximately ten years before Jesus's birth, there were serious riots during Passover. The Jews actually took back control of Jerusalem and held it for fifty days, until the Feast of Shavuot, the celebration of Moses hearing Yahweh's voice on Mount Sinai. On that fiftieth day, Rome sent in its centurions. Although the outcome was briefly in question, Rome's greater power ultimately prevailed, and Jerusalem was returned to the empire's control. But hundreds of Roman soldiers and thousands of Jewish rebels and innocent pilgrims lost their lives in the conflict.

Despite their defeat, the Jewish community spent the next six decades completing a major expansion of the Second Temple, their zeal and determination undiminished. This was done in the midst of Rome's brutal occupation—and was perhaps even encouraged by it. King Herod—himself half-Jewish—led the construction, hoping to win the Jewish people's affection. Indeed, when the Second Temple was completed in about the year 50 CE, it was thereafter called Herod's Temple, and it was considered the architectural jewel of the eastern Mediterranean. Once again, high on its hill, the Temple was the repository of Jewish faith and hope. Certainty about the permanence of this Temple was widespread, as was an increasing belief that the Jewish Messiah would soon come. Fueled by pride, long-burning resentments against Roman rule increased and smoldered, occasionally breaking out in violence.

By the year 60, small Jewish uprisings had proliferated, and over the next decade fighting broke out across Palestine. A full-scale revolt appeared imminent. In 70, as tensions boiled, the newly elected Roman emperor,

Vespasian, decided to permanently deal with this group he viewed as combative and problematic. Not satisfied to merely add to the Jewish body count, determined to completely and finally destroy the Jewish power base, Vespasian prepared the most devastating blow possible.

On the precise anniversary of the date that Babylon destroyed Solomon's Great Temple, the Roman guard—under the command of General Titus, Vespasian's son—arrived in full and terrifying force. In disciplined and thundering cadence, the massed troops marched to the center of Jewish life, Herod's Second Temple, and undertook to level it completely. There is no known equivalent to what Rome did that day. The Temple's high altar, the heart of worship, was shattered into tiny pieces. While some troops took down the massive walls stone by stone and removed them from the city, others burned all of the Torahs and scrolls and destroyed the holy vessels.

This time, Rome wanted no ambiguity and no contentious survivors in exile. Titus's men massacred virtually all of the Temple authority—the priests, the scribes, and their families and tribal members. They slaughtered tens of thousands of Jews. Emperor Vespasian wanted absolute certainty that not one scrap of scroll nor any tiny vestige of the Temple remained. There would be nothing at all left upon which the proud Jewish people could pin their hopes.

Much of Jerusalem was sacked that day, but the Temple was a different matter. The soldiers' instructions were specific and crystal clear: no looting of the Temple was permitted—only its total annihilation. When the troops were done, nothing more than a flat platform and a bereft community survived. Vespasian's horrifying and decisive action accomplished its goal. The Temple, all of its authorities, and all of its worship had ceased to exist.

Even the earlier fall of the First Temple had not fractured Judaism as did this second and total destruction. This loss threatened the foundations of Hebrew cosmology and wiped out almost every leader of the faith. Somehow, everything the Temple had represented in the hearts and spirit of its people had to be rebuilt if the Jewish faith was to survive. In this time of great danger, a rebirth was necessary.

Birthplace of the Gospel of Matthew:
Great Antioch on the Orontes, 70s CE

After the massacre, the few remaining Temple leaders fled to the city of Antioch. Its Jewish community quickly became the new center for the remnants of the Hebrew faith, though in total chaos and preoccupied with great challenges. It was also the crucible of inspiration for Matthew's gospel.

Antioch, Alexandria, and Rome were the three great centers of the Greco-Roman world. Antioch lay about three hundred miles due north of Jerusalem, only a week's journey away. Because there were several cities named Antioch throughout Asia Minor, Matthew's particular Antioch, which stood on the banks of the Orontes River, was called Great Antioch. The Orontes opened to the Mediterranean Sea, providing a sheltered deep-sea port and a strategic location for Rome's regional military control. A contemporary map reveals that the Orontes is known today as the Asi River, and the Turkish city of Antakya now lies over the remains of Great Antioch.

In the year 70 CE, Antioch's Jewish population was exceeded only by that of nearby Jerusalem. The city's synagogue was grand and had special status, because it contained items originally from Solomon's Temple (the First Temple) that had been secreted away to Antioch when the Babylonians pillaged. Prideful worshippers, perhaps presumptuously, even referred to Antioch's synagogue as a "second temple." Additionally, Antioch's large base of Jewish leaders included many descendants of Temple authorities who had fled there after the unsuccessful Passover uprising some eighty years earlier.

This city was a natural crucible in which Judaism could begin to reorganize and recast itself. Reform efforts began in the chaos of a bitter factional struggle that raged throughout the faith. Four factions arose and fought for the heart of the Jewish community. One segment believed that all hope was lost and was certain that an apocalyptic end time had arrived. They maintained that the destruction of the world—either by flood or by fire—was imminent, and that the Temple's destruction had been the first sign of the final days.

The Pharisees, lower-level teachers risen to greater power when the priests and scribes were slaughtered in Jerusalem, headed a second group.

They maintained that the Great Temple's destruction had resulted from God's wrath, brought on by laxity of religious observance. They therefore sought to unify Judaism through diligent observance of Mosaic law and ritual practice. They maintained it was only by these means that the Temple would be restored and the promised Jewish Messiah would finally arrive.

Another faction, perhaps numerically the largest, was confused, unsure of what to believe or which way to turn. Many of these people simply wanted to get on with their lives. Others were fearful of any course and waited for the "right" answer to appear—one that would provide them with a sense of stability and safety.

The final contingent was the Messianic Jews. The members of this group were extremely vociferous and very determined, though small in number. They viewed their context and their challenge as starkly different from those of the other factions. They believed that their Messiah had already come and that Jesus was that Messiah. Their challenge lay in trying to understand what the Messiah expected of them in the wake of the loss of the Temple (and thus of their accustomed rituals), and in navigating through the Jewish community, the majority of which did not share their beliefs.

Today, we recognize this final group as the early Christians, and they were Matthew's intended audience. He directed his gospel specifically to them in their time of chaos, trial, and difficult beginnings. Matthew wanted them to understand that their Messiah who had come, Jesus the Christ, taught about a new temple to be built within the heart of each follower as a direct and personal relationship with God, supported by a community of like believers. No longer was a huge edifice or a special location needed. Matthew's inspired gospel became the prayer and practice of the Messianic Jews, forming their spiritual foundation.

In this book, we will use the words "Messiahnians" and "Messianic Jews" to refer to these early followers, who believed that Jesus was their Messiah. We will also use the expression "Christus followers," the language found in early documents. These terms are applied primarily in the periods prior to the formal break with Judaism (therefore in discussions of the Gospels of Matthew and Mark).

Approaching Matthew Today: Facing the Mountain

Even though Mark was the first gospel written, Matthew was first in the ancient reading cycle. A gospel of endings and new beginnings, Matthew offered ancient Sunday listeners the beginning of a divine process. This gospel put forward to the Messianic Jews of Antioch a message of hope and fresh promise. It presents the same to us. It clearly conveys an understanding of the first spiritual path of quadratos. Matthew's metaphorical mountain and rock perfectly describe our own landscape in this first phase. As we make our way up our own mountains, we trip over pebbles, jump over rocks, and try to climb over the boulders of our actions, preconceptions, and fears. How often do we continue to believe in their permanence and solidity, even as we watch them shift and crumble, both from their essential instability and in the face of our stubborn persistence?

The patterns in which Matthew structures his lessons are as inexorable as the lessons we must ourselves learn in the first path. They circle back over and over again, each building on the previous lesson, leading to the inevitable, unavoidable conclusion. As we study this gospel sequentially, we'll see how Matthew's writing specifically addresses the first path, using every segment of Jesus's life to direct us to the development of our own inner resources, most particularly those of self-honesty, self-compassion in the face of loss, and trust in the divine.

Fallible Icons: The Genealogy

Inspirations and reassurances begin immediately in the opening chapter of Matthew's gospel, principally provided by a lengthy recounting of the genealogy of Jesus the Messiah. No other gospel has this recitation. (Luke has a genealogy, but it is much less prominent and contains different names.) By starting out in this manner, Matthew accomplishes a dual purpose for the Messianic Jews of Antioch. He holds up the entire line of names, allowing them to roll sonorously off the page in a majestic procession of historical Jewish icons. This told the Antiochians that they came from a great and long line of people who had suffered tremendous loss, but who had prevailed. It reminded them that they were descended from Abraham, with whom God had directly covenanted, and that they had inherited the warrior might of King David. They too were special, and they too were strong. This function of the recitation is explicit—clear to us even today.

Also explicit to the Messianic Jews were the losses, betrayals, and historic twists and turns represented by the names in the list. The labyrinthine narratives signaled that they, too, needed to expect the unexpected and should not be overcome by fear. It reassured them that their forebears had not only survived, but had even discovered treasure in their reverses and thrived. Indeed, a further message within the genealogy emphasized that there are instances when challenging traditional structure, rather than maintaining it, can bring great honor. This was profound counsel and deep affirmation for the Messiahnians, and it came at a time when they found themselves unwelcome and disrespected by their more conventional Jewish counterparts.

These messages held by the genealogy are less obvious to a present-day reader. Some of us may recognize the names, but we generally associate them with the pinnacles those icons reached by the end of their successful life journeys. Matthew's audience, however, knew the entire stories—successes and failures—of these real, struggling human beings. Chronicles of Jewish heroes and heroines comprised the glorious heritage repeated regularly throughout their lives. They had grown up knowing the full drama of each person named.

There is no way that in these pages we can replicate the quality of knowing that comes from oft-repeated tales learned from birth. However, we have selected a few stories and fleshed them out from information that can be found in the Hebrew scriptures. As we go through the genealogy, we'll see how the icons become human—fallible and beset by woes, just like us. This lets us absorb Matthew's message with an understanding that more closely approximates that held by the Messianic Jews.

Matthew's first line, a summary sentence, goes straight to the heart of the entire recitation. It begins with the central belief that Jesus is the Jewish Messiah, and immediately moves on to combine his name with those of the greatest of the great leaders, David and Abraham. To Matthew's original listeners, these words intoned, in effect, "This is your heritage; this is your belief, and this is the core of its truth."

An account of the genealogy of Jesus the Messiah, the Son of David, the son of Abraham. (1:1)

Matthew's lineage recites the direct line of Abraham: to Isaac, one of Abraham's sons; then to Jacob, Isaac's son; and then to Judah, one of Jacob's sons; and methodically on, clear to Solomon—and eventually to Joseph, husband of Mary, who was the mother of Jesus. What can we learn from this genealogy?

Following early tribal tradition, Abraham had two wives, Sarah and Hagar. Hagar had a son, Ishmael, but Sarah was sadly barren until very late in her life. Then an angel appeared and told Abraham that Sarah would conceive. While she would have gloried in this news earlier in her life, at her advanced age the prospect seemed so ridiculous that she laughed when she heard the angel's prophecy. Nonetheless, a son, Isaac, was born to her. After his birth, ill will between the wives began, growing to such a degree that Abraham, at Sarah's insistence, cast out Hagar and Ishmael. (Ishmael was later named the patriarch of Islam.) Abraham's choice of Isaac over Ishmael flew in the face of tribal tradition, which clearly held that the birth of a son, particularly a first son, was a concrete sign of God's blessing, just as the lack of a son was a curse.

The human dilemmas in this story are huge. Sarah, miserable and "cursed" with barrenness most of her life, had to contend with an infant as an old woman. Abraham had a houseful of angry, fighting women and had to throw one of them out, along with a blessed son! Together, Abraham and Sarah, while comfortable and settled in their life in Ur, subsequently found themselves forced to leave everything they knew and move to Palestine, a land completely alien to them. Their human lives were filled with unanticipated losses, predicaments, and change.

The lineage continues with more elements considered highly nontraditional. According to ancient tribal custom, eldest sons always inherited and younger sons frequently received little or nothing, yet for generations Matthew's list does not contain a single eldest son. Abraham completely broke with custom when he made Isaac his inheritor instead of Ishmael, his eldest son. Jacob, the second son of Isaac, tricked his way into his inheritance in place of Esau, his elder brother. In turn, Jacob named his fourth son, Judah, as heir, bypassing three older sons and again deviating from the community's beliefs and expectations.

> Abraham was the father of Isaac, and Isaac the father of Jacob, and Jacob the father of Judah and his brothers. (1:2)

Judah had three sons: Er, Onan, and Shela. Although Er and Onan married, they were killed before either of their wives bore children. Judah, attempting to lift the curse of (male) childlessness from his family, ordered Tamar, Er's widow, to stay unmarried until Judah's youngest son, Shela, was old enough to marry her. Tamar acquiesced, but when Shela matured, Judah reneged. Tamar, needing children (preferably sons) to provide for her in her old age, took action. She veiled herself and, in disguise, seduced Judah. Being smart and prudent, she also persuaded Judah to give her his signet (seal) and staff before he lay with her. When she became pregnant, Judah sentenced her to death for the shame she had brought on his name through her disobedience and promiscuity. When Tamar proved Judah's fatherhood with the signet and staff, Judah revoked his sentence and welcomed her back. She bore him twin sons, Perez the elder and Zerah.

> . . . and Judah the father of Perez and Zerah by Tamar. (1:3)

Matthew's "calling of the roll" moves through many brave and iconoclastic men and women and eventually gets to King David, his wife Bathsheba, and Solomon, a story that all Jews of the time knew very well indeed. They were rightfully and immensely proud of David, even though he had significant human flaws and a biography rife with betrayals. After all, he had built their holy city Jerusalem, united and expanded the Promised Land, and ruled benevolently. Yet Matthew's wording also specifically identifies David as an adulterer (saying that he fathered Solomon "by the wife of Uriah"). David's shame, however, went far beyond the betrayal of marriage vows. King David slept with Bathsheba, wife of his faithful servant Uriah, impregnating her, while Uriah gallantly fought one of David's wars. Worse, he tried unsuccessfully to deceive Uriah about the paternity of the child, and when the deception failed, he sent Uriah back into the heart of the battle in a move tantamount to murder. Worse still, his hope that Uriah would die on the battlefield came true.

With Uriah's death, David was able to marry Bathsheba, but the child that came of that union died, a sure sign that God had cursed them. David, in his old age, passed over his eldest son (by a prior wife) and chose another child, Solomon, to inherit his throne. Solomon became the Jewish icon who represented wisdom, and to him fell the honor of building the Great Temple.

... and David was the father of Solomon by the wife of Uriah. (1:6)

Matthew's choice of the genealogy was a wonderfully wise and compassionate opening for the Messianic Jews of Antioch. With the rhythms of a chant, it speaks a proud and ancient history and brings that history forward into a hopeful future. Though most of the names seem foreign to our eyes, to the eyes, ears, and hearts of Matthew's audience, the litany must have seemed like the rising of a giant army of affirming angels carrying a message far more potent than a procession of glorious names.

To people who knew the stories, the genealogy certainly did not read like a list of devout and holy people with circumspect lives of perfection, humility, and generosity. These were *imperfect* humans—indeed, their very imperfection was often the source of their heroism and their reputation. They had been tested. In lives that twisted and turned, they had suffered great periods of loneliness and estrangement, and they had known confusion and conflict. Yet these heroic figures had endured—and their path of trial had led directly to the coming of the Jewish Messiah.

Matthew's genealogy completely contradicted the Pharisaic Jews' belief that the Messiah would come only from perfection, a blessing from God for flawless behavior and diligent religious practice. More than anything else, the genealogy affirmed the Messianic Jews. It inspired them with their great lineage, and encouraged them to eschew the beliefs and customs of other Jews who were caught in a legalistic, perfectionist notion of the Messiah.

WE SHARE SO many of the lessons of Matthew's genealogy on the first path. Remember the beginning of this chapter? We each start with a history—a particular matrix that is only, and individually, our own. This is the hard ground on which we stand, facing the mountain arising before us. We have, however, an inheritance greater than just ourselves. We each have prophets and warriors in our past, people of great depth and endurance and spirit.

We are following in the footsteps of the daughters and sons of our own Davids, our own Abrahams. As we begin our journey, we will be wise if we take the time to identify these significant people in our history. We need to establish our heroes and heroines, our inspirational figures. We may be able to find them within our direct lineage, or we may discover a kinship further afield in our human family. In either case, what we are looking for are real humans whose frailties, challenges, and successes have relevance to our own.

We will find these inspirations especially useful during the stumbles of the first path. However, as we continue, we will likely wish to revisit and even expand the search for our personal genealogy. Doing so, we will learn more about ourselves, and we will better discover which heroes and heroines we need and want to keep around us for support. Will we require the fortitude of Sarah, the careful prudence of Tamar, the self-forgiveness of David, the wisdom of Solomon? Or the practical nature of our grandmother? Or Nelson Mandela's unfailing ability to smile?

Receiving the Call: The Announcement of Jesus's Birth

Matthew concludes the genealogy with the story of Joseph, and clearly shows that the historical line of the Messiah came through Joseph, even though he was not Jesus's biological father.

> . . . and Jacob the father of Joseph the husband of Mary, of whom Jesus was born, who is called the Messiah. (1:16)

Matthew is telling a story of faith, and of faith tested—not a biography of Jesus. So his focus is on Joseph, a man who found himself with a great dilemma. Betrothed to Mary, which by Judaic law meant they were married but not yet living together, he learned that Mary was pregnant. Joseph was devout, prayed regularly, tried to help others, and followed all the rules. He was considered "righteous." He knew, when he learned of Mary's pregnancy, that the child could not possibly be his. He felt betrayed and trapped. His mind certainly swirled with questions and protests, and we can be sure he began an internal search. Why had this pain come to him? Had he committed some terrible wrong to be so punished?

Joseph's predicament was more than personal. Semitic life demanded adherence to accepted custom. Villages were governed by social approval, and neighborly gossip was the arm of correction. If a couple argued at the breakfast table, the village knew every word and gesture by lunchtime. The small, tight society had clear expectations of behavior and response. Deviation caused shunning by the entire village, a fate genuinely worse than death, because the shame would forever taint the family name and lineage.

Descended from David and, by extension, linked to the Messiah, Joseph bore an even greater responsibility to the community. Should he risk ruining his family name by continuing the charade of his upcoming marriage to a now-pregnant woman? Should he cast out the woman who had betrayed him? While neither option offered a painless solution, Joseph initially gave in to tradition, and decided to quietly ask Mary to leave.

> Now the birth of Jesus the Messiah took place in this way. When his mother Mary had been engaged to Joseph, but before they lived together, she was found to be with child from the Holy Spirit. Her husband Joseph, being a righteous man and unwilling to expose her to public disgrace, planned to dismiss her quietly. (1:18–19)

History indicates that as a conventional and "righteous" man, Joseph unreflectively lived the life expected by his society. Suddenly, an "angel . . . in a dream" came to him and instructed him that he was not to cast Mary out, but to keep the child, raise it as his own, and name it Jesus. Undoubtedly, as he received these divine instructions, he felt everything he knew of the world collapse.

Yet Joseph faithfully complied and, in doing so, became a powerful exemplar of courage and trust. Antioch needed this example of acceptance, which said, "Stay open to the inner messages of God. It is important that the feelings that may arise within you that contradict those messages—your assumptions and fears—are not allowed to impede you. Neither should the demands of your people and their traditions. If God asks, you must be willing to move forward, no matter the cost."

> But just when he had resolved to do this, an angel of the Lord
> appeared to him in a dream and said, "Joseph, son of David, do not
> be afraid to take Mary as your wife, for the child conceived in her is
> from the Holy Spirit. She will bear a son, and you are to name him
> Jesus, for he will save his people from their sins." All this took place
> to fulfill what had been spoken by the Lord through the prophet:
> "Look, the virgin shall conceive and bear a son, and they shall name
> him Emmanuel," which means, "God is with us." When Joseph
> awoke from sleep, he did as the angel of the Lord commanded him;
> he took her as his wife, but had no marital relations with her until she
> had borne a son; and he named him Jesus. (1:20–25)

THE FOCUS ON Joseph instead of Mary in the nativity of the Gospel of Matthew is the first place where the gospel inconsistencies truly illuminate the quadratos journey. We are not yet aware of our new life being birthed, but our lives haven't been working out too well, and consciously or not, we are awaiting the invitation. Or maybe we have received it, but we haven't wanted to acknowledge it. We are like Joseph, questioning our situation and circumstance. And, also like Joseph, we must trust in the call. The fog will lift and the next part of the path will unfold. Remember, Joseph did not seek his dream—it sought him—and only with a similar calm and stillness can we discover the holy condition of our own journey.

It takes time to learn these new ways. Our experience is limited, and it may prove inadequate to generate genuine conviction. When we encounter doubt and anxiety, we can muster up those heroes and heroines for support as we grasp for solid footing. We can call friends who are further ahead on the journey. We can read this gospel over and over again if needed. And we can pray. Matthew reminds us through Joseph that "God is with us! God is with *me*."

Homeward Star: The Nativity of Jesus the Christ

Matthew next tells the story of Jesus's birth. The account opens with the name of King Herod—historically a very dangerous figure—and then goes on to the sighting of a new star and the tale of "the Magi," wise ones, coming from the east. Signifying the rising of the sun and the direction the priests faced for morning sacrifice, the east represents the direction of new beginnings, of hope arising in the face of darkness. There was also a Greek belief of the time that all people received the gift of a star at birth that served as a guiding spirit, similar to many people's trust today that each of us has a guardian angel or spirit surrounding us.

King Herod, consumed by fear over the threat of the Messiah, a new and unknown element, asked his scribes and priests to discover where the Messiah was to be born. In a subterfuge, Herod then relayed this information to the Magi, asking them to find the child and report back the precise location so that he could also go and "pay him homage." The Magi left King Herod, saw the guiding star, followed it, and were led directly to the newborn Jesus.

> In the time of King Herod, after Jesus was born in Bethlehem of Judea, wise men from the East came to Jerusalem, asking, "Where is the child who has been born king of the Jews? For we observed his star at its rising, and have come to pay him homage." When King Herod heard this, he was frightened, and all Jerusalem with him; and calling together all the chief priests and scribes of the people, he inquired of them where the Messiah was to be born. They told him, "In Bethlehem of Judea; for so it has been written by the prophet: 'And you, Bethlehem, in the land of Judah, are by no means least among the rulers of Judah; for from you shall come a ruler who is to shepherd my people Israel.'" Then Herod secretly called for the wise men and learned from them the exact time when the star had appeared. Then he sent them to Bethlehem, saying, "Go and search diligently for the child; and when you have found him, bring me word so that I may also go and pay him homage." When they had heard the king, they set out; and there, ahead of them, went the star that they had seen at its rising, until it stopped over the place where the child was. (2:1–9)

The star led the Magi to Joseph's home. In Matthew's gospel, despite the story depicted in holiday school plays and children's books, Mary and Joseph lived in their home in Bethlehem, where they were presumably comfortable. They did not wander, looking for a place to have their child, nor did they take refuge in a stable or lay their baby in a manger. Powerful and symbolic gifts, represented by the Magi and their gold, frankincense, and myrrh, came to them—much as the dream had come to Joseph.

The Magi were deemed the wisest of men, and they followed heavenly and prophesied signs to the birth. Their gifts, brought from the east, were all profound references to the Great Temple. Frankincense and myrrh had been the precise and essential components of the most important Temple rituals, and were as costly as the gold of the Temple's vessels. The highly aromatic resin of myrrh was added to the oil used for royal and priestly anointing. Frankincense was burned only for the highest sacrificial offerings.

With these precious materials, Matthew symbolically transfers the components of the old physical Great Temple to the infant Jesus, the Messiah and emissary of the new, inner temple. Through the use of extraordinary messengers—angel and Magi—Matthew makes sure that every Messianic Jew in Antioch clearly understood that Yahweh had granted his blessing and power to the new Lord. For added emphasis, Matthew incorporates another dream vision, which cautions against a return to Herod's realm.

> When they saw that the star had stopped, they were overwhelmed
> with joy. On entering the house, they saw the child with Mary his
> mother; and they knelt down and paid him homage. Then, opening
> their treasure chests, they offered him gifts of gold, frankincense, and
> myrrh. And having been warned in a dream not to return to Herod,
> they left for their own country by another road. (2:10–12)

HOW DOES THE story of the Magi at Jesus's birth fold itself into our lives? First is the image of the star. This is an enduring metaphor for a spirit that guides us, which can be found firmly embedded in our language and our psyches through all these ages. The word "disaster" literally means "dis-star"—to be separated from one's star, from one's inner guidance. We need to recover this understanding now. We face *disaster* when we are separated from our deep wisdom.

And disaster is not too strong a word: although new inspiration is rarely welcome at first, we ignore it at our peril. Dangers abound. Herod was implacable in his determined efforts to locate the threat represented by Jesus. He wanted to protect the center of his power. Similarly, our fears and ignorance threaten the nascent life within us. Fear moves in hidden places and holds secrets. It is quiet, sneaky, and unrelenting.

The fears we feel at our personal new birth mirror the difficulties of Jesus's arrival. Our birth, equally unexpected, is also a home birth. The spiritual journey begins in the middle of our ordinary life. We have no exotic locales to distract us. We are usually alone, or feel so. What we have thought to be our normal world has crumbled, turned completely upside down, and become chaos. Still, we have somehow heard our invitation to a new life, mustered our courage, and—despite our trepidation—moved ahead.

But our difficulties have continued unabated. The messengers of the King of Fear, our ego, are still on the hunt; they dog our every step. However, in the midst of our disorientation, the Magi will pay us a visit, as they did Jesus. We don't know what form they will take, or what specific gifts of wisdom they will bring. The presents they offer may be small—a piece of the past resolved—or very large—an unshakeable communication with Inner Spirit—but they are always precious and powerful. We will find these presents to be tools for our journey, holding the same prominence and solemnity of the ancient gold, frankincense, and myrrh. We need to watch for our Magi, and when we receive their messages, be attentive, so that their wisdom can unfold for us as we travel.

Returning to Pain: The Flight to Egypt and Galilee

After Jesus's birth, an angel came again to Joseph, telling him to take Mary and the tiny, defenseless new baby away from the comfort of their home. Even more distressing, the angel instructed Joseph that he should take them to Egypt, the country of Jewish slavery, a place of deep danger, of historical alienation and pain. Joseph must surely have felt that he had again received an enormous, incomprehensible—even mistaken—charge. However, the move was needed to protect the child from Herod, who was determined to find the baby and kill him. In his efforts, Herod slaughtered all male children two years old and younger throughout the region of Bethlehem.

Joseph acceded to these instructions, but his trials were not over. Herod died, and though Joseph might safely have returned home to Bethlehem, once more an angel appeared to him in a dream, this time telling him he was to remain away, separated from his parents and siblings. Matthew's audience would have understood the extreme nature of this command. It flew in the face of all custom and the deepest responsibilities felt by a man of his time. Leaving one's family was an act tantamount to abandonment, and it was considered a sure sign that one's ancestors had been cursed and one's descendants would be shamed. For the third time, Joseph bore the burden of a horrible requirement whose purpose he could not possibly comprehend.

Yet once again, Joseph obeyed the angel. Departing from Egypt, he chose Nazareth, in Galilee, as his new destination. Nazareth was a distant northern region that southerners like Joseph considered a crude, heathen, poverty-stricken, undesirable place. The Messiahnians would have empathized with Joseph, since their decisions had thrown them into a state that felt equally unfamiliar, far away from friends and cherished traditions. Their inner lives were in similar turmoil.

> Now after they had left, an angel of the Lord appeared to Joseph in a dream and said, "Get up, take the child and his mother, and flee to Egypt, and remain there until I tell you; for Herod is about to search for the child, to destroy him." Then Joseph got up, took the child and his mother by night, and went to Egypt, and remained there until the death of Herod. This was to fulfill what had been spoken by the Lord through the prophet, "Out of Egypt I have called my son." When Herod saw that he had been tricked by the wise men, he was infuriated, and he sent and killed all the children in and around Bethlehem who were two years old or under, according to the time that he had learned from the wise men. Then was fulfilled what had been spoken through the prophet Jeremiah: "A voice was heard in Ramah, wailing and loud lamentation, Rachel weeping for her

children; she refused to be consoled, because they are no more. When
Herod died, an angel of the Lord suddenly appeared in a dream to
Joseph in Egypt and said, "Get up, take the child and his mother, and
go to the land of Israel, for those who were seeking the child's life are
dead." Then Joseph got up, took the child and his mother, and went
to the land of Israel. But when he heard that Archelaus was ruling
over Judea in place of his father Herod, he was afraid to go there. And
after being warned in a dream, he went away to the district of Galilee.
There he made his home in a town called Nazareth, so that what had
been spoken through the prophets might be fulfilled, "He will be
called a Nazorean." (2:13–23)

THE ANGEL'S INSTRUCTION to Joseph that he take his wife and tiny baby,
leave the comfort of his home, and flee to Egypt is one of the most profound
of Matthew's passages, perhaps because we can relate so deeply to the truths
it holds. Our angel, our inner voice, will also come to us in stillness. It will
tell us that we must hurry back into our Egypt, our place of inner wounding. It will tell us that we must psychologically take our whole selves—our
inner child-self *and* our inner parental aspect—when we make that most
difficult trek. In this exile, we will discover and examine our early pain,
and then come to know it well enough that it no longer paralyzes us or has
mastery over our lives, no matter how difficult that is or how long it takes.

And it might take awhile. The strength of our resolve may well turn out
to be measured like Joseph's, in patience and fidelity, by our willingness
to endure and remain vigilant as time passes and old understandings die.
We too will likely have to go from the first exile into a deeper and wilder
place. Only through our commitment to this process can we safe-keep the
precious nativity we hold. This is the first and critical part of the agreement
we made with ourselves when we accepted quadratos. We took on the responsibility to make the journey, and also to be its guardians.

Will we yield to our inner voice and accept the necessary exile? Will
we risk living in foreign and very uncomfortable places? Will we honor
the promises we made to ourselves? The Magi and Joseph all went into
the unknown, following a star, listening to an angel. Our course up the
veiled mountain likewise feels unknown, mysterious, and frightening, but

it is the gestation of the Messiah's birth in us, and I tell you that our feet fall securely on a well-worn path.

Courage! Trust! Walk onward.

Repentance and Blessing: Jesus's Baptism

Next in the gospel is John the Baptist, who appears in "the wilderness of Judea." Antiochians knew that this wilderness lay below and south of the old Temple mount in Jerusalem, in the direction of Egypt. They remembered the fate of the Temple, the murder of the priests, the ensuing despair encountered by the Jewish people, and the wildness into which the great city had fallen. Yet John the Baptist called out that the kingdom of heaven—the reign of Spirit—was near. And he called for repentance!

These words must have puzzled the Jews in Antioch. They may well have asked, "What could he possibly mean? Wasn't the destruction of our Temple enough? How deep must our suffering be, and how can our despair bring the Messiah nearer?" Could John's words mean that we ourselves have to repent? But why? Surely the disasters that befell us were not of our making! This confusion was precisely Matthew's intention.

In Matthew's gospel, John used the word "repent." The choice is significant. The root of "repentance" is the Greek word *poina,* which means "pain." Historically, this word took three linguistic forks. One was *poine,* referring to legal compensation and, later, to expiation and punishment. Another was *poena,* meaning the taking of vengeance. The third, *poenire,* took the meaning of conscience and absolution, becoming the word "repentance" (and also becoming part of "penitentiary," which meant "house of correction").

Matthew's choice of words conveys an understanding that repentance is a correction of one's conscience—an act of personal, voluntary, inner transformation—very different from the frequently held view that repentance connotes punishment or vengeance. I believe that Matthew intended the Jews of Antioch to understand that they had to repent in order to mark the change from their old ways to new practices that would generate greater meaning and vitality in their lives.

In those days John the Baptist appeared in the wilderness of Judea, proclaiming, "Repent, for the kingdom of heaven has come near." This is the one of whom the prophet Isaiah spoke when he said, "The voice of one crying out in the wilderness: 'Prepare the way of the Lord, make his paths straight.'" (3:1–3)

John's ensuing ritual of repentance—the baptisms—took place at the Jordan River, just east of the city of Jericho, precisely where the Hebrews had crossed into the Promised Land. It is important to understand that the ritual of washing in this gospel is not the same baptism practiced today by Christians. The ritual Matthew refers to is first-century Judaic baptism, an ancient rite of moral cleansing, which today Jews refer to as *mikvah*.

Gathered at the river were multitudes from Jerusalem and Judea, places of power and privilege. Among them were Sadducees and Pharisees, members of elevated levels of society. Matthew takes careful and precise aim. These two groups in Antioch supported the "old order." The remnant Sadducees advocated a return to Temple worship, while the Pharisees, who had become the leaders of Judaism outside Jerusalem, sought to centralize Judaism under a codified law and strict ritual observance.

In Matthew's telling, John the Baptist stood at the Jordan's ancient crossing place and asked for a journey that reversed the odyssey the Jews had made. John cried out, "Repent!" and called for a commitment to go back into the wilderness, to make profound change and correction. He invited the gathered multitudes to enter the river and accept a new time of exile from their historic communities. Going further, John specifically challenged the elite groups, inveighing against them as a "brood of vipers," warning of "wrath" and fire and burning, even denying their claim to the lineage of Abraham. In this way, Matthew warns the Jews of Antioch that if they hold to the old Temple and its traditions, they choose a sure path to destruction—one that equals the quick and painful death of a viper's bite. No past glories would protect them. All would perish.

At the same time, Matthew uses John's voice to send a dramatic message of hope: "The new temple has arrived. Abraham's true lineage is through Joseph to Jesus. Leave. Face completely away from the comfort of the old, accept your insecurities, and walk forward. Enter the water and repent. Be corrected. You will be cleansed of your desires to hold on to your yester-days. Repent and allow Spirit's heart within you to beat anew!"

Now John wore clothing of camel's hair with a leather belt around his waist, and his food was locusts and wild honey. Then the people of Jerusalem and all Judea were going out to him, and all the region along the Jordan, and they were baptized by him in the river Jordan, confessing their sins. But when he saw many Pharisees and Sadducees coming for baptism, he said to them, "You brood of vipers! Who warned you to flee from the wrath to come? Bear fruit worthy of repentance. Do not presume to say to yourselves, 'We have Abraham as our ancestor'; for I tell you, God is able from these stones to raise up children to Abraham. Even now the ax is lying at the root of the trees; every tree therefore that does not bear good fruit is cut down and thrown into the fire." (3:4–10)

Matthew recounts that Jesus arrived "from Galilee" in the north, where Joseph and Mary lived in exile, to join John's baptism gathering at the Jordan. John felt himself unworthy to baptize his Messiah, seeing him as an exalted presence, and thus he resisted performing the ritual. Jesus, however, insisted that John serve, making the point that correction was a necessity for everyone, even Jesus himself. John consented, and Jesus entered the water. Coming up out of the water Jesus beheld a great vision. The heavens opened and the Spirit of God arrived "like the dove." Again, Matthew carefully chooses a highly resonant metaphor for the Antiochian Jews, reminding them of the dove that returned to Noah on the ark holding an olive leaf in its beak, heralding the appearance of "new land" after the devastation of the great flood.

Matthew uses the language of Genesis, replacing fear-filled visions with images of hope and love. Genesis describes the world as flat and enclosed within a dome that separates us from surrounding and threatening water. If the dome opened, there would be a deluge and the earth would be destroyed, as it was for Noah. By his reference to the alighting dove, Matthew is implicitly offering a new vision and a different ending, designed for wavering Hebrew hearts, and particularly for those who believed that the end of the world was imminent: "If you repent, you will receive the blessing of a loving God. You will be called 'beloved.'"

Then Jesus came from Galilee to John at the Jordan, to be baptized by him. John would have prevented him, saying, "I need to be baptized by you, and do you come to me?" But Jesus answered him, "Let it be so now; for it is proper for us in this way to fulfill all righteousness." Then he consented. And when Jesus had been baptized, just as he came up from the water, suddenly the heavens were opened to him and he saw the Spirit of God descending like a dove and alighting on him. And a voice from heaven said, "This is my Son, the Beloved, with whom I am well pleased." (3:13–17)

⁓

WHAT DOES JOHN'S clarion call to "Repent!" mean to us on the first path of quadratos? It reminds us that we each have inner voices of Sadducees and Pharisees that roil and breed ceaselessly within us like a nest of "brooding vipers." Speaking through our ego-self, they often seem to be in a superior, or elevated position, yet their true faces are our woundedness and fear of change. When we are held in their grip, we are inflexible. We know only one answer, and are unable to entertain a new question. The poison in their terrible fangs will kill any possibility of the new life we are trying to discover—quickly, silently, and certainly.

When we receive the invitation for change, we are in much the same position as the Jews in Antioch to whom Matthew wrote these strong words. Do we think the end times have arrived and there is nothing to live for? Do we believe that whatever devastation has occurred has happened because we did something wrong or not right (the words "if only," "should have," and "ought to" echoing in our minds)? Do we fall into despair or resignation or denial, substituting work or addiction or other escapes to avoid dealing with our dilemma? John spoke to Antioch and now speaks to us. We need to make the vital decision to become aware of these outworn inner voices and recognize that they no longer serve us—then respectfully dismiss them. We must "repent" and have the willingness to grow and walk in a new direction.

In Jesus's insistence that John perform the baptism, we are reminded that the Christ is an exemplar of our own individual journey. Inner correction is a responsibility to be welcomed, and if the opportunity arises and there is assistance and community participation, so much the better.

Confronting the dilemmas of the past and attempting to correct their effect on us has particular prominence in the first path of quadratos. One of the greatest blessings we discover is that as the process of transformation circles back through our lives again and again, our ability to detect the need for correction increases. As this happens, so does our capacity and comfort level in completing the task.

Just as Matthew has done, we should call particular attention to the role of taking concrete—even public—action to mark our decision to enter a journey. Many established religious rituals began with this purpose, but we can certainly craft our own. Even if they remain private, or are shared only with a single friend, these acts reinforce our intention and provide an external marker to which we can refer in times of trial. If we choose a more public acknowledgment, we benefit even more, because our chosen community will stand beside us and can be marshaled in our support.

The most important communication Matthew sends to us across the centuries comes at the very end of Jesus's vision. It is the gorgeous word spoken by the voice from heaven to Jesus, who stands in our stead. "Beloved," the voice pronounced: "Beloved, with whom I am well pleased." What a remarkable message to hear in our first path, when we are not always feeling very pleased, or particularly lovable. We need this message; we need to hold it tightly and to remember it. This is the firm foundation of quadratos and of our journey. We are not alone and we are loved. We are the Beloved. These are the words that can sustain us as we continue to make our way up the treacherous and rocky path.

Saying No to Illusion: The Temptations

The gospel next recounts that immediately after receiving his vision and hearing God's blessing, Jesus was led into the wilderness. Again, Matthew is directing his words to the internal experience of the Messianic Jews, who had voluntarily entered a spiritual wilderness. Their choice to follow Jesus as the Messiah had led to the sacrifice of friends, family, community, and tradition. Their feelings of isolation and abandonment were strong.

And a voice from heaven said, "This is my Son, the Beloved, with whom I am well pleased." Then Jesus was led up by the Spirit into the wilderness to be tempted by the devil. (3:17–4:1)

After fasting for forty days in the wilderness, Jesus became famished, and in his deep exhaustion, "the tempter" arrived. When the tempter came to Jesus, he immediately challenged Jesus to make bread from stones to assuage his hunger. Jesus ignored the challenge, completely rejecting the tempter; he refused to participate in a meaningless demonstration of power and maintained that better nourishment would be found through Spirit, in "every word that comes from the mouth of God." Matthew is telling the Messiahnians, equally wearied after the fall of the Temple, that they are at risk of a similar temptation, of picking up the old ways. In the first century, bread was everyone's daily staple, and Matthew intends the stones to represent the building blocks of the old Temple, which lay scattered.

He fasted forty days and forty nights, and afterwards he was famished. The tempter came and said to him, "If you are the Son of God, command these stones to become loaves of bread." But he answered, "It is written, 'One does not live by bread alone, but by every word that comes from the mouth of God.'" (4:2–4)

The tempter came a second time and placed Jesus atop "the temple." This time, he asked Jesus to prove his divinity by throwing himself from the great height without harm. In effect, the tempter whispered to Jesus, "Surely your God is not a God of such pain. Surely 'the Beloved' would not have to suffer so." Matthew speaks directly to the newly converted Messiahnians in this passage, knowing that they were particularly vulnerable to this temptation. They must have found it very difficult to reconcile the pain they were experiencing with their understanding of being "loved by God."

Then the devil took him to the holy city and placed him on the pinnacle of the temple, saying to him, "If you are the Son of God, throw yourself down; for it is written, 'He will command his angels concerning you,' and 'On their hands they will bear you up, so that you will not dash your foot against a stone.'" Jesus said to him, "Again it is written, 'Do not put the Lord your God to the test.'" (4:5–7)

In the third trial, Matthew offers another clear-eyed vision of the temptations the Messiahnians faced. The devil placed Jesus on a very high mount and showed him "the kingdoms of the world and their splendor." He offered Jesus the glittering temptation to set himself above others, as a "special" or specially anointed man.

This temptation of self-righteousness—a risk to which all "new believers" are especially susceptible—would also have resonated with the Messianic Jews in their time of external chaos and internal trial. In this allegory, preying on the anxiety of fear and separation, Jesus is promised great treasures if only he will take a few small steps toward worshipping the devil.

> Again, the devil took him to a very high mountain and showed him
> all the kingdoms of the world and their splendor; and he said to him,
> "All these I will give you, if you will fall down and worship me." Jesus
> said to him, "Away with you, Satan! for it is written, 'Worship the
> Lord your God, and serve only him.'" Then the devil left him, and
> suddenly angels came and waited on him. (4:8–11)

MATTHEW'S TEMPTATIONS WERE not just on target for Antioch—they are the perfect stories for us on the first path of quadratos. Emotionally, we find ourselves in a strange and unaccustomed place—a mountain path, a wilderness. Most of us have been taught by our families and culture that we have to pass some kind of rigorous test to become worthy to hear the deep voice of love, that love is something we need to *earn*. Matthew reverses this belief. He tells us that hearing the "voice of love" is only a matter of opening our hearts to an ever-present invitation. God's call challenges us to walk through a bleak landscape so that we may get to the place where that love will mature. The tests we undergo arise as we remove the obstacles within ourselves to hearing the voice of love more clearly. From this perspective, each crisis we meet is a fresh invitation. As we succeed, in small steps, the elation we discover along the way helps to sustain our resolve.

As we make our way through these challenges, we too become famished, exhausted, and susceptible to temptation, just as Jesus did. And it is when we are most exhausted, when we feel that we have reached the limits of what we can do, or endure, that Jesus's three temptations become clearest to us.

The illusion proffered by the first temptation might be called, "Why deny myself this pleasure?" It asks, "Why settle for stones? Why not take that drink? Why not escape my intention by burying myself in family or work?" We need to recognize the real fears and insecurities that reside within these questions and the pitfalls that acting on them represents.

The second temptation whines. Its imploring voice says, "Surely this path is not about suffering?" When we listen to this voice, we try to maintain our lives in a rosy world where we never face our pain, only deny it. We indulge in fantasies and long for worlds without unfairness or conflict. Sometimes we slip into the role of victim and identify all of our pain as coming from outside ourselves, from "them." Our confused ego-mind offers us this illusion as it struggles to stay in control. If we allow this cycle to continue, the tragic next step is an inevitable whisper that urges, "If this is from God, then God has abandoned us, and we should abandon God." All of us who have suffered loss or trauma or tragedy will recognize the power of this suggestion and the risk of accepting it; but if we are to move toward our inner freedom, we must resist.

The third temptation may be the most pernicious, because it can be very, very sneaky. Its vehicle is self-righteousness. It tells our ego-mind that it can be in charge, and it can be "special," elevated above others, a "king." This temptation subverts our elation. It converts our sense of being "beloved" into being "*most* beloved." The instant we begin to believe that our personal and hard-won certainties are the truth for anyone other than ourselves, we have fallen prey to this temptation and have begun to "worship" the devil. Why? Because we have allied ourselves with the devil of division, who thrives when we diminish the experience and inner wisdom of others. We are started on a grim course leading inevitably to a type of grandiosity that seeks the elevation of self at the expense of others—and the avoidance of pain through a false sense of merit or privilege.

This third temptation affects our world on a daily basis. It can start with something as simple as the desire of a child for a particular kind of clothes, or toy, so that he or she will feel more "special," be more popular—and hence "better"—than his or her peers. As those "special" children grow into adulthood, many of them continue to be convinced that outer signs and material goods equate to entitlement. Communities divide instead of unite as walls go up around "gated developments." Mental and emotional gates follow the physical gates. And on both sides of the walls, people speak of "them."

In religion, we see the same pattern. One church, or synagogue, or mosque—equally self-elevated and separated from full human brother-hood—condemns the practices of another, predicting God's wrath and shunning, sometimes even killing the members of another sect it perceives to be offending. In global politics, one country calls another "evil" and acts on that perception; yet in its self-righteousness, it employs policies as extreme as those of the opponent it denounces, even making war. All of this is the "temp-tation" that Jesus resisted and that Matthew's inspired prose condemns.

These words are not ivory-tower idealism of any kind. There are real differences between people. There are genuine and valuable distinctions, true merit, earned rewards, and a multitude of problems created by these differences that must be addressed pragmatically. However, there is also a simultaneous truth: when our inner selves convert distinctions into a per-ceived right to diminish others, we are not on a holy path. We are submit-ting to the mighty enticements of the third temptation, and we are serving the devil. God, whom we seek and serve, does not devalue our differences. God holds us all as equally beloved.

Another caution: when we find ourselves praying a prayer of restora-tion, asking for a return of the past, or of our old, comfortable ways—even if it is a very small request—it is wise to stop immediately and reflect upon our motives. Most often, self-reflection will reveal that such prayers are really an attempt to quell our uncertainty. While this is understandable in these early days on the first path, and we should view our yearning self-compassionately, we need to realize that we cannot go back. It is much more useful when we can understand that our uncertainty is necessary and holy. If we could somehow dispel it, we would also destroy Mystery—the very thing we seek. Uncomfortable though we may feel, Mystery is the deep companion of our journey and cannot be cut down to human size. It cannot be made comprehensible and monolithic. It is Mystery. It is God.

The genuine path that opens before us does not lead in the direction of greater control, but toward a new kind of intimacy. It releases us into learning to live within great unknowing, instead of being frightened of incomprehension and attempting to exert power over it. Our journey will be walked through unknowing, and the ways we choose to contend with our fear about this will constitute the greatest peril of our pilgrimage. Matthew's allegories of Jesus and the tempter awaken us to the most significant of these risks.

Climbing with a Practical Heart: The Sermon on the Mount

Chapters five through twenty-five of Matthew's gospel comprise the heart of what have come to be called Jesus's "wisdom teachings." The opening portion of this enormous section—chapters five, six, and seven—is known as "the Sermon on the Mount." Among its many passages, it contains the Lord's Prayer. Its core teachings, "the Beatitudes," are found in chapter five. We will study these closely.

Chapters eight through twenty-five are largely composed of lessons called "parables," which amplify and elucidate the previous instruction. Matthew included them as additional tools for those in Antioch, and designed them as conundrums, an ancient method of wisdom teaching. Each is intentionally structured to confound, to tie the rational mind into knots, and to assist in the deconstruction of old ways of thinking. The theory holds that while the mind is thus occupied, something may be loosened in the heart, thereby allowing for the grace of fuller understanding. The parables are lengthy and we will not study them here, but we strongly recommend that you read them. They can be valuable in wrestling with the new ways that begin to arise in the first path—and they contain beautiful poetic passages.

In chapter five, we see that Matthew, ever cognizant of the symbolic efficacy of the Great Temple, sets Jesus's great sermon atop a high mount in Galilee. Seated, in the expected posture of an elder teaching in the Temple, the Messiah began to speak. Yet we should note that this mountain has no name. It is not one of the traditional Jewish holy places, and there is no physical structure of any kind. Furthermore, Jesus's words of wisdom did not remonstrate or demand in the traditional manner, but instead tumbled out poetically and lovingly, reflecting a new way of teaching.

The section begins with the lyrical verses of the Beatitudes. Their lilting words transmit a ninefold blessing from Jesus to his disciples and to the Messiahnians whom Matthew addresses. Each of the nine couplets invokes supportive and constructive attitudes of heart—practical assistance for beginning and withstanding the inner challenges of a spiritual journey.

When Jesus saw the crowds, he went up the mountain; and after he sat down, his disciples came to him. Then he began to speak, and taught them, saying:

"Blessed are the poor in spirit, for theirs is the kingdom of heaven.
"Blessed are those who mourn, for they will be comforted.
"Blessed are the meek, for they will inherit the earth.
"Blessed are those who hunger and thirst for righteousness, for they will be
*   filled.*
"Blessed are the merciful, for they will receive mercy.
"Blessed are the pure in heart, for they will see God.
"Blessed are the peacemakers, for they will be called children of God.
"Blessed are those who are persecuted for righteousness' sake, for theirs is the
*   kingdom of heaven.*
"Blessed are you when people revile you and persecute you and utter all
*   kinds of evil against you falsely on my account. Rejoice and be glad, for*
*   your reward is great in heaven, for in the same way they persecuted the*
*   prophets who were before you." (5:1–12)*

After reciting the Beatitudes, Jesus continued with a clear and uncompromising teaching, found in no other gospel. In it, he laid out new ways of evaluating and dealing with traditional practices. Like a repeated chant, Jesus first recited, "You have heard it said to those of ancient times . . . ," and then he inserted a particular religious or cultural practice. Then Jesus gave his directive, beginning with the words, "But I say to you . . . ," and thereafter provided his new, expanded interpretation of the practice in question. Through this very explicit section, Matthew uses the revolutionary words of

Jesus as a sort of instruction manual that directly addressed the Messianic Jews of Antioch, who found themselves deeply embattled by the Pharisees and Sadducees.

Matthew's intention is twofold. First, he uses wording that makes it explicit that perfect religious practice would not bring the Messiah to Antioch. That is one purpose of the repeated recitation of the words "you have heard it said." The Messiah had already arrived, so anyone who was still calling for perfection was clearly wrong. Antiochians could relinquish any onerous burden of perfection (and any sense of shame that it generated) with a clear conscience.

His second goal is to convince the Messiahnians of the need to think in new ways about rules of conduct. Just because a respected external authority establishes a code of behavior does not make it correct. Meaningless acquiescence is not a holy course; a genuinely holy path requires individual responsibility, effort, and scrutiny. As Jesus the Messiah taught, learning, reflection, and evaluation reveal the essence of "rules," enabling them to become a meaningful practice flowing naturally from love and compassion.

"Do not think that I have come to abolish the law or the prophets; I have come not to abolish but to fulfill." (5:17)

"You have heard that it was said to those of ancient times, 'You shall not murder'; and 'whoever murders shall be liable to judgment.' But I say to you that if you are angry with a brother or sister, you will be liable to judgment; and if you insult a brother or sister, you will be liable to the council; and if you say, 'You fool,' you will be liable to the hell of fire." (5:21–22)

"You have heard that it was said, 'You shall not commit adultery.' But I say to you that everyone who looks at a woman with lust has already committed adultery with her in his heart." (5:27–28)

"Again, you have heard that it was said to those of ancient times, 'You shall not swear falsely, but carry out the vows you have made to the Lord.' But I say to you, Do not swear at all, either by heaven, for it is the throne of God, or by the earth, for it is his footstool." (5:33–35)

"You have heard that it was said, 'An eye for an eye and a tooth for a tooth.' But I say to you, Do not resist an evildoer. But if anyone strikes you on the right cheek, turn the other also; and if anyone wants to sue you and take your coat, give your cloak as well; and if anyone forces you to go one mile, go also the second mile. Give to everyone who begs from you, and do not refuse anyone who wants to borrow from you." (5:38–42)

"You have heard that it was said, 'You shall love your neighbor and hate your enemy.' But I say to you, Love your enemies and pray for those who persecute you, so that you may be children of your Father in heaven; for he makes his sun rise on the evil and on the good, and sends rain on the righteous and on the unrighteous." (5:43–45)

⁓

THE WISDOM TEACHINGS in Matthew contain such an abundance of sensible counsel that we would do well to keep them close. They are a poetic guide to the promises and the dangers that greet us on the first path. The recommendations and responses they hold are truly Be-Attitudes designed to move us forward. They challenge us to:

- Accept that we do not and will not know results in advance. We often feel "poor in spirit."
- Make farewells to our yesterdays and embrace the grief we feel.
- Be humble in our willingness to journey. Yielding to exile will yield riches of Spirit.
- Know that our true hunger and thirst are for Spirit, and only Spirit, despite all trials and temptations.
- Greet all we encounter, within and without, in mercy, and reap the rewards of gratitude. Recognize that mercy derives from *merces,* a Latin word that translates as "reward." (It continued into French as *merci,* meaning "thanks," or "gratitude.")
- Be full of heart. Do not seek to remove any thought, any feeling, or any person from our inner life. Each is an aspect of Spirit. Welcome them all.
- Believe in "Jeru-Shalom" as a home of welcome that accommodates the true peace of respect for differing voices, if we will but listen.

- Accept inner and outer hardship as needed for the sake of living a new life in the presence of God. Power and applause are not what we seek. Our journey leads instead to humility and service.
- Anticipate lack of esteem. Be prepared instead for conflict—and meet it with respect and love.

The nine Beatitudes reflect diverse parts of a harmonious unity which endlessly reflect and touch each other as we go through our lives. As the very heart of Jesus's teachings, their practice opens us to compassion. If we are able to place these on our hearts, walk with them on our feet, hold them in our hands, and seal them in our thoughts, we will have more insight along our journey. They will become our walking staff and guide for the arduous times we will face.

We can certainly find equal relevance in the rest of the Sermon on the Mount. All of us have "heard it said"—by parents, by friends, by society, by religious institutions—that we ought to "do this" or "avoid that." Unreflectively, we may have accepted or rejected what we have heard. Jesus's words ask us to become more conscious. He tells us that truth is not found on the surface. We are encouraged to explore the original purpose and meanings of the things we have been told, as well as their genuine truth and relevance in our hearts and lives today.

We have talked about the risk of returning to older, seemingly simpler ways, but an equal peril lurks within this first path: the urge to rush in the opposite direction. Our ego-mind can just as readily deceive us into thinking that all of yesterday's wisdom is empty folly—that nothing we have ever learned or been told has merit or benefit; that we are without guidance. Rejecting everything and racing off to the "new and better" can be a sprint to isolation and despair. Either one of these extreme positions is only a trick, not a truth. Quadratos requires that we ignore these deceptions and dig deeper, explore further. Although many people and institutions have become protectors of empty practices, there are others who still hold truthful, living attitudes of heart. We are on a journey to discover which have real veracity for us and endeavor to claim them in our own personal way.

Meeting Betrayal with Friendship: The Passion

Each of the four gospels has an account of Jesus's final days and death. These accounts are commonly called "the Passion," deriving from the Latin root *pati-,* which means "to suffer or endure." Each gospel recounts the Passion story in a different way—no less dramatic, no less inspirational, no less spiritually valuable—but very, very different. In each telling, the intensity of the Passion crystallizes the answers to the spiritual question offered by that gospel. The community to whom the story is directed understands Jesus the Christ's death and resurrection as the necessary and logical culmination of the lessons that precede it. Furthermore, the writer of each Passion carefully nests the account in circumstances that enable that community to poignantly and personally internalize Jesus's experience.

In Matthew's gospel, remember that the Jewish community of Antioch was dispirited and anxious. Matthew's Passion account is directed at the small, beleaguered group of Messianic Jews and is designed to provide very precise guidance. Throughout this account, Jesus the Christ is the exemplar of remaining emotionally and spiritually present in a time of distress and uncertainty. Matthew's Passion brings the gospel's question into the realm of the very specific: In the midst of anxiety and fear, how do we embrace change with love rather than succumb to victimhood?

Arriving in Jerusalem

After preaching the Sermon on the Mount, Jesus continued to teach in Galilee and Judea, telling stories and challenging the authority of the Temple and its leaders at every turn. The chief priests and Temple elders in Jerusalem were quite naturally becoming increasingly incensed over the potential rebellion these teachings represented. They were afraid the power, authority, and perquisites of the Temple were at risk. Jesus finally arrived in Jerusalem itself, and the Temple leaders decided it was time to dispose of this upstart teacher. But they were apprehensive. Jesus was so popular that they feared riots might break out among the people if they arrested him, and then Rome would hold the Temple responsible.

Overtaken by both urgency and opportunity, the authorities opted for a plan offered by Jesus's disciple Judas. The arrest was scheduled during the Feast of Unleavened Bread, the celebration today known as Passover. Though the chief priest and elders were reluctant to interfere with the festivities because they feared inciting a riot, Judas's scheme called for confronting Jesus late at night and in a private setting, when the public would hopefully have little, if any, reaction.

> When Jesus had finished saying all these things, he said to his disciples, "You know that after two days the Passover is coming, and the Son of Man will be handed over to be crucified." Then the chief priests and the elders of the people gathered in the palace of the high priest, who was called Caiaphas, and they conspired to arrest Jesus by stealth and kill him. But they said, "Not during the festival, or there may be a riot among the people." (26:1–5)

In the midst of this account, Matthew takes a few verses for a pointed digression. During a meal in the home of Simon the leper, an unnamed woman is described as anointing Jesus's head with expensive oil. Five verses later, Matthew recounts the large amount of silver that Judas Iscariot received for betraying Jesus. The entire purpose of this juxtaposition is to pose a question to the Messiahnians: "In times of difficulty and isolation, there will be choices to make. Will you pay the cost to honor the beliefs of your soul? Or will you collect the price of shame and betray them? The expense of either will be high, and you will have to decide."

> Now while Jesus was at Bethany in the house of Simon the leper, a woman came to him with an alabaster jar of very costly ointment, and she poured it on his head as he sat at the table. (26:6–7)

> Then one of the twelve, who was called Judas Iscariot, went to the chief priests and said, "What will you give me if I betray him to you?" They paid him thirty pieces of silver. And from that moment he began to look for an opportunity to betray him. (26:14–16)

The Last Supper

The Last Supper, clearly identified as the Passover meal, was held at an unidentified house. Conversation began abruptly and focused on impending betrayal, which Jesus accepted in a matter-of-fact way. In the custom of the time, meals were served in a single, common bowl. Tearing a piece of bread to use as a scoop, each person reached into the bowl, got food, and then ate. Jesus announced that his betrayal would come from "the one who has dipped his hand into the bowl with me." These words literally specified that *everyone* at table that night would betray him; Jesus did not differentiate between Judas and the other disciples.

Jesus knew that *none* of the disciples were sufficiently ready, sufficiently mature in their faith, to be capable of constancy. He knew that they would cling to their old behaviors, the old order. He knew that betrayals of all kinds would occur over and over and over again—that this was an inevitable and predictable part of the early stages of the spiritual journey—and he wanted to prepare his followers for this reality. He wanted to bring them forward to the much more important lesson of "what remains to be done after betrayal."

Everyone at the table, even Judas, responded, "Surely not I?" Matthew notes, however, one small—but extremely significant—difference concerning Judas. Eleven disciples addressed Jesus as "Lord," in recognition of Jesus's higher nature and authority, but Judas addressed Jesus as "Rabbi." In that time, rabbis were not the specially educated heads of congregations they are now. Largely self-appointed teachers who had the capacity to attract a following, they were often completely unlettered. With this address, Judas therefore minimized Jesus's station, treating him as simply another man. Judas could, with impunity, ignore and even disrespect a mere rabbi. It is likely that this is more a message to the Messiahnians than an accurate historical detail. Matthew is probably much more concerned that those in Antioch acknowledge Jesus the Christ as "Lord" instead of "Rabbi" than Jesus would have been. Nonetheless, it is an important distinction in this gospel with respect to the character of Judas.

On the first day of Unleavened Bread the disciples came to Jesus, saying, "Where do you want us to make the preparations for you to eat the Passover?" He said, "Go into the city to a certain man, and say to him, 'The Teacher says, My time is near; I will keep the Passover at your house with my disciples.'" So the disciples did as Jesus had directed them, and they prepared the Passover meal. (26:17–19)

When it was evening, he took his place with the twelve; and while they were eating, he said, "Truly I tell you, one of you will betray me." And they became greatly distressed and began to say to him one after another, "Surely not I, Lord?" He answered, "The one who has dipped his hand into the bowl with me will betray me. The Son of Man goes as it is written of him, but woe to that one by whom the Son of Man is betrayed! It would have been better for that one not to have been born." Judas, who betrayed him, said, "Surely not I, Rabbi?" He replied, "You have said so." (26:20–25)

Gethsemane, Arrest, and Trial

After the meal, Jesus went with the remaining disciples to the Mount of Olives, knowing he would be arrested there. Jesus reiterated that all of the disciples would desert him. Peter protested that he would never abandon Jesus, no matter what others did. In response, Jesus predicted Peter's three-time denial "before the cock crows." Peter again promised his total fidelity, as did the rest of the disciples. Yet within a few hours, they were all to desert him. The irony of this repeated promise added to the litany of betrayals we find in Matthew's story.

When they had sung the hymn, they went out to the Mount of Olives. Then Jesus said to them, "You will all become deserters because of me this night; for it is written, 'I will strike the shepherd, and the sheep of the flock will be scattered.' But after I am raised up, I will go ahead of you to Galilee." Peter said to him, "Though all become deserters because of you, I will never desert you." Jesus said to him, "Truly I tell you, this very night, before the cock crows, you will deny me three times." Peter said to him, "Even though I must die with you, I will not deny you." And so said all the disciples. (26:30–35)

Jesus then went with the disciples to Gethsemane to pray. Gethsemane was on the Mount of Olives. The Aramaic word *Gethsemane* means a place where olives are pressed, and using it here as the named location clearly reinforces the core message of this gospel: the effort, strain, and attentiveness necessary to produce the oil of balm and anointing. Selecting the three most loyal and experienced disciples—Peter, James, and John—Jesus took them further, leading them away from the others. There, he requested that they remain with him and stay awake as he prayed. Three times the Messiah prayed, "If it is possible, let this cup pass from me; yet not what I want but what you want." Three times, the three disciples, tired and distressed, proved unable to stay awake and fell soundly into sleep. Jesus remonstrated with Peter that he was not yet strong enough to endure difficult tests of faith.

An often-debated question arises here about which cup Jesus prayed not to drink. Earlier, at the Passover meal, Jesus had said he would not take wine again "until that day when I will drink it new with you in my Father's kingdom" (26:29). Yet in this verse, perhaps only an hour later, Jesus prayed to let "this cup" go by if possible. Did he mean the cup of his imminent death, or a metaphorical cup of bitterness caused by the desertion of his intimate friends and disciples? We cannot know for certain. However, because Matthew consistently emphasizes betrayal and its consequences throughout the Passion (as well as Jesus's almost nonchalant acceptance of his fate), we believe this prayer was metaphorical, asking for release from inner pain over the desertion, and was not a prayer to avoid physical death.

> Then Jesus went with them to a place called Gethsemane; and he said to his disciples, "Sit here while I go over there and pray." He took with him Peter and the two sons of Zebedee, and began to be grieved and agitated. Then he said to them, "I am deeply grieved, even to death; remain here, and stay awake with me." And going a little farther, he threw himself on the ground and prayed, "My Father, if it is possible, let this cup pass from me; yet not what I want but what you want." Then he came to the disciples and found them sleeping; and he said to Peter, "So, could you not stay awake with me one hour? Stay awake and pray that you may not come into the time of trial; the spirit indeed is willing, but the flesh is weak." (26:36–41)

When Judas appeared at Gethsemane with a crowd sent by the Temple authorities, he identified Jesus by kissing him, again using the word "Rabbi" and not "Lord." In return, Jesus lovingly addressed Judas as "friend," completely embodying the principles he had taught in the Sermon on the Mount. He then calmly accepted his arrest. Could there have been a more dramatic example for the divided Jewish community of Antioch of responding to betrayal with equanimity and compassion?

> While [Jesus] was still speaking, Judas, one of the twelve, arrived; with him was a large crowd with swords and clubs, from the chief priests and the elders of the people. Now the betrayer had given them a sign, saying, "The one I will kiss is the man; arrest him." At once he came up to Jesus and said, "Greetings, Rabbi!" and kissed him. Jesus said to him, "Friend, do what you are here to do." Then they came and laid hands on Jesus and arrested him. (26:47–50)

Following the arrest, the chief priests held a trial (quite different than the trial we will read of in the Gospel of John). Throughout this trial, Jesus remained silent. Finally, when placed under oath, he responded to the high priest and did not claim to be the Messiah. Jesus spoke instead of the "Son of Man," an implicit reference to the Hebrew book of Daniel (7:13), which contains a vision in which Daniel saw "one [who is] like a human being" acting as God's agent, winning a battle for God, and restoring harmony between heaven and earth. The chief priests were enraged when they heard Jesus predict that "the Son of Man" would sit in a place of power. This vision implied that high priests sacrificing animals on altars would become unimportant, which clearly denounced the authority of the Temple and foretold nothing less than a spiritual revolution.

In effect and under oath, Jesus had drawn a line—and historically, he was proven correct. Ultimately, the presence of Jesus the Christ and the ensuing growth of Christianity was a major factor in the crumbling of the Temple's inner authority. Only a few decades later, Rome completed the job by destroying the Temple's outer shell. Matthew, always determined to communicate this parallel to the Jews in Antioch, never missed an opportunity to reiterate: "Let your old beliefs and desire for a physical temple go. These allegiances are outworn. They are like a heap of dry bones. Kick them aside on your path up God's mountain. Embrace the unknown. You are beloved. Do not fear."

> Now the chief priests and the whole council were looking for false testimony against Jesus so that they might put him to death, but they found none, though many false witnesses came forward. At last two came forward and said, "This fellow said, 'I am able to destroy the temple of God and to build it in three days.'" The high priest stood up and said, "Have you no answer? What is it that they testify against you?" But Jesus was silent. Then the high priest said to him, "I put you under oath before the living God, tell us if you are the Messiah, the Son of God." Jesus said to him, "You have said so. But I tell you, From now on you will see the Son of Man seated at the right hand of Power and coming on the clouds of heaven." Then the high priest tore his clothes and said, "He has blasphemed! Why do we still need witnesses? You have now heard his blasphemy. What is your verdict?" They answered, "He deserves death." (26:59–66)

Betrayals continued in the Passion story. Peter, the most intimate of Jesus's disciples, fearing arrest, fulfilled Jesus's prediction and denied knowing Jesus on three separate occasions. However, Matthew uses this example as the opportunity for a deeper teaching. Despite his betrayal, Peter subsequently experienced not only remorse, but more importantly, self-understanding. Consequently, he remained not only a full disciple but also a witness throughout the narrative. This underscored Matthew's point to the Antiochians that facing one's weaknesses with honesty and mercy leads to greater strength and should be welcomed by the community.

> Now Peter was sitting outside in the courtyard. A servant-girl came to him and said, "You also were with Jesus the Galilean." But he denied it before all of them, saying, "I do not know what you are talking about." When he went out to the porch, another servant-girl saw him, and she said to the bystanders, "This man was with Jesus of Nazareth." Again he denied it with an oath, "I do not know the man." After a little while the bystanders came up and said to Peter, "Certainly you are also one of

them, for your accent betrays you." Then he began to curse, and he swore an oath, "I do not know the man!" At that moment the cock crowed.

Then Peter remembered what Jesus had said: "Before the cock crows, you will deny me three times." And he went out and wept bitterly. (26:69–75)

Judas, meanwhile, also felt remorse over his betrayal of Jesus. Returning to the priests, he claimed repentance and gave them back the silver he had been paid. They dismissed him contemptuously. In complete despair, Judas left and killed himself. Matthew has put Judas's and Peter's behavior in clear contrast. Peter reflected on his actions; he "remembered what Jesus had said." He acknowledged Jesus's power as greater than his own. So even though he had briefly given in to his fears, he had the stability for self-forgiveness and the capacity to move forward. He could return to the Messiah and walk on, despite his failings.

Judas, on the other hand, lacked the inner resources to reflect beyond his own misery. In quadratos's terms, he was spiritually immature. He had no humility, as Peter did, but instead remained trapped by the narrowness of his arrogance. He was unable to reflect and "remember" in the way Peter did. When shame and despair overwhelmed him, and his conscience wanted to make a correction, he was unable to do so. He didn't know how. He returned to the only ways his ego-self actually knew—the old ways, personified by the "chief priests and elders." Caged in his fears, Judas was vulnerable to temptations and never truly understood Jesus's invitation or his message of forgiveness. Death was the only option he could discover in the limitations of his closed imagination and heart.

Judas's suicide appears only in the Gospel of Matthew. It was a message to the Messiahnians, but it endures as one of the great teachings of Christianity: forgiveness is always available for a believer in Jesus the Christ. The voice of love is ever-present. We are the only ones who can close the door to forgiveness, and we close it on ourselves, through our own lack of understanding and self-compassion.

When Judas, his betrayer, saw that Jesus was condemned, he repented and brought back the thirty pieces of silver to the chief priests and the elders. He said, "I have sinned by betraying innocent blood." But they said,

"What is that to us? See to it yourself." Throwing down the pieces of silver in the temple, he departed; and he went and hanged himself. (27:3–5)

Subsequent events have a tone of increasing bitterness. The "chief priests and elders" persuaded "the crowds" to demand that the Roman governor, Pontius Pilate, grant clemency to Barabbas, another prisoner and known criminal, and sentence Jesus to death. Pilate acquiesced. Matthew frequently links "crowd" and "chief priests and elders." He uses this vocabulary at Jesus's arrest, and again at the sentencing. In other words, this "crowd" was not just any group of people from Jerusalem, or even an innocuous group of Jews, but a specific group of Temple followers, doing the bidding of the Temple authorities—a distinction critical for our comprehension of events that follow.

After his condemnation by Pilate, Jesus was taken away and flogged. But first, the soldiers placed a scarlet robe on him. Although all four gospels record the robe, the color varies in each, reflecting the core message of that particular gospel. Matthew robes Jesus in the color of blood, wanting to call attention to the link between Jesus's imminent death and ritual sacrifice, a central component of Jewish traditional religious life. As we noted earlier, in the hour before each dawn, the chief priest poured the blood of a lamb over the high altar. Jews believed that the life force of a creature or a person resided in their blood, which made it the most significant element of the animal and therefore of the sacrifice. The meat itself was discarded and burned.

Images of blood are woven throughout this gospel. The lengthy genealogy dramatizes the *blood*line of the Messiahnians. Herod shed the blood of innocents when he searched for the infant Jesus. Judas's silver, received for betraying Jesus, became known as "blood money." Pilate washed his hands of Jesus's innocent blood, and the Temple authorities and their crowd cried out: "His blood be on us and on our children!"

For centuries, this cry of blood from the crowd has been read as a curse, and used to justify the torture and killing of Jewish people. Did Matthew intend this as a curse on the Jews? All biblical texts have many possible readings, but because of the particularly horrible uses to which this phrase has been put, it is very important that we analyze this thoroughly. We do not believe that Matthew intended to curse Jews or the Jewish religion at all.

Our belief is based on several obvious realities. The first is the clear metaphorical meaning Matthew has ascribed to the Temple authorities and the "crowd" of Temple followers around them. Throughout the gospel, these figures symbolize the old ways of thinking and doing. They represent groups and people who, over time, became complacent and allowed inspiration to diminish so that increasingly rigid structures could be accommodated. These same people became unreflective and obedient to authority and tradition for its own sake. So when they cry out after Pilate's decision, their words are the desperate words of a threatened belief system, which Matthew has characterized as "corrupt" and useless.

The second reason for a rejection of the customary interpretation is because Matthew has a complete grasp of the early stages of the spiritual journey: His Passion is a profound analogy. His account tells Jesus's story and simultaneously reveals its deeper revelation: spiritual growth requires an internal death and a renunciation of the previous ways. Understood in this sense, the phrase "His blood be upon us and our children" would mean that Jesus's blood would fall upon the crowd (and their descendants); and when it fell upon them, it would change them. The new would transform the old. We realize that this is an unorthodox reading of the crowd's cry. However, we find its message of encouragement and hope for the Messiahnians—that their fellow Jews would eventually join them in their beliefs—to be far more consistent with Matthew's gospel than the traditional (and to us, hateful) interpretation.

The "curse" theory cannot be valid for an even greater reason: it would be completely antithetical to Jesus's behavior and teachings, and certainly to Matthew's inspired gospel that recounts them. Scholars agree that the Beatitudes contain the clearest example of Jesus's principal lessons, and these explicit instructions, in our view, mandate that Matthew's messages throughout his gospel be interpreted in that spirit. Matthew wants the Messianic Jews to be transformed by love, not hampered by hate.

Now the chief priests and the elders persuaded the crowds to ask
for Barabbas and to have Jesus killed. The governor again said to
them, "Which of the two do you want me to release for you?" And
they said, "Barabbas." Pilate said to them, "Then what should I do

with Jesus who is called the Messiah?" All of them said, "Let him be crucified!" Then he asked, "Why, what evil has he done?" But they shouted all the more, "Let him be crucified!" So when Pilate saw that he could do nothing, but rather that a riot was beginning, he took some water and washed his hands before the crowd, saying, "I am innocent of this man's blood; see to it yourselves." Then the people as a whole answered, "His blood be on us and on our children!" So he released Barabbas for them; and after flogging Jesus, he handed him over to be crucified. Then the soldiers of the governor took Jesus into the governor's headquarters, and they gathered the whole cohort around him. They stripped him and put a scarlet robe on him, and after twisting some thorns into a crown, they put it on his head. They put a reed in his right hand and knelt before him and mocked him, saying, "Hail, King of the Jews!" They spat on him, and took the reed and struck him on the head. After mocking him, they stripped him of the robe and put his own clothes on him. Then they led him away to crucify him. (27:20–31)

Crucifixion and Death

Except for his preparatory prayer in Gethsemane, Matthew gives no hint that Jesus suffered, or even took much note of the terrible events of the Passion. He responded simply and quietly to Pilate at his trial and, it seems, responded not at all to the flogging or sustained mockery.

When the time finally came for his painful death, Jesus's demeanor still did not change. At Golgotha, the place of crucifixion, Matthew tells us that Jesus was offered gall, a bitter substance that deadens pain when mixed with wine. Jesus rejected the potion. He chose to remain fully awake, to face and feel every moment with an open mind, heart, and body, not resisting pain. His noble behavior demonstrated the legitimacy of his place in the genealogy as "the son of David, the son of Abraham." This served as an excruciating message to Antioch: "Suffering is of value. This time is your necessary trial, your unavoidable inner death. Stay present. Stay awake to the experience. God will sustain you."

And when they came to a place called Golgotha (which means Place of a Skull), they offered him wine to drink, mixed with gall; but when he tasted it, he would not drink it. (27:33–34)

Jesus hung on the cross, where he withstood the jeers and mockery of the Temple followers. Matthew clearly references Jesus's first temptation when he describes how the Temple authorities and their group at the crucifixion challenge Jesus to come down and escape his torment. Matthew makes an explicit parallel when he equates the demands of the priests with the temptations of the devil. He unequivocally avers that the Temple is corrupt, no longer useful, and obstructing the new ways. "Do you think the Pharisees abuse their power in Antioch?" Matthew asks. "Look at how the old Temple structure abused your Messiah!" No opportunity is lost to make his point.

Those who passed by derided him, shaking their heads and saying, "You who would destroy the temple and build it in three days, save yourself! If you are the Son of God, come down from the cross." In the same way the chief priests also, along with the scribes and elders, were mocking him, saying, "He saved others; he cannot save himself. He is the King of Israel; let him come down from the cross now, and we will believe in him. He trusts in God; let God deliver him now, if he wants to; for he said, 'I am God's Son.' " The bandits who were crucified with him also taunted him in the same way. (27:39–44)

As Jesus's last moments drew near, he called out the first line of Psalm 22: "My God, my God, why have you forsaken me?" To be certain it is properly identified, Matthew puts it both in its original Aramaic and in its translation. Any devout Jew in the first century, who had prayed all his life, would have hoped to be able to pray this psalm at his death. Its misinterpretation by some of the "crowd" is a pejorative comment by Matthew about the crudeness of their character and their lack of piety.

And about three o'clock Jesus cried with a loud voice, "Eli, Eli, lema sabachthani?" that is, "My God, my God, why have you forsaken me?" When some of the bystanders heard it, they said, "This man is calling

for Elijah." At once one of them ran and got a sponge, filled it with sour
wine, put it on a stick, and gave it to him to drink. But the others said,
"Wait, let us see whether Elijah will come to save him." Then Jesus cried
again with a loud voice and breathed his last. (27:46–50)

Only the Gospel of Matthew records the next phenomenon: a great
earthquake and a simultaneous tearing of "the curtain of the temple" that
occur precisely at the moment Jesus dies. This is a reference to the curtain
that shields the entrance to the Holy of Holies in the Temple, making this a
powerful and climactic image for the Messianic Jews.

The Messiahnians of Antioch could certainly relate to an earthquake,
as every aspect of their lives was being shaken. Their connection to the
divine must have seemed especially precarious. Without the Temple, could
they still reach God, know God, and see God? The picture Matthew presented must have awed and frightened them. Nevertheless, the stories they
could find within this metaphorical imagery also fully affirmed their hope
in the blessing at the heart of Jesus's teachings. The curtain in the Temple
tore because it had lost its usefulness. The Messiah had come, and God was
now omnipresent. The treasures, until then kept behind the curtain, now
rested everywhere, accessible at any time and to all believers—not just the
priests. Furthermore, this cataclysmic opening had also raised the saints,
who would presumably now be available, directly, to them.

> Then Jesus cried again with a loud voice and breathed his last. At
> that moment the curtain of the temple was torn in two, from top to
> bottom. The earth shook, and the rocks were split. The tombs also
> were opened, and many bodies of the saints who had fallen asleep
> were raised. (27:50–52)

NOW, MOVING TOWARD the end of the first path of quadratos, how
shall we summarize the significance of Matthew's Passion? We have been
greeted with hope and grief, promise and resentment. That is the first path.
We know that no matter the depth of our previous spiritual growth, each
time we stand on the threshold of deep change, we will feel the sting of
anxiety that marks our crossing into the new unknown. Will we choose

to set out, even if others around us do not? Will we choose to be awake as we hike up the mountain? Will we choose to confront our fears, even unto the death of our small beliefs and to the uncompassionate corners of our most hidden hearts? Will we choose kindness—at this juncture, mostly for ourselves? And as we are able, for others?

Our first deep practice in this phase requires self-responsibility and presence. We need to be "with" ourselves—mind, body, and spirit—in a condition of self-honesty and openness. Although we must not descend into isolation, we cannot allow ourselves to be distracted by anything or anyone. We can take no gall. Instead, our course is prayer, and the asking for wise counsel therein.

Our second practice is patience. Our walk up the mountain will have many missteps, many "self-betrayals." We must expect this, and meet each of these with love instead of piling self-criticism and shame on the fragile new self emerging. Can we name ourselves "friend"? Can we comprehend that our journeys are as individual as we are, and even our mistakes are a part of the odyssey that Spirit has chosen for us? We must learn self-honor and say, over and over again, "Thank you." Our self-embrace will give us the courage and freedom to go further.

Moving Past Tribe: The Resurrection of the Messiah

Just as each of the four gospels has a distinct Passion account, so too are there four very different resurrection accounts. In each gospel, the story of the resurrection serves to both resolve and carry forward into practice the core set of concerns on which the gospel is focused.

Matthew's resurrection account is a buoyant conclusion to his gospel. The gospel teaches the words of Jesus the Christ in inspiring, yet uncompromising prose. Throughout a purposeful journey, the travails and abuse of his trial and crucifixion, and even his death, Matthew has shown us a tranquil and loving Jesus. Now, at the end of the gospel, the resurrection holds out the magnificent vision of a world that can become reality if the challenge of Jesus's transcendent example can be met.

After Jesus's burial, as both Mary Magdalene and Mary (the mother of James and Joseph) waited by the tomb, Matthew recounts a second

earthquake and the simultaneous rolling back of the tombstone by an angel. Sitting on the stone, the angel proclaimed Jesus's resurrection, saying,
"He has been raised from the dead, and indeed he is going ahead of you to
Galilee; there you will see him." Like the earlier combination of earthquake
and curtain-tearing, this reiterated Matthew's central message: "God, the
promise of the Messiah, has moved out of the Temple, out of the tomb. He
lives and is with you. You are invited to a new and larger life."

> After the sabbath, as the first day of the week was dawning, Mary
> Magdalene and the other Mary went to see the tomb. And suddenly
> there was a great earthquake; for an angel of the Lord, descending
> from heaven, came and rolled back the stone and sat on it. (28:1–2)
>
> The angel said to the women, "Do not be afraid; I know that you are
> looking for Jesus who was crucified. He is not here; for he has been
> raised, as he said. . . . 'He has been raised from the dead, and indeed he is
> going ahead of you to Galilee; there you will see him.' This is my message
> for you." (28:5–7)*

In Galilee, the place of the promised second sighting, the disciples encountered the risen Jesus as the angel had promised. But this did not happen on either of the great historic Jewish mountains—Mount Moriah or
Mount Sinai. It was simply "a mountain" in Galilee, significantly unnamed,
just as the mountain had been for the Sermon on the Mount. Matthew, once
again, is explicitly leaving the Temple mount in Jerusalem behind. The new
mountain of the Messiah is not in a particular place. It is anywhere, and
everywhere. It is within.

Since there is only a single appearance of the risen Christ in this gospel,
Matthew clearly wishes his summary to be focused on the points he makes
here. He chooses to reiterate and expand the same words Jesus referenced
in his trial before the high priest—the revolutionary and extraordinary

---

* There is a small section (28:9–10) that tells of an encounter between the two Marys
and the risen Jesus. It was almost certainly added to Matthew a century after the gospel
was originally written. This is believed partly because its placement at this point in the
text disrupts the gospel's otherwise seamless narrative. When this section is omitted
and the gospel is returned to the original, Jesus appears only once, on an unnamed
"mount in Galilee."

vision of the prophet Daniel. These final words defied the foundation of traditional Jewish belief. When the resurrected Jesus appeared in Galilee to his disciples, he decisively announced that the full power and unity of both heaven and earth were *his,* and his alone. He claimed all divine and temporal authority. He spoke in the name of the one God, and he gave a command that must have completely astounded his listeners.

Jesus the Messiah, the risen Christ, told the disciples to leave the mountain. He instructed them to take the power of God—the inner power they had gained and all that they had learned—out to every place and everyone. He instructed them to teach discipleship—the process of intimate relationship with Spirit they had learned from him—to one and all, near and far. He directed them to share the lessons of love, to tell others that the divine has only one source, and that every person is a son and daughter of that source.

Messianic Jews surely found this instruction not only revolutionary but horrifying. They were Jews. They trusted, in an understanding as deep as their history, that the God to whom they prayed was uniquely *their* God, not everyone's. God's covenant with Abraham had made them first among all people, specially privileged. Now the Jewish Messiah had come—and of course he had come *for them alone.* It must have been almost impossible for them to believe that after two thousand years of Jewish suffering, hoping, and waiting, they were not going to receive any exceptional acknowledgment.

Jesus's instruction told them that their centuries of expectation were unfounded and that they had to completely renounce any privilege they might have believed was theirs. Even further—they were instructed to give their privilege away to "all nations," even to the oppressors! It must have seemed impossible—almost absurd. After all, their world already felt as though it were rocking with theological earthquakes, and the logical course in an earthquake is to hold on to what is solid, not to let it go. How could their precious Messiah ask them to give up the belief in their privilege when they had already lost so much? This had to have been a deeply dismaying challenge for the suffering Messiahnians.

The direct and simple beauty of the gospel's last line must have allayed the dismay and confusion, however. With the same full power and authority of heaven and earth used for his difficult instructions, Jesus the Messiah pronounced, "Remember." He told his followers never to forget that they were not alone. He was with them, loving them, always and forever. This is, indeed, the fitting and final message to which Matthew has brought everything in this gospel: "And remember, I am with you always, to the end of the age."

> Now the eleven disciples went to Galilee, to the mountain to which
> Jesus had directed them. When they saw him, they worshiped him;
> but some doubted. And Jesus came and said to them, "All authority
> in heaven and on earth has been given to me. Go therefore and make
> disciples of all nations* . . . teaching them to obey everything that I
> have commanded you. And remember, I am with you always, to the
> end of the age." (28:16–20)

WHEN WE CONSIDER how this last section of Matthew's gospel resonates within our own lives, we might at first be tempted to think in terms of how dissimilar our experience is today. After all, we know that in the Mediterranean basin, as in most parts of the world, early human groupings were tribal. Each village had its own god, and the villagers' beliefs determined their entire understanding of the world. Indeed, tribal culture still dominates in many third-world regions. Yet the essentially tribal fears and trepidation of Antioch relate to us right here in the first world even more than we might realize. The idea of something larger and more cooperative than the tribe, a "nation state," is really very recent in the history of humankind.

We talked in the Preface about the close sense of "village" found in an extended Lebanese family. Right now, today, in tribes throughout the world, including Lebanon, people are taught that they only "know" people from their village, even if they can see the villages of outsiders in the distance. These tribal understandings shape everyone's early development, and they are, in some ways, not so different from those of many Americans in rural areas and even large, urban neighborhoods.

---

* Present-day Bibles include the phrase "baptizing them in the name of the Father and of the Son and of the Holy Spirit" at this point in the text. This phrase, commonly referred to as "the baptismal commission," was added to the gospel some years after the original text was written. We know this because the concepts of Father, Son, and Spirit did not crystallize until after full separation from Judaism had occurred and self-identification of early followers as "Christians" had commenced.

Most of us no longer live in places we would call villages, and we have told ourselves that our awareness is different and more "sophisticated." Yet we still retain many vestiges of the old patterns. We are often suspicious of those who differ from us in ways large and small. We keep company with those most like ourselves, and we refer to outsiders as "them"—in our families, our work, our churches, our countries.

So while the fearfulness of Jesus's command may have lessened somewhat over the centuries, its basic challenge has not. The words are still inspiring, and their practice is still daunting, no matter how much we may believe in the principle of equality. We are, after all, on the first path.

The self-honesty we have begun to gain on our trek up Matthew's mountain has given us a glimpse into our next challenge, the stormy sea. Throughout Matthew we have been called—like Joseph, husband and dreamer—to accept emotional exile and make an original journey. To accomplish this, we have had to put our usual ways of knowing aside and begin walking to an inner voice, as Joseph did. We have had to lose a few of our normal "markers," a bit of our self-confidence. In these last lines of Matthew, we begin to realize, as Joseph did, that the cost to heed this inner voice will be enormous.

At the beginning of his gospel, Matthew recounted the story of the Messiah's lineage and the coming of a child to be named Emmanuel, which means "God is with us." The last line of the Gospel of Matthew has given us the power to continue and sustain our journey. It is an unequivocal promise: "Remember, I am with you always, to the end of the age."

This is the answer to all of our questions and all of our fears. The earthquake we are feeling is also opening the tombs for our saints to arise. They are with us. God is with us. Now we are headed for Rome and the very stormy sea of the Gospel of Mark. We will carry Matthew's final message as a staff, holding it firmly as we stride toward the waves that glint before us. The second path, and its gospel, will be another great challenge, but I promise you we will make our way through it. Remember—there is not just one gospel. Nor are there two gospels, or even three. There are four gospels in the Journey of Quadratos. We can, and will, traverse the second path—and the third—and the fourth. We have the map. Do not forget: we are not alone—we are *never* alone. With God's promise in our hearts, let us move into Mark's gospel.

Prayer for the First Path

PSALM 121

I lift my eyes to the mountain peak—
Where does my help come from?
It comes from you
Maker of heaven and earth
Who holds my foot firm on the path up
Who's constantly present
Everywhere aware

Look!
With you there's no obscurity
Nothing is dim, asleep, inert
To those who question and struggle
You respond, keep hold, give cover
So that by day the sun won't burn
Nor by night the moon mesmerize

You guard against evil
Enfold and reveal the soul

Guard my arrival
Secure my departure—
Now:

Always
        translation by Norman Fischer

EXERCISES FOR THE FIRST PATH

Create Temenos

Temenos is a Greek term that literally means "to make a cut or furrow in the ground." It was particularly used to indicate the unbroken cut that marked off the spiritual area where a temple was to be built. The unbroken trench thereby created was intended to assuage fear that the divinity might escape from the holy place. The Greeks understood that to go to a temple was risky behavior. One went there to ask a question, and asking meant that one did not know—a frightening admission for the ego-self. The self therefore wanted to be sure that it was going to a place of genuine divinity and safety before making the journey into the unknown. Temenos provided that assurance.

In our present-day world, temenos is a very useful way of understanding the balance between safety and risk. Too much safety easily leads to complacency, and we can we slip into the illusion that security and a lack of danger are our prerogatives. The opposite is equally true. Too much risk, and emotional paralysis can be the result. If we are overstimulated or overwhelmed, we can fall into the opposite illusion and decide the journey is simply too painful, beyond our capacity.

The practice of the first path requires a continual discovery of learning your emotional and psychological strengths and vulnerabilities, which you will do as you proceed through the fits and starts of making progress and falling back. Then your challenge will be to put your knowledge to work in keeping your balance between inspiration and a sense of being overwhelmed.

Therefore, to genuinely begin a practice of temenos requires quite a number of serious tasks. You are, after all, trying to establish a balanced environment for your journey. You need to contemplate, find, and gather the words, people, and stories that you think will enable trust and inspire movement or the desire for movement in you. Stories and films that inspire you and remind you that this journey has successfully been made by others are also helpful.

You will also need to secure a trusted adviser, or a spiritual guide, or a mentor. And most importantly, it is critical that you begin a daily practice of reflection, meditation, and/or prayer. These matters are not optional. Without them, you will not be able to travel the long journey ahead. But we assure you, every single effort you put forth toward accomplishing these tasks will result in untold riches and enormous benefits for you—not only in the completion of the Journey of Quadratos, but throughout the rest of your life.

Welcome the Heyoeka

The Lakota people of North America have a concept called the *heyoeka,* or "the other." A person identified as a heyoeka, whether male or female, becomes an official "opposite," feeling and thinking and expressing what others will not. The heyoeka dresses in heavy clothes in the summer and lightweight fabrics in the winter, walks backward, laughs when others are sad, and is sad when others are happy. His or her most important role is served when the people are in deliberation at council. As a decision begins to gain approval, the heyoeka must speak loudly and strongly to the opposite opinion. The Lakota believe that every voice and every position on an issue must be given a respectful hearing before the people can make a correct discernment. Heyoeka is a specific name from a specific people, but this practice of offering respect to every voice and position is generally found throughout the indigenous people of the Americas.

Therefore, as you are setting out, it is essential that you begin to listen for the annoying, irritating opinion inside yourself, amongst your family members, your friends, your church, your region and country. When you hear it, and when you sense resistance to it inside yourself, make an effort to respectfully entertain the new position. Indeed, try to think about *all* positions, especially those you would normally reject automatically, even (or especially) if they make you uncomfortable or angry. Attempting to welcome these ideas does not mean following them—but it does mean getting to know them, and trying to understand differing positions and the people who hold them. It is possible that one of these seemingly foreign ideas may provide the key to your next step—or even your entire journey.

HOW DO WE FACE CHANGE?

is the core question of the Gospel of Matthew

The great, overarching message of Matthew is courage and trust. In writing to the early Messiahnians, who didn't know they were to be among the founders of a new religion, his steadying words still echo with prophetic insight and pragmatic counsel invaluable to all who are on the first path of the Journey of Quadratos. How often are we, too, surprised by the completely unexpected way events turn out in our lives?

The genealogy of Matthew, the story of Joseph, the arrival of the Magi, and the baptism of Jesus all tell us to search not only our individual histories, but the experience and stories of others, for inspiration. Every great example we find reminds us that arduous journeys can be accomplished—and that they are worthwhile. Remain open to surprise. Great gifts can come from unexpected, seemingly improper, contradictory, or uncomfortable sources. And above all else, remember—even when ash falls from the sky, or the earth trembles—we are beloved.

Herod's example and Mary and Joseph's return to Egypt ask us to confront our fears about making a new journey, and learn from them. When we then return and recognize our places of deep wounding, Spirit will help us begin to loosen pain's hold and lead us to larger freedom. We need to discipline ourselves to disregard "what if?" and "should have" and "if only."

The devil's temptations ask us to be mindful of our motives at every minute of our journey, for many self-illusions can lead us astray. Self-righteousness can be a particular problem when we claim our beliefs as right for anyone other than ourselves and try to aggrandize ourselves at the expense of others.

The Beatitudes give us standards to emulate, goals to choose, and beautiful words to pray. They will help us stay on the road if we keep them close at hand.

The Passion account affirms that if we truly accept our invitation to the journey offered by Jesus the Christ, we will stay "awake" to the entire process. Through prayer and self-reflection, we will embrace change with a full heart and not blame others and take on a victim's mantle when difficulties befall.

The resurrection account tells us we have to take personal responsibility for our spiritual lives and accept the challenge to make our journey. We need to renounce self-righteousness and any sense of being special that we may feel because of Jesus's charge to share our faith. There is no need for us *ever* to feel alone, because we have Jesus's promise: "Remember, I am with you always, to the end of the age."

· · ·

4

Crossing Mark's Stormy Sea

WILDERNESS PRAYER
I am not asking you
to take this wilderness from me,
to remove this place of starkness
where I come to know
the wildness within me,
where I learn to call the names
of the ravenous beasts
that pace inside me,
to finger the brambles
that snake through my veins,
to taste the thirst
that tugs at my tongue.

But send me
tough angels,
sweet wine,
strong bread:
just enough.

Jan L. Richardson

The Second Path:
How Do We Move Through Suffering?

The second path is without a doubt the most agonizing of the four paths—so it is a very good thing that it is also the least complicated and can be the shortest. In the first path, we chose to thrust ourselves directly back into our greatest fears and insecurities. Now, in the second path, they fight back. Although we are in a time of great discovery, our revelations happen in an environment of terrific emotional and spiritual trial. The profound question of the second path is, How do we move through suffering?

We feel as though we are in a small boat on a stormy sea—terrified, exhausted, fragile. The winds and water lash us as we are tossed about in a gray, horizonless, directionless world. Is help coming? There is no way to tell, and in any case, we are not sure how to discern what would help and what would harm us further. We are thirsty, but only salt water surrounds us. We are filled with doubt that drains our strength like the deepest failure. We feel pretty certain we will die.

We know we can't return to the beginning. At this point, we probably could not even find that place—but we don't really wish to anyway. We want to get through this time. We have only one genuine possibility, and that is to fall back on ancient and proven practice. We pray, or we meditate. We stay attentive for a hopeful sign or voice—a navigational star, a neighborly and knowledgeable sailor who knows the waters better than we. We pray and listen more. Then we follow the instructions we receive, in whatever way we receive them, without question. We pray and listen still more. We surrender yet again to whatever greater knowledge is expressed to us. And we continue to pray.

The bleak condition in which we find ourselves now is precisely the same condition in which the early Christians of Rome in the middle of the first century found themselves—lost, alone, struggling to have hope. The Gospel of Mark was written as a compassionate beacon to light the way through their enduring journey of faith, and it now illuminates our second path.

Birthplace of the Gospel of Mark:
Rome, Mid-60s CE

In the first century, Rome was the great Mediterranean center of power. Anyone who wanted to exert influence, or just wanted to be in the middle of things, had to go to Rome. By the year 60, Rome numbered some two million people, thirty to forty thousand of whom were Jews. Even though that was only two percent of the population, the Roman government paid a significant amount of attention to this minority, ensuring and sustaining a long-established pattern of discord and contention. Roman Jews would live in relative peace for a time. Then a problem would arise and they would be evicted. They would return, enjoy a bit of peace, and then endure another eviction. Evictions took place in 139 BCE, and again in 19 and 49 CE.

In the year 41, Emperor Claudius came to power. He immediately restricted the Jews by prohibiting the use of public places for worship, which effectively shut down the synagogues. The Jews regrouped and began using private homes as gathering places for Sabbath worship and other Jewish feasts and celebrations. Everything remained quiet on the surface until the year 49, when disturbances broke out in the Jewish quarter. Claudius responded by decreeing the expulsion of all Jews from Rome. Although we lack clear historical evidence, we do know that tension had been mounting in the quarter between traditional Jews and Messianic Jews who believed in the Christus (the Christ), and we conjecture that the conflicts behind the expulsion were between these two groups.

After Claudius died and Nero became emperor in the year 54, the Jews were allowed to return. The apostles Peter and Paul, the two most prominent figures of first-century Christianity, both lived in Rome during those mid-century years. Peter may initially have come in the 40s, been evicted, and returned in 54. Paul is thought to have been brought to Rome as a prisoner, and lived there under house arrest, sometime between 56 and 60. We do know, for certain, that in the agonizing years of Mark's gospel, they both lived in Rome—almost certainly in close proximity to each other in the Jewish quarter, a marshy area across the Tiber River from the hills on which the aristocracy resided in elevated splendor.

The Christian church was ultimately to be founded on the differing gifts of these two powerful leaders, but their approaches were so dissimilar that conflict between them was inevitable. By all accounts, until coming to Rome they had successfully avoided each other for years. Now they found themselves in the same city. Both were members of a troubled minority in a time of great tumult at the center of Roman power. Their personal and theological differences stood in stark contrast as each vied for influence and loyalties in the Jewish community. It is strange irony indeed that the Christian church later gave them a shared feast day: June 29 is the Feast of Sts. Peter and Paul.

Peter was a fisherman who grew up in Galilee, far from Jerusalem and its perceived high culture. He had known Jesus personally, had been one of the inner circle of disciples, and was the titular (and cautious) leader of the Messianic Jews. Although we have almost no writings by Peter beyond two possible letters in the New Testament, tradition has frequently described his personality with words such as "gentle" and "accepting."

By contrast, Paul was a scholar and orator who produced an extensive body of writings. His are the first and oldest Christian writings we have, dating from approximately 45 to 60 CE, prior to the first gospel. Although he grew up in what is today known as Turkey, he was well educated and very much at ease in Greco-Roman culture. Paul had a fiery heart and tongue, and carried the message of the Christ across Asia Minor and Greece as a committed evangelist, although he never personally knew the historical Jesus. Accused of being a dangerous radical and enemy of the emperor, Paul—unlike Peter—was a Roman citizen.

On July 19 in the year 64, an immense fire erupted in Rome. It blazed for five days, stilled, then ignited again and burned for another forty-eight hours. The flames raced through most of Rome, and when the conflagration finally ended, most of the city had been reduced to embers. Little remained—not even the stately hillside homes of the aristocracy had been spared. Many people died. Common gossip spread among the devastated Romans saying that Emperor Nero was responsible for the fire—that he had started it so that his proposals to raze buildings and rebuild Rome in a grand, classical manner could proceed unhindered. The tales proliferated, and Nero soon found himself under attack by his senators. He needed to find the real culprits, or at least someone to blame, and he needed to do it quickly.

Fate—and ghetto geography—provided his answer. The Jewish quarter, untouched by the fire, made the Jews perfect scapegoats for Nero. The fact that the Jewish section was far away, across the river and on the outskirts of Rome (which is why it didn't burn), was ignored. Word raced through the quarter that the Jews were about to become Nero's way out of his predicament. Feelings resurfaced from the earlier disturbance and expulsion in 49. The Jews had been back in Rome for only ten short years. Understandably, they dreaded another eviction, and dreaded even more the likelihood of worse punishments exacted by the desperate emperor. Fear and anxiety rose to near panic. Predictions of mass suffering and executions spiraled out of control.

Desperate to forestall what they were certain would be Nero's terrible wrath, a small group went to the emperor and confessed that a fringe group of Jews had indeed set the fire. They identified the culprits as the Messianic Jews, the Christus followers. Centuries later, it is impossible for us to know precisely what anxieties or divisions drove them to Nero with this story or what they expected that Nero would do. Today, we know only what Nero's horrific response actually was.

Nero immediately demanded that the Jewish community collaborate with Roman soldiers to identify those who belonged to the Christus group. Presented with a completely untenable situation and trying to reduce casualties, the Jewish community agreed. What ensued was a mini-genocide. Roman soldiers knocked on every door of the quarter, demanding to know if anyone in each house was a Christ believer. The answer determined the fate of the householder and everyone else in that house.

If a believer was identified, either by others in the community or his own admission, everyone in his house was seized and publicly executed. The normal execution involved leading victims to the floor of the Circus Maximus, shackling them, splattering them with blood, and then loosing starving dogs to eat them as Roman citizens watched. Today, twenty centuries later, when we visit St. Peter's Basilica and walk on its great *piazza* or watch televised ceremonies held there, it is difficult to imagine that this was a place of terrible torture and slaughter.*

If the head of the household denied being a believer, he was nonetheless required to name someone who was. There was no exemption from

---

* One archaeological opinion says that the Circus Maximus was temporarily moved across the Tiber River to the vicinity of Vatican Hill after the fire of 64 CE.

horror. The named individual was summarily arrested and executed, with no opportunity for appeal or protest. Neighbor was forced to turn on neighbor. As the number of executions mounted, self-preservation was the order of the day. Family members even reported on other family members. Fear and paranoia reigned.

In the end, the Roman Messianic community was totally destroyed. Among its many casualties were the great leaders, Peter and Paul. Although Peter initially fled Rome to avoid the slaughter, accounts written years later told that his escape was stopped—not by Romans, but by a vision of the Christ. As the story goes, Christ appeared and asked, "Peter, where are you going?" Chastened, his conscience and faith reawakened, Peter reversed his footsteps and returned to Rome, where he was immediately arrested and executed. Later unsubstantiated accounts relate that he died after being lashed upside down on a post or cross.

Paul had already been charged as an enemy of the emperor and taken to Rome as a prisoner to await trial some years prior. However, as a Roman citizen, he was permitted house arrest and had been languishing there, still awaiting trial. Now, however, as a self-avowed leader of the Christus community, his guilt was deemed clear and no trial was needed. Yet Paul was spared the agonies of the Circus Maximus. All Roman citizens were entitled to the dignity of a "quick" death and could not be tortured. Reports say that he was beheaded. This is in part why many statues and paintings of Paul show him holding a sword. (The other reason is his zeal and fiery oratory.) Other purported leaders of the Christus group were set afire and used as human torches at Nero's debauched banquets for the aristocracy.

What could possibly have been worse for the believers in Jesus as the Messiah? They identified themselves as faithful Jews. (Self-identification as Christians would not come for another twenty years.) Their community had totally betrayed and abandoned them. Their families, their children, their elders—even Peter and Paul—had been gruesomely murdered. We can only imagine the overwhelming extent of their isolation and pain, and undoubtedly there were times when the promise of the Christ, the prophesied Messiah, seemed hollow and empty. Terror, shame, abandonment, and death are the context of the Gospel of Mark.

Approaching Mark Today: Adrift in the Storm

The Gospel of Mark is not only the earliest written; it is also the shortest of the four gospels. Correspondingly, this will be the shortest gospel chapter of this book. The size does not imply that Mark, or the second path of quadratos for that matter, holds any less importance than the other three. In fact, its concision has deep significance. Mark and the second path house some of our deepest and most complex feelings—our fears, our resentments, and our early wounds. Indeed, if we were to spend too much time annotating and examining this particular path, we would likely defeat, or at least conceal, its unique power and gift. We might easily fall into masochism, perversely relishing the struggle and elevating it beyond its place as part of a greater process. Therefore, as we move through the gospel, perspective requires us to be content with its brevity.

Although Mark's gospel was the earliest written, it was placed second in the reading cycle. And this completely matches our experience in the second path of quadratos. This path will offer knocks on the doors of our hearts, and some of them will be as fearsome as those heard in Rome millennia ago. The way in which we will choose to answer these knocks is the profound question we meet in this part of our journey.

As we proceed through the gospel, we will have very little lyrical language for company. Mark's words are terse and spare. He gives us nothing but the barest outlines. He does not paint the landscape with flowery descriptions. His stories are stark and revelatory. Why? First, because he addresses Rome's Messianic Jews, who lived under a death sentence. They had no use for hearts and flowers. Second, because the core message of the gospel itself is simple, direct—even tough. That message is embodied, in this gospel, by a Messiah who fully understood the suffering of his followers—who came to earth, took human form, and withstood agonizing pain. This Messiah wanted those who followed him to know that while their pain was necessary—because they were part of a much larger process—their Messiah not only genuinely understood their suffering but was there, in their very midst, with them, as they suffered. And Mark didn't need a lot of words to convey that.

Nonetheless, we will encounter some significant literary devices. Mark uses the metaphor of wilderness, as well as two equivalent-to-wilderness metaphors drawn from Jewish history and tradition: deserts and bodies of water. In order to escape Egypt centuries earlier, the Jews had had to enter and traverse the Red Sea. It was their nemesis, the great barrier to their freedom. Seas in general were wild and unruly places, treacherous. In Hebrew writings, seas, lakes, and rivers represented deep anxiety and even death, and so did the desert. The great flood of Noah was strong in memory, as were the myriad stories of the forty-year desert trial of the Jewish people, from which few survived to enter the Promised Land. Mark compassionately uses these three images—wilderness, bodies of water, and desert—throughout his gospel to represent the inner landscape of frightening and uncharted territory.

Despite Mark's often bleak language, he does not—ever—deliver a singular message of difficulty. Nor does he depict trials that lead only into despair. We will see that each image of wilderness is coupled with an image of comfort or hope. John the Baptist eats both locusts (yuck!) and wild honey. When sin is confessed, cleansing is received. Heaven is torn apart and a dove descends. Jesus goes into the wilderness and encounters both beasts and angels. The sparseness of language may make this coupling difficult to grasp at first. Our initial impression is anything but hopeful. Mark writes nothing but the barest outlines: no long descriptions, or even a list of the temptations. He acknowledges the angels with little more than a nod. Patience and close reading, though, will reveal the pairings. Mark *always* includes hope.

As we enter this next stage of quadratos—the deep chaos of the second path and our own stormy sea—this straightforward style provides its own kind of comfort. It suits the needs of the place we are in and the ways we are able to hear. And Mark's specific words, through the principal parts of his gospel, will illuminate the path—expanding on and guiding us through this most difficult part of our journey.

What Good News? Beginning the Gospel

Mark's gospel begins with a call to fill hearts with hope and gather strength. Clearly inspired, he announces, "Good news!" Yet Rome's Messianic Jews didn't have much to celebrate. Even though they had professed Jesus as Messiah, as asked by their faith, their obedience to his call threatened their lives and had resulted in the senseless slaughter of their family and friends.

"*What* good news?" they might well have asked. Yet—with his opening words, Mark insists that those hearing this text cast off all doubt. He reminds them of their most central truth, and calls them to the glory and joy it holds—the glory and joy that summoned them to believe in the first place. From this point of beginning, Mark will carry the Christus followers into the deepest understanding of their beliefs, and the possibilities of meaning and purpose that lie within their great suffering.

The beginning of the good news of Jesus the Christ, the Son of God. (1:1)

One of the most startling differences between this gospel and that of Matthew is the complete absence of any kind of birth narrative, or indeed anything about Jesus's early life at all. Mark moves immediately to one of the most powerful, persuasive, and meaningful parts of the story of the Messiah for his audience—the account of John the Baptist and Jesus's baptism. Mark says that Jesus has arrived, and with nothing intervening, he starts to recount the specific events he knows will matter most to the Messianic Jews in Rome.

To open the baptism narrative, Mark significantly calls attention to the prophecy of the "messenger" who was foretold by Isaiah in the eighth century BCE, as the coming of a Messiah who would suffer for his people, who would "not grow faint or be crushed until he has established justice in the earth" (Isa. 42:4). Mark also makes his first of eight separate references to the metaphor of "wilderness" in this initial twelve-verse passage.

As it is written in the prophet Isaiah, "See, I am sending my messenger ahead of you, who will prepare your way; the voice of one crying out in the wilderness: 'Prepare the way of the Lord, make [the Lord's] paths straight.'" (1:2–3)

At the Jordan River, multitudes answered John the Baptist's invitation, just as they did in Matthew's gospel. But this is a very different baptism than that reported by Matthew. Although John the Baptist issued a call for repentance in both gospels, in Matthew his words were directed primarily to the Temple officials and privileged classes. Mark, with a different audience and objective, creates a completely different atmosphere. There is no mention of officials in this baptismal scene. Mark's multitudes are "people" who came to the Jordan for baptism and confession of their "sins." In this context, how does Mark intend the word "sin"?

Shunned by the larger Jewish community, the Roman Messianic Jews carried great burdens of shame. The scapegoating and divisions within their faith community, and Nero's subsequent executions, had given them the experience of the most brutal realities of human behavior. They harbored terrible feelings of disappointment and anger that ate at their inner lives and contaminated all of their relationships. These were the "sins" that Mark calls on them to confess as he describes John's mass baptism at the Jordan. He is showing them a way to release their pain and begin a process of forgiveness—forgiveness of themselves, of their families, and of their community—so that they might move forward and once again live full lives.

> John the baptizer appeared in the wilderness, proclaiming a baptism of
> repentance for the forgiveness of sins. And people from the whole Judean
> countryside and all the people of Jerusalem were going out to him, and
> were baptized by him in the river Jordan, confessing their sins. (1:4–5)

John next announced that Jesus would soon arrive to perform baptisms, and not "with water, but . . . with the Holy Spirit." The message was clear to the multitudes—and to the Roman Messiahnians. "Sin" had been cleansed, and repentance, the correction of one's conscience, could be claimed. Through confession, the barrier of unresolved inner burdens had been removed. Now Spirit could truly enter through Jesus the Christ. Now was the time to receive baptism.

> [John] proclaimed, "The one who is more powerful than I is coming after
> me; I am not worthy to stoop down and untie the thong of his sandals.
> I have baptized you with water, but he will baptize you with the Holy
> Spirit." (1:7–8)

In the verses that follow are several of those careful juxtapositions that we mentioned previously as being characteristic of Mark. All are written in his typically stringent language. Each begins with an image of great challenge and ends with an image of promise. Every word assures the Messiahnians that trial is always accompanied by hope and that they may rest eternally assured that God remains with them in their suffering and will never abandon them. The message's simplicity calls believers to use the gospel in a practical way—as a tool to transcend despair. Implicitly, Mark charges, "Read on!" and "Read again!"

Notice the structure of these consecutive verses. These couplings—their apposed concepts, their sequence, their one-by-one narration, and their stripped-down words—give the sense of a litany, or mantra. When we realize that first-century Messianic Jews probably did not read these words, but rather prayed them aloud, often over and over, we can begin to grasp their beauty and effectiveness. There are many more passages like these in Mark's gospel—some before these and others that follow them.

In those days Jesus came from Nazareth of Galilee and was baptized by John in the Jordan. And just as he was coming up out of the water, he saw the heavens torn apart and the Spirit descending like a dove on him. And a voice came from heaven, "You are my Son, the Beloved; with you I am well pleased." (1:9–11)

And the Spirit immediately drove [Jesus] out into the wilderness. He was in the wilderness forty days, tempted by Satan; and he was with the wild beasts; and the angels waited on him. (1:12–13)

Now after John was arrested, Jesus came to Galilee, proclaiming the good news of God, and saying, "The time is fulfilled, and the kingdom of God has come near; repent, and believe in the good news." (1:14–15)

OUR INCREASED AWARENESS of inner opposites and the connections between them will define the second path of our spiritual journey. Mark's juxtapositions typify many of the divisions we are now beginning to feel. We started out hoping to gain larger life, more meaning, and more vitality—or at least to jettison the worst of our problems. We entered the process knowing it would be difficult. We followed the instructions in this book: we found heroes and heroines, we created safe space, we sought wise advice, we opened ourselves as best we could, we meditated and prayed. But so far, it seems that everything we have done has been unavailing. We often feel disheartened as we move further into the second path, because the first path has left us in such a state of high anticipation. With more questions than answers, we experience increasing despair and weariness.

We give you fair warning and fair promise: the real stripping is about to begin. Yet this peeling of layers, this shedding of old beliefs, habits, and assumptions, is absolutely necessary. Patience must become our core practice, and we need to recognize that "mindless" strength is its underpinning. Our brains will not help us in this place. We are beginning the process of what psychology calls "ego death." Mystics and shamans describe it as dismemberment, as being torn apart, limb from limb. In this time, psychologically, in all practical ways we are still unborn. Our *belief* in new life, not its experience, gives us legs to keep walking.

Many of us try to shorten the process at this point, finding it just too painful. We feel that the sooner we return to the "light," the better. Frequently, our struggling ego-self rushes to forgiveness. Having visited the painful parts of our personal history, we choose to end our work on our past, "deciding" to view troublesome people and events with loving equanimity. These efforts initially seem positive and successful. We receive praise and support from others for our "forgiveness" and "changed attitudes"—but we are actually just making maneuvers to avoid our path. These are mere surface adjustments that accomplish nothing lasting.

The deep river of anger and fear and pain still runs within us, no matter how far we try to conceal it behind a facade of loving words. Our work does not end until we thoroughly strip ourselves to the core of our painful emotions. Before we can truly alter these feelings, we must embrace and fully experience them with sufficient patience, for sufficient time.

If, however, we choose to stay in this uncomfortable place, and use the quadratos sequence of the gospels as a guide, we will see how the baptism in Mark's account builds on the instruction given in Matthew's. Having left our old ways, we must now confess our "sins." Gradually, we learn that confession is not a recounting of unearned shame. It has nothing to do with the relentless inner punishment we often exact from ourselves when someone betrays us, or when we fall short of unjust parental or societal expectations.

Rather, confession requires us to scrutinize our inner life, in part so that we may lift the weight of debilitating shame.

Making "a searching and fearless moral inventory of ourselves" constitutes the fourth step of twelve-step recovery programs. This inner examination is what we must do now. As much as we would like to avoid this process, we need to become aware of our limitations, our inner pain, and the transgressions of ourselves and others. At the same time, we must accept the equally significant challenge to identify our strengths, our gifts, and our good deeds. In this manner, we will also begin to better develop the ability to hear, know, and accept the clarity of our own inner voice.

As we take responsibility for our transgressions, we also need to assume "appropriate" guilt—in other words, fully understand and accept our wrongdoing—and then express, when that is possible, our genuine desire for forgiveness. Also, when possible, we need to make restitution, taking care to do so in a self-compassionate way. In our rigorous striving for self-honesty, we learn to grant to ourselves the same understanding and latitude we freely grant to others.

When we take responsibility, we must also acknowledge "inappropriate" guilt. This is a deeper issue. Many of us hold shame resulting from our instinct to blame ourselves for burdens that are not truly ours. They can result from emotional or physical neglect, or physical, sexual, or psychological abuse. They are most often things we internalized as children, usually placed upon us by society or our parents, often unknowingly, sometimes not. Whatever they are, if we are doing our deepest journeying, the second path is where we will discover their deadly impact on our lives—and where we will stop and take whatever steps are needed to heal them if we are to continue our spiritual quest. In this instance, the second path can become much lengthier.

Although we will be able to take much of this "inner inventory" by ourselves, we don't have to. We can, and should, enlist all the help we need. But when we are done, and begin to achieve sincere understanding through our evaluation, any aloneness will end, regardless. Because our next step is to stand humbly before another human being and fully, honestly, and voluntarily share ourselves with them. Once we reach this difficult, poignant, and wondrous point and open ourselves to being truly known, we can begin the process of fundamental change. We can truly absorb and accept help and wisdom. We can begin to actually release our pain. At last!

These steps of inner repair are the "sins" and the "repentance" revealed by the Gospel of Mark.

If we have more serious burdens of shame, such as those caused by childhood neglect and abuse, then we will need further help. We cannot turn away from this necessity. Our solitary perspective, even in prayer, will not be sufficient to move us through these difficult passages. Counselors who are specially trained in the work of reprocessing early childhood development and trauma or a variety of twelve-step groups such as Adult Children of Alcoholics are the resources to seek out.

Yet, no matter what level of confusion or pain we uncover, it is important to remember that our suffering is temporary—and we have chosen to bare ourselves. We have done this because we know it is necessary to clearly reveal the Christ within in order to touch love.

Confusion and Discernment:
On and Around the Sea of Galilee

Mark's next set of lessons employs topography to metaphorically frame his stories, alternating his narratives between the wilds of the desert and the terrors of the Sea of Galilee. With the same constant cadence of the Sea of Galilee's tides, Jesus prayed, then went out; returned to pray, then went out again. Earlier in the chapter, he was baptized (prayed), and then driven out into the desert. Next, we find that he sought solitude to pray, and then returned to minister to the crowds. He both circled and crossed the sea. Mark uses this pattern to reinforce some of his wisest counsel: "Amidst confusion," he advises, "amidst the demands of others and one's internal clamoring, stop. Leave. Go to prayer. The true course is found in a quiet, centered heart."

> In the morning, while it was still very dark, [Jesus] got up and went out to a deserted place, and there he prayed. And Simon and his companions hunted for him. When they found him, they said to him, "Everyone is searching for you." He answered, "Let us go on to the neighboring towns, so that I may proclaim the message there also; for that is what I came out

to do." And he went throughout Galilee, proclaiming the message in their synagogues and casting out demons. (1:35–39)

From chapters two through eight, Mark continues his narrative by describing Jesus's ten-city tour, historically known as the Decapolis (in Greek, literally "ten cities"). As Jesus encircled the shores of the Sea of Galilee, he made no fewer than four crossings with his disciples. The core teachings of this gospel are within these crossing accounts.

The dramatic first account exemplifies all four. The Messiah demanded that the group make the trip by night, creating an especially terrifying and incomprehensible experience. A great storm arose, leaving the disciples trapped in a small boat; tossed around in the dark, unable to see, knowing only that their lives were in imminent danger. What was Jesus's response to this terror and chaos? He slept peacefully in the rear of the boat on a cushion, while his disciples were seized by panic. In despair, they finally roused him and pleaded that he rescue them: "Teacher, do you not care that we are perishing?"

The hysteria felt by the disciples in the boat paralleled the emotional state of the Roman Messianic Jews. Stranded by their faith in the Messiah and assailed on all sides, their lives were also in peril. Like the disciples, they were very, very frightened. We can almost hear their anguished queries: "Has the Messiah really come? Is he with us? Has God abandoned us?" Mark's inspired message assures them that the Christ is with them, just as he had been with the disciples in the storm-tossed boat.

In the raging storm, when the disciples begged in fear, Jesus's voice called out: "Be still!" Immediately, the wind stopped. Awed by this demonstration of Jesus's omnipotence, the disciples immediately accepted it as indisputable evidence of Jesus's divinity, discussed it, and rushed to deify him. Similarly, in each of the next crossing stories, when Jesus commanded, any and all turmoil ceased. These demonstrations of divine power and authority amazed and comforted the disciples. Jesus pronounced loudly and restored order. He *was* the all-powerful Messiah. He *would* protect them. They had no reason to fear death!

However, the progression of the crossing stories demonstrates a much greater message. Although Jesus continued to use his power to still storms, in each crossing Mark recounts that Jesus grew increasingly impatient with the presumption of his disciples that he would simply perform a divine act and in every instance relieve them of their fear. They seemed to completely ignore that they also had responsibilities. They had an obligation to endure and to find inner calm through faith. By the final crossing, Jesus was totally exasperated and demanded to know if his disciples had yet learned anything whatsoever.

Mark's message, an invaluable lesson for the Roman Messianic Jews, is that the disciples still sought a God who rescued them, who removed obstacles. They wanted to remain safe—as children—with a God who acted as an all-powerful, protective parent. They could not yet fathom a God who not only did not do this, but who actually pushed his followers into dark, nighttime storms. They did not yet have the spiritual maturity from which they could derive inner equilibrium and serenity in the midst of trial. They had not yet discovered an inner place of God.

> On that day, when evening had come, [Jesus] said to them, "Let us
> go across to the other side." And leaving the crowd behind, they
> took [Jesus] with them in the boat, just as he was. Other boats were
> with him. A great windstorm arose, and the waves beat into the boat,
> so that the boat was already being swamped. But Jesus was in the
> stern, asleep on the cushion; and they woke him up and said to him,
> "Teacher, do you not care that we are perishing?" He woke up and
> rebuked the wind, and said to the sea, "Peace! Be still!" Then the
> wind ceased, and there was a dead calm. [Jesus] said to them, "Why
> are you afraid? Have you still no faith?" And they were filled with
> great awe and said to one another, "Who then is this, that even the
> wind and the sea obey him?" (4:35–41)

> "Do you still not perceive or understand? Are your hearts hardened? Do
> you have eyes, and fail to see? Do you have ears, and fail to hear? And do
> you not remember?" (8:17–18)

UNCERTAINTY, DEPRESSION, AND anxiety run rampant along this second path. We teeter on the cliffside edge of chaos. But we must jump off that cliff. Like Jesus's followers, we are called to step out in faith and make a fearful journey through the conflict of opposites for the sake of our souls. Like the disciples, our frightened hearts call out: "Fix it! Fix me! Show me the strength I was promised. Use that strength on my behalf—please, please!" We remember the first path of Matthew fondly—at least we could discern the top of the mountain then, even if the path was rocky and difficult. We pray that someone—or something—will arrive to dispel the fear in our hearts, subdue our panic.

The simple, unadorned maxims of twelve-step programs often seem appropriate to this time. Developed for people caught in dismal circumstances, determined to escape without resorting to old patterns, these clear words provide tools for coping with trial. Note how well the effortless simplicity and beauty of the well-known Serenity Prayer,* adopted by Alcoholics Anonymous, captures the essence of Mark and the second path:

> *God, give me the serenity to accept things which cannot be changed;*
> *Give me courage to change the things which must be changed;*
> *And the wisdom to distinguish one from the other.*

We have to describe—encircle—the inner places that hold our chaos and conflicts, in the same way that Jesus circled the Sea of Galilee. As our faith grows, so does our courage, and we choose to walk directly into that chaos and pray. We will learn the deepest, most important lessons in the tempests of our own stormy seas, and emerge ready to engage in proper action—action born not of ego, but of the Christ within.

It is also vital that we not travel alone. We will absolutely require at least one human being to steady us, and more are highly recommended. The presence of wise counselors in our life cannot be underestimated, and groups who are on the same path that we are, or who have traveled it ahead of us, are invaluable. Self-isolation and "go it alone" attitudes come from

---

* This prayer has been variously attributed to American philosopher Reinhold Neibuhr; to a Common Prayer of Fourteenth-Century England (by Johann Christoph Oetinger); to a deacon in Weisberg, Germany (1762–1769); and to German theologian Friedrich Christoph Oetinger (1702–1782).

our fearful selves, resisting being known and changed, and it is important for us to resist them back.

Although the Gospel of Mark doesn't have much joy, it does have a continuing and resounding message of strength and faith. Despite all the differences in the crossing accounts, the core truth remains the same: the Christ is always with us. This truth must constitute the foundation of our daily spiritual practice, as we strive to stay in trust. Gripping the gunwales of the small boat of our humanity, we cannot forget that we are never alone. Even if we are blinded, whether by avoidance or fear or pain; even if we make mistakes; even if we feel abandoned, tossed to the heavens at one moment and to the depths at the next—we will never be alone.

Teachings About Power: Caesarea Philippi, the Transfiguration, and the Journey to Jerusalem

In Mark's eighth chapter Jesus and his disciples have moved to the foot-hills of Caesarea Philippi, recognized today as Israel's northern boundary with Lebanon and Syria. In the first century, well-known natural springs flowed from these mountains into the Sea of Galilee and from there to the Jordan River, where they finally emptied into the Dead Sea. Mark has care-fully selected this topography because it evokes the Jewish creation story in Genesis that tells of a domelike vault protecting the earth from the seas of chaos. A crack in the vault would release a flood and wash the world away—and the waters gushing from above would look exactly like spouting springs. Furthermore, these particular springs were already the source for great seas and rivers that played significant parts in a terrifying history for the Jews. Yet at the same time, Mark presents another of his paradoxes: life cannot exist without water. We will see that this chapter is a metaphorical turning point for the entire gospel.

Jesus asked his followers a daunting question: "Who do you say that I am?" Peter responded: "You are the Messiah." Mark then details Jesus's instruction that his disciples keep his divinity confidential, seemingly a strange request. Yet the command did not come from a need for secrecy or a sense of modesty or shame. Jesus made this demand lovingly, because he knew that his disciples still did not understand the full path of true discipleship. They lacked the maturity to comprehend all the complexities and implications of "Messiah" themselves, and thus were not competent to communicate it to others. He therefore used his question and Peter's answer as the prelude to a great teaching.

First, Jesus recounted the series of events he knew were imminent—his suffering, rejection, death, and resurrection. Upset, Peter began to rebuke Jesus for his prediction. Abruptly, Jesus snapped at him: "Get behind me, Satan! For you are setting your mind not on divine things, but on human things." Why use the word "Satan"? Because Peter's reaction proved that he was still "young" in his faith, and tempted by immature notions about an omnipotent God. Peter had become accustomed to thinking of the Messiah as a wonder-worker, with the power to banish every difficulty. He assumed that Jesus could—and would—save himself from death. Jesus's response dramatically emphasized the message from the crossing stories: "If you are looking for a miracle-working Messiah, then you have not yet understood the nature of your faith."

Jesus then addressed the true path of discipleship. He told those gathered that if they wanted to follow him, they would experience great trial and conflict. They could not avoid, evade, or divert their fate, nor could they count the cost. They could only accept and endure. Finally, he promised them that if they chose to do this, if they followed the path, they would come to know God. These inspired messages were specifically directed to the Messiahnians, who regarded Peter not only as a great hero who died for his faith, but as the founder of their community. This narrative inspired them that they too could be like Peter—whose faith had wavered, had been immature, but who still had gone forward and eventually prevailed.

From this point on, the narrative changes dramatically. All the circling ends, and just as the spring waters rushed straight downhill to become sea and then river, so does the route of Jesus and his disciples. The increase in the size and potential danger of the water corresponds to the increased peril for the travelers. Every step they take on their journey from the spring to the Sea of Galilee, then down the Jordan River valley and finally into Jerusalem, moves them closer to the moment of Jesus's crucifixion. Mark dramatically juxtaposes these elements of overflowing life and imminent death.

Jesus went on with his disciples to the villages of Caesarea Philippi;
and on the way he asked his disciples, "Who do people say that I am?"
And they answered him, "John the Baptist; and others, Elijah; and still
others, one of the prophets." [Jesus] asked them, "But who do you say
that I am?" Peter answered him, "You are the Messiah." And [Jesus]
sternly ordered them not to tell anyone about him. Then [Jesus] began
to teach them that the Son of Man must undergo great suffering, and be
rejected by the elders, the chief priests, and the scribes, and be killed,
and after three days rise again. He said all this quite openly. And Peter
took [Jesus] aside and began to rebuke him. But turning and looking at
his disciples, [Jesus] rebuked Peter and said, "Get behind me, Satan! For
you are setting your mind not on divine things but on human things."
[Jesus] called the crowd with his disciples, and said to them, "If any want
to become my followers, let them deny themselves and take up their cross
and follow me. For those who want to save their life will lose it, and those
who lose their life for my sake, and for the sake of the gospel, will save it.
For what will it profit them to gain the whole world and forfeit their life?"
(8:27–36)

Six days after the teaching at Caesarea Philippi, Jesus took three
disciples—Peter, James, and John—to an unnamed high mountain. There
they witnessed their Messiah suddenly appear even brighter, nobler, more
holy and beautiful than he had been. Mark says he was "transfigured before
them." Then, as the three looked on in amazement, Jesus was joined by the
Hebrew prophets Moses and Elijah. These are the two pillars of Judaism,
and they represent opposites. Moses is the law-giver, the aspect of tradition. Elijah is progressive, the aspect of compassion. Mark uses the vision
to show Jesus the Christ as the joining of these aspects.

Although the disciples actually saw Jesus in his full glory, once again
Jesus ordered them to conceal their knowledge. He knew they still didn't
understand many things. They lacked understanding that conflict and suffering were essential parts of God. Consequently, they were not yet ready
to speak.

Six days later, Jesus took with him Peter and James and John, and
led them up a high mountain apart, by themselves. And [Jesus] was

transfigured before them, and his clothes became dazzling white, such as no one on earth could bleach them. And there appeared to them Elijah with Moses, who were talking with Jesus. Then Peter said to Jesus, "Rabbi, it is good for us to be here; let us make three dwellings, one for you, one for Moses, and one for Elijah." [Peter] did not know what to say, for they were terrified. Then a cloud overshadowed them, and from the cloud there came a voice, "This is my Son, the Beloved; listen to him!" Suddenly when they looked around, they saw no one with them any more, but only Jesus. As they were coming down the mountain, [Jesus] ordered them to tell no one about what they had seen, until after the Son of Man had risen from the dead. So they kept the matter to themselves, questioning what this rising from the dead could mean. (9:2–10)

After descending the mountain, Jesus led his disciples directly to Jerusalem. They were quickly moving closer to the painful end of their teacher's physical life. Along the way, Jesus never stopped teaching, though he knew they would not fully understand many of the lessons he taught them until after they had actually witnessed his death and resurrection.

Over and over again, through story and image and phrase, Mark reiterates the primary tenet: "Walking a path of faith is not only worthy; it is of greater value than life itself." As they drew closer to the city, Mark recounts Jesus's language as suddenly filled with dreadful and horrific imagery. Severed limbs, ravaged flesh, and the fires of hell became pervasive, but these images helped prepare the disciples for the intense pain and conflict they would soon feel in their hearts, souls, and minds. Two thousand years later, we can see that the psychological accuracy of these metaphorical descriptions is stunning.

Mark wants to emphasize the depth of commitment needed for the Roman Messianic Jews to survive. In essence he demands that they must, in their prayers, ask for the very fire in which they will burn. He further insists that they will have to be "salted with fire," a reference found only in Mark's gospel. Why "salted"?

In the first century, salt was more valuable than almost anything else—equal to gold. It could preserve meat and therefore gave protection from starvation and illness. Furthermore, it protected against dehydration in the arid desert. In short, it meant survival. Wars were launched and fought over it. In the Temple, only meat that had been treated with salt was offered. Infants' lips were rubbed with salt to protect against evil. Romans tied salt to the heads of those they executed and wished to offer to the gods.

Those who believed that Jesus was the Messiah were very likely to be executed—sacrificed in the arena—and were therefore likely to receive the precious salt. This is perhaps the most powerful paradox stated in Mark's gospel: salting as a sign of sacrificial death and also as a metaphor for the inestimable worth of God's love. When Messiahnians heard, "Everyone will be salted with fire," they understood that they were receiving a promise and a blessing that would make their death immensely valuable.

> "And if your foot causes you to stumble, cut it off; it is better for you
> to enter life lame than to have two feet and to be thrown into hell.
> And if your eye causes you to stumble, tear it out; it is better for you
> to enter the kingdom of God with one eye than to have two eyes and
> to be thrown into hell, where their worm never dies, and the fire is
> never quenched. For everyone will be salted with fire. Salt is good;
> but if salt has lost its saltiness, how can you season it? Have salt in
> yourselves, and be at peace with one another." (9:42–50)

THE LESSONS THAT Jesus taught in Mark's crossing accounts and at Caesarea Philippi are some of the most challenging in all of the gospels to comprehend and to adapt for our daily lives. They force us to purge our traditional conception of God as a super-parental divine rescuer. These lessons have a clear message: God is certainly capable of rescuing us, but God will not rescue us, because rescue would stop our journey. The journey is long and full. It contains peacefulness, joy and ecstasy, pain, conflict and paradox—all of which we must eventually learn to balance in order to reach a capacity for inner serenity. This is the way of quadratos. This is the way of the Christ.

In this second path, it is as if we were in a tiny boat on a menacing sea in a great storm. The storm is so fierce that we feel completely directionless. We hope that the pattern we are learning and trying to follow is true, but we really haven't a clue. On an emotional level, it is clear to us that we know nothing about anything useful that can save us. What should we do? We have only two helpful choices. We can perform the one simple task we have: we can row. And we can pray. Through these two, we can surrender all of our habits and assumptions. We can practice our faith and not allow the demons in the depths below nor the thunder and lightning above to deter us.

One of the dangers of this path is our desire to choose one opposite over another. We often want to move in the direction of Moses or Elijah— precisely why Mark gives us the image of the transfiguration. When challenges arise, we have to realize that our impulse to force a resolution, or move in one extreme direction or another, is due to our immaturity. Our best course for now is simply to remain aware, attempt to stay in the middle and resist extremes, and try not to fall back on our old ways.

When faced with pain and conflict and left to our own limited resources, we tend to overuse our intellect. We attempt to *think* our way out of the dilemma or be distracted from our pain by arguing. We can find ourselves arguing with everyone, even with Mystery itself. It is not unusual to hear people who are struggling with this path make derisive comments about God. These are narrow courses, driven by our fearful, threatened egos. However difficult, we must try to ignore that inner "chatter." We must pray to enter our necessary trials more deeply, rather than to be rescued from them. Most importantly, we need to accept and accept and accept some more, even though we often don't understand exactly what is happening, or how our experience "fits" into the process.

The second path of quadratos is about "losing life" to gain it. We are attempting first to learn what that means, and second to accept it. Through prayer and proven counsel, we learn to receive our trials as they arrive in our lives and live with them, knowing that we cannot hasten or alleviate the rigors of the path itself. Every time we attempt to avoid a situation, we only reduce our opportunity to grow, to learn from the journey. Like the immature disciples looking for a God who merely provides, we are, in fact, asking that God become smaller. Fortunately, God is not so paltry. Mystery will not be diminished; nor will it ever abandon us, no matter how childishly we are behaving.

Mark's particular attention to Peter holds two lessons for us. One is the critical practice of self-compassion—absolutely crucial as we make our inventory. Wisdom can travel only through error, difficult though that is, and we must forgive ourselves the many errors that are our good teachers. The other reiterates the counsel we received in Matthew: find help. However, in this case, the advice is much more specific. Peter is a real mentor. He is someone who has traveled the path, a person who has made the journey successfully and can serve as a trusted spiritual guide, a soul-friend. At this point in our journey, we need someone like this—a living example with whom we can share our travails, and whose advice we can trust.

Yet, especially without help, the stresses of this path will cause many of us to make a choice to stop right now, right here, and return to what we think is a safe harbor. But stopping now comes at great cost, for this is the place where we discover our level of commitment and our true willingness to rely on God's grace. If we abort the journey at this point and retreat to our old ways, we will gradually discover (or others will tell us) that our lives take on a pattern of increasing narrowness and rigidity. Therefore, though we are tempted to stop, to negotiate—to make bargains to shorten or ease the burden of the inner work that must be done—we press on. We want more than a less-than-complete life in the less-than-satisfactory company of a less-than-perfect and mysterious god. We want the "good news."

Facing Conflict: Confrontations in Jerusalem's Temple

After their long trek, the group finally arrived in Jerusalem. Jesus went directly to the Temple, where a bustling scene of commerce confronted him. People buying and selling animals for sacrifice filled the courtyard. The "holiest" sacrifices were designated the most expensive by the Temple system—but even modest offerings bore exorbitant prices. Jesus, outraged over the injustice, which forced humble petitioners into corrupt practice, unhesitatingly began overturning tables and pronounced that the Temple was no longer a "house of prayer" but a "den of robbers." Recognizing a direct threat to their authority, the priests and scribes intensified their talk of murdering the charismatic and contentious interloper.

Mark knows that the Christus community is in direct opposition to Roman Jewish leaders. He wants to fortify his audience with the example of the Messiah he shows here—confident, forceful, walking directly into conflict. This is encouragement for the Messiahnians, in order to give them the strength to face their own conflict, regardless of what they might have to endure as a result.

> Then they came to Jerusalem. And [Jesus] entered the temple and began to drive out those who were selling and those who were buying in the temple, and he overturned the tables of the money changers and the seats of those who sold doves; and he would not allow anyone to carry anything through the temple. He was teaching and saying, "Is it not written, 'My house shall be called a house of prayer for all the nations'? But you have made it a den of robbers." And when the chief priests and the scribes heard it, they kept looking for a way to kill him; for they were afraid of him, because the whole crowd was spellbound by his teaching. (11:15–18)

The following day, Jesus returned and directly confronted the Temple authorities. The men argued, tension mounting quickly as Jesus emphatically and clearly responded to their inquiries. He left, but then returned to Jerusalem and the Temple once more. This time he spoke in parables, each crafted for Mark's Roman audience. One story told of heartrending conflict and loss endured by "a man who planted a vineyard." Nonetheless the man persisted, and the parable closed telling of a "rejected stone" that eventually became a "cornerstone." This parable, with its references to planting, building, and a vineyard that would produce new wine, was a powerful message to the Messianic Jews. "Persist," it said. "Even though you are cast aside, the vines will still be planted, and recognition of the Messiah will yet come. You and your community are the cornerstone of the foundational changes in your faith. Your lives, your sacrifices, are not in vain."

> Again they came to Jerusalem. As he was walking in the temple, the chief priests, the scribes, and the elders came to him and said, "By what authority are you doing these things? Who gave you this authority to do them?" Jesus said to them, "I will ask you one question; answer me, and I will tell you by what authority I do these things. Did the baptism of John come from heaven, or was it of human origin? Answer me." They argued with one another, "If we say, 'From heaven,' he will say, 'Why then did you not believe him?' But shall we say, 'Of human origin'?"—they were afraid of the crowd,

for all regarded John as truly a prophet. So they answered Jesus, "We do not know." And Jesus said to them, "Neither will I tell you by what authority I am doing these things." (11:27–33)

Then he began to speak to them in parables. "A man planted a vineyard, put a fence around it, dug a pit for the wine press, and built a watchtower; then he leased it to tenants and went to another country. When the season came, he sent a slave to the tenants to collect from them his share of the produce of the vineyard. But they seized him, and beat him, and sent him away empty-handed. And again he sent another slave to them; this one they beat over the head and insulted. Then he sent another, and that one they killed. And so it was with many others; some they beat, and others they killed. He had still one other, a beloved son. Finally he sent him to them, saying, 'They will respect my son.' But those tenants said to one another, 'This is the heir; come, let us kill him, and the inheritance will be ours.' So they seized him, killed him, and threw him out of the vineyard. What then will the owner of the vineyard do? He will come and destroy the tenants and give the vineyard to others. Have you not read this scripture: 'The stone that the builders rejected has become the cornerstone; this was the Lord's doing, and it is amazing in our eyes'?" When they realized that he had told this parable against them, they wanted to arrest him, but they feared the crowd. So they left him and went away. (12:1–12)

Mark's next chapter brings the conflict with the Temple authorities to a dramatic conclusion. Again, Jesus spoke using vivid imagery, this time of destruction and rebirth. Mark wants the Messiahnians to understand the nature of fundamental change—and to understand that serious conflict is one of the necessary and predictable steps of all transformation. In the same way that Jesus the Christ died but was resurrected, their faith would not end with the terrible tribulations they were experiencing in Rome. Belief in the Christ would continue to live. "This is how change works," Mark is teaching. "This is how strong foundations are built. You must clear out the old. There are always extreme struggles as the old beliefs fight back, then crumble to make room for the new ones arising." These principles gained even greater impact (and irony) to readers in subsequent decades, because only a few years after Mark wrote his gospel, Jerusalem's Temple was leveled in Rome's great assault.

Jesus's final exhortation in this chapter was to "keep awake!" All three synoptic gospels—Matthew, Mark, and Luke—use these words, but each places them at a different point in the account, presumably to call specific attention to the matters of greatest import to each author. Mark locates them directly at the close of the contentious debate with the Temple authorities and ensuing lessons on the nature of deep change—and immediately prior to the Passion account. He does this as a reminder to his audience, telling *them* to remain awake and vigilant because there is no escape from necessary suffering. It is part of their journey.

> When you hear of wars and rumors of wars, do not be alarmed;
> this must take place, but the end is still to come. For nation will
> rise against nation, and kingdom against kingdom; there will be
> earthquakes in various places; there will be famines. This is but the
> beginning of the birthpangs. As for yourselves, beware; for they will
> hand you over to councils; and you will be beaten in synagogues;
> and you will stand before governors and kings because of me, as
> a testimony to them. And the good news must first be proclaimed
> to all nations. When they bring you to trial and hand you over, do
> not worry beforehand about what you are to say; but say whatever
> is given you at that time, for it is not you who speak, but the Holy
> Spirit. Brother will betray brother to death, and a father his child, and
> children will rise against parents and have them put to death; and you
> will be hated by all because of my name. But the one who endures to
> the end will be saved. (13:7–13)

> "Truly I tell you, this generation will not pass away until all these things
> have taken place. Heaven and earth will pass away, but my words will not
> pass away." (13:30–31)

> "And what I say to you I say to all: Keep awake." (13:37)

WHEN PEOPLE FEEL anxious and out of control, psychologically, they search for messages and outer signs to help calm themselves. And they tend to find them, even if such signs don't objectively exist. Through the centuries, it has been easy for people to read Mark's words about apocalyptic happenings, look around their world, and take his words literally. But we do not need to prepare for external "end times." There is more relevance in universal truths, particularly as they relate to quadratos. We comprehend that if we transform our inner selves, we will not cause or be party to the external events that lead to catastrophe. In this journey of inner transformation, we can understand that the images in Mark's gospel are invaluable metaphors for the powerful feelings that we undergo in the second path, when death and destruction and collapse, dressed in depression and despair, surround us.

Our message today echoes Mark's message to believers in Rome long ago: "This is not the end, even though it feels as though it might be. Inner and outer conflict are to be expected. So are the uncertainties that always arise with conflict. Try to remember: when deep change occurs, this is what the beginning of something new looks and feels like. Hold on. Hold on! Later, you will be able to remember this moment, and see how unexpectedly the new cornerstone was chosen, and with what deep purpose it was laid."

As we walk this path in faith, our immature ego-self reluctantly begins to crumble. Resistant to change, it fights back, just as the Temple authorities did, and it does so with great skill and determination. Do not be surprised. "Keep awake!"

Staying Present: The Passion

Mark's Passion account sharpens the focus of all the lessons he has presented thus far, bringing the main spiritual question of the gospel to a more precise point: How do we have trust in the path we have chosen despite our pain and fear? In keeping with the rest of Mark's gospel, this account of the Passion is the shortest of the four (and remember, it was the first written by about a decade). Starkly and unsparingly, Mark weaves an emotional fabric of powerful conflict and deep, painful abandonment. Written with the certain knowledge that many of the Christus followers would relate very directly to the feelings it conveyed, he knew that they would not simply recollect the death it described; they would see their own deaths reflected in every word.

The Last Supper and Gethsemane

Mark's telling of the Last Supper is particularly poignant. Jesus foresaw his betrayal by an intimate, someone "dipping into the same bowl," and he said so. Rome's Messianic Jews knew this same perfidy. When the centurion knocked on their door, they knew the likelihood that they had been given away by someone close to them. When they heard the words of the gospel, it was as though the Messiah himself was warning them not to be disloyal to each other, and not to abandon the new community of the Son of Man.

After Jesus's meal with his disciples, the group went to the Mount of Olives. There, Jesus told his followers that even though only one would betray him, all of them would desert him. Peter protested, specifically reiterating the word "desert." As always, Mark chooses his words with extreme care. Matthew, less precise a wordsmith, and with a different purpose, uses the words "deny," "desert," and "betray" interchangeably in his gospel. Mark, however, has subtle distinctions for each of these.

In Mark's gospel, Jesus used the word "betray" to refer to those who totally gave up their belief or who, like Judas, turned someone else over to the authorities. He used the word "desertion"—which literally means to turn one's face in another direction—to describe those who gave in to the impulse to avoid conflict—something that, as Jesus predicted, all the followers did.

By the time Mark wrote this gospel, it is likely that Peter had already deserted Rome, then returned and been killed for his faith. We believe that Mark is encouraging his audience not to flee as Peter had while simultaneously extending great compassion to them. When he focuses on Jesus's prediction that, given the circumstances, inevitably "all" would desert, he is telling the Messiahnians he understands their emotional and physical *need* to flee. Jesus knew that the combination of young faith and terrible challenges could lead to a lapse in faith, in vigilance. He also knew that desertion, unlike betrayal, would not critically damage the soul—deserters could redeem themselves, turn around again, and return to the path. Mark's choice to emphasize these words of Jesus vividly conveys essential counsel to the Christus followers in Rome.

Mark also chooses the word "denial" in this passage, to connote the lowest level of abandonment. He uses "denial" when someone claims "not to know"—even when one actually does—illustrated by Peter's denial of knowing Jesus. This choice of words tells the Christus community that even the most faithful of disciples can have momentary lapses and abandon their faith. But they can also immediately understand their error, repent, and be restored.

Mark knew that before the knock on the door came, the Messiahnians would have ample time to reflect. However, the moment the door opened and the centurion asked his question, there would be time for only one answer. Mark therefore wanted his readers to understand that they, like the disciples, had four choices, and each one had different spiritual and moral consequences. His examples and his language were precise. "When you are asked, 'Are you a follower of the Christus?' you can answer yes, or you can deny, or you can desert, or you can betray. Those are your four choices, and your *only* choices." Mark implores them to directly examine their beliefs ahead of time, and to do so thoughtfully and deeply for their own sake, and for the sake of their community.

When it was evening, [Jesus] came with the twelve. And when they had taken their places and were eating, Jesus said, "Truly I tell you, one of you will betray me, one who is eating with me." They began to be distressed and to say to him one after another, "Surely, not I?" He said to them, "It is one of the twelve, one who is dipping bread into the bowl with me. For the Son of Man goes as it is written of him, but woe to that one by whom the Son of Man is betrayed! It would have been better for that one not to have been born." (14:17–21)

When they had sung the hymn, they went out to the Mount of Olives. And Jesus said to them, "You will all become deserters; for it is written, 'I will strike the shepherd, and the sheep will be scattered.' But after I am raised up, I will go before you to Galilee." Peter said to him, "Even though all become deserters, I will not." Jesus said to him, "Truly I tell you, this day, this very night, before the cock crows twice, you will deny me three times." But [Peter] said vehemently, "Even though I must die with you, I will not deny you." And all of them said the same. (14:26–31)

Then Jesus took the disciples to a section of the Mount called Gethsemane and took aside the same three disciples who had accompanied him at the transfiguration: Peter, James, and John. Jesus requested them to stay awake with him as he prayed in his time of grief. Since these were the three who had witnessed the transfiguration, one might assume that they were more mature disciples and would have taken these instructions with great seriousness. Nonetheless, they did not; they slept. During their slumber, Mark recounts, the solitary Jesus prayed the central message of this gospel: "Dear Father, even though you are omnipotent, and could remove this suffering, please provide me with what you know to be best, even if it isn't what I want (or yet understand)." Furthermore, this passage notes that Jesus was greatly "distressed and agitated" and "threw himself on the ground" to pray. The Greek word used in this text conveys a sense of intense distress. After his prayer, Jesus awakened the sleeping disciples and remonstrated only with Peter. Once again, Mark is keeping the focus on Peter, and his words are gentle and deeply compassionate, witness to his understanding of the heart-rending dichotomies between desire and reality. Indeed, Mark's words from Gethsemane are so apt that Matthew used them also, and they have fallen into common parlance: "The spirit indeed is willing, but the flesh is weak."

They went to a place called Gethsemane; and [Jesus] said to his disciples, "Sit here while I pray." [Jesus] took with him Peter and James and John, and began to be distressed and agitated. And Jesus said to them, "I am deeply grieved, even to death; remain here, and keep awake." And going a little farther, [Jesus] threw himself on the ground and prayed that, if it were possible, the hour might pass from him. [Jesus] said, "Abba, Father, for you all things are possible; remove this cup from me; yet, not what I want, but what you want." He came and found them sleeping; and he said to Peter, "Simon, are you asleep? Could you not keep awake one hour? Keep awake and pray that you may not come into the time of trial; the spirit indeed is willing, but the flesh is weak." (14:32–38)

Pilate and the Crucifixion

The scene next moves to the high priest's courtyard after Jesus's arrest. Twice asked by a serving girl and once by a bystander whether he is one of Jesus's followers, Peter denies that he is. After the three denials, there is a very slight but very meaningful difference from Matthew's account. In Matthew, Jesus said that Peter would deny him three times "before the cock crows." In Mark, Jesus said that the thrice-repeated denial would happen "before the cock crows twice." But wouldn't Peter have remembered Jesus's words when he heard the cock crow the first time? This is a tiny detail; however, it intensifies the impression of Peter's helplessness in the face of his all-too-human fear. Even when reminded by the initial crowing, he was unable to stop himself, unable to change course.

Well aware that Rome's genocide was continuing over a protracted period, Mark knows that no one who betrayed his neighbor or his friend could legitimately use the excuse of surprise. They had plenty of time to consider their answer before the soldier's knock came. Peter's example emphatically drives that reality home.

> While Peter was below in the courtyard, one of the servant-girls of the high priest came by. When she saw Peter warming himself, she stared at him and said, "You also were with Jesus, the man from Nazareth." But he denied it, saying, "I do not know or understand what you are talking about." And he went out into the forecourt. Then the cock crowed. And the servant-girl, on seeing him, began again to say to the bystanders, "This man is one of them." But again he denied it. Then after a little while the bystanders again said to Peter, "Certainly you are one of them; for you are a Galilean." But [Peter] began to curse, and he swore an oath, "I do not know this man you are talking about." At that moment the cock crowed for the second time. Then Peter remembered that Jesus had said to him, "Before the cock crows twice, you will deny me three times." And he broke down and wept. (14:66–72)

The Passion account proceeds to Jesus's appearance before Pontius Pilate, where the parallels between Jerusalem and Rome continue. Pilate chose to ignore what he knew to be the truth about Jesus and accepted the judgment of the "crowd," agreeing to Jesus's crucifixion. Nero, in scape-goating the Messianic Jews for the fire in Rome, had also abandoned truth and taken an expedient course. Mark intensifies the pain of these betrayals, which moved beyond a personal matter into a public catastrophe.

> Now at the festival [Pilate] used to release a prisoner for them, anyone for whom they asked. Now a man called Barabbas was in prison with the rebels who had committed murder during the insurrection. So the crowd came and began to ask Pilate to do for them according to his custom. Then he answered them, "Do you want me to release for you the King of the Jews?" For he realized that it was out of jealousy that the chief priests had handed [Jesus] over. But the chief priests stirred up the crowd to have [Pilate] release Barabbas for them instead. Pilate spoke to them again, "Then what do you wish me to do with the man you call the King of the Jews?" They shouted back, "Crucify him!" Pilate asked them, "Why, what evil has he done?" But they shouted all the more, "Crucify him." So Pilate, wishing to satisfy the crowd, released Barabbas for them; and after flogging Jesus, he handed him over to be crucified. (15:6–15)

After the trial, in the courtyard, Mark gives us a dramatic image: the soldiers stripped Jesus and robed him in purple—a color reserved for royalty (and completely different from the red robe described in Matthew). They crowned him with thorns and mocked him as "King of the Jews." Mark uses the ugliness and childishness of this scene—and Jesus's lack of response to it—as an illustration of brutality contrasted with the maturity and dignity of Spirit. And brutality was clearly consigned to the representatives of the Temple and the soldiers who belonged to Pilate, to Rome. When the time arrived for Jesus the Christ to be led to his greatest physical trial, the crucifixion, the purple robe was removed, and he was described as in "his own clothes." Mark is precise: spiritual power needs no outward trappings.

> Then the soldiers led him into the courtyard of the palace (that is, the governor's headquarters); and they called together the whole cohort. And they clothed him in a purple cloak; and after twisting some thorns into a crown, they put it on him. And they began saluting him, "Hail, King

of the Jews!" They struck his head with a reed, spat upon him, and knelt down in homage to him. After mocking him, they stripped him of the purple cloak and put his own clothes on him. Then they led him out to crucify him. (15:16–20)

Mark's depiction of the crucifixion is very brief. It contains no extra words and few explanations. He does write that Simon of Cyrene, described as the "father of Alexander and Rufus," carried the cross for Jesus. It is possible that Alexander and Rufus were members of Rome's Messianic Jewish community. If true, this mention provides another link to these followers. Furthermore, if Alexander and Rufus had accepted execution in Rome, their mention here would have provided further inspiration to the Christus believers. In an account with language as sparse as Mark's, their mention would seem to have some significance, but we can only conjecture.

They compelled a passer-by, who was coming in from the country, to carry [Jesus's] cross; it was Simon of Cyrene, the father of Alexander and Rufus. (15:21)

Jesus was led to Golgotha, stripped naked, and crucified with two bandits. Contrary to what has often been thought, the stripping of Jesus was not a specific attempt to dishonor him. Nakedness was the norm for Roman executions, but it was especially shameful for all Jews, who considered public nudity a terrible disgrace. As Jesus hung on the cross, awaiting death, everyone taunted him: bystanders, the bandits, the chief priests, and the scribes. Finally, at three o'clock, six hours after being nailed to the cross, Jesus cried out the beginning words of Psalm 22: "Eloi, Eloi, lama sabachthani?" which means, "My God, my God, why have you forsaken me?"

Mark's gospel records these as Jesus's only words—and through the millennia, they have been subject to myriad interpretations. Many have believed that Mark's Passion shows Jesus betrayed and consumed by feelings of despair, but we believe this interpretation is neither correct nor supported by the text itself. Furthermore, it is completely inconsistent with Mark's message to Rome's Messianic Jews. We believe this crucifixion account is both heartrending and heartfilling, an image of Jesus painfully, yet exultantly, moving into the final moments of his human life, fully awake.

In the first century, as we noted in our study of Matthew's gospel, it would have been no aberration, nor any great surprise, for Jesus—or any Jew—to have recited the words of this particular psalm at the moment of death. Jewish tradition called for pious Jews to die with the words of Psalm 22 on their lips, so reciting the first words would have indicated the same thing as a Christian today starting to pray, "Our Father . . ." Strengthening my belief in this crucifixion as a moment of triumphant suffering is the nature of Psalm 22 itself, a work that every devout Jew would have known from beginning to end. This psalm does, indeed, begin in lament. However, it continues as a celebration of trust and faith in the midst of agony and even death. If we understand that Jesus was *quoting* from a great and jubilant prayer, a core piece of Hebrew scripture, it makes absolutely no sense to think of him sagging from the cross, bloody, abandoned, and inconsolable.

Psalm 22 ends with these words: "To [God], indeed, shall all who sleep in the earth bow down; before him shall bow all who go down to the dust, and I shall live for him. Posterity will serve [God]; future generations will be told about the Lord, and proclaim the Lord's deliverance to a people yet unborn, saying that [God] has done it" (Psalm 22:29–31). This is the full picture that Mark gives the Roman Christus followers of this defining moment.

In Mark's gospel, Jesus the Christ was indeed betrayed, and when he gave a "loud cry and breathed his last," he was certainly bloody and he was certainly alone. Not a single one of his disciples is noted as having been around him when he died—not even Mary, his mother—although it is mentioned that some women, including Mary of Magdala, watched "from a distance." Yet Mark gives no indication that Jesus surrendered to bitterness or resentment. On the contrary, he calmly predicted his fate to his disciples, and though he was distressed in Gethsemane, his prayer was clear: he accepted the necessity of his suffering and death if that was God's will for him. The shame and mockery heaped on him by the soldiers and on the cross did not affect him. He refused the palliative wine he was offered.

While there is no bitterness or resentment in this account, there is intense suffering and great sadness. Jesus's final moment was a crying out, a proclamation of being present to pain, as Jesus marshaled all his energy, all the strength of his belief, in a last, great triumphant outbreath. We must weep as we read these words. Ever since the teaching at Caesarea Philippi's springs (8:27), Mark's gospel has been focused on lessons that suffering must be endured because suffering is part of the nature of God—and this crucifixion shows the terrible and moving and unforgettable image of that truth.

After the death, Mark recounts that among the watching strangers and enemies, a centurion, upon seeing the serene and stately strength of Jesus, exclaimed, "Truly, this man was God's son!" How immensely meaningful these six words were! When the Messianic Jews went to be sacrificed in Rome, they too would face a centurion. Surrounded by strangers and enemies, shackled and dying, they would also be taunted. Mark called on them to understand that the manner of their death contained the seed of conversion residing in the power of great spiritual example and would proclaim the reality of Jesus the Christ that could be carried forward to coming generations.

> Then they brought Jesus to the place called Golgotha (which means
> the place of a skull). And they offered him wine mixed with myrrh;
> but he did not take it. And they crucified him, and divided his clothes
> among them, casting lots to decide what each should take. It was
> nine o'clock in the morning when they crucified him. The inscription
> of the charge against him read, "The King of the Jews." And with
> him they crucified two bandits, one on his right and one on his left.
> Those who passed by derided him, shaking their heads and saying,
> "Aha! You who would destroy the temple and build it in three days,
> save yourself, and come down from the cross!" In the same way the
> chief priests, along with the scribes, were also mocking him among
> themselves and saying, "He saved others; he cannot save himself. Let
> the Messiah, the King of Israel, come down from the cross now, so
> that we may see and believe." Those who were crucified with him also
> taunted him. When it was noon, darkness came over the whole land
> until three in the afternoon. At three o'clock Jesus cried out with a
> loud voice, "Eloi, Eloi, lema sabachthani?" which means, "My God,
> my God, why have you forsaken me?" When some of the bystanders
> heard it, they said, "Listen, he is calling for Elijah." And someone
> ran, filled a sponge with sour wine, put it on a stick, and gave it to

him to drink, saying, "Wait, let us see whether Elijah will come to take him down." Then Jesus gave a loud cry and breathed his last. And the curtain of the temple was torn in two, from top to bottom. Now when the centurion, who stood facing him, saw that in this way he breathed his last, he said, "Truly this man was God's Son!" There were also women looking on from a distance; among them were Mary Magdalene, and Mary the mother of James the younger and of Joses, and Salome. (15:22–40)

IN THIS VERY difficult second spiritual path, we must hold tenaciously to the lessons of Jesus the Christ and the example of Peter that we find in the Gospel of Mark. Through the actions of these two figures, more powerfully than through their words, we can gain counsel to help us through this chaotic sea.

Aside from Jesus himself, Peter is the primary figure of this gospel, placed in every chapter except those of the crucifixion and resurrection. Why? Because Peter was very much like us. He struggled to remain "awake." He faithfully followed all the steps. He was present, bodily and spiritually, at all of the important moments. Yet Peter fell asleep at a critical moment. He denied Jesus, despite having been warned and in the face of a vivid reminder—the first cock's crow. Yet he did not stop himself. And then he cried. And then he disappeared, and was not at the crucifixion. He is nowhere for the remainder of the gospel. Why?

For Mark, Peter represents a living, breathing historical example, one filled with large measures of human weakness and uncertainty. Peter was a great hero of the Messianic faith who ultimately died for his beliefs, but Peter failed—and did so more than once. This is a message that failure and guilt are redeemable, regardless of the number of lapses and even though resolution might take a very long time and be filled with uncertainty. Once Peter shed his sincere tears of regret, his spiritual and literary purpose was ended as far as Mark was concerned, and he disappeared from the recital. But Peter's usefulness to us as an echo of the second path is immeasurable and unceasing: attentiveness, struggle, repeated failure, and no resolution.

Congruent with the Serenity Prayer (quoted earlier in the chapter), Jesus was presented with challenges he "knew he could change." He ascertained this through prayer that made him decisive and forceful. Over and over, Mark characterizes Jesus's response with the word "immediately." In the Passion account, however, Jesus faced trials he knew he could not, and should not, change.

Therefore, in the Passion, with full understanding, Jesus the Christ embodied the deep and true power of surrender. He accepted. He stayed centered, calm, and dignified. He did not speak out, for there was nothing to say. His example conveyed that there was nothing external that could or should be fought. His only battle was the same as ours in this second path—to stay awake, to stay connected to Mystery, and to use all of our energy to proclaim God's love, even in the midst of pain and conflict.

The Resurrection Announced

Mark's resurrection narrative is a puzzling, even startling, end to a profound gospel. It contains four elements that are completely unique to it—particulars not found in any of the other gospels.

After Jesus's burial, the same women who watched him die "from a distance" went to the tomb to anoint the body. They did this, not because they believed in resurrection, but because they wanted to be certain that Jesus's burial was in accordance with Jewish law.

When the women got to the tomb, they saw what Mark describes as a "young man dressed in a white robe." This is the first puzzlement. Although it has been assumed by many that this figure was an angel, Mark does not tell us this.

The young man presented the second surprise when he informed the women that Jesus had "been raised." He went on to issue instructions that the women inform the disciples of a pending meeting with the risen Christ. In the narrative that follows, however, clear to the end of the gospel itself, we read of *no* actual sighting. It simply isn't there. Decades later, another ending was added that did contain a sighting, but the original gospel has none.

The instructions that the women were asked to relay to the disciples called for a meeting with the risen Christ *in Galilee*. This is the third oddity. In the first century, a reference to Galilee customarily meant the entire region of the Sea of Galilee. Mark pointedly directs the disciples to see their risen Messiah in the place he has used in his gospel as the metaphorical locale for chaos and wilderness.

The fourth enigma is the most interesting of all. The text says that the women did not fulfill their instructions. Instead, they fled and "said nothing" to anyone. They were clearly frightened. Indeed, the word "afraid" is the final word of the gospel that Mark writes to the Messianic Jewish community of Rome. Christian readers in subsequent years found this ending so unsettling, it seems, that not only one but two more "satisfactory" endings were added in the second century. No one has ever been able to give a coherent, logical reason for Mark's original closing.

The original ending is not obscure, nor is it some kind of odd lapse or digression. Mark's gospel is extremely precise, pointed, accurate, and consistent. The word "afraid" was chosen because it best resonated with the terrified Messianic Jews of Rome to whom Mark wrote. It served as a direct challenge to them—a rhetorical question. It asked: "When the soldiers come to your door, what will your answer be? Will you betray, or desert, or deny? Or will you give witness to the Messiah?"

When the sabbath was over, Mary Magdalene, and Mary the mother
of James, and Salome bought spices, so that they might go and anoint
him. And very early on the first day of the week, when the sun had
risen, they went to the tomb. They had been saying to one another,
"Who will roll away the stone for us from the entrance to the tomb?"
When they looked up, they saw that the stone, which was very large,
had already been rolled back. As they entered the tomb, they saw
a young man, dressed in a white robe, sitting on the right side; and
they were alarmed. But he said to them, "Do not be alarmed; you are
looking for Jesus of Nazareth, who was crucified. He has been raised;
he is not here. Look, there is the place they laid him. But go, tell his
disciples and Peter that he is going ahead of you to Galilee; there
you will see him, just as he told you." So they went out and fled from
the tomb, for terror and amazement had seized them; and they said
nothing to anyone, for they were afraid. (16:1–8)

MARK'S ORIGINAL—AND HERETOFORE perplexing—ending fits us, on the second path of quadratos, as precisely as it fit the Jews in Rome. It challenges us. Will we manage to endure our continuing death, and also bear witness to it? Will we betray it and give up, amid all the temptations with which we are faced? Will we desert, turn our faces away, and run? If we do, will we return? Will we accept one (or many) of the possible distractions and deny the path? If we do, how long will it take us to recover our direction? Will we ever recover? Or, heeding Mark's counsel, will we somehow manage to have trust in our chosen journey and make our way through the uncertainty and confusion?

Our walk through this second path will not be likely to look as unswerving and true as that of Jesus's from the flowing spring down to the city. Eventually, when we are more mature in our journey and as we make more cycles of quadratos, it may straighten a bit; but now, at this early stage, we are much more like the disciples, like Peter. Jesus said they would "all" desert him—and despite their sincerity, they all did. We will probably desert, too, in some way or another—but remember, Peter showed us that desertion is redeemable.

This is a miserably uncomfortable process, but through it, we will learn what we "can change" and what we "cannot change." As we paddle across the choppy sea of chaos, sometimes we will fall over the side of the boat and gulp a fair amount of seawater. We will get seasick. But as long as we keep praying—and rowing—we will not be lost at sea.

Indeed, the Christ promises us that the far shore will grow closer and closer. Awareness of the grace that guides us will begin to dawn, surely and certainly. The storms will quiet, and land will appear. Our boat will slide smoothly onto the sand of a golden beach, and right over a rise, just behind the sea grass, the most beautiful and fragrant garden we can possibly imagine awaits. John's glorious garden is preparing our welcome. In the shade of a bending tree, amongst the blossoms, we will find a bench, and we will see our name engraved upon it. Hold to faith; let our courage be blessed. We will soon rest.

Prayer for the Second Path

PSALM 22

My God, my God, why have you forsaken me?
Why so far from my delivery
So empty in the anguish of my words?
I call to you in the daytime but you don't answer
And all night long I plead restlessly, uselessly

I know Your holiness, find it in the memorized praises
Uttered by those who've struggled with you
Through all the generations
These, my forebears, trusted you
And through their trusting you touched them
Held and delivered them
They cried out to you and you met them face to face
Their confidence was strong and they were not confounded

But I am not as they
Utterly alone, I am cast out of the circle
A worm, a living reproach, scorned and despised, even less than despised
Unheard, unseen, unacknowledged, denied
And all who encounter me revile me with cynic laughter
Shaking their heads, parting their nattering lips, mocking
"Let him throw himself at God—for God's deliverance," they say
"Since that is who he trusts let the Lord save him."

And they are right:
How not to trust You, and what else to trust?

You I entered on leaving the womb
You I drank at my mother's breast
I was cast upon you at birth
And even before birth I swam in you, my heart's darkness

Be not far from me now
When suffering is very near
And there is no help
And I am beset all around by threatening powers
The bulls of Bashan gaping their dismal braying mouths
Their ravenous roaring lion mouths

I am poured out like water
My bones' joints are snapped like twigs
My heart melts like wax
Flooding my bowels with searing viscid emotion
My strength is dried up like a potsherd
My tongue cleaves woolly to the roof of my mouth
And I feel my body dissolving into death's dusts

For I am hounded by my isolation
Am cast off and encircled by the assembly of the violent
Who like vicious dogs snap at my hands and feet
I count the bones of my naked body
As the mongrels shift and stare and circle
They divide my clothes among themselves, casting lots for them

So now in this very place I call on you
There is no one left

Do not be far from me
Be the center
Of the center
Of the circle
Be the strength of that center
The power of the absence that is the center
Deliver my life from the killing sharpnesses
Deliver my soul from the feverish dogs
Save me from the lion mouths
Answer me with the voice of the ram's horn

And I will seek and form and repeat Your name among my kinsmen
In the midst of everyone I will compose praises with my lips
And those who enter your awesomeness through my words will also praise
All the seed of Jacob will glorify you
And live in awe of you
All those who question and struggle
Will dawn with your light
For they will know
You have not scorned the poor and despised
Nor recoiled disgusted from their faces
From them your spark has never been hidden
And when they cried out in their misery
You heard and answered and ennobled them
And it is the astonishment of this that I will praise in the Great Assembly
Making deep vows in the presence of those who know your heart
Know that in you the meek eat and are satisfied
And all who seek and struggle find the tongue to praise
Saying to you:

May your heart live forever
May all the ends of the earth remember and return to you
And all the families of all the nations bow before you .
For all that is is your domain
Your flame kindles all that lives and breathes
And you are the motive force of all activity
The yearning of the grasses, the lovers' ardor
And they that rise up, live and eat the fat of the earth will bow before you
Before you will bow all those who lie down, find peace, and enter the dust
For none can keep alive by his own power—you alone light the soul
Distant ages to come shall serve you, shall be related to you in future times
Those people not yet born
Will sing of your uprightness, your evenness, your brightness
To a people not yet born, that is still yet to come
That this is how you are.

                              translation by Norman Fischer

EXERCISES FOR THE SECOND PATH

The exercises of quadratos are cumulative. On the second path, we continue the practices of temenos and heyoeka. These are present throughout all four paths. They are particularly essential on the second path, where we often feel exhausted, conflicted, and anxious, needing trust and the experience of every voice. Remember, this is transformation. We are moving through a type of death—and it is very difficult.

Hold the Tension of the Opposites

Christianity provides a powerful image of the practice of holding the tension of the opposites. The tradition's earliest form of the cross was a simple + drawn with four arms of equal length. This is the same form known and venerated in the years the earliest gospels were composed. When we read Jesus's words "pick up your cross and follow," it was this kind of cross Mark was referring to. Its equal arms formed a symbol representing the joining of all opposites—left to right, and up to down. Even those distinctions disappear when this potent and apparently simple symbol is laid flat or turned in a circle. When you meditate or pray, see this + mark in your mind, or find (or make) such a cross and keep it by you.

In prayer and in practice with others, listen to all perspectives and sides. This is a deepening and expansion of the heyoeka exercise we advanced in the first path. When you now try to find truth in each and every perspective, no matter how opposed you feel initially, know that if you are sincere, you will also discover great interior conflicts. Resist every tendency to take one side over another. Understand that truth is your objective. Examine the fact that the tendency to choose *any* one side at the expense of its opposite is an ego-defense that serves no purpose except to makes us feel better in the moment. The ego feels calm after such a choice because it has something definite to latch onto—no uncertainty, no dilemma, no shades of gray, no anxiety. But this tendency is extremely harmful, almost by definition. Human interaction is complex, and if it is to be approached maturely, it can almost never be judged with the kind of simplistic exactitude that soothes the ego. Observe your own inner reactions to each perspective and continue to refrain from choosing specific positions.

When we do this, and accompany it with prayer and spiritual practice, an even greater truth will be revealed that goes still further—a way that folds the opposites together. But we are not yet there. On this second path, our challenge is to endure and learn from the opposites, listening intently to all sides, choosing neither. Holding the tension of opposites and living through our anxiety is our necessary trial as we keep to our journey, hoping and believing in a new epiphany.

Ask to Be Deepened

The lyrical poetry of Psalm 22 holds great mystery, grace, and wisdom. It is possible that a time of deepest abandonment can open feelings of hope and even praise within us.

A Buddhist prayer used before meditation recites: "I pray that I may be given the appropriate difficulties and sufferings on this journey so that my heart may become awakened, and my practice of compassion and liberation for all beings may be fulfilled."

Václav Havel, writer and former Czech president, has said: "Hope is not the conviction that something will turn out well, but the certainty that something makes sense, regardless of how it turns out."

Our practice in the second path, in the midst of great concern, pain, and emotional deprivation, is to pray that the meaning in these moments will be made clear to us, and that we will have the courage to live the answer that the meaning provides.

HOW DO WE MOVE
THROUGH SUFFERING?
is the core question of the Gospel of Mark

Good news! The Gospel of Mark opens with the hopeful reassurance that our trials actually represent good news—a further advance of our spiritual journey, along which we will continue if we persevere through faith.

John the Baptist calls us to "repent our sins": to scrutinize our lives, recognize the core source of our pain, acknowledge appropriate guilt, correct our conscience through asking for forgiveness, and then move on.

The storms at sea ask us to remember that we are not alone in the boat. They also tell us to listen for our inner "Rescue me! Fix me!" voice. When we hear it, we can know that this is a temptation to fall into feelings of helplessness and victimization. Mark asks us to respond with our greatest inner strength and determination to keep going, without losing compassion for ourselves and our frailties.

The transfiguration advises us that the nature of divinity is the joining of opposites, and that it holds both structure and compassion. We also need to be mindful that we lack understanding, and that we should wait and learn more before we speak, especially about our supposed wisdom.

The teachings on the road to Jerusalem tell us that we are on a deep and mysterious journey of transformation that will often be filled with pain and will seem completely incomprehensible. We will be unable to continue unless we pray to Spirit for help and accept that this is the nature of the second path.

The confrontations in the Temple teach us to take courage and walk directly into our inner and outer conflicts. The tension and anxiety we find in conflict is necessary and inevitable as the old ego-self struggles with Spirit.

Jesus's teaching about tribulation cautions us that when we find ourselves wanting to point fingers—externalizing our conflicts onto others—our practice instead should be to focus on the necessary transformation of our own inner lives. In this way our journey continues, and we do not become party to increasing the conflicts of others.

Mark's Passion account tells us to look to Peter's example and the example of the Christ. Peter's story shows that we can expect to fall into denial, or even desertion, and resolution may not come quickly. Jesus the Christ gives us an image of suffering as part of God and teaches us that, through surrender, we will come to know Spirit more deeply.

The resurrection announced asks us a significant question: What will our response be when we are challenged to step out in faith—especially when the cost is discomfort or turmoil or fear unto death? In the second path, it seems that almost every moment holds this question.

5

. . .

Resting in John's Glorious Garden

PSALM 126
When you bring us out from enclosure
We will be like dreamers
Our heads thrown back with laughter
Our throats vibrating with song
And the others will say

Yes
Great happenings
Have happened to them
The ones who have struggled
Long with their questions

Yes
Great things would have happened to us
And we would be dizzy with the joy of them
Drunk on water in an arid land
Our tears our joy's seed
We'd go out weeping
And come back singing
Our arms full of sheaves

translation by Norman Fischer

The Third Path:
How Do We Receive Joy?

In one electric, life-changing instant, it seems as though everything in us shifts and a blinding new reality enters. Until this point, so much has been struggle. Our toes searched for firm purchase on the mountain path of decision, and we cowered in the battering storms as we were tossed in the treacherous sea of the second path. Nonetheless, we remained faithful through all difficulties and missteps. We prayed that our yearning, out-stretched hand would be met by a firm, answering grip that would lead us ashore. That is not what we get, though. We get infinitely more. Yet no step we have taken, nor prayer we have prayed, could have prepared us for the wonder of this moment.

What arrives and opens in us feels like the everlasting embrace of an eternal guardian or an intimate lover. We are filled with an immediate and unexpected experience of union—full, unreflected, visionary, totally inde-scribable. The sensations of this moment will be different for each of us. Some of us will be aware of a new energy; we may tingle or tremble. Some will feel a deep stillness. A great calm—or exuberance—may arise. Sight may seem brighter, clearer. Flashes of creativity and new insight may burst into life. Minds may race into full engagement—or blissful emptiness. Al-most universally, we will perceive everything as gift.

With this opening, it is as though we have walked through a gate into the most beautiful springtime garden imaginable. Immeasurable beauty and bounty surround us. Our senses are confounded. Breezes ruffle our hair as we stroll, and birds call out their jubilant songs. We can feel how our fragile footprints are being overlaid by the Great Spirit, the infold-ing of Mystery, the Christ. We have a clear sense that we have entered a new plane of understanding where this largesse is freely available, a gift bestowed on all—not earned by any action of ours and completely uncon-ditional.

This is the third path and the Gospel of John. As the path unfolds through the apostle's metaphor of a garden—specifically, the Garden of Eden—we discover a bounty that feels as though it truly holds everything. We feel as though we have arrived at the point we have been headed for—at last! It is the culmination. We have made it. And in one way that is true.

John's gospel is a vision that is simultaneously unitive and illuminative—and there is absolutely nothing that can equal its inner experience. This feeling is precisely what poets and mystics try to describe and certainly one of the main reasons people use drugs and alcohol. They are trying to achieve an encounter with this bliss. It is the pinnacle, the apogee, and the heart of all.

When we rest and surrender to this epiphany, our attention gradually refocuses and our perception expands and sharpens. We notice much more than the garden flowers and the warmth of the new embrace. We become aware of the expanding roots, leaves, buds, and blossoms—the foundation and the future. Time expands. We sense the past and realize that our garden also contains dirt and worms and the sere brown memories of last season's blooms. We feel the rhythm of its unceasing cycles of decay into beauty into decay into beauty.

As powerful as our bliss is, it is only an instant, and the feelings of epiphany are only one part of one path of a full journey, in the same way that blossoms are only one brief season of a garden. Paradox is the treasure and essence of the third path. The third path's capacity to hold ambiguity means it can—and does—contain *everything*. It holds joy. It holds conflict. It holds boredom. It holds compassion. It holds cruelty. It holds ecstasy. It holds pain. It holds love. It holds cynicism. It holds hope. It holds misery. It holds striving. It holds hate. It holds peace. It holds every gradation of light and dark of each day and every passage of the seasons. It holds our full human complexity. It invites and accepts and celebrates every aspect of our human enigma.

Therefore, the glorious garden of John's gospel also holds a profound caution—not against the gift, but against the limitations of our understanding. In the third path, our insights are not yet fully mature, *although they feel so*. In fact, the world is full of people who reached the point of epiphany and immediately rushed out to share their supposed wisdom, and instead created only havoc. Wisdom is a much longer journey. These new revelations need space and careful sheltering. Matthew and Mark asked us to continue moving. John asks us to abide and receive. If we do, we will find that our awareness of complexity and interconnection expands. We will gently move toward a comprehension of our proper place within the whole. When questions about meaning and purpose begin to arise from that awareness, we will better understand, and then be ready to leave and take up the fourth path.

A critical equilibrium, the face of maturity, will reveal itself to us. If we leave too soon, we won't completely absorb our lessons. The young stalks planted by our journey thus far will never grow strong enough to support the blossoms that try to open. New buds filled with promise will wither. Yet, if we remain too long, our journey is incomplete, and our inner reformation is obstructed. A glorious garden must be sensitively tended. Too little water, and flowers will shrivel. Too much, and roots will rot. With either extreme, we will find our garden reduced to its soil and we will have to begin again—or be satisfied with plastic flowers.

The core question of this third path is, How do we receive joy? And the answer is that it is all about balance. How many times has each of us turned our back on joy through fear and cynicism? How many times have we each clung to joy and watched as it remorselessly thinned into illusion? The greater tragedy is to abandon the journey itself through the pain of our trepidations and losses, never understanding how close we came to finding real vitality and peace. Psychology cites the three primary ways we defend ourselves against perceived threat and also against the risks of change as sentimentality, cynicism, and assertion of power over another. These, too, are among the risks of the third path.

At first glance, the directions for this path seem simple. They are, basically, "relax and enjoy"—but for most of us, this is not so easy. Most of us are better trained for "doing" than for just "being," and when we manage to relax, we don't tend to do so in an attentive way, which is exactly what is required now.

Surprisingly, "enjoy" may present even more challenges than "relax." Many of us can't even rationalize enjoyment as our reward for the suffering we have endured. We are unaccustomed to feeling worthy. We are used to giving, but we don't know a single thing about receiving. However, "enjoy" means we must learn the deep truth of all gifts: a receiver with an open and thankful heart is absolutely essential, or the gift does not exist. It disappears. For many of us this comes as entirely new, and very difficult, information. But it is critically important. We are now in an eternal, unconditional embrace we can actually see and feel, thanks to the inner "stripping" we have undergone on the previous two paths. There is one catch:

our enjoyment is needed to complete the relationship. We don't have to do anything to earn the love—that is ours, no matter what—but without our enjoyment of that love, we deprive Spirit, and the universe, of our "resounding joy," which can reach far indeed.

Simply enjoying love may seem a gentle insight compared to the drama and hard-fought struggles of the first and second paths, but for many of us, this matter is anything but simple. The experience of union actually throws some of us into an acute depression, because we are so certain we don't deserve what we have received. To a smaller or greater degree, our time on the third path requires us to acknowledge our own worthiness. We cannot progress until we learn to put away the internal whips with which we remind ourselves of even our tiniest inadequacies. In this garden, it is our time to embrace the fact that we are loved simply because we are alive, not because of anything we do.

We will luxuriate in the words of this gospel as well as study its demanding challenges. What were the needs and conditions of the culture two millennia ago that inspired John to such beauty, mysticism, and rigor? We saw the unsettled Messiahnian beginnings in Antioch and empathized with the agonies of the Christus believers in Rome. Now we will visit the teeming complexity of the Aegean port of Ephesus, at the end of the first century, to share in the excitement and promise of its blossoming Christian community.

Birthplace of the Gospel of John: Ephesus on the Aegean Sea, 100 CE

At the end of the first century, Ephesus was a major seaport and the fourth largest city in the Greco-Roman world (after Rome, Alexandria, and Great Antioch). Chosen by the Roman Empire as the capital of its Asian provinces, it sat due east of Athens on the Aegean Sea in what is today known as Turkey. Both port and capital city, it boasted a culturally diverse and thriving population.

Ephesus was also very significant in early Christianity and most likely provided a haven for some of the greatest icons of the faith. The apostle Paul arrived in Ephesus in the mid-50s CE to teach, and did so for about three years. He (or someone who accompanied him) is credited with founding the community there that later came to call itself "Christian." Stories abound that the apostle John, author of the gospel, took Jesus's mother, Mary, there to live out her life after her son's death. Mary of Magdala is also thought to have taught in Ephesus before moving to Gaul, where she died. These figures provided a rich soil of faith and experience in which the followers of the Christ could learn and mature.

It is generally believed that the Gospel of John was written in Ephesus sometime between 98 and 105 CE, though some scholars posit that the gospel was written in Alexandria. (The cultural dynamics of the two cities were similar in so many respects that this debate regarding location makes little difference to our thesis.) For many years, it was thought likely that both this gospel and the book of Revelation had the same author— "John"—since both were written at approximately the same time, in almost the same place. It is now believed that there were two "Johns." Most scholars think John the apostle wrote the gospel, while a zealous Christian known as John the Seer who wrote from the nearby Isle of Patmos (where Emperor Domitian had imprisoned him for his beliefs) authored the book of Revelation.

John the apostle (the only apostle not martyred) is thought to have left Jerusalem for Ephesus before the Great Temple's destruction. In Ephesus, he found a community that had enjoyed rich teaching and practice for more than a decade—particularly that of the apostle Paul, its founder. John remained in Ephesus until his death of old age, continuing to teach and write. As we read his work, it is important that we keep ourselves anchored in history. A fervent evangelist, John had no interest whatsoever in accommodating his views to those of Judaism. He believed that the path of Jesus the Christ was superior to Judaism and never hesitated to express that view. His job, as he saw it, was to enlighten the people of Ephesus and to advocate for the Messiah who had come.

The Ephesian Christian community matured very differently from those in Rome and Antioch. The matrix was unique. The city had a diverse population with many well-traveled citizens, no religious persecution, and highly skilled religious teachers. In Ephesus, in contrast to Rome and Antioch, many non-Jews became followers. The congregation, therefore, developed to address the spiritual needs and beliefs of a wide assortment of pagan believers, as well as those of Messianic Jews. Building a coherent Christian community that encompassed this multiplicity of tradition was a vibrant process that required many years—and benefited especially from the wisdom of great inspiration.

When the Gospel of John was written, it was seeded in the rich soil of Paul's teaching, which had been nurtured by additional learned teachers and the deep practice of almost fifty years. Furthermore, the community had, by that time, been totally separated from Judaism for ten years—distinctions unique to this gospel. The Ephesians firmly considered themselves members of a separate new faith and self-identified as "Christians." They did not regard Jesus as the Jewish Messiah who had come only for the Jews. They were a multi-tribal community that followed a universal Christ who had come, died, and been resurrected for all. Their Messiah would lead them to an inner temple in a new Jeru-Shalom where everyone would find welcome.

The new faith, needing a way to form community and confirm members, developed a new "baptism" that, by the time of John's gospel, had become Christianity's rite of entrance. In the first century, the actual form and purpose of baptism varied. As noted earlier, the type of baptism that John the Baptist performed was a version of the Jewish ritual washing for cleansing and purification today called *mikvah*. In the writings of the apostle Paul, we see the transformation of the Jewish baptism ritual into a process of initiation that joined an individual to the Christ. Gradually, this new Christian rite achieved equal stature with the traditional Jewish ritual of circumcision and then, after the break with Judaism, replaced it.

Building on the traditional washing ceremony, Christian baptism went far beyond "cleansing," and required much more commitment than a mere willingness to be dunked in the river. Christians seeking to be baptized—men and women alike—were required to undergo a lengthy period of reflection and practice. It was mandated that baptismal candidates make a commitment to service that involved heavy responsibilities within the faith community. Only if they fulfilled these criteria were they eligible for the final ritual, which was designed to provide an internal experience of Jesus the Christ's life, death, resurrection, and call to service. The process was so complex that it was tantamount to what we would today consider ordination. Indeed, one eminent scholar, Raymond Brown, suggests that John's entire gospel may have been written as a series of reflections for those preparing to be baptized.

Christianity's impact in Ephesus far exceeded the ritual of baptism, however. For millennia, each village, city, and region had its own god or goddess, which could never be the god of anyone outside the tribe. Religious beliefs held the gravity of survival practices, because all religions of the time believed that everything in life was in the hands of these powerful beings. It was believed that the sun literally rose each day based on the wishes of the gods. Therefore, universally in law and custom of the time, tribal outsiders were not only regarded as unbelievers, but also represented concrete threats to the harmony and existence of the world. Thus there were unceasing quarrels, and even battles, over the supremacy of the various deities and the practices followed in the service of each.

It is important that when we think of the quarrels and eventual rift between Judaism and Christianity, we realize that, historically, neither religion held the forms we see them in today. Although Judaism marked an unmistakable departure from the practices in the region by becoming a monotheistic religion, recognizing God as a single God, above all other "false gods," it remained strongly tribal. Even though the Torah pronounced that all people came from Yahweh (G–d), were created in his image, and were therefore to be respected, the deity's omnipotence was available only to Jews—who carefully negotiated with, and appealed to him through elaborate rituals developed over the centuries.

Christianity, by the time of John's gospel—although it had not yet become a formal religion of any kind—had broken the ancient tribal pattern. Ephesus had heard the apostle Paul preach the invitation that women and men, Greek and Jew, free and slave, all share their lives with each other following one God. The new faith wanted everyone to understand and follow its vision. The gospel shouted out the affirmation of this joyous summons: "*All* are one; no one is excluded; join us!" The Christian approach to social structuring was a stark departure from the long-held practices of the Hebrew tribes, the Old Temple, and the traditional strictures of tribalism itself. Historically, all tribes consisted of a core group whose membership evolved primarily through blood or marriage or locale (although other members might be allowed in by agreement of the group). Judaism, for example, granted automatic membership through the blood of a Jewish mother. Christianity, however, changed the rules of tribe by actively inviting *everyone*. In the Mediterranean region of the time, this was a radical—even blasphemous—concept, but the cultural diversity of Ephesus welcomed these deeply inclusionary beliefs and Christianity quickly grew.

Using the core teachings of the Hebrew Testament, particularly those in the book of Genesis, John reworks them into a more Christian perspective. Beyond penning new metaphors for the garden, and for Adam and Eve, his fresh stories transform the old accounts of trial and suffering into tales resonating with the jubilant message that through the Christ, Paradise is *now recovered*. This reshaped garden of Christianity *welcomes* people rather than casting them out. It doesn't consider them usurpers of the divine; rather, it invites them to share in its bounty and beauty. In this way, John illuminates the new faith to his diverse audience in a way that would be familiar to the Christ followers and comprehensible to everyone.

Unmistakably visionary, John's poetic words also make vast metaphysical pronouncements quite different from those in the Hebrew Testament. Although that testament holds many passages of immense beauty, and Yahweh certainly extends understanding to his people, a great many of its passages recount swift punishment and little mercy. Much of Yahweh's awesomeness derives from the vast power he readily wields. In direct contrast, the Gospel of John also proclaims Jesus the Christ as eternal and immensely powerful, but leaves out the images of punishment. John wants to emphasize that the Christ's power and authority originate from a divinity based in wisdom and love—a difference that must have startled his readers.

The comportment of Jesus and his "pronouncements" differentiate John from the Gospels of Matthew, Mark, and Luke. In John, a divine Jesus, completely in charge of every single event that is recounted, always spoke first, bestowed wisdom and miracles, and carried his own cross. He was sure, confident, and serene. There are no passages that portray or discuss the aspect of Jesus as a divine being incarnated as a human, here on earth to relate to humans as an almost-peer and to suffer with humans. In fact, the topic of suffering is altogether absent in this gospel.

In another departure exclusive to this gospel, Jesus the Christ engaged in cordial discourse with a wide assortment of people whom tribal custom of the time would have deemed socially inferior or unacceptable. And though Jesus was clearly respectful and welcoming to these diverse peoples—among them women, Greeks, and a blind man—his presence in the accounts was nonetheless unfailingly powerful and divine. He stood, always, with the authority of God and did not hesitate to use that authority to *bestow* truth, mercy, and miracles. With this royal demeanor, not found in the other gospels, Jesus used language that was assured, emphatic, and not in the least collegial. There are no soft and approachable beginnings to Jesus's sentences, and "friend" was a rare address. By contrast, although Jesus certainly directed events and performed miracles in Matthew, Mark, and Luke—often forcefully—we would probably not characterize his actions in those accounts as *bestowing,* which we can readily do in John's gospel.

In this gospel, Jesus the Christ graciously, gracefully, and *very* firmly laid down the core principles on which he wished believers to focus: union and complexity and compassion. He made it clear that when he gave this instruction he did so with the full force and authority of God's divine power, which he claimed for himself. He further charged that believers had a duty to accept these precepts as immutable truths. Finally, his commands for action were explicit: "Go out and practice these principles in your lives!"

John's gospel is a full-hearted proclamation that all is unified. The diversity and exuberance of the Ephesian Christian community is inextricable from the gospel itself. Each came from the other; each led the other forward. In this exciting synergy, for a few remarkable years Ephesus became the heart of Christianity, in precisely the same way Jerusalem had been the heart of Judaism.

Approaching John Today: Resting in the Garden

The poetry and depth of John's words represent the third path in its fullest blossoming. John was a mystic. His language resonates with continuous ecstasy and deep peace. Of the four gospels, John's was the last written, and is placed last in the Christian Testament. However, as we have noted, when taught in the ancient church, certain passages were chosen to be used primarily for the seasons of Lent and Easter, the traditional church periods for reflection on death and new life. This was likely done because this gospel describes the third path—epiphany and rebirth—and because John's gospel and the third path are completely different in form, in tone, and in substance from the other paths.

As we proceed on our spiritual journey, we will discover the succor of John's gospel on an ongoing basis in our inner lives. We will be able to find and feel the many tiny epiphanies that are continually occurring all around us, no matter what specific "path" we are focused on. I am certain this is why almost all the ancient reading cycles, with full inspiration, placed sections of John's gospel within the other gospels. "Behold!" its words cry out, "See the flowers. Smell the air. Appreciate the dirt and the bugs. Be blessed. Know joy. Feel worthy. Share the gift." Let us move to examine some concepts that will help us to enter into John's gospel—and the experience of the third path—as fully as possible.

Western spirituality has used terms like "enlightenment" and "illumination" to describe what we call the third path. These words result from attempts by mystics to express a sense of their experience through the use of a "light arising" metaphor. We are moving from not-seeing to seeing, and it is easy to characterize this, in terms of our bodily senses, as a movement from the "dark," where our physical sight is limited, into the relative clarity of "light." But this is too small a metaphor for what we are experiencing.

Further, the use of these terms can lead us into difficulty, because they imply a sense of switching from a flat, one-sided state into another equally flat state. The third path is not so limited. In its complexity, it is neither light nor dark, but rather an infolding of the two, of up and down, of right and left, of all opposites into a whole, intricate, and ever-changing harmony. It doesn't proceed in "steps" and "stages" like the other paths tend to do. It isn't linear at all. It is nonsequential, its aspects frequently simultaneous, undifferentiated.

With regard to this third spiritual path, the word "path" itself is almost a contradiction. It arrives as a complete and unitive experience. And once we are on it—*in* it—we don't walk or engage in much activity at all. We stay still and observe. We stay still and feel. We stay still and pray. In a mature spiritual life, these are the practices that will fill and illuminate everything we do. Here our habit of self-and-other-reflection begins to truly deepen and become threaded into the tapestry of our lives.

Another concept that can help us comprehend the nature of this path is an understanding of the word "symbol." Symbol comes from two Greek words, *sum* and *ballein. Sum* means "together" and *ballein* is "to throw." Thus, *sumballein,* which became "symbol," is "to throw two or more things together." When we use or make a symbol, we throw together disparate elements: word and picture, heart and head. This is the capacity to deal with paradox, an essential aspect of the truth of union, and the third path.

Contrast the meaning of symbol with the Greek word *diabol,* from which *diablo,* or "devil," is derived. *Dia* means "across" and, again, *bol* derives from *ballein,* "to throw." *Diaballein,* or *diabol,* is, therefore, "to throw across." Using this understanding, we can see that the second spiritual path—which we recently traversed—was a diabolic inner landscape, a tempestuous place of obstacles thrown across our path, where opposites appeared separate, distinct. The temptations of ego surfaced continually, and we felt lost as opposites tore at us.

Now, at the third path, in a surprising flash, we have been given the capacity to know *sym-bol.* Harmony has replaced our experience of searing trial, and we are resting in our garden instead of battling the stormy seas of *dia-bol.* The strain and exhaustion of the second path begin to fade and we move into our springtime garden. Green buds appear on the wizened brown twigs of our soul. What we feared damaged beyond repair—dead—comes back to life. We look back with a sense of meaning, knowing that the course of events could not have been otherwise and was worth the pain. We begin to relax into our blessings and the self-value they imply. We dare to believe that we hold a blossom within.

As we revel in the harmonious union John has given us, we must remember that much of the historical teaching about John's priceless words is not remotely consistent with his original, deeply loving, and mystical intention. Instead, many readers, teachers, and institutions—over many centuries—have misinterpreted John's priceless and *symbolic* words through the eyes of *diabol.* Indeed, they continue to do so. Unfortunately, once the original fourfold reading cycle was abandoned, churchgoing Christians lost the possibility of the full journey of psychological and spiritual transformation in the gospels, and with it, the complexity of *symbol.* The joyous message of John's gospel—of oneness—was crushed into the one-dimensional meanings that conformed to the more linear narratives of Matthew, Mark, and Luke. This is the tragic and inevitable result of an incomplete spiritual journey—and reinforces the importance of restoring the full understanding of quadratos now.

The words of this gospel have been—and are—viciously misused, and have metamorphosed into weapons for the razor-sharp sword of self-righteousness. Historically, they have all too often been converted into justifications for enslavement and even murder. While appalling, this is not surprising, for it is precisely what happens if one leaves the third path too quickly or fails to continue on to the lengthy and transformative practice of the fourth path. It is the terrible hidden peril of the third path, which we will learn about as we continue. In this gospel we will read passages that seem at odds with John's core message and realize, with compassion, that John himself fell victim to the very same shortcomings against which his gospel cautions.

Among the deeply inspired, beauteous, and resonant words lurk an array of strident passages that are clearly angry and much less inspired. Many people today consider John's gospel to be anti-Semitic, because John frequently rails against "the Jews." However, we must remember that John himself was a Jew, as was Jesus. When John penned his angry words, he was inveighing against the Pharisees and Jewish authorities who had, half a century after Jesus's death, cursed the Messiahnians and driven them out of the synagogues. (We can relate this to those abroad who curse "Americans"—but mean those in charge of American government policies that they find onerous, and not American people in general.) John's harsh words are a historical window into the tremendous pain and trauma of the fight among the ancestral family of Judaism at the end of the first century.

An unfulfilled spiritual journey risks becoming mired in the distortions of *diabol,* and John's discordant words provide us with a precise and terrible mirror for what can happen when those malformations are broadly misused. For his own personal and historical reasons, John separated the Jewish authorities from his extraordinary universal vision, and made resentful judgments against them in his gospel. Horrific consequences developed. During the Middle Ages—a period that follows the loss of the three-year reading cycle—John's words against "the Jews," although *not* directed against an entire faith or tribe, began to be especially singled out by those with an anti-Jewish agenda. The accepted church interpretation of

John's words became literal, the verses stripped of their message of vision-ary unity and *sym-bol*.

This simplistic interpretation focused on the surface meanings of John's words, and particularly seized on John's flashes of anger and frus-tration against the Pharisees—on *dia-bol*—shaping the gospel into a strident tool for an evangelism that focused on Christian self-righteous superiority and dominion over other religions. Instead of inspiring har-mony, it inspired hate, pogroms, and murder. It has produced division within us, within our churches, and between Christianity and other world religions. It continues to divide us today, far beyond misapprehension, as an ongoing, active tragedy.

It is imperative that we reach for the ancient view of wholeness avail-able to us in this gospel and couple it with our understandings of history and psychology. By doing so, we will understand the necessity for the full four-path spiritual journey and become empowered to restore our richest and most meaningful practices, refreshing them in ways that are useful now, today. John's rhythmic verses and metaphors carry us into the truth of a Oneness beyond categories, beyond words, into the rich paradoxes of *sym-bol* and Mystery.

So let us begin our study of the third path, starting with the Pro-logue, which contains some of Christianity's most significant passages. We'll move on to John the Witness (John the Baptist in a new role) and the wedding at Cana, then the teaching stories of Jesus and Nicodemus, the woman at the well, the man born blind, and the raising of Lazarus. Lastly, we will discover John's unique Passion, which culminates in his resurrection accounts.

Remember that, unlike Matthew and Mark, John is not distracted by any of the requirements of telling a linear story, but remains focused only on the eternal. His words are sure, steady, and beautiful, exuding a confi-dence that leaps into our hearts. They describe that transcendent and soul-filled place celebrated by prophets and sages, by poems and symphonies, and by every enduring painting and hymn. John's glorious garden is before us. Let us open the gate and enter its bounty.

The Most Crucial Words in Christianity:
"The Christ"

The introductory eighteen verses of the Gospel of John, commonly known as the Prologue, contain some of Christianity's most important concepts—ideas with such far-reaching implications that they need extra preparation and attention from us.

First, let us go back a bit. You may recall that at the beginning of the book, we discussed the importance of recovering the full name, Jesus *the* Christ, rather than the currently used single name, Jesus. The three-word name was the normal expression used by all early believers. Within it is a great truth that the apostle Paul wrote about, and that greatly influenced all of the gospel writers, particularly John.

Paul wrote, in a passage from Colossians that we quoted earlier, that the Christ was "the image of the invisible God, the firstborn of all creation; for in him all things in heaven and on earth were created, things visible and invisible, whether thrones or dominions or rulers or powers—all things have been created through him and for him. He himself is before all things, and in him all things hold together" (Col. 1:15–17).

The apostle Paul, through this and many other influential writings, made it clear that he understood "the Christ" to be an overarching reality that existed eternally, and Jesus as an individuated embodiment of that reality. This became accepted belief, and it is why the religion is named Christian, and not Jesusian. It is also why early baptism proclaimed believers as becoming "a Christ" as they rose up out of the water and entered into that new, greater reality.

As we are about to read, this truth is proclaimed in its most certain and poetic words in the Prologue of the Gospel of John. John's Prologue is very clear. It speaks of a reality existing in a time before time—before Genesis. John uses the term "the Word" (*Logos,* in Greek) to express the same eternal reality that Paul expressed by "the Christ" (*Christos*).

In the beginning was the Word, and the Word was with God, and the Word was God. He was in the beginning with God. (1:1–2)

Subsequently, the Prologue tells us, Jesus came to us as a human manifestation of the Christ.

He came to what was his own, and his own people did not accept him.
(1:11)

Why is this distinction between eternal reality and human manifestation so vitally important?

If "the Christ" began with Jesus's conception, which has been the increasingly mistaken belief for nearly a thousand years, then it is quite natural for our religion to be focused—as it is—on the personality of Jesus, because his personage would constitute the end-all and be-all—the entire point. Precisely what words Jesus actually spoke and when he spoke them would assume immense importance. Biographical details would be endlessly fascinating and significant. The quest for new excavations and interpretations would be never-ending. *And that's exactly the focus we see today!* Yet despite devoted study of that historical personage, people would be filled with confusion that could never be satisfied and conflicts that could never be resolved. *Exactly as they are today!* Why? Because the lifelong spiritual needs (not to mention psychological and emotional needs) of millions of people worldwide, who think of themselves as Christian, are focused on the biographical details of a brief human history in ancient Palestine that they will never completely know. And there will *never* be enough bones or papyrus—or analytical wisdom—to meet those needs.

If we grasp the depth of the Prologue, however, we open ourselves to a new understanding. Jesus the Christ is a divine and unified reality that presents two faces to us: one that is loving and familiar and another that is vast and mysterious. We can pray to them both, just as Christians have for many centuries. Jesus walked with us on the earth as the human, visible manifestation of the Christ. We know that when we pray to Jesus, our sense of relationship is close and intimate. We can feel that he holds our hand firmly in his. The Christ, our God, is the other face. The Christ is ineffable Mystery, and comes to us in our times of deepest need, when we offer up the feelings and experiences we cannot endure by ourselves—our greatest pain and our overwhelming joy. The Christ is boundless, powerful, far beyond anything we can know or comprehend, with no beginning and no end. It is to the Christ that we turn in our humility. The Christ shares and supports us in everything we ask. Jesus and the Christ are two expressions of a great and creative process, which we are invited to enter and make our own.

When we shed our immature Jesusian focus and engage the Christ fully, we begin to see how much Christendom has confused us by using the two parts of the great name interchangeably. They are *not* interchangeable. Jesus was born. The Christ was not. Jesus died. The Christ did not. Jesus rose. The Christ did not. Jesus went away. The Christ did not and never will. Every prayer we speak and every hymn we sing asks to be heard with this new discrimination from both our hearts and our minds.

Many philosophers and metaphysicians have described our world as being separated from the timeless truth of All, as if by a veil through which we can dimly see. Two thousand years ago in the Middle East, Jesus came and "ripped the veil" so that we might enter into greater truth of the Christ. That truth encompasses the reality of all things in the universe. In each succeeding generation, we have been granted more and more access to tools enabling us to widen our understanding and appreciation of Mystery. Today, when we ponder God and the process of creation, we use religion, philosophy, psychology, science, sociology, anthropology, and many other disciplines—as well as the quiet places of our hearts. When we do this, we are following the instructions in John's Prologue and becoming the "children of God, . . . born, not of . . . the will of man, but of God" (1:13).

The answer to the confusion and conflict of today is not to run back to Jesus's biography when we seek answers about our faith. That dooms the very promise for which Jesus came. Instead, we must focus on the reality of the Christ, who has *always* been at work. St. Paul tells us that the Christ was "the spiritual rock" from which Moses drank (1 Cor. 10:4). The Christ was one with Jesus in the first century. The Christ is with us now and will be with us for eternity. If this is the presence that we come to know today, then we will have no fear of tomorrow. Let us hold this in our hearts as we enter the majesty of the Prologue's eternal vision.

Beyond Time: The Prologue

The opening passages of the Gospels of Matthew, Mark, and Luke link history and geography as metaphorical guideposts for their intended audiences, providing places from which to begin, or continue. The opening of John, however, does not concern itself with such small, earthbound matters. History, place, and time—none of these mundane human conceptions are found in the extraordinary first words of the Gospel of John.

The Prologue is exquisite, mystical poetry. Its serenity and sonorous majesty immediately carry its readers to the time before time, the unfolding of the deepest of mysteries. Echoing the pronouncements and rhythms of Genesis—"In the beginning when God created the heavens and the earth" (Gen. 1:1)—its words rise far above both personal and didactic discourse. They recite only the greatest of truths, and expound only on the most elevated realms of the heart and soul. Intended to inspire, not reassure, they pronounce what John clearly *knew.* They are the most expansive context possible for the series of meditations on Jesus the Christ that forms this gospel.

John's Prologue clearly and joyfully proclaims the Christ as the alpha and the omega, an eternal presence with no beginning and no end. These rapturous verses must have echoed profoundly in the Christian hearts of Ephesus—particularly when spoken in their original Aramaic language. When one says the word "Messiah" in Aramaic, it ends with an outbreath. Each time "Messiah" was spoken, there was a sensory re-creation of the single breath from which all and everyone began. Even with the apostle Paul's translation to the Greek word *Christos,* and the loss of this visceral experience, the poetry remains so powerful that we are deeply moved by it two thousand years later.

The Prologue uses "the Word"—*Logos,* in Greek—which was a concept promulgated much earlier by a Hellenistic Jew named Philo. Well understood by Jews of the time, Philo's *Logos* represented a sort of emanation from God that was not really separate from God. John, who uses several Greek-based ideas in his gospel, chose Philo's word for his Prologue, overlaying *Logos* onto Paul's concept of *Christos*—the eternal reality which Paul had titled, expressed, and taught in Ephesus for many years.

John writes that the Word was with God in the beginning, and that later the Word was made flesh in Jesus. Without John's insight, we might think today that "the Christ" and "Jesus" were synonymous, and that "the Christ" came into being only with Jesus's conception. John's mature vision also clarifies the birth stories of the child Jesus found in the Gospels of Matthew and Luke, helping us see that these are accounts of Jesus's fleshly incarnation as an *aspect* of the Christ but do not in any way tell of the *beginning* of the Christ.

> In the beginning was the Word, and the Word was with God, and the Word was God. He was in the beginning with God. All things came into being through him, and without him not one thing came into being. What has come into being in him was life, and the life was the light of all people. The light shines in the darkness, and the darkness did not overcome it. (1:1–5)

> He was in the world, and the world came into being through him; yet the world did not know him. He came to what was his own, and his own people did not accept him. But to all who received him, who believed in his name, he gave power to become children of God, who were born, not of blood or of the will of the flesh or of the will of man, but of God. (1:10–13)

> And the Word became flesh and lived among us, and we have seen his glory, the glory as of a father's only son, full of grace and truth. . . . From his fullness we have all received, grace upon grace. The law indeed was given through Moses; grace and truth came through Jesus Christ. No one has ever seen God. It is God the only Son, who is close to the Father's heart, who has made him known. (1:14, 16–18)

"THE WORD BECAME flesh." With these words, John identifies Jesus as a commingled reality of spirit and humanity, the exemplar of all aspects of oneness: of heaven and earth, life and death, east and west, light and dark, male and female, height and depth, past and future—all existing eternally. The sublime meditations of John help us to enter into this understanding, an experience of deep unity, enabling us to join what is outside of time to that which is within time. This is the great gift of the Prologue of the

Gospel of John. Through faith and love, it leads us to the truth of the cosmos and shows us that all else is illusion we can ignore.

Although it is possible for us to transform any part of the gospels we find meaningful into a prayer for regular use, the foundation of our deepest belief is expressed in the Prologue. Many have adapted it for their own as a profound personal invocation, as the following text illustrates.

In the beginning was the Christ, and the Christ was with God, and the Christ was God. The Christ was in the beginning with God. All things came into being through the Christ, and without the Christ not one thing came into being. What has come into being in the Christ was life, and the life was the light of all people, of all creation. The light shines in the darkness, and the darkness did not overcome it. The Christ was in the world, and the world came into being through the Christ; yet the world did not know the Christ. The Christ came to what was the Christ's own, and the Christ's own people did not accept the Christ. But to all who received the Christ, who believed in the Christ's name, the Christ gave power to become sons and daughters of God, who were born, not of blood or the will of the flesh or of the will of man and woman, but of God. And the Christ became flesh and lived among us, and we have seen the Christ's glory, the glory as of the Creator's only offspring, full of grace and truth. From the Christ's fullness we have all received, grace upon grace. The law indeed was given through Moses; grace and truth came through Jesus the Christ. No one has ever seen God, the Creator. It is God—the only offspring—the Christ —who is close to the Creator's heart, who has made the Creator known.

To open a more personal, image-filled, intuitive prayer that still illuminates the essence of the creation experience, experiment with other changes. Substitute "Wisdom" or "Love" or "Compassion" in all the places that "the Christ" appears above. As you slowly read each altered text, notice the tiny cues that the body and the soul give you. Which image best speaks to your heart? Which best helps you capture a sense of Oneness and Mystery? Pray with the adaptation that forges the best inner connection for you.

Much of John's Prologue, and indeed his entire gospel, is preoccupied with the concept of illusion. Scholars believe that this may well have become part of John's work due to his almost certain familiarity with the Greek philosopher Plato. Plato wrote that our everyday minds live in what he characterized as a shadowy cave of veiled sight. If we are deep in a cave, we cannot see light directly; all we see is its reflection on the floor and walls. While we may believe that the reflection is the source of light, our belief is illusion. Similarly, the experiences we have in unopened lives and hearts feel as though they are "real," but they are not. We are merely living in a state of illusion. Everything we think we're learning is still just inference, rather than direct experience.

Some have held that when John writes, "The Word was in the world," he implies that spirit and matter are separate, with spirit holding a higher value than matter. In this text, however, "world" does not mean the physical place we occupy. John understood that if we do not enter into the Christ and experience spirit and matter as one, we are caught in "the world" and yet do not realize it. Therefore, whenever we read the word "world" in this text, it is this limited, illusory sense that is intended. When we enter the Christ, this small, shadowed, illusory "world" shatters to reveal the fullness and unlimited nature of God. John does not condemn body or physical matter; he condemns only our *illusion* that body and matter are separate from spirit and heaven. All are one, without separation, in John's glorious garden.

Yet the habits of acting as though things *are* separate—a perspective of dualism rather than unity—are pervasive and well rooted, nourishing the misconception that opposites are conflicting realities. Dualism accepts no middle ground. It tells us that things or people are either one thing or another with no degrees of difference or nuance, and celebrates or denigrates extremes of behavior such as asceticism on the one hand or material success on the other. Acting from these rigid and unrealistic attitudes limits our humanity. When we are faced with them, most of us are filled with confusion and anger. This is the face of *dia-bol* in action. Do we wish change? If yes, then we must use discernment with each and every extreme attitude we hold.

Sym-bol, the truth of unity, demands that we reexamine a famous line from the Prologue and another of our fondest presumptions, so often quoted in churches: "The light shines in the darkness, and the darkness did not overcome it" (1:5). Commonly and completely misinterpreted, this line, if properly understood, could start our churches on a profoundly transformative path—or at least lead us to question much of what we have been taught.

The misunderstanding occurred gradually and perhaps, in some ways, inevitably. Although we know that Israel is in the Middle East, in our desire to see Jesus in our own lives, we sometimes forget all the implications of the fact that Jesus's home was actually in Asia. The worldview of Jesus the Christ had (and has) at least as much resonance, if not more, with the philosophies of Asia as with those of Greece and Rome, and particularly with how those philosophies expressed themselves in language. The native language of Jesus and all the apostles was Aramaic. John attempted to convey his understanding and experience of an Aramaic Christ to the very diverse Ephesian population. Following Paul's earlier example, he wrote in Greek, the predominant language of Ephesus, and as we have noted, he also used many widely circulated Greek ideas.

The Aramaic worldview was entirely different from the Greek one, forcing John to translate whole cultures, as well as words. Aramaic is a poetic, image-based language filled with metaphors of the earth, of nature and agriculture. By contrast, the Greek language of the first century was more conceptual. Its focus was comparative values based on thought, and its metaphors naturally inclined to the more cerebral and metaphysical. Unfortunately, the dichotomy of culture and language that John encountered when he translated Aramaic poetry into Greek concepts led to much of the tragic narrowing and the misinterpretation from which we still suffer today.

Our understanding of the last line of the first stanza of the Prologue, quoted above, is perhaps one of the most lamentable results. In Aramaic, each and every segment of the night and day has a singular word that paints a particular picture of that time, shaded by the balance between light and dark. No segment is either wholly dark or wholly light. All the "night words" contain an aspect of light and all the "day words" contain darkness and shadow. Wholeness is implicit in every single descriptor.

When we read, "The light shines in the darkness, and the darkness did not overcome it" with the more Aramaic understanding (and the sense of reality that John fully understood and, we must presume, intended), we can clearly see how far common belief has retreated from this early truth. Light is not *overcome* by the dark. Light and dark *coexist*. John's line is not about light banishing darkness; rather, it acknowledges and honors the reality that light and dark always play together in infinite variations. John probably never imagined the limited interpretation that would ensue from his words. If he had, he might have written, "*The light shines in the darkness, and the darkness did not overcome it, as the two played together in harmony, and shadows formed.*"

Yet today, in places of worship, we hear again and again that God is light (and light only), and that light reigns over the dark. This perception has spilled into every aspect of our culture: good guys wear white hats; bad guys wear black ones. When we attain holiness, we are en*light*ened. Dark people and dark emotions are considered extremely dangerous, and we often feel it necessary to shun them, conceal them, enslave them, and even kill them. We have demonized the dark, and in so doing have cut off parts of ourselves, of each other, and of our world.

For a long time, vestiges of this earlier, fuller, more Aramaic understanding remained and were expressed in Christianity. The builders of the Chartres Cathedral, the first example of Gothic architecture, surely grasped the depth of John's poetry. They built a cathedral specifically designed so that neither light nor dark overtook the other. Instead, a dynamic interplay between them allowed light to pour from the vividly colored windows into the cathedral's shadowy darkness, where the two met to form new shades of color.

Unfortunately, by the eighteenth century, the rhythms and understandings of the reading cycle had been lost for a very long time, and the cathedral was remodeled, although perhaps "defaced" would be the word more appropriate to the standards of John's text. An overzealous bishop replaced about a third of the colored windows with uncolored opaque glass. This dramatically altered the balance of light and dark in the space. Nonetheless, it is possible for visitors today to still get some sense of the earlier, more shadowed effect.

But the terrible error persists. By now, almost everyone believes without question the misinterpretation of John's poetic, unifying line. For centuries upon centuries, most churchgoers have learned that light banishes, destroys, and wipes out the evil dark. So, of course, places of worship have quite naturally enshrined this interpretation through architecture that is over-illuminated by sun or electricity. These gleaming edifices are making a philosophical statement, as is their intention. However, when they proclaim the superiority of light over the dark, they unknowingly reject the genuine wholeness of light and dark in harmony. And we are lulled into a false and shallow comfort, flattened and *dia-bolic*.

The prayers we pray, the hymns we sing, and the daily language we speak have not gone unscathed. A one-sidedness of language that raises up *only* light and ease and purity as "holy" feeds our instinctual fear of the dark. Because our eyes don't work as well in the dark, after the sun sets we fall headlong into the unexpected. We naturally retreat to a place of light—imagined or real—forgetting in the process that much of our spiritual challenge requires us to come to terms with our instinctual nature.

Yet, how often do we vainly attempt to shun these "dark" aspects? We ignore what we know: that when we cut off psychological or emotional aspects of ourselves, they do anything but disappear or rest quietly, benignly neglected. Even if they sometimes operate under our conscious "radar," they grow anxious, stronger, more needing of attention and understanding. They move out of balance and find ways to slip into our lives and, collectively, into the world. The more we try to focus only on the bright and sunny aspects of our existence, the more the hidden and unknown in us will call out. The dark, the difficult, and the foreign are holy also, and the Gospel of John specifically calls us to the task of recognizing them, loving them, and giving them welcome as part of our wholeness.

The third path's proclamation of wholeness—the vision wherein all opposites are unified—is not only a spiritual condition. Psychology tells us that unless we are able to perceive ourselves in this entirety, we will continually "split off" the aspects of ourselves that we have not accepted or integrated, stunting the creativity and vitality that make us human, and in extreme cases putting us in danger. On a communal level, even if we believe that we have erased racism from our conscious minds, we need to bring much deeper discernment to this question. The habits of our languages, our lives, and every aspect of our cultures have been embedded for a very long time and run deep indeed. Let us be thoughtful and welcome both *words* and *images* of darkness in all their manifestations—visible and invisible, places that are dark, people who are dark, and our own individual darkness and difficulty. Only in this way can we hope to find a course that leads out of the divisions of fear, racism, and war that continue to tear our bruised souls and the world apart.

John the Witness: Transforming John the Baptizer

This gospel gives John the Baptist a new role. Here he becomes John the Witness, though his importance is in no way lessened. Whereas John in this gospel did baptize believers, he did not baptize Jesus. Instead, John's main purpose in this text was to serve as a witness to revelation. He identified Jesus as divine and illustrated his presence as the "Lamb of God," referencing Exodus and Isaiah. This shift in John's function matched the evolution of the new Christian baptism ritual in Ephesus, reinforcing its internal and transformative nature.

> The next day he saw Jesus coming toward him and declared, "Here is the Lamb of God who takes away the sin of the world! This is he of whom I said, 'After me comes a man who ranks ahead of me because he was before me.' I myself did not know him; but I came baptizing with water for this reason, that he might be revealed to Israel." And John testified, "I saw the Spirit descending from heaven like a dove, and it remained on him. I myself did not know him, but the one who sent me to baptize with water said to me, 'He on whom you see the Spirit descend and remain is the one who baptizes with the Holy Spirit.' And I myself have seen and have testified that this is the Son of God." (1:29–34)

An Ancient Story Retold: The Wedding Feast at Cana

The story of the wedding feast at Cana concludes the opening section. In it, John once again skillfully and sensitively recovers Hebrew narratives, bringing them forward and restating them in persuasive Christian terms. Messianic Jews identified with the stories and found increased promises in them, while non-Jews felt the warm welcome of new traditions full of openness, celebration, and meaningful ritual. John's account of the wedding feast evoked Adam and Eve in the Garden of Eden—the second chapter of Genesis—just as his Prologue echoed the first chapter—the seven-day creation—when God spoke and the world came into being.

Although not obvious to us today, a story about a wedding implicitly referenced Genesis to the Ephesians. In the first century, weddings were always held outdoors in gardens or courtyards—never in public buildings—so the first words, "On the third day there was a wedding," automatically meant "garden," which in turn recalled the story of Adam and Eve.

Genesis described that Adam and Eve's life in the Garden of Eden was blissful and completely carefree. Yet that untroubled state could not last. The pair's innocent delight had been coupled with a grant of self-will, and an irresistible inner longing called them to exercise the free choice they had been given. With the intervention of a snake (the ancient symbol of rebirth), they chose to try to become more connected with God—more "like gods"—by eating the fruit of knowledge. When they ate, their carefree life vanished and, in effect, they began the process of growing up. Although they gained a more mature relationship with God, their decision had hard consequences. God exacted heavy prices for their temerity, the most distressing of which was ejection from the garden. Paradise, a trouble-free world of beauty and abundance, was lost forever.

John wants to communicate to the Christians in Ephesus that through the power of Jesus the Christ, Paradise has been regained, and the story of the wedding feast is his new metaphor covering the same ancient territory. He expands the story of Adam and Eve into a vital and present experience. Adam and Eve become Everyman and Everywoman. In this account, Jesus and Mary, his mother, exemplified the great promise of Genesis—a deep connection with God. However, instead of receiving punishment for becoming more closely connected, as Adam and Eve did, at Cana they celebrated!

Remember that there were similar "updates" in the Gospels of Matthew and Mark in the story of Jesus's baptism, when the heavens tore and the voice of God spoke. Instead of the voice pronouncing floods or destruction or punishment, as might have been expected from traditional Hebrew belief, the voice in the Christian gospels conferred blessing. John's account of Cana's wedding feast similarly reforms the story in attitude, metaphor, and meaning.

Cana's wedding echoes Adam and Eve in its focus on Mary and Jesus. Throughout, Jesus referred to Mary only as "woman" and not by name, a literary device that John uses to clearly designate her as Everywoman, as Eve, the first woman—just as Jesus parallels Adam. By choosing the Messiah and his mother, however, John makes a vastly important change in his "update" of Genesis. These figures are perfect and completely incorruptible. They aren't like Adam and Eve, after all, mere humans who, through the effrontery of their actions, lost their purity and were punished by God. John therefore makes a powerful and inspiring argument for the promise of the new faith: its garden is all-powerful, all-encompassing, and will last forever.

Further in the wedding story, Jesus ordered that huge vessels made of stone (an "incorruptible" material) be filled with water, presumably for use in the traditional Jewish mealtime washing ritual. However, once again John converts a well-known Hebrew ritual into something larger and more expansive. In this case, the water meant for cleansing is transformed into the joyous wine of a wedding—a celebration of *symbol,* of two becoming one, of unity in the Christ.

> On the third day there was a wedding in Cana of Galilee, and the mother of Jesus was there. Jesus and his disciples had also been invited to the wedding. When the wine gave out, the mother of Jesus said to him, "They have no wine." And Jesus said to her, "Woman, what concern is that to you and to me? My hour has not yet come." His mother said to the servants, "Do whatever he tells you." Now standing there were six stone water jars for the Jewish rites of purification, each holding twenty or thirty gallons. Jesus said to them, "Fill the jars with water." And they filled them up to the brim. He said to them, "Now draw some out, and take it to the chief steward." So they took it. When the steward tasted the water that had become wine, and did not know where it came from (though the servants who had drawn the water knew), the steward called the bridegroom and said to him, "Everyone serves the good wine first, and then the inferior wine after the guests have become drunk. But you have kept the good wine until now." Jesus did this, the first of his signs, in Cana of Galilee, and revealed his glory; and his disciples believed in him. (2:1–11)

JOHN COULD NOT have given us more perfect allegories for the third path. In Matthew and Mark we strove mightily, and like the Baptist we declared the coming of change in our souls. Now suddenly, it has arrived. The wedding day is here! While not really unexpected, its jubilant feelings are unfamiliar; we have a sense of being caught unaware, as though Cana's water were suddenly, remarkably, converted into wine. We have been engrossed in survival—abruptly we are now filled with the elixir of celebration. We feel so completely new and different that we wonder if our cells have changed, if somehow we have been transubstantiated.

In her great work *The Interior Castle,* the sixteenth-century abbess Teresa of Avila described the feeling with precision (writing in the third person): "Unexpectedly—while she is praying aloud, for instance, and not thinking about interior things—she seems to suddenly burst into sweet flame. It is as if a powerful fragrance had engulfed her and spread through all her senses, though this is a phenomenon that utterly transcends the sensual."*

Four centuries later, Thomas Merton described the feeling in *No Man Is an Island:*

> For if we continue in our prayer, we "remember" Him, that is to say, we become conscious, once again, of Who He really is. And we see that He has found us. When this consciousness is the work of grace, it is always fresh and new. It is more than the recovery of a past experience. It is a new experience, and it makes us new men. This newness is the "delight" and the "exercise" which are the living evidence of contact with the Spirit of the Lord. It makes us "swoon" in our spirit in a passage from death to life. Thus are our eyes opened. We see all things in a new light. And we realize that this is a new beginning.†

In John's gospel, his metaphors of the wedding and the Garden of Eden are apt. As we move into the third path, we feel deeply accompanied—and somehow safer. Our personal, interior experience blooms with new beginnings, fresh vitality, and a sense of purpose. At this moment, we feel that

---

* Teresa of Avila, *The Interior Castle,* translated and with an introduction by Mirabai Starr (New York: Riverhead Books, 1955), p. 171.

† Thomas Merton, *No Man Is an Island* (New York: Harcourt, Brace, 1955), p. 231.

the pieces have come together and all taints have been removed. The vision we hold seems whole and incorruptible.

Possibility surrounds us like the expanding, colorful images we see when we look through a kaleidoscope. We experience Cana's wedding feast, yet on some level we know that the glorious feelings of the wedding celebration are temporary. We understand that while our vision is absolutely pure and true, building our vision into a mature marriage that deepens with our lives will require patience and practice. And yet today we celebrate—fully, even ecstatically. As we should.

Unlocking the Doors: The Great Teaching Discourses

The next ten chapters of John are known as the great teaching discourses. In them, the writer employs a natural and persuasive evangelism, designed for the melting-pot city of Ephesus. The stories reference the beliefs prevalent among the local tribes and build upon the principles set forth in his first chapter—each story offering up reflections of a specific truth as though John were turning a diamond and examining the glistening brilliance of a particular facet. Further, he does this with a lyrical pacing, so the rhythm of the stories themselves helps the reader move gently into increasingly fresh and deepened perspectives.

Early Christianity used the four stories we will study as final reflections before baptism. Today all four are read on the Sundays of Lent in many Protestant churches (the Roman Catholic Church leaves out Nicodemus's story). They share the same structure, which begins with a question representing a specific danger of separation, of *dia-bol*. The central figures in each story initially appear trapped by their normal, logical, ego-based thought processes—essentially, they are locked in a room of dim sight and preconception. As each conversation progresses, we see that Jesus offers a "key" that, if accepted, will unlock the door and allow egress to a place of clear sight and the truth of limitless union.

In each story, a solemn Jewish convention is also broken. Even conversing with a "Messiah for all tribes" verged on heresy for a Pharisee like Nicodemus. And Jesus broke both tribal and gender taboos by having a conversation with a Samaritan woman in the second story. When Jesus mixed a healing poultice for a blind man on the Sabbath, he shattered the commandment not to work on the Jewish day of rest. Finally, in the last tale, he violated ancient custom when he ordered a tomb unsealed and commanded others to touch a dead body.

Each discourse, each story, has the same design, and then the stories combine to form an overall progression. In the first, Nicodemus the Pharisee made little progress and departed from his encounter with Jesus as an unchanged man. As John continues, in each story repeating the same pattern of question and answer (but with a different questioner in a slightly different setting), he shows comprehension increasing slowly. Step by step, with each story, acceptance of paradox grew. Ultimately, by the time of the last story, the gifts of wisdom offered by Jesus were accepted, and a new truth was absorbed. Let us turn to the discourses and observe the process of inner unlocking.

Impenetrable Barrier: Nicodemus the Pharisee

Nicodemus, a Jewish Pharisee, came to query Jesus about his purported divinity and the principles he proclaimed. This is the only place in all of the gospels in which Jesus is portrayed in genuine conversation with a Pharisee, rather than in a disputatious power struggle. It is especially remarkable because Nicodemus is no lowly questioner; he is clearly identified as a "leader of the Jews" and a "teacher of Israel." John uses this story to examine what he sees as the overarching challenge to new believers: being wedded to tradition and therefore closed to new belief and revelation.

As with so much in John, a duality instantly emerges when the sense of honest inquiry in the conversation is juxtaposed against the detail that Nicodemus came to Jesus "by night." Nicodemus certainly did not want anyone to see him talking with Jesus, deemed by the Pharisees a dubious teacher at best and, at worst, a blasphemer. However, maybe this isn't stealth at all. Recall that in Judaism, sunset marks the time when day begins and God's action starts anew. By setting the conversation at night, John may have been raising the possibility that the Pharisee himself was considering a new path, filled with questions as a potential believer, yet beset with inner turmoil, a poignant dilemma that must have verged on sacrilege for Nicodemus.

Nicodemus's central question was whether or not Jesus was just another teacher among many, or truly the Messiah. Although the miracles Jesus performed seemed to verify his divinity, Nicodemus found the teachings confusing and in conflict with what he had been taught: that the Messiah would come only through devout obedience to every precept of Mosaic law, that he would arrive only for the Jews, and that Jews were Jews because they were born to Jewish mothers. Most importantly, Nicodemus believed these things because Mosaic law said they were true, rendering any contradiction of them false. How could a different truth be possible?

"How could a Jew not be a Jew?" Nicodemus asked. How could a Jew be a Christian? How could the Messiah not be exclusively for the Jews? Similarly, how could a Savior come for everyone? How could something new grow? How could some kind of rebirth be possible? Nicodemus was trying to understand the same issues that were almost certainly dwelling within the hearts of many citizens of Ephesus, no matter what tribe they came from, whether they were already converted or prospective believers.

Jesus responded that the ties of "flesh," though real, were spiritually meaningless. The real birth was a new birth through Spirit, "from above." These words are the first words directly spoken by Jesus in John's gospel about transcending the strictures of tribe, and they gave Ephesus a revolutionary new commandment: "The new faith calls you to abandon your old teachings and be obedient to a new and wider teaching." Still, Nicodemus questioned.

> Now there was a Pharisee named Nicodemus, a leader of the Jews. He
> came to Jesus by night and said to him, "Rabbi, we know that you are a
> teacher who has come from God; for no one can do these signs that you
> do apart from the presence of God." Jesus answered him, "Very truly, I
> tell you, no one can see the kingdom of God without being born from
> above." Nicodemus said to him, "How can anyone be born after having
> grown old? Can one enter a second time into the mother's womb and
> be born?" Jesus answered, "Very truly, I tell you, no one can enter the
> kingdom of God without being born of water and Spirit. What is born

of the flesh is flesh, and what is born of the Spirit is spirit. Do not be astonished that I said to you, 'You must be born from above.' The wind blows where it chooses, and you hear the sound of it, but you do not know where it comes from or where it goes. So it is with everyone who is born of the Spirit." Nicodemus said to him, "How can these things be?" Jesus answered him, "Are you a teacher of Israel, and yet you do not understand these things?" (3:1–10)

In the face of Nicodemus's continued disbelief, Jesus gave a fuller response, its primary text quoted below. The Ephesians, who had years of background in Paul's teaching, and who understood the Prologue as the great pronouncement of Jesus the Christ, surely grasped the intention of John's words, which are an open, expansive, and compelling vision: "If you can understand the totality that I represent, then the illusion in which you live will be dispelled and you will enter into the fullest comprehension of God. In *that* presence, separation of any kind is meaningless. Through this awareness will come the true saving of your soul."

Tragically, in the long centuries of misunderstanding that have followed those early, joyous years in Ephesus, John's gospel has been seen in a narrower and more literal sense. The great Prologue has been read as a mere announcement of Jesus's birth, and the gospel itself as one of four accounts of Jesus's life. Words from the story of Nicodemus—specifically, the "God so loved the world" passage found in 3:16–18—have been equally viewed through this literal interpretation. They have become a statement of a Christian duty of salvation in its smallest and most divisive sense for the entire world, and—worse—an implicit right of condemnation of all other religions. At their most innocent levels of misuse, these three verses have been at the forefront of rejection and self-righteous condescension. At their worst, they have been the justification for so-called holy wars and the slaughter of Jews, Muslims, and other non-Christians.

Yet the entire story of Nicodemus is about overturning narrow vision and tribalism, and John's consistent use of the word "world" as a place of immature spiritual understanding confirms this. Therefore, we read in John's words that God cared so much about trying to remedy our spiritual backwardness that he sent Jesus the Christ to help us be more open and mature, promising that if we could transcend our limitations, we could rejoin God in timeless eternal life. Therefore, it is the greatest irony that these particular words have been so misused—when their specific intention was precisely the opposite—to offer the greatest spiritual awareness and reward by a loving Jesus who refrained from even the smallest emotional force to persuade the obstinate Pharisee of his truth.

> [Jesus said,] "For God so loved the world that he gave his only Son, so that everyone who believes in him may not perish but may have eternal life. Indeed, God did not send the Son into the world to condemn the world, but in order that the world might be saved through him. Those who believe in him are not condemned; but those who do not believe are condemned already, because they have not believed in the name of the only Son of God." (3:16–18)

Ask and Be Filled: The Woman at the Well

In the story of the woman at the well, Jesus asked a woman of Samaria to give him a drink of water. Until this point in the text, Jesus had limited himself to conversations and contacts within his customary levels of class and tribe, but now he crossed well-drawn boundaries. When he spoke to the woman at the well, he not only broke gender taboos, but also tribal proscriptions, because he was a Jew and she was a Samarian. Note that John again uses only the word "woman" when he refers to her, which in the Greek style is a designation for Everywoman.

Their discourse was genuine and thoughtful. Jesus regarded the woman's inquiries with as much seriousness as he did those of Nicodemus, the "teacher of Israel." This behavior on Jesus's part would have been regarded as completely radical. Jews were particularly forbidden to step outside tribal boundaries, and absolutely no one spoke to women as equals, publicly or privately. With what appears to us today to be an uncomplicated story, John conspicuously elevates the status of women, as he does in other instances in his gospel.

Jesus the Christ's simple request for a drink would also have been fraught with drama and meaning for John's readers. His clear request to "serve me," addressed to the non-Jewish Everywoman, was an allegorical and universal call to worship. Jesus, the Jewish Messiah, was inviting *all* to serve—women and men and people of all tribes. The use of water in the request, the essence of all life from which everything ushers forth, added to the power of this deeply symbolic act.

Water takes on further meaning here. The first story of the Hebrew book of Genesis spoke of "a wind from God [sweeping] over the waters" (1:2). John echoes Genesis yet again, and we read the words of Jesus sweeping over the old story of Jacob, which John uses as shorthand to refer to all the patriarchs of Judaism. Jacob merely provided a simple well for his people that satisfied their bodily needs. By contrast, Jesus offered "living water."

Examine the layers of meaning: Jacob's well was only for *his* people, while Jesus's water was offered to all who were willing to take the initiative of asking for new understanding. John emphasizes that the water for Jacob's tribe was merely water, from the temporal "world," and therefore limited in power. John's implicit instruction to Ephesus was, "You are now filled with the living water of Jesus the Christ. This 'living water' is for more than mere life, more than the body. It is sustenance for life everlasting. And it is for all of you—men and women from every background."

He left Judea and started back to Galilee. But he had to go through Samaria. So he came to a Samaritan city called Sychar, near the plot of ground that Jacob had given to his son Joseph. Jacob's well was there, and Jesus, tired out by his journey, was sitting by the well. It was about noon. A Samaritan woman came to draw water, and Jesus said to her, "Give me a drink." (His disciples had gone to the city to buy food.) The Samaritan woman said to him, "How is it that you, a Jew, ask a drink of me, a woman of Samaria?" (Jews do not share things in common with Samaritans.) Jesus answered her, "If you knew the gift of God, and who it is that is saying to you, 'Give me a drink,' you would have asked him, and he would have given you living water." The woman said to him, "Sir, you have no bucket, and the well is deep. Where do you get that living water? Are you greater than our ancestor Jacob, who gave us the well, and with his sons and his flocks drank from it?" Jesus said to her, "Everyone who drinks of this water will be thirsty again, but those who drink of the water that I will give them will never be thirsty. The water that I will give will become in them a spring of water gushing up to eternal life." (4:3–14)

Jesus's next words to the woman were not lengthy, but to the readers of Ephesus they were packed with significant implications. With clear reference to Jerusalem's Great Temple, Jesus predicted that new places of worship would arise; the old acknowledged mountains and temples would not remain the sole sources of spiritual power. Jesus then said that the time had come to worship in "spirit and truth." This was a specific reference to the dual prophets: Elijah as the Hebrew representation of compassion and Moses as that of the law. Once again, John transforms Hebrew traditions, renouncing old metaphorical separations. John is saying that in Jesus the Christ, Moses and Elijah are remade into an undivided spiritual principle, a union of apparent paradox, in which the two elements constantly negotiate with each other. In the Christ, "spirit and truth," law and mercy, wisdom and compassion are fluid parts of an indivisible whole.

The chapter closes with the words that "many Samaritans" accepted Jesus's teachings. This indicated that some transition to new understanding was made—and spread to others. This is a further step from the case of Nicodemus, who was unable to accept the new revelation at all.

Jesus said to her, "Woman, believe me, the hour is coming when you will worship the Father neither on this mountain nor in Jerusalem. You worship what you do not know; we worship what we know, for salvation is from the Jews. But the hour is coming, and is now here, when the true worshipers will worship the Father in spirit and truth, for the Father seeks such as these to worship him. God is spirit, and those who worship him must worship in spirit and truth." (4:21–24)

Many Samaritans from that city believed in him because of the woman's testimony. (4:39)

Who Truly Sees, and Who Does Not? The Man Born Blind

In the next story, Jesus saw a blind man and restored his sight by mixing spittle with mud, and the man was subsequently questioned by the religious authorities about the cure. This story has the same basic elements as those of Nicodemus and the woman at the well: references to the water that

brings new life and understanding, the limitations of old beliefs and tribalism, and a questioning of Jesus's divinity. However, the focus in this story—
its particular facet of the diamond—lies in the emotional dilemma faced by
believers when voices outside the new Christian community question their
faith and their decisions. How should they best sort out their complicated
feelings?

Remember, John is not literal. He gives no details of the man, nor does
he name him. Instead, John once again uses this person to represent Adam,
or Everyman. And in John's overall metaphor, "sight" always denotes "inner
sight." The account simply relates that Jesus applied the crude, elemental
substance of mud to the man's eyes, enabling him to "see." The lesson John
is teaching is that when the man regained his sight, he could then realize a
truth different from that which he had been taught since birth. He could
"see" the reality of the Christ.

John uses other figures in the story to represent inner voices to which
the Ephesians could relate. The Pharisees stand for close-minded obstruc-
tion and judgment, while the man's parents, who do not speak actual words
of condemnation, typify those who were unconscious, not searching and
not open to revelation. In effect, they represent the progenitors, the genesis
of blindness. These characters enabled the Ephesians to view themselves
and engage in self-scrutiny without the sting of a pointed finger.

Within John's metaphor of inner sight, he further uses the parents to
directly carry the message of revelation. "Don't be unconscious," John
urges. "Ask yourself the deep questions. Are you still blind? What parts
of you cannot yet see? What will it require for you to find sight?" With
great wisdom and subtlety, John is calling attention to the reality that,
as beautiful as epiphany may be, stepping out of tribalism and the traditions of centuries will present enormous emotional, spiritual, and cultural
challenges.

This story offers practical counsel that addresses the confused feelings
of the newly converted Christians whose friends and families had not followed their path and were naturally full of uncertainties. "Of course they
are unable to comprehend," John is saying. "They haven't had your experience. How can you expect them to see what you see? And when they reject
your experience and fall into self-righteousness, they are *twice* blinded. It is
natural for them to assault you with questions and doubts."

Then, in closing, the blind man said, "I believe," showing that he had absorbed the "new" understanding—and demonstrating a further movement toward acceptance than was made in the previous story.

They brought to the Pharisees the man who had formerly been blind. Now it was a sabbath day when Jesus made the mud and opened his eyes. Then the Pharisees also began to ask him how he had received his sight. He said to them, "He put mud on my eyes. Then I washed, and now I see." Some of the Pharisees said, "This man is not from God, for he does not observe the sabbath." But others said, "How can a man who is a sinner perform such signs?" And they were divided. So they said again to the blind man, "What do you say about him? It was your eyes he opened." He said, "He is a prophet." The Jews did not believe that he had been blind and had received his sight until they called the parents of the man who had received his sight and asked them, "Is this your son, who you say was born blind? How then does he now see?" His parents answered, "We know that this is our son, and that he was born blind; but we do not know how it is that now he sees, nor do we know who opened his eyes. Ask him; he is of age. He will speak for himself." (9:13–21)

He said, "Lord, I believe." And he worshiped him. (9:38)

The story does not end with the blind man's statement of belief. John goes on to amplify the theme of "blindness," his metaphor for lack of spiritual truth. When challenged by the Pharisees, Jesus responded that if they had been merely "blind" (that is, ignorant of truth), they would be free of sin. However, since they stubbornly refused to acknowledge their ignorance, accepting the illusions of the "world" and persisting in claiming to "see," they did, indeed, sin. In the progression of the stories leading to increased comprehension and acceptance of truth, this picture of the Pharisees is a vivid image of the opposite position—self-satisfaction and the rejection of truth. John knows it is critical that the new believers of Ephesus grasp this principle. In the midst of their ecstatic self-transformation, they—like all new believers—would have found it very easy to slip into a belief that their learning was over and their position was right—and from there, the perils of self-righteousness were a mere hairsbreadth away.

> Jesus said, "I came into this world for judgment so that those who do not see may see, and those who do see may become blind." Some of the Pharisees near him heard this and said to him, "Surely we are not blind, are we?" Jesus said to them, "If you were blind, you would not have sin. But now that you say, 'We see,' your sin remains." (9:39–41)

Allow the Tears to Fall: The Raising of Lazarus

The story of Lazarus's raising is generally considered one of the consummate biblical proofs of Jesus's divinity. And though John includes details that emphasize the miraculous nature of Jesus's actions, there are other, deeper messages in this account revealed through its dialogue.

Mary and Martha were sisters whose brother, Lazarus, was very ill. They asked Jesus for help. Giving no reason, he refused. Lazarus subsequently died, and four days later Jesus met with Mary, who was still grieving deeply. John recounts that Jesus the Christ was "greatly disturbed in spirit and deeply moved," and that he wept. Then, at Lazarus's tomb, Jesus was "again greatly disturbed." When he commanded that the stone be removed from the tomb, Lazarus emerged, still in burial bandages. Jesus instructed that he be "unbound" and freed.

We have made note of the fact that in John's gospel, Jesus was never less than a divine presence—he was the initiator of every action, the ultimate bestower of everything good, in full control of all events, and apparently unaffected by any requests or entreaties. Yet here, John shows Jesus in great emotional distress. In this passage, Jesus the Christ actually wept—only one of two instances in any of the gospels where he did. What precipitated the divine tears? Why was Lazarus raised? Because Jesus the Christ's heart was open, and when he met with Mary and went to the tomb, confronted in each case by genuine grief in the face of genuine loss, he needed to respond. *Compassion* was the divine impetus to restore life.

Jesus firmly stated, "Unbind him and let him go." The story of Lazarus was an analogy for the Ephesians about their new Christian revelation. It told them it was good—even necessary—for the old ways, the old dogma, to die so that resurrected life could appear. It told them their grief was appropriate and all right. It told them that through feelings of compassion, an epiphany would burst through their hearts into reality, and that that same compassion would guide them into a free, "unbound" new life.

> When Mary came where Jesus was and saw him, she knelt at his feet
> and said to him, "Lord, if you had been here, my brother would not
> have died." When Jesus saw her weeping, and the Jews who came with
> her also weeping, he was greatly disturbed in spirit and deeply moved.
> He said, "Where have you laid him?" They said to him, "Lord, come
> and see." Jesus began to weep. So the Jews said, "See how he loved
> him!" But some of them said, "Could not he who opened the eyes of the
> blind man have kept this man from dying?" Then Jesus, again greatly
> disturbed, came to the tomb. It was a cave, and a stone was lying against
> it. Jesus said, "Take away the stone." Martha, the sister of the dead man,
> said to him, "Lord, already there is a stench because he has been dead
> four days." Jesus said to her, "Did I not tell you that if you believed, you
> would see the glory of God?" So they took away the stone. And Jesus
> looked upward and said, "Father, I thank you for having heard me. I
> knew that you always hear me, but I have said this for the sake of the
> crowd standing here, so that they may believe that you sent me." When
> he had said this, he cried with a loud voice, "Lazarus, come out!" The
> dead man came out, his hands and feet bound with strips of cloth, and
> his face wrapped in a cloth. Jesus said to them, "Unbind him, and let
> him go." Many of the Jews therefore, who had come with Mary and had
> seen what Jesus did, believed in him. (11:32–45)

JOHN'S GOSPEL FOCUSES on the challenges of paradox and the truth of union, and these matters are at the center of all his teaching discourses. In our earlier paths, we were asked to overcome obstacles, but on this path, we are invited to sit and peacefully ponder each encounter as we are led on an expedition through reality and illusion. Each of John's stories presents us with a contradiction of the great unitive vision. Reflection on these, and on corresponding instances in our own lives, will give us the opportunity to observe the main psychological work of the third path. Our untransformed ego-self will persistently try to spring traps, tempting us to perceive our world and ourselves as a series of divisions instead of an indivisible whole. It will keep asking us to separate things and to make either/or judgments. It will try to force everything into black or white. This is our opportunity to study the beauty and subtleties of the many shades of gray.

Nicodemus's struggle reminds us that, at the moment when the glorious, undifferentiated vision arises, the Nicodemus aspect inside us will feel uncomfortable. We all share some of Nicodemus's characteristics. We have a well-worn way with which we are accustomed to looking at the world and approaching new things. Many of us also have at least a touch of *dia-bol*. We rush to find an appropriate category for every new experience. In this story, we see that Nicodemus was obviously drawn to Jesus, but his questions could not be satisfied through logic alone, which made him uncomfortable. When we feel likewise drawn, and desire fully rational answers, we will simply have to withstand our discomfort and understand that we may not be able to get them. Our path asks us—just for a moment—to suspend our deductive minds. This is a new reality. We need to simply remain awhile and let it soak in. Patience, patience.

The story of the woman at the well was placed after the story of Nicodemus for a reason. Intellectually, Nicodemus knew everything; yet in a deeper sense, he knew nothing. The woman at the well had none of Nicodemus's kind of knowledge. She was "only" a woman, and she was from Samaria, a region deemed unsophisticated, inhabited by "hicks." Yet Jesus selected her to receive two great acknowledgments: the call to service, and knowledge of the difference between the old well water and the new "living water." She accepted Jesus's statements from her heart and not from her rational mind, and therefore understood their meaning immediately. She made no philosophical inquiries at all and had a question only about her worthiness as a non-Jew.

The lesson of this story is a call to a practical form of self-examination, asking us to think about how we understand events. How do we move beyond the ways we think about ourselves and our past experiences? If we reflect on the self-definitions we use (as the woman did), it is likely that the limitations we have been holding about others and ourselves will be revealed and fall away. Those limitations are driven by the untransformed ego-self, which would self-protectively have us live out of our narrowest, fear-driven natures, rather than our most expansive. This diminishes our creativity and vitality and that of others. Our work here is to become aware of our narrowness. We need to become conscious of all the places that the tendrils of fear and division have reached. How are we less open than we might be? What parts of our garden are being watered from the old well rather than from our unceasing supply of living water?

The third path also places us in a new context with respect to others and our actions toward them. The story of the man born blind affords us the opportunity to examine the sources of feelings we carry, and how we deal with them in a social setting. It tells us that we cannot expect those who have not had a like experience to understand or appreciate our "new sight." At the same time, we are neophytes and thus are unable to see ahead very clearly ourselves. Our new vision increases our clarity when we look backward, as we have learned—but does not easily predict what lies ahead. So if we think we know exactly what is going on and what we should do and how others should behave, the consistent advice of the third path is . . . Do nothing except meditate and pray. Sit still. Rest in the garden and reflect. Close your eyes and use your inner sight. Watch the vision unfold around you.

The story of Lazarus serves us as a reminder: his dead corpse is like our old ways of thinking and the self we are leaving behind—bound up, stinking, and keeping our emotions blocked, as though hidden behind a rock in a dark cave. Let us use this image of Lazarus to energize ourselves, to release the trapped and limited places inside us. We long to act from our inner truth but often feel unable to do so, because fear or a sense of narrowness or emptiness stops us. Each time we pretend, each time we act from someplace false, our soul registers a small inner betrayal. Now is the time to grieve for those accumulated betrayals—our lost truths—and shed our long-held genuine tears. Our weeping is a critical component that helps us release new sources of vitality that we need for our journey. Our bindings fall away and we gain energy for our real freedom.

A Truth Greater Than Suffering: The Passion

No Great Drama: Entering Jerusalem

By the time the Gospel of John was written, Jerusalem was more than a city. It had become a symbol—one of the most powerful in talmudic and biblical lore. It was King David's great accomplishment. Jerusalem represented the historical, emotional, and spiritual center of the Hebrew faith, and was the location of the First and Second Temples. It was where the heads of the twelve tribes had met. Jerusalem was the vision of a place where the diversity of the Hebrew people could find creativity and harmony.

Part of this derives from the name itself. As noted earlier, Jeru-Shalom would translate as City of Peace. However, the peace of *shalom* is complex, differing greatly from our normal English sense of the word. *Shalom* comes from a root word that means "wholeness," thus in the Hebraic way of thinking it means the joining of opposites. That is the reason *shalom* is used as a greeting when meeting, as well as when leaving someone—times that contain both beginning and end, coming and going. The word *shalom* makes the unity of opposites implicit.

Therefore, John takes full advantage of Jeru-Shalom, its deep meaning and its iconic status. It is his preeminent symbol for an inner reality of "communion," a place where all tribes, not just Jews, could live in dynamic harmony. He carries the concept further, in support of his deeper theology, and makes Jerusalem a place in which opposites can reconcile and a new vitality can reign. This gave the Ephesians a communal image as they struggled to define themselves and move forward into the challenges that faced them as a diverse group of new Christians.

In the Gospels of Matthew, Mark, and Luke, Jesus took long journeys throughout Israel and the surrounding region, all of which ended in Jerusalem. However, since the city itself is a thematic focal point, John's gospel is located almost entirely in Jerusalem and its Temple. Many of the lessons were taught there, and others (such as that of Lazarus) took place only a few miles outside the city. In this gospel, Jesus's entrance into Jerusalem was not the climax to a lengthy and arduous journey, and although assembled crowds did shout acclaim, there were no accounts of the journey or preparations, or instructions for entry. A mere three verses describe the entry, and one of them contains the small notation that Jesus found his own donkey and sat himself down upon it. John's focus is clearly elsewhere.

> The next day the great crowd that had come to the festival heard that Jesus was coming to Jerusalem. So they took branches of palm trees and went out to meet him, shouting, "Hosanna! Blessed is the one who comes in the name of the Lord—the King of Israel!" Jesus found a young donkey and sat on it; as it is written: "Do not be afraid, daughter of Zion. Look, your king is coming, sitting on a donkey's colt!" (12:12–15)

Stripped, Selfless, and in Service: The Last Gathering

Subsequent to his understated arrival into Jerusalem, which occurred just before the Feast of Passover, Jesus gathered with his disciples for John's version of the Last Supper. This account is entirely different from those found in the other gospels.

John's depiction gently and affectionately shows that Jesus and his followers were devoted to each other. He doesn't focus on the meal; there was no bread, no passing of a cup—indeed, no description of food whatsoever. Only four verses into the chapter, Jesus arose and began a poignant, intimate ritual, washing the feet of each and every one of the disciples. Peter objected vehemently, but Jesus insisted that they would all understand "later."

Throughout John's gospel, there are continual references to water— the transformed water at Cana, the "living waters" of the well, the pool in which the blind man was instructed to wash, and Jesus's tears. An essential component of any garden (and therefore a seamless accompaniment to John's other core metaphor), water is also the basic requirement for life on earth. It is present at birth, and its absence leads to death. Because of its necessity and the vitality it brings, water is a component of many sacred rituals. Now, in John, it is used during a tender and symbolic ceremony of footwashing.

The Christian ritual of baptism uses water to express the elements of death and rebirth. In the early church, deacons performing baptism were instructed to grasp the initiate around the chest from the back, lowering the individual under the water in such a way that a "startle response" was triggered, thereby providing an experience of near death. Arising, the person was then blessed and announced to the community as moving forward into new life with Jesus the Christ. In the early part of this chapter, we mentioned the scholarly theory that John's entire gospel might have been written as the requisite contemplations and teachings in preparation for baptism.

Now remember that each gospel writer uses the intensity of the Passion to emphasize and make specific the answers to the spiritual question offered by his text. John's core question is, How do we receive joy? The Passion moves this question to the specific: How do we move from our old beliefs into the new? How do we resurrect into new balance and move forward in the Christ? When we know that the words of this gospel were originally used for baptism and that the ensuing ritual was a graphic representation of this question, John's use of water symbolism here in the Passion becomes an even more delicate, startling, and powerful image.

The recitation of the footwashing is simple and quietly paced, yet John's words touch upon all of his major themes: baptism, communion, and service. Jesus rose from the table and removed his robe, leaving only his underwear, which he covered with nothing more than a towel. Jesus the Christ, God on earth, who has heretofore moved through this gospel as nothing less than a divine presence, stripped down and presented himself to his disciples in a way that would have been appropriate only for a servant or a slave. And then he washed their feet—*their* feet! There could have been no more perfect exemplar of the selflessness of Spirit in service, and it reinforced the dialogue between Jesus and Peter that followed.

Peter strenuously objected to his feet being washed by Jesus. Jesus told Peter, quite firmly, that if he were unwilling to receive the gift he was being offered, he could no longer continue as a disciple. Peter capitulated and agreed to the washing, even finding enthusiasm for the prospect. John is sending a twofold message to Ephesus about the genuine nature of union: first, the example of humility in *giving* as Jesus washes feet, and second, the example of humility in *receiving* as a chastened Peter accepts his bounty with real gratitude. John knew that the abilities to discern, understand, offer, and accept genuine relationships could prove critical to the Christian community.

Jesus also singled out one of the disciples from the rest, noting that he was "not clean." John identified this "one" as Judas, the betrayer. What did

Jesus mean by "not clean"? The meaning becomes clear if we recall the new process of Christian baptism, which was designed to provide *an internal experience of Jesus's death and resurrection leading to rebirth.* According to the Gospel of Matthew (written before John, and almost certainly known to John and John's readers), Judas fell into despair after betraying Jesus, chose suicide, and did not live through the experience of Jesus's death and arising. Judas, therefore, never completed his journey—the "washing" portion of it—and thus was not "cleansed."

In words that rang with authority, Jesus lastly commanded all those present that they continue the footwashing with other believers as a symbolic ceremony of humble service. Now known as "the mandatuum," this ritual was earnestly embraced for a period of approximately one hundred years, and every time Christian followers met, when the bread was broken and the wine from the cup was poured, those present also washed each other's feet. Today, in many Christian churches, the ritual is still performed—but generally only once a year at Easter. In this gospel, the mandatuum also introduces the themes that John pursues in the next chapters.

> Now before the festival of the Passover, Jesus knew that his hour had
> come to depart from this world and go to the Father. Having loved his
> own who were in the world, he loved them to the end. The devil had
> already put it into the heart of Judas son of Simon Iscariot to betray
> him. And during supper Jesus, knowing that the Father had given
> all things into his hands, and that he had come from God and was
> going to God, got up from the table, took off his outer robe, and tied
> a towel around himself. Then he poured water into a basin and began
> to wash the disciples' feet and to wipe them with the towel that was
> tied around him. He came to Simon Peter, who said to him, "Lord,
> are you going to wash my feet?" Jesus answered, "You do not know
> now what I am doing, but later you will understand." Peter said to
> him, "You will never wash my feet." Jesus answered, "Unless I wash
> you, you have no share with me." Simon Peter said to him, "Lord,
> not my feet only but also my hands and my head!" Jesus said to him,
> "One who has bathed does not need to wash, except for the feet, but
> is entirely clean. And you are clean, though not all of you." For he
> knew who was to betray him; for this reason he said, "Not all of you

are clean." After he had washed their feet, had put on his robe, and had returned to the table, he said to them, "Do you know what I have done to you? You call me Teacher and Lord—and you are right, for that is what I am. So if I, your Lord and Teacher, have washed your feet, you also ought to wash one another's feet. For I have set you an example, that you also should do as I have done to you." (13:1–15)

Held in the Arms of Love: The Discourse on Intimacy and Union

Following the footwashing, John delivers four entire chapters best described as mystical poetry. In Christian scholarship, this narrative is variously known as "the discourse on intimacy and union," or "the eucharistic discourse." In three of the four chapters, Jesus addressed his disciples. Jesus's words in the last chapter of the discourse—words that are particularly elevated—are addressed directly to God the "Father," in the form of a prayer.

The lengthy verses of the discourse, among John's most significant, are deeply inspirational. They resonated with the disciples and, through them, with all of Ephesus. They announce an eternal truth—a message that comes from "before the foundation of the world." They tell of a loving, personal, and intimate God who addresses followers by the title "friend." This would have been an astonishing change to many of the new Christians. Tribal gods had not been friends; Greek gods of the time were distant and whimsical, and the Hebrew god sat in judgment. Proximity was unexpected.

In these chapters, we again find the same beautiful, poetic prose that began this gospel, and much of the vocabulary duplicates John's core metaphors: "world" and "see" are frequently inserted to represent the secular world of illusion and divine sight, for example. However, the text is set in a long, elegant discourse on intimacy from Jesus to his disciples at the final meal. Jesus spoke about their sense of fear and isolation, and early in the recitation he proclaimed that an Advocate would be sent, who would not only accompany them, but hold them in the arms of eternal love.

Within the verses we can discover another of John's garden metaphors—a vineyard, with words that, interestingly, refer to Jesus himself being pruned of branches that "bear no fruit." Jesus went on to talk of

friendship and to use dramatic images of childbirth to illustrate the pain
and division experienced by those who are without faith and beset by illusion. Over and over again, he used words that could be treasured by the
Christians in Ephesus as new wisdom to ponder and reinforcement of their
inner certainty. The final words of Jesus's prayer at the end of the meal (and
of the discourse) are another lyrical promise of eternal accompaniment: "I
made your name known to them, and I will make it known, so that the love
with which you have loved me may be in them, and I in them" (17:26).

"And I will ask the Father, and he will give you another Advocate,
to be with you forever. This is the Spirit of truth, whom the world
cannot receive, because it neither sees him nor knows him. You know
him, because he abides with you, and he will be in you." (14:16–17)

"I am the true vine, and my Father is the vinegrower. He removes every
branch in me that bears no fruit. Every branch that bears fruit he prunes
to make it bear more fruit." (15:1–2)

"This is my commandment, that you love one another as I have loved you.
No one has greater love than this, to lay down one's life for one's friends."
(15:12–13)

"You are my friends if you do what I command you. I do not call you
servants any longer, because the servant does not know what the master is
doing; but I have called you friends, because I have made known to you
everything that I have heard from my Father. You did not choose me but I
chose you." (15:14–16)

"Very truly, I tell you, you will weep and mourn, but the world will
rejoice; you will have pain, but your pain will turn into joy. When a
woman is in labor, she has pain, because her hour has come. But when her
child is born, she no longer remembers the anguish because of the joy of
having brought a human being into the world." (16:20–21)

"The hour is coming, indeed it has come, when you will be scattered,
each one to his home, and you will leave me alone. Yet I am not alone

because the Father is with me. I have said this to you, so that in me you may have peace. In the world you face persecution. But take courage; I have conquered the world!" (16:32–33)

"As you, Father, are in me and I am in you, may they also be in us, so that the world may believe that you have sent me. The glory that you have given me I have given them, so that they may be one, as we are one, I in them and you in me, that they may become completely one, so that the world may know that you have sent me and have loved them even as you have loved me. Father, I desire that those also, whom you have given me, may be with me where I am, to see my glory, which you have given me because you loved me before the foundation of the world. Righteous Father, the world does not know you, but I know you; and these know that you have sent me. I made your name known to them, and I will make it known, so that the love with which you have loved me may be in them, and I in them." (17:21b–26)

AS WE READ the passages from this first part of John's Passion and contemplate them, the most difficult thing we must do is to pause now. Our desire is to race ahead. Even reading these words probably seems slow, even redundant. We know that the heart of the Passion is next, and it seems that the very best lessons are surely there. Yet waiting is one of the great lessons of John. Every bit of the bountiful spring garden in which we are now resting is worthy of our attention. As we quietly sit, in this third path of our Journey of Quadratos, we aren't climbing mountains, nor are we enduring stormy seas. The angst in our lives has calmed somewhat. Of course, we still have to pay careful attention—but instead of tensing for danger, we are more able to be focused on discerning complexities and details as they reveal themselves.

Jesus's entry into Jerusalem is not presented as very important to us; but Jerusalem itself looms large—indeed, it is vital. It represents the place where the twelve tribes met: Jeru-Shalom, where diversity sought the complex harmony of ever-changing opposites. Once again John asks us: What is the true picture of our inner and outer complexity? This question must be followed by: How can we be known in our fullest, richest reality? These are the natural queries that begin to arise as we rest in awareness of union, and they will gradually increase as the close of the third path draws nearer. And these flowering buds will then lead us into the primary challenge of the fourth path: How are *we* Jeru-Shalom?

We observe with wonder that everything is one—undivided, unbroken, and unswervingly whole. At the same time, everything is unique and individual. Both realities are limitless, yet our entire journey is in vain if we attempt to comprehend this truth (or believe we have done so) with any separated part of ourselves—with only our intellect or our emotions or our senses or our spirit. We must continue to sit, meditating upon the wondrous garden, and—as Jesus did—meet each aspect as it arises with as much of ourselves as we are able. If we can summon our *full* presence, we will discover that each encounter reveals a unique meaning and shows us its interplay with the whole, and we will gain a sense of undivided comprehension. This is John's assurance to us from across the centuries. If we do not take the time to receive this full pattern, then we will stand no chance of its fulfillment in the fourth path. Be in peace and patience. There are no shortcuts here.

John also gives us the opportunity to wrestle with some of our deepest feelings about self-worth—those feelings that can divide us from spiritual development and the richest relationship with God. Can we feel our own difficulty with unworthiness in the poignant imagery of Jesus's final meeting with his disciples? Can we open to its intimacy and sensuality? Can we begin to sense a new set of inner questions? How would *we* feel if Jesus the Christ, clad only in a towel, were on his knees before us and wanted to wash our feet? Would we be able to receive that extraordinary gift with a whole heart? Or would we, like Peter, resist? Jesus the Christ was firm with Peter, and his admonition applies to us as well. We cannot be on the journey unless we are able to receive. We must be able to participate in both sides of a relationship—giving *and* receiving. This is not easy, since we are so often raised to believe that thinking of ourselves is "selfish" and negative. Indeed, most of the third path is devoted to the practice of receiving, of just being still, and becoming aware of what is offered by the Great Mystery all around us.

Jesus's demeanor in the footwashing could scarcely be more humble, and we understand that we are called to a similar humility. However, it is equally important to realize that there was nothing weak about Jesus's humility. On the contrary. Jesus understood to his core that he was *accompanied* on his journey—that he would never be alone or bereft. He therefore walked forward in confidence, clarity, and command. Humility does not imply that we must be soft or timid or weak. Humility derives from the most profound strength.

The sensuality of the footwashing opens up another issue in this gospel that is both important and—unsurprisingly—paradoxical. John's gospel is extremely "earthy": Jesus asks for a drink of water; he mixes spit with mud for the blind man's poultice; he weeps; he strips to a towel; he washes feet; he carries his own cross; he cooks breakfast on the shore. Indeed, his physical presence is probably stronger here than in any of the other gospels. Yet, as noted earlier, John's gospel has often been accused of elevating spirit over body. And it does. In the Prologue and in Jesus's discourse with Nicodemus, John uses the word "flesh" synonymously with "world." And we know by now that "world" is pejorative in John's lexicon. "Flesh" is therefore clearly relegated to the territory of illusion and is certainly not equal to "spirit." Yet John has told us that he believes in divine, timeless wholeness wherein spirit and matter are unified. Where do we find the answer to this apparent paradox, and to the several inconsistencies created by it in the gospel? In the same place that accounts for John's stridency about the Pharisees: in the personal disharmonies of the man himself. And we should treat this paradox in the same way—by focusing on what are clearly the more compelling and inspired elements of John's great verses.

When we properly focus on John's inspiration, we should include, rather than dismiss, the elements of earthiness and sensuality. Indeed, we need to give them our close attention. With his earthy and physical language, John proclaims unity despite himself. We are in physical bodies, just as Jesus the Christ came to a physical earth in a physical body. Our physical senses give us our information about the world. In fact, as we sit in the garden and allow ourselves to become open to the fullness of God's bounty, what do we notice? As our senses sharpen, we pick up the buzzing of the bees and the rustling of the wind through the leaves. We become aware of the remarkable artistry in the veining of every leaf and bird feather. Inevitably, at some point, we sense the musculature beneath our own thin skin that miraculously holds us at 98.6 degrees in both snow and blistering sun. We wiggle our toes and stretch our arms and enjoy the sun or perhaps the taste

of a raindrop on our tongue. This is God's gift of sensuality awakening—
becoming more sensitive and appreciative. Our reflection is twofold: first,
wholehearted enjoyment; second, sensory epiphany—thoughts about the
ways in which we have rejected and neglected our bodies and our sensuous
selves in the past. For many of us, this has had significant personal, family,
and even community impacts. Now it is time to examine the fullness of the
physical natures we have been given by God, without fear or self-rejection.

The beautiful, meditative discourses on intimacy and union poetically
restate all of John's great themes. They speak of new birth. They wash us
with words of care and loving kindness. When we read them, we can—and
should—find vast and resonant reassurance in their eloquence: all is connected and all is well. Within the verses, however, we will also sense the
coming of more challenge and more growth—note the sharp metaphorical
pruning shears in the vineyard. As much as John wants us to keep our focus
in the garden, he cannot avoid reminding us that there is more walking
ahead, and the cutting is not done.

Inner Strength and Calm: In the Garden and Courtyard

In chapter eighteen, as John moves to Jesus's arrest, he sets this account
within his primary metaphor: a literal garden. There is no reference to the
Mount of Olives, or to Gethsemane, the place of "pressing" and agonized
heart of which we read in Matthew and Mark. John's story is as dramatic in
what it does *not* say as it is in what it *does* say.

Jesus's arrival with the disciples at the garden was followed by the almost simultaneous arrival of Judas and a detachment of soldiers, accompanied by police sent from the chief priests and Pharisees. Jesus walked
forward and inquired as to their mission. Although he knew what they had
come to do, Jesus (again) initiated the action and offered himself. Shocked,
the group fell back. They had expected a powerless victim. Instead, they
were met with unexpected strength and calm.

In the face of their bewilderment—and in an echo of the Hebrew Testament's "I Am"—Jesus twice proclaimed, "I am he." The apparent strength
of the soldiers paled against the real strength of Jesus the Christ as he met
his oppressors. This is John's lesson to Ephesus: the soldiers were merely of

"this world"—crippled by illusory, dichotomized thinking. It was evident that they had no real power. Not a one of them laid a hand on him. Even so, Peter rushed to defend Jesus, and in doing so cut off the ear of the high priest's slave. Jesus gently chided Peter, telling him to put his sword away. Then, in this garden, free from agony and indecision, Jesus merely asked Peter, in an almost offhand way, "Am I not to drink the cup that the Father has given me?" There was no prayer, no questioning, and seemingly little or no sense of inner turmoil.

> After Jesus had spoken these words, he went out with his disciples across the Kidron valley to a place where there was a garden, which he and his disciples entered. Now Judas, who betrayed him, also knew the place, because Jesus often met there with his disciples. So Judas brought a detachment of soldiers together with police from the chief priests and the Pharisees, and they came there with lanterns and torches and weapons. Then Jesus, knowing all that was to happen to him, came forward and asked them, "Whom are you looking for?" They answered, "Jesus of Nazareth." Jesus replied, "I am he." Judas, who betrayed him, was standing with them. When Jesus said to them, "I am he," they stepped back and fell to the ground. Again he asked them, "Whom are you looking for?" And they said, "Jesus of Nazareth." Jesus answered, "I told you that I am he. So if you are looking for me, let these men go." This was to fulfill the word that he had spoken, "I did not lose a single one of those whom you gave me." Then Simon Peter, who had a sword, drew it, struck the high priest's slave, and cut off his right ear. The slave's name was Malchus. Jesus said to Peter, "Put your sword back into its sheath. Am I not to drink the cup that the Father has given me?" (18:1–11)

John's Passion account next moves to the courtyard of Annas, a former high priest and the father-in-law of Caiaphas, the current high priest. Remember from the story of the wedding at Cana that "courtyard" is a garden metaphor? John is therefore moving the tale from one garden into another. The confrontation in Annas's courtyard is a more complex account than the arrest scene, however, and it replaces the stories of Jesus's trial before the high priest that are found in all of the other gospels.

Two disciples—Peter and an unnamed man—followed the officers who arrested Jesus. However, a woman acting as guard stopped Peter at the gate. (Note that John once again records a woman in a nontraditional foreground role.) The unnamed disciple is able to get Peter through the gate, after which the guard inquired of Peter whether or not he followed Jesus. Peter denied that he did. The pair continued into the courtyard, where Annas, Jesus, the soldiers, and others were gathered, warming themselves around a charcoal fire. Despite the story line of Jesus's inquisition, in this second gathering the real focus is on Peter and on discipleship.

Annas began his interrogation, asking only about Jesus's relationships with "his disciples and his teaching." Jesus responded that he had nothing to hide and suggested that Annas inquire of "those who [had] heard what I said." Though present, neither Peter nor the unnamed disciple spoke. Annas continued. Jesus, completely composed, rebuked Annas for his questions. A soldier slapped Jesus for his effrontery, but that did not deter him. Jesus was then sent on to Caiaphas, and the disciples remained in the courtyard around the fire. While they were waiting, Peter twice more denied his discipleship, and the other disciple never spoke a single word.

This was John's perfectly inspired mirror for the Ephesian Christian community. During Annas's questioning, everyone was present around the charcoal fire: leaders of the old faith traditions, their minions, the enforcers of secular power, disciples of the "new way," and Jesus the Christ. The new and the old, the temporal and divine worlds, John's "truth" and "illusion"— all stood together, speaking and not speaking.

Special attention should be drawn to the figure of "another disciple," who is not named and who appears only here. There has been much conjecture about his purpose and which disciple he is, especially since there is another figure identified as the "unnamed disciple," who is also designated as "loved" by Jesus, who appears at the footwashing, the crucifixion, and the resurrection. It is our belief that "another disciple" is *not* the "unnamed" disciple. John is scrupulous about naming and not-naming in his gospel and we think that John intends the figure here in Annas's courtyard to serve as an "everyman," or, in this case, as "every disciple"—a representative of those especially committed Christians on whom the future of the faith rested.

With that in mind, we now look again at this small vignette of people around the fire and ask, What did the disciples do? The other disciple remained silent—in this account it is clear that he was still connected to the old order, he "was known to the high priest." He had influence sufficient to get Peter through the gate into the group who were solely people connected to the high priest plus soldiers and slaves. (Remember that Peter, once inside, disavowed Jesus when questioned.) The "other disciple" represented those in Ephesus who were engaged and vigorously moving forward, but still retained active connections to the Jewish community. John wanted them to realize how damaging their silence and dual allegiance might be.

Peter denied Jesus thrice, but we see his actions in a very different way than in the other gospels. The denials all come in the context of the preceding discourse on intimacy, which speaks about willingness to lay down one's life for a friend. Peter's first denial was necessary so that he might stay close to Jesus—as were the second and third denials. Peter was, in effect, in enemy territory. As he asserted at the final meal, Peter was determined to show his willingness to follow his lord anywhere and lay down his life for him. In these efforts, however, he continued to display his spiritual immaturity, slicing off an ear and denying his path—even though Jesus's fate was foreordained and unstoppable by him. Yet in this gospel Peter's errors are clearly shown within the context of love and friendship. After the triple betrayal, the scene ends abruptly, with no statement of remorse at all. The primary issues for the Christians of Ephesus are the dangers of acting from spiritual immaturity and their need to think through their motives before they act.

So the soldiers, their officer, and the Jewish police arrested Jesus and bound him. First they took him to Annas, who was the father-in-law of Caiaphas, the high priest that year. Caiaphas was the one who had advised the Jews that it was better to have one person die for the people. Simon Peter and another disciple followed Jesus. Since that disciple was known to the high priest, he went with Jesus into the courtyard of the high priest, but Peter was standing outside at the gate. So the other disciple, who was known to the high priest, went out, spoke to the woman who guarded the gate, and brought Peter in. The woman said to Peter, "You are not also one of this man's disciples, are you?" He said, "I am not." Now the slaves and the police had made a charcoal fire because it was cold, and they were standing around it and warming themselves. Peter also was standing with them and warming himself. Then the high priest questioned Jesus about his disciples and about his teaching. Jesus answered, "I have spoken openly to the world; I have always taught in synagogues and in the temple, where all the Jews come together. I have said nothing in secret. Why do you ask me? Ask those who heard what I said to them; they know what I said." When he had said this, one of the police standing nearby struck Jesus on the face, saying, "Is that how you answer the high priest?" Jesus answered, "If I have spoken wrongly, testify to the wrong. But if I have spoken rightly, why do you strike me?" Then Annas sent him bound to Caiaphas the high priest. Now Simon Peter was standing and warming himself. They asked him, "You are not also one of his disciples, are you?" He denied it and said, "I am not." One of the slaves of the high priest, a relative of the man whose ear Peter had cut off, asked, "Did I not see you in the garden with him?" Again Peter denied it, and at that moment the cock crowed. (18:12–27)

Facing Off at High Noon: Pilate and Jesus Meet

After the encounter with Annas and Caiaphas, Jesus was sent to Pilate's headquarters. The Hebrew authorities who had been questioning him refused to enter, however, because it was the day before Passover. The Jews had ritually cleansed themselves (specifically of yeast, according to ritual requirements), and since Pilate was a gentile, in meeting with him they would risk coming into contact with "unclean" elements, which would prevent them from partaking of the Passover meal. After conversation outside with the priests, Pilate ascertained this and had Jesus brought inside for questioning, which meant that in John's gospel, there were no priests present during Jesus's meeting with Pilate.

All alone, Jesus—*Logos,* the representative of divine truth incarnate—then faced off against Pilate, embodiment of the temporal world of illusion and of Rome's power. In their exchange, Jesus confidently proclaimed his

sovereignty of the world of spirit, and Pilate, locked into the world of illusion, failed to understand him. This encounter was a stark statement of John's
two opposing principles, and it stands in marked contrast to all of the other
gospels. In Matthew, Mark, and Luke, Jesus remained mute; he refused to
answer Pilate. In the Gospel of John, however, Jesus the Christ was never
hesitant, never silent. He always demonstrated the full force of his divinity.
Pilate, remaining trapped in his ignorance and self-righteousness, had Jesus
removed for flogging. Although mocked and struck in the face, Jesus never
wavered. He was impervious to every assault, every question, insult, and
blow. This was the divine model John wanted to present to his audience—the
picture of one who was confident, even loving, in the face of all trials.

> Then they took Jesus from Caiaphas to Pilate's headquarters. It was
> early in the morning. They themselves did not enter the headquarters,
> so as to avoid ritual defilement and to be able to eat the Passover.
> (18:28)

> Pilate entered the headquarters again, summoned Jesus, and asked him,
> "Are you the King of the Jews?" Jesus answered, "Do you ask this on
> your own, or did others tell you about me?" Pilate replied, "I am not a
> Jew, am I? Your own nation and the chief priests have handed you over
> to me. What have you done?" Jesus answered, "My kingdom is not from
> this world. If my kingdom were from this world, my followers would be
> fighting to keep me from being handed over to the Jews. But as it is, my
> kingdom is not from here." Pilate asked him, "So you are a king?" Jesus
> answered, "You say that I am a king. For this I was born, and for this I
> came into the world, to testify to the truth. Everyone who belongs to the
> truth listens to my voice." Pilate asked him, "What is truth?" (18:33–38)

> Then Pilate took Jesus and had him flogged. And the soldiers wove a
> crown of thorns and put it on his head, and they dressed him in a purple
> robe. They kept coming up to him, saying, "Hail, King of the Jews!" and
> striking him on the face. (19:1–3)

> [Pilate] entered his headquarters again and asked Jesus, "Where are you
> from?" But Jesus gave him no answer. Pilate therefore said to him, "Do

you refuse to speak to me? Do you not know that I have power to release you, and power to crucify you?" Jesus answered him, "You would have no power over me unless it had been given you from above; therefore the one who handed me over to you is guilty of a greater sin." (19:9–11)

Critical Distinctions: The Counting of the Days

Over and above the dissimilarity of the events themselves, one of the most striking differences in John's Passion is the timing of the events. In the Gospels of Matthew, Mark, and Luke, the Last Supper was the Jewish sacred meal of Passover. Indeed, most Christians today believe that Passover is *the* definitive date for the final meal. But in John's gospel, that last gathering was not held on Passover—an immensely significant fact.

In the Gospel of John, the ritual of footwashing and the meeting with Annas occurred on the evening of Preparation Day—the day *before* Passover. (Remember that Hebrew days begin at sundown, not midnight.) The subsequent meeting with Pilate and the crucifixion itself happened during the daylight hours of Preparation Day, again *before* Passover began. Not only does this change of timing allow John to (again) reframe Hebrew tradition, but it also provides an intensely different and dramatic backdrop for the entire Passion. To get some sense of the context that John is trying to set up, it is helpful to read an excerpt from Exodus describing Preparation Day:

> The Lord said to Moses and Aaron in the land of Egypt: This month shall mark for you the beginning of the months; it shall be the first month of the year for you. Tell the whole congregation of Israel that on the tenth of this month they are to take a lamb for each family, a lamb for each household. If a household is too small for a whole lamb, it shall join its closest neighbor in obtaining one; the lamb shall be divided in proportion to the number of people who eat of it. Your lamb shall be without blemish, a year-old male; you may take it from the sheep or from the goats. You shall keep it until the fourteenth day of this month; then the whole assembled congregation of Israel shall slaughter it at twilight. (Exod. 12:1–6)

These verses, recounting sacred rituals practiced for centuries, would have been familiar to all of John's Jewish readers. Passover, one of the holiest of Hebrew holidays, required that ten nights after the new moon and three nights before the Passover meal, every house was to choose and "keep" an unblemished male lamb for three days. And "keep" didn't mean simply that the animal was set aside; "keep" meant that the youngling actually lived within the household, honored and cared for. Imagine the tangled emotions of the family as the day of death for this little creature approached.

In the days of the Great Temple, animals were frequently sacrificed for many rituals and reasons. On regular days, the animal was delivered to the Temple, the priest took the animal from the bearer, slaughtered it, removed a portion of the meat as payment, and burned the remainder. On Preparation Day, however, the head of the house was required to personally bear the lamb to the Temple for sacrifice. There, the priest handed the ritual knife to the householder, who had to slit the lamb's throat himself and then drain its blood into a large bowl that was given to the priest. The priest emptied the bowl, filled with the lamb's blood, over the Temple's high altar. The bloodless carcass was then taken back home, where it was prepared and eaten for the Passover meal.

It has been estimated that ten thousand lambs were slain at the Great Temple on each Preparation Day in the first century. It is likely that blood was flowing down the Temple's steps and running through the streets of Jerusalem by noon on that day. The city must have been filled with the sight and stench of butchery. This may even have been an intentional part of the ritual, serving as a graphic reminder of the massacre visited upon the first-born in Egypt on that same day some twelve hundred years earlier.

It is on this day of bloody slaughter, and of the memorial of bloody slaughter, that John situates Pilate's judgment and Jesus's crucifixion. Lest there be any confusion about the clear parallel he is drawing, John has Pilate issue his judgment "about noon," the time of the height of the ritual carnage, and it is pronounced from the "Gabbatha." This is a term that appears only in this gospel and refers, in Aramaic (though John calls it Hebrew—the languages are closely related), to a high stone platform—a clear reference to the ancient Temple mount.

The analogy is clear, and with it, John's inspiration once more focuses on the larger point, perhaps overturning actual history a bit. Passover memorializes the liberation of the Jews. First-century Jews expected the Messiah to come for them—and to be another Moses when he came, acting as a warrior-liberator, freeing them from the heavy yoke of Roman rule. John wants to be very clear that Jesus was indeed the Messiah; however, his definition is quite different. First, the arms of John's Messiah are wide open in active invitation to all of humanity, not only Jews. More importantly, he is not a warrior-liberator figure at all. Instead, this Savior is defined as "one who serves." Therefore, in John's Passion, Jesus does *not* celebrate the Passover meal; rather, he washes feet and actively chooses the role of the lamb. He is the servant—he is even willing to be a physical sacrifice. John is telling Ephesus to look beyond the events of history. John's statement is that Jesus's life was not taken from him by either Jew or Roman. Instead, he offered his physical body, so that through his resurrection, it would be revealed that death is simply an illusion.

> When Pilate heard these words, he brought Jesus outside and sat on
> the judge's bench at a place called The Stone Pavement, or in Hebrew
> Gabbatha. Now it was the day of Preparation for the Passover; and it
> was about noon. (19:13–14)

A Peaceful and Willing Death: The Crucifixion

Following Pilate's sentencing, John says only that Jesus went to Golgotha, and that he personally carried the cross on which he would be crucified. There is no mention of suffering, no exhaustion, no agony. Indeed, reading the passage, one might well assume that the cross was very light.

As noted about the timing of the judgment, during those same hours Jews would have been taking their lambs to the Temple for slaughter before returning home to prepare the Passover meal. They would have been standing in long lines, clutching their male lambs, as they waited to mount to the altar, their arms tired from holding the squirming bodies. The air would have been filled with bleating, and with the sights and smells of death.

In contrast to this noisy, bloody, chaotic mess, Jesus the Christ, the Lamb of God, walked calmly, willingly, and triumphantly amidst the sight and stench of death. Throughout John's Passion, only a majestic and serene

Jesus the Christ is recounted—a figure completely present to every moment of his human life, supremely at one, even at ease, with its events—again, startlingly different from the Passion accounts in the other three gospels.

When Jesus reached Golgotha, the Place of the Skull, John simply states, with no adjectives, no elaboration, that he was crucified. John adds only that Jesus was between "two others." Even in this physical description, John places Jesus in the center of two—a position of *sym-bol,* of joining, of the union that is the omnipresent theme of this gospel.

> Then [Pilate] handed [Jesus] over to [the Temple authorities] to be crucified. So they took Jesus; and carrying the cross by himself, he went out to what is called The Place of the Skull, which in Hebrew is called Golgotha. There they crucified him, and with him two others, one on either side, with Jesus between them. (19:16–18)

Watching the crucifixion, close to the cross, was a small group that included Mary the mother of Jesus, Mary Magdalene, Mary the wife of Clopas, and "the disciple whom [Jesus] loved," who was possibly John himself, the author of this gospel. This differs from the narratives in Matthew, Mark, and Luke, which mentioned no disciples being present and described the women as viewing the death from quite a distance.

Jesus on the cross spoke only a few words—some to his mother and to the "disciple whom he loved." His words had nothing to do with death. He didn't recite Psalm 22, as noted in Matthew and Mark. Instead, Jesus explicitly joined the disciple and his mother, announcing him as Mary's new "son." And oral tradition holds that John took Mary into his household, first in and around Jerusalem and then later in Ephesus. From John's perspective, however, these words gave divine instruction to Ephesus that, in the Christian faith, families could be formed by ways other than by blood, which had been the accepted practice for generations beyond number. Tribal and familial bonds could be loosened, and families could be formed by love and by intention and by commitment.

Once again in complete control of events, though near death, Jesus said, "I am thirsty." John notes that this was "in order to fulfill the scripture." John is referring to Psalm 69, King David's prayer for deliverance from his enemies, wherein he was given poison to eat and vinegar to drink. Jesus on the cross drank wine from a sponge held by a "hyssop" branch, a shrub whose branches were used for sprinkling both blood and water during Jewish rituals. In Matthew and Mark's gospels, wine was put to Jesus's lips but he did not drink. In Luke, no wine was offered. In John's gospel, water transformed into wine celebrated the union of marriage at Cana, and now wine marks the reunion that would soon occur with the resurrection. By drinking voluntarily, Jesus "fulfilled" the ancient Hebrew prophecy. In the psalm, David prayed for deliverance. On the cross, Jesus symbolically "drank" the illusions of the world, transforming them into illuminating truths through his resurrection.

His earthly purpose completed, Jesus spoke three words—"It is finished"—then bowed his head and died. In this gospel, we have a clear sense that Jesus *chose* the precise moment of his death and that his earthly life was in no sense taken from him. And we feel certain that, until this final moment, Jesus's head was upright and unbowed. Although this end is astonishing in its outward circumstances, it is deeply metaphysical and completely consistent with the themes of this gospel. What did Ephesus take from John's writing? We have no way to know, but certainly any person praying these words as preparation for baptism could not have failed to be both challenged and uplifted by Jesus's message and demeanor in this scene.

> Meanwhile, standing near the cross of Jesus were his mother, and his mother's sister, Mary the wife of Clopas, and Mary Magdalene. When Jesus saw his mother and the disciple whom he loved standing beside her, he said to his mother, "Woman, here is your son." Then he said to the disciple, "Here is your mother." And from that hour the disciple took her into his own home. After this, when Jesus knew that all was now finished, he said (in order to fulfill the scripture), "I am thirsty." A jar full of sour wine was standing there. So they put a sponge full of the wine on a branch of hyssop and held it to his mouth. When Jesus had received the wine, he said, "It is finished." Then he bowed his head and gave up his spirit. (19:25b–30)

After the crucifixion, in another part of the account unique to John, soldiers came to break the bones of those crucified so that their deaths would be hastened. John recounts that when they came, they didn't break Jesus's legs, because "he was already dead." There was a prohibition against breaking any of the bones of the sacrificial lamb, so this detail completes John's analogy with the Passover lamb.

Then a soldier pierced Jesus's side with his spear. "Blood and water" issued forth. What an amazing—even shocking—image! For Ephesus, it combined the familiar old blood rituals of sacrifice with the "living waters" of Christianity, and also with the new ritual of water baptism, which contained the experience of death and resurrection.

> Then the soldiers came and broke the legs of the first and of the other
> who had been crucified with him. But when they came to Jesus and
> saw that he was already dead, they did not break his legs. Instead, one
> of the soldiers pierced his side with a spear, and at once blood and
> water came out. (19:32–34)

Return to the Garden: The Burial

The passages about Jesus's burial contain more references that are obscure to most contemporary readers, but were extremely significant to John's audience. Joseph of Arimathea and Nicodemus asked to take Jesus's body so that they could bury him properly—an affront to Jewish authority and tradition. First, men never prepared bodies—only women—and certainly not men of high position. (Nicodemus was a Pharisee and Joseph had sufficient stature to speak with Pilate.) Second, handling a dead body made a person ritually unclean. The fact that Joseph and Nicodemus were willing to defile themselves just hours before the Passover meal broke another taboo. Furthermore, Nicodemus himself brought the traditional myrrh and aloes for embalming—and a huge and expensive quantity of them—making it quite clear that neither he nor Joseph expected Jesus would rise.

Unsurprisingly, John once again sets his story in a garden—this time near the burial tomb at Golgotha. As we've learned, the Garden of Eden metaphor figures prominently in this gospel, but as a general metaphor gardens represent places of perpetual death and resurrection. Living things die, or appear to, just as living things are reborn, or seem to be. The entire process is a dynamic interaction of opposites. The future of its dying is held by the living plant, and the fallow ground holds the seeds and power of rebirth. Together those aspects of life and death echo the same eternal reality, so John provides yet another image that is a powerful preparation prayer for the baptism ritual.

> After these things, Joseph of Arimathea, who was a disciple of Jesus, though a secret one because of his fear of the Jews, asked Pilate to let him take away the body of Jesus. Pilate gave him permission; so he came and removed his body. Nicodemus, who had at first come to Jesus by night, also came, bringing a mixture of myrrh and aloes, weighing about a hundred pounds. They took the body of Jesus and wrapped it with the spices in linen cloths, according to the burial custom of the Jews. Now there was a garden in the place where he was crucified, and in the garden there was a new tomb in which no one had ever been laid. And so, because it was the Jewish day of Preparation, and the tomb was nearby, they laid Jesus there.
> (19:38–42)

AS WE KNOW, John's gospel is read in pieces in the lectionary, wisely interspersed throughout the other gospels. Because of this, in the Sunday reading cycle we get morsels of visionary joy and ecstasy, spread out as intermittent illuminations. When we move through the gospel from beginning to end in quadratos's third path, we get the full measure of John's wisdom.

Once again, in two settings of his garden metaphor, which inherently offer a context of change and complexity, John teaches lessons about spiritual immaturity. In the first, the calm of Jesus is contrasted with the zeal of Peter and his drawn sword. This is a picture of us in the third path. We want to jump ahead, right *now*! But we can easily miss the mark, because we are not yet ready. In the courtyard scene, we are given more complexity on which to reflect. Both Peter and the unnamed disciple have confused allegiances. Those of the unnamed disciple are clear to us—we may still have lingering attachments to people, places, and attitudes that seem expedient, but are actually detriments to our transformation. Peter's misalignment is more subtle. Peter is creditably following his loyalty to his friend and teacher, Jesus—but in doing so, he is being disloyal to the principles of his faith, which are more rigorous. This is a trap for us also, equally subtle. If we genuinely examine our motives, how often are we attracted to the teacher rather than the teaching, the surface rather than the substance?

In the rest of the Passion account, the focus is on Jesus as a spiritual model. Throughout, Jesus maintained his demeanor of humility and inner strength. Literally stripped, even of his clothing, Jesus the Christ could not be seen as weak in any way when he washed the feet of his disciples. Nor, subsequently, with Annas and Pilate, who sought to harm him, was he sub-servient at all. Not arrogant, he was forthright—even forceful—in every instance. Although Jesus is largely silent in other gospels, John shows him freely responding to the questions he is asked by these powerful men as an equal, without rancor or resentment. This illustrates the wholeness of the third path. The antagonists represent many of our inner voices which, in these scenes, we see as ever-present, yet balanced with our deepest spiritual nature. Asking and answering, we are able to make an assessment of what is real and what is illusion.

Jesus's calm, strength, and confidence are our model. Secure in the knowledge that he was not alone and capable of seeing through the illusions of the temporal world, he was cognizant of his true purpose. When the de-cision went against him, he accepted it as part of his destiny and raised no objections, refusing to be a victim in any way whatsoever. The Romans may have sentenced him, but he gave himself freely to the crucifixion—even car-rying his own cross—because he realized the truthful odyssey of his earthly life. This is the attitude we must pray to claim as our own, knowing it to be critical in the latter part of the third path. We will not always find fairness. Illusion will win out many times, in many places, and in many ways, just as it did with Jesus, just as it did for the Ephesians, and just as it has thousands of times in the millennia since then. We must continue our reflection until we can truly discern this difference and avoid the trap of resentment and victimhood. Then we will be able to move forward into the fourth path. However, if we find ourselves unwilling to carry our own cross, that is a sign that we have reverted to the second—or even the first—path.

As a bit of an aside, but an important one, notice that through John's symbolism, Jesus's confrontation with Pilate personifies the battle between two great opposing forces: Jesus the Christ as the representative of what is divine and real and of God, and Pontius Pilate as that of the temporal "world" of illusion. This scene, which took place at high noon, has a lot of the same dramatic tension as the famous showdown at the OK Corral. Notably, no Jews—not even the Temple authorities John finds so obnoxious—witness the two powers squaring off, still more evidence that John does not blame the Jews for Jesus's death.

Jesus's instruction that Mary form a new family with "the disciple whom [Jesus] loved" mirrors our own progression. Mary symbolizes our progenitor, our parent, our culture. She gave us birth and also transferred many things of value to us—as well as some beliefs we have had to overcome, such as tribalism, categories about ourselves and the world, and other limited, untrue, and unproductive judgments. The beloved disciple, on the other hand, is making a journey like ours. He has been following a difficult path, and will soon see through death and the torn veil and find the truth of unity. Mary and the disciple, the old and new, will form a family; blood and water will flow together. Likewise, when we, too, are able to join that which has been separate, or that which we have believed to be separate, our old assumptions and resentments will die and new possibilities will flower.

Jesus's simple declaration of his death, "It is finished," exemplifies his acceptance—heart, mind, body, and soul—of pain as an inevitable part of wholeness. When the undivided reality of everything becomes our reference point, it then becomes possible for even the most excruciating experiences to open into a calm transcendence. Emotion, mind, spirit, and flesh must be held together as one, as hospice workers and chaplains in war zones, for example, have often reported.

There is a caution here—revealed perhaps through the words of John's own gospel and suffered by the writer himself: balance is the key to the third path. It is possible to become spiritually overexalted; indeed, this is not uncommon for mystics. They come to see the mind and spiritual planes as most important, and their emotions or their physical body as obstructions to their spiritual growth. This often leads them to fall out of balance with their humanity and to denigrate emotions or physicality. Earlier we discussed John's possible discomfort with "the flesh," and psychologically the lack of pain in the crucifixion account could reflect such discomfort. Overexaltation is not unusual, to be sure. Extremes in diet, emotional or sexual repression, and self-mutilation are all among the many ways a lack of balance asserts itself. When these behaviors are present, we can be certain that, at least in those parts of our lives, our journey has stopped, even regressed.

It is just as possible to unbalance in the other direction. When exposed to the vision of union, some feel an ego-response of desperate unworthiness. John recognized this voice of unworthiness and acknowledged it through Jesus's answer to Peter's question at the footwashing, chiding Peter. But because John was concerned primarily with the euphoria of Ephesus, the possibility of a plunge in the other direction—down into unworthiness—remained a mere mention. We, however, need to be aware that this plunge is a real risk. We can slide right out of feeling elevated—or never feel any rising at all—and fall into deep despondency, even depression. Again, such a response is an indication that our journey has halted and needs help.

The Passion tells us to open our hearts and souls in joy, to receive all that is before us, and to expand far beyond our intellect and our ever-yammering ego-self. If we can do this, our openness will change how we meet the world and how the world meets us. We need to sit in the garden, sing in the garden, paint in the garden, contemplate in the garden, pray in the garden. Inevitably, we will be engaged so deeply that our toes will become roots and our embrace will be as solid as the trunk of an oak tree. We won't be "in" the garden anymore. We will *be* the garden.

Touching Eternity: The Resurrection Accounts

John's gospel has three appearances of the resurrected Jesus in the original text (plus another added later, for a total of four). There is only one appearance in Matthew's gospel; and in its original form, Mark has no appearance at all, only an announcement. And we will see that Luke recounts two appearances of Jesus after the crucifixion. Why are there more appearance accounts in the Gospel of John?

The main reason lies in the nature of the gospel itself. John uses very specific teaching methods. Just as we compared John's approach at the beginning of the gospel to the slow turning and examination of the carefully cut facets of a diamond, at the gospel's close we can see the pattern of infinite glimmers within that diamond, especially those that reach far below its surface. The remarkable structure of this gospel is a multidimensional journey through spirals that simultaneously ascend and descend.

The Gospel of John is structured masterfully. It begins with the poetic pronouncement of exalted themes and divine truths in the Prologue, and leads the reader to the poignant recounting of the crucifixion of a single human body and its resurrection as the proof of those truths. The resurrection accounts use the same dramatic arc—from the immense, then back down to the particular. In them, John begins with the clearly divine—and somewhat overwhelming—event of the resurrection and brings the revelation of its exalted truths straight back down to human, everyday life.

In every section of the appearances, John provides meditations that focus on a particular principle. First he asserts a truth; then he either expands it or exhorts against failure to understand it. John illustrates his points either through several stories, each focusing on a figure with distinctive characteristics and a dilemma, or through the use of differing and vivid metaphorical locations. Sometimes he employs both techniques, which we see with clarity in the resurrection accounts. These four accounts summarize, reinforce, and complete John's core messages. The gospel is like a great symphony, with its melodies brought together in the resurrection accounts like an inspirational and resolved climax.

The Prologue presents all of the truths with which John is concerned, and the balance of the gospel elucidates them. Likewise, the first appearance account reiterates John's primary message, and the subsequent ones comment on that message or, more accurately, contain important caveats. Increasing the richness, all the elements of the first appearance—the setting, the participants, their actions, the tone, the words themselves—echo the Prologue's themes, but this time in a pragmatic, comprehensible human context. Indeed, these concluding chapters stand in clear contrast to the central part of the gospel, which consists of lengthy discourses and lengthy sentences. These chapters are simple and direct, the sentences short and commanding.

Recall that in our discussion of the Prologue, we examined John's use of a Platonic metaphor—Plato's shadowy cave of veiled sight—to refer to the illusion of the "world" versus the reality of divine truth. Note two things in the following chapters: the setting of each appearance and the use of the words "see and believe." John is moving his inspirational principles into the realm of lived reality—and he wants to be sure no reader misses the connections he is making.

The Way of Heart: The First Appearance of
Jesus the Christ Resurrected

Jesus's death fell on a Friday afternoon, just before the Sabbath (or "Shabbat," the "day of rest" at the end of the Jewish week, which starts at sundown Friday and continues until sundown Saturday). In that peaceful time of dark before dawn, "on the first day of the week"—that is, early Sunday morning—Mary of Magdala arrived at Jesus's tomb and saw that the stone had been removed from the entrance. Consistent with his other updates of Jewish tradition for his Ephesian audience, John eliminated the references to Shabbat, using instead the more secular phrase, "first day of the week." All of the other gospels describe the resurrection as having occurred on the day after Shabbat.

This may seem like a small change in language. However, it is actually not so small. By not referencing everything to Jewish tradition, John validated developing Christian practice, thus setting the stage for the eventual adoption of Sunday as the Christian feast day and "day of rest." Keep in mind that another two hundred years would pass before Christianity was fully acknowledged and legalized by secular authorities and Sunday could officially become a non-workday. Until then, Christians followed the custom of the Messianic Jews. Saturday was their traditional Sabbath and their rest day. Then they met in the first hours of Sunday morning in remembrance of Jesus's resurrection, and went to work for the rest of the day.

In the early morning of the first day, as John tells it, Mary of Magdala raced to tell Simon Peter and "the other disciple" that Jesus's body had been removed from the tomb. At a run, they followed her back, and upon arrival at the tomb, each of the men entered and confirmed it empty. John notes that the wrapping linens were "lying there," implying that Jesus's body had been stolen and defiled. The men "saw and believed" that the body had been taken and, assuming theft, they returned to their homes.

Mary remained, grief-stricken and weeping. She looked in the tomb as the men had, but experienced an entirely different vision. She saw angels who asked why she wept. She responded with her sense of deep loss—her "Lord" had been "taken away." From behind her, she heard the question repeated. Turning, Mary saw someone she thought to be "the gardener." She begged him to tell her where Jesus's body had been taken. The gardener then called out, "Mary!" Recognizing him as Jesus, Mary responded, "Rabbouni!" ("My teacher").

Throughout the gospel, Jesus has used only a kind of philosophical address, calling his mother "woman," for example—one of the ways in which John emphasizes that his intention is in the nature of a meditation on themes rather than a narrative about specific individuals. Until now, the single exception was Lazarus, whom Jesus summoned from his tomb by name. Suddenly, in this poignant moment of grief at his own tomb, an engaged, risen Jesus spoke directly and uncharacteristically. "Mary!" he called out, startling her.

This encounter at Jesus's tomb, unlike the after-death scenes found in any of the other gospels, occurred with only one witness, Mary of Magdala. Further, the other three gospels make no mention of a garden at the burial site, the two angels, nor the actual appearance of Jesus at the tomb itself. John clearly has his usual allegorical intentions in mind. Beginning with the Prologue and continuing throughout the gospel, he has determinedly worked to provide a new Garden of Eden metaphor for Christianity. In this first resurrection account, through the construction of extraordinary symmetries, he perfects his task.

Centuries prior, the Great Temple of Jerusalem was specifically constructed and sited so that everyone who entered it would have an inner and symbolic reentry into the Garden of Eden. Its main gate faced east to the rising sun—the same direction as the entrance to the ancient garden of Hebrew scripture. By continuing into the heart of the Temple, one reached the Holy of Holies, the Inner Sanctuary, where images of palm trees and flowers covered the walls. Two immense sculptures of cherubim (angels)—a reminder of the two angels who guarded the entrance to Paradise—arched over the heart of the room, protecting the Ark of the Covenant, the most sacred relic of the faith, containing Moses's tablets and pieces of manna from the arid desert where the Jews had suffered for so long.

John's Jewish readers are now offered a consummate vision of a new garden. Here at Golgotha, exquisitely timed just before the sun rose in the east, John has matched each gospel image with all the historical Jewish symbols. Grief-stricken Mary, in a fresh, living garden (symbolic of Eden), looked into the opened tomb where she beheld two angels centered over an empty space. John has constructed a metaphorical Holy of Holies. Observe, however, the vast difference between the two settings: one is outdoors, freely reached, expansive—while the other was in a closed-up, guarded room deep within the Great Temple. And the new holiness, seen between the angels, is not a "mere" object. Instead, it is the site of a mysterious, divine event—Jesus's resurrection—whose truth is the gateway to all of the promises of the Christian faith.

Mary's silent, lonely weeping deepens the Eden allegory. First there was only Adam. Then one became two, in partnership. Here, in this garden of resurrection, we also see a solitary figure—weeping for her lost teacher and companion. Her tears of grief summoned the resurrected Jesus, to be in relationship with her, through faith, forever. John is using Mary's tears to reiterate and complete a point he has made many times before: the journey to wholeness cannot be accomplished through intellect alone. The path to the Christian inner sanctuary—its Holy of Holies—requires that the heart be opened and joined to intellect and spirit.

The simplicity of Jesus's appearance to Mary is also significant. He came quietly, almost seeming to glide into the scene. Neither his entrance nor his manner was extraordinary. There were no radiating beams of light, no sounding trumpets. This was a very emotional, but quiet and intimate, setting. Its peacefulness holds the most astonishing revelation of Christianity: Jesus died; yet Jesus lives. John is communicating that the most trustworthy path is based on direct experience. His words are an implicit caution against relying solely on the received knowledge of history or traditions or writings, and their tone provides assurance that truth proceeds quietly and steadily.

Great attention was paid to naming in Genesis, which is echoed and modified by John here. In Genesis, "the man gave names" to the creatures of the earth, thereby acknowledging their unique nature and assigning them their role. Upon expulsion from the garden, as they went into trial, he named the woman Eve, which means "mother of all." We find no less significance in John's retelling. In this peaceful, heart-filled scene, Jesus, appearing as a gardener, addressed Mary directly by her given name.

"Mary!" Jesus called. The sudden calling of Mary's true name in this garden is a repeated and larger version of his earlier direct address to

Lazarus, whom he told to "come out" of his tomb. John's dramatic moment here says, in effect, "Mary, your tears have shown that your heart has truly opened to me. Therefore, I know that you are able to understand this moment and the path before you, which is the path into Paradise. We have been bound together now, in union, by the revelation of my rising. I will be your eternal companion." The "naming" is also a reference by John to the ritual of Christian baptism, which included the announcing of one's name on arising from the waters.

Another level of meaning, almost certainly more obvious to the original audience than to readers today, can be found in the name Mary itself. Mary is *Miryam* in Hebrew, rabbinically translated as "bitterness" (from the root *merum*). Presumably, John's readers would have made the connection readily, but he makes certain of it by having Mary weep, both here and in the previous account of Lazarus. Although some texts offer up to seventy possible sources and translations, the interpretation of the name Mary as "bitterness" seems most logical because all of the Marys weep. Mary, Lazarus's sister, wept (but the other sister, Martha, did not). Jesus himself wept in response. Mary of Magdala wept profusely at the tomb, crying for help. However, in every instance, the tears of loss shed by the Marys evoked compassion, and were turned to tears of joy through Jesus's intervention.

> Early on the first day of the week, while it was still dark, Mary
> Magdalene came to the tomb and saw that the stone had been
> removed from the tomb. So she ran and went to Simon Peter and the
> other disciple, the one whom Jesus loved, and said to them, "They
> have taken the Lord out of the tomb, and we do not know where
> they have laid him." Then Peter and the other disciple set out and
> went toward the tomb. The two were running together, but the other
> disciple outran Peter and reached the tomb first. He bent down to
> look in and saw the linen wrappings lying there, but he did not go
> in. Then Simon Peter came, following him, and went into the tomb.
> He saw the linen wrappings lying there, and the cloth that had been
> on Jesus' head, not lying with the linen wrappings but rolled up
> in a place by itself. Then the other disciple, who reached the tomb
> first, also went in, and he saw and believed; for as yet they did not

understand the scripture, that he must rise from the dead. Then the
disciples returned to their homes. But Mary stood weeping outside
the tomb. As she wept, she bent over to look into the tomb; and she
saw two angels in white, sitting where the body of Jesus had been
lying, one at the head and the other at the feet. They said to her,
"Woman, why are you weeping?" She said to them, "They have taken
away my Lord, and I do not know where they have laid him." When
she had said this, she turned around and saw Jesus standing there, but
she did not know that it was Jesus. Jesus said to her, "Woman, why are
you weeping? Whom are you looking for?" Supposing him to be the
gardener, she said to him, "Sir, if you have carried him away, tell me
where you have laid him, and I will take him away." Jesus said to her,
"Mary!" She turned and said to him in Hebrew, "Rabbouni!" (which
means Teacher). (20:1–16)

WHEN WE READ this appearance story two millennia later, we do not
share the connections with the Temple that John's readers did. Yet the spiritual wealth available to us is nonetheless abundant. Although all of John's
major themes can be found in the appearance of the resurrected Jesus the
Christ to Mary of Magdala in the garden, there are three that are of particular importance for us in the third path. The first is how we may come
to "see and believe"—or not. The second is hearing the sound of our true
name. The third is having the patience to know bitterness—to endure the
difficulties that are a necessary part of spiritual growth.

Brought by Mary, Peter and the other disciple looked into the tomb.
They believed they saw an empty tomb. That was, after all, what they expected to see. Before their eyes was a pile of unwrapped linen—no body
and no rational explanation. Mary then looked into the tomb—but brought
more of herself to the experience. She looked with her heart, not simply her
mind. *She* saw cherubim. And afterward, as she grieved, the resurrected
Jesus the Christ joined her. We face the same choice many times daily. Our
lives will largely flow from our expectations. The more we are able to be
present in our fullest selves to any moment or situation in our lives, the
more likely we are to see angels instead of emptiness—and to know how
deeply we are accompanied.

For some of us, this will not be terribly difficult. It is our natural inclination. For others of us, it will be a rigorous task. And for all of us, the process of opening at an emotional level will present challenges, chief among which are addressed by the second and third appearance accounts. Onerous or not, this third path moves primarily, though not exclusively, through our hearts. There is no possible way to comprehend wholeness with intellect only—or, for that matter, with body only. Heart is where we are able to feel the range and reach of the All, and allow its entry into us for the work of transformation, so that we may joyously proclaim, "Rabbouni!"

If we are not fully present—not open to possibility—we will be unlikely to hear our "true name" when it is called. When the full experience of deep new vision arrives, it somehow creates in us a refreshed, even a new, sense of identity. We feel more aligned with the deepest, most powerful and authentic ways in which we can know ourselves. We move our focus from the beautiful blossoms of John's garden and gain comprehension of the roots. We feel anchored, centered.

Traditions and rituals throughout the world acknowledge the opening of this extraordinary and very personal inner awareness. In all cultures, at birth or shortly thereafter, a name is chosen for each new life. Many of the world's rituals allow people to take a new name when they cross to some designated level of awareness or commitment, including the ritual of Christian baptism. In most religious communities, a name change was once mandatory. Now either a new name is selected or the old is reaffirmed. The pope of the Roman Catholic Church, for example, chooses a highly symbolic new name after he is elected. These rituals are designed to recognize, honor, and assist with what is acknowledged as a core change.

Understanding "bitterness," exemplified by the name Mary, is complex, a bit unexpected, and often difficult to manage. It is also an unavoidable element of full transformation. It is no accident that throughout the centuries, one of the names for Mary, the mother of Jesus, has been Mater Dolorosa, Mother of Sorrows—and that many images of great art depict her weeping. We encountered suffering in our first and certainly our second paths, and had to move through it. But now it is time to deepen that reality and transcend mere endurance.

Whole *does not mean idyllic*. No life is lived without the reality of pain. When pain arises in our lives, we are confronted with choices—and again, the degree to which we hold ourselves present to each moment will largely determine what we decide. We may bring only our small ego-mind and respond from the categories of *dia-bol*. If we do, then gradually we will end up with an embittered heart. If instead we can stay open, as Mary did after Lazarus's death—even though she was surely disappointed that Jesus had not come soon enough to save her brother—then our pain can transform into compassion. If we can grieve without losing our faith, as Mary of Magdala did, then we will be rewarded with divine awareness. A compassionate heart carries both the reality of pain and the hope of joy. It moves us forward. These elements are the fullness of the extraordinary and uplifting feelings of the third path—not their contradiction. The garden overflowing with flowers is simultaneously a picture of death and decay. At the joyous moment of a baby's birth, in the ecstasy of new life, the baby cries. Grief and sorrow can be profound and enriching, just as the cello and bass are the deep tones that keep a symphony from flying off into sentimentality.

In the Locked House:
The Second Appearance of Jesus the Christ Resurrected

The second appearance of Jesus the Christ resurrected, as down-to-earth as the first, narrows its thematic focus to the letting go of anger and resentment. It is essentially cautionary. The story opens with the disciples in a house that is "locked for fear of the Jews." This is John's shorthand to Ephesians for their trepidations and uncertainties about moving forward despite the pressure they feel from the authorities of the old religion. They could "lock the doors" of their lives and their attitudes, says John, or they could choose another, more positive course.

Jesus appeared before them. After a greeting in the name of "peace," repeated twice, he commanded the disciples to receive "the Holy Spirit," which he conferred by breathing upon them. This is an echo (once again) of Genesis, where it is said that God "breathed into [Adam's] nostrils the breath of life; and the man became a living being" (Gen. 2:7). John is emphasizing that the intaking of Spirit needn't be a complicated ritual involving sacrifices in a temple. It is a simple, natural, and regular practice—as easy, yet profound, as breathing.

The resurrected Jesus then proceeded to talk to the disciples about their responsibilities, now that they had received the infusion of Spirit. The Oxford New Revised Standard Version (NRSV), which is used throughout this book, translates the two Greek verbs in this passage as "forgive" and "retain." These translations are technically correct and theoretically possible. However, they are more congruent with the practice of priests granting (or denying) forgiveness than with the consistent message of John's gospel, which is the release of pain from one's heart and life. The original Greek words have great subtlety, and other possible translations make more sense.

The first verb in the verse is *aphiemi,* which means "to send away, cancel, or release." The second is *krateo,* which means "to hold, hold fast, or keep." Using these definitions, we might translate Jesus's words as: "Receive the Holy Spirit. If you send away sins from another, they are sent away from them; if you hold onto them, they are held fast." These words are about the work of the Holy Spirit within the heart of each individual and that individual's responsibilities. John is pointing out both a promise and a caution to his readers.

In a more expanded version, we might restate this verse as: "If, *within yourself,* you are able to unlock your heart's doors and send away your feelings of judgment over differences with others and over being wronged, then *your* heart will be freed. If, however, you do not choose to release *yourself,* then the trespasses you hold against others will remain alive, held fast *within you* and in the world."

John's specific inclusion of Jesus's words about forgiveness in his gospel to Ephesus was a practical mandate promoting amity and shalom in a diverse Christian community and city. The more commonly accepted interpretation of this passage, that Jesus was conferring the privilege and responsibility of forgiveness specifically on his disciples (and, by extension, on the priesthood), makes much less sense. That interpretation is not only contradictory within the gospel, but is also contrary to John's clear intentions to foster harmony in the Christian community of Ephesus.

When it was evening on that day, the first day of the week, and the
doors of the house where the disciples had met were locked for fear
of the Jews, Jesus came and stood among them and said, "Peace
be with you." After he said this, he showed them his hands and his

side. Then the disciples rejoiced when they saw the Lord. Jesus said
to them again, "Peace be with you. As the Father has sent me, so I
send you." When he had said this, he breathed on them and said to
them, "Receive the Holy Spirit. If you forgive the sins of any, they
are forgiven them; if you retain the sins of any, they are retained."
(20:19–23)

WHAT CAUTIONS MIGHT we, in today's world, take for ourselves in this
second appearance? One is the challenge of balance. Jesus, in his human
body, "showed" his hands and side. One of the critical dangers of the third
path is that, in our attempts to remain in ecstasy, we may fail to find a
productive way to sustain matter and spirit together. There is a great risk
that we will try to supersede our wounds by moving out of our bodies into
some ethereal place that is "only spiritual." Conversely, we may risk "over-
embodying" our wounds by moving from acceptance into indulgence.

What does this mean? It means that our human journey is exactly that—
human. Our human experience is embodied, and our journey can proceed
only through acceptance of that reality. "Human" (and "humility") derives
from *humus,* earth. This reminds us that we are made of the same elements
as the soil. Many teachers assert that we are not bodies being spiritual, but
rather spirit, or spiritual beings, having the experience of a body. This is a
difference without a distinction. We are both matter *and* spirit, human *and*
divine. We do ourselves no service in our quest for spiritual maturity when
we try to supersede our bodies or, in fact, when we separate ourselves in
any way, rather than bending our efforts to encourage the harmony of our
complexity.

The opposite extreme—over-embodying—presents an equal challenge.
Quadratos tells us that all is whole, and all is well, and gives us a path of
acceptance on which we can walk. As we inhabit the third path, we can
peacefully observe and become conscious of how many "inner tribes" make
up our individual harmony. However, we must remain cognizant that many
of the behaviors we carry are ones we developed as adaptations in our earlier, less mature stages in the "locked house." "All is well" does not in any
way mean that all the behaviors within us are good or productive. We still
need to assess what serves our mature life, and what does not. If we use the

third-path revelation as an excuse for indulgence, we will find ourselves merely circling through the rooms of our personality, instead of moving through the door of transformation.

So what does Jesus, in the second appearance, tell us about how to open that door? First, the disciples "rejoiced." This parallels Mary of Magdala's tears of joy. The disciples moved into the realm of their feelings, giving us guidance to the path we also have to follow. Then Jesus pronounced, "Peace be with you." We, too, must strive to maintain a peaceful, open, and willing inner diversity. Then Jesus exhaled the Holy Spirit into the disciples, who gratefully accepted it.

This sense of personal advocacy, of companionship and perpetual memory, is the essential understanding of the Holy Spirit we must grasp and accept in the third path. We need to inhale it fully, breathing deeply, contemplating, meditating, and praying. This is the perfume of the garden of our lives. When we have it, we will know we are no longer alone. We will never be paralyzed by fear again, and the door to the house will swing open.

The final words of the second appearance are like a fresh breeze rushing in through the door, displacing the old, stale air inside. Jesus commanded his disciples to "send away" their sins and judgments, to free themselves from the narrow vision of one-sidedness, lest they cause suffering within themselves and the world. This understanding varies considerably from what has been widely accepted as the meaning of these verses, and it is crucial that we understand this in the third path.

In this time of new revelation, the danger of imbalance continues its threat. Gravitating toward partial truths, for example, prevents genuine forgiveness. We can move to forgiveness only from a steadied center that balances both our intellect and our emotions. This is best accomplished through a learned practice of compassion. Without it, we may rely too heavily on our intellect, fall into judgment and cynicism, and fail to access the leavening of the heart. If, on the other hand, we tip the other way and place too much emphasis on our emotions, we can easily fall into sentimentality and fantasy, losing the necessary guidance of our reason. Only in our attempts at balance will the door stay open, so that the breath of the Holy Spirit coming through the portal may enliven our compassion.

Further complicating matters, our culture's understanding of the word "forgiveness" has become distorted in a way that makes the conventional translation of John's verses very misleading. Forgiveness does not mean that we sit in judgment of others and then condescend to be "understanding" of what we deem to be their failings or their sins against us. This is false forgiveness and will keep us locked in self-righteousness, breathing fetid air. Genuine forgiveness allows us to move to a posture outside the need for judgment and requires us to, instead, release judgment *within ourselves*. The "sins" we forgive are actually the attitudes we hold within our *own* hearts. This resurrection appearance helps us to compassionately understand the actions of others anew—as their emanations of fear, loneliness, or loss.

With Thomas in the "Shut" House:
The Third Appearance of Jesus the Christ Resurrected

A week later, Jesus visited the disciples, and again they were described as being in a house, although this time it wasn't locked—merely "shut." This time, the disciple Thomas was present. In Greek, Thomas is Didymus, which means "twin." John uses this name to explore the voices of faith and doubt—internal and external—which inevitably buffet and challenge believers.

As Christianity exploded in size in the early years, many problems and opinions naturally arose. Who would claim authority and marshal support? When and how were ritual circumcision and ritual cleansing going to be converted to the new rite of Christian baptism? What size table was needed for all the new members, men and women, to sit and converse? Which accounts of Jesus were most correct? Which teachings could be trusted?

Even if these matters could somehow be settled, there were pragmatic challenges in day-to-day dealings with diversity. How could people and their practices be harmonized into a coherent and loving whole? How could an individual transform inner conflicts into resolute faith? John offers the image of Thomas as a way to address these specific dilemmas.

Thomas was, in effect, John's "straight man." He questioned everything, always required literal proof, and is now memorialized in the expression "doubting Thomas." True to his nature, Thomas was completely unable to believe in the resurrection based on the story told him by the other disciples. He needed specific, concrete evidence and said so. "[I need to] put my fingers in the mark of the nails and my hand in his side," said Thomas. So Jesus, without comment or criticism, offered Thomas the chance to verify the injuries—and Thomas's skepticism vanished.

As we noted when we discussed the teaching discourses, John is always working on many levels—turning the diamond, as it were. Doubt is scarcely the sole issue in this appearance, albeit the primary one. In all four appearances, Jesus appeared in human form, but in both the second and third appearances, John notes that he appeared with the holes of the crucifixion still in his body. The resurrected body was not miraculously made undamaged, a detail found only in John's gospel. John is proclaiming to Ephesus that resurrection occurs in a regular human life and that faith is not flawless. It has doubts and it has wounds, neither of which need be hidden.

Additionally, John uses a profoundly inspirational choice of words in the third appearance account. The holes in Jesus's body are referred to not as wounds, but as "marks." John is clear that Jesus *chose* his crucifixion. Therefore, Jesus could not have been "wounded," but he was certainly "marked"—and he did not flinch or hesitate to show those marks. This was a distinction of great value to the Ephesian Christians, building a community among diverse people. The group's ability to receive each other's differences as marks of glory rather than pejorative tribalistic damage, or "wounds," enabled the individual members of the group to act more freely and potentially avoid assuming the roles of victimhood.

Jesus's final words in this appearance rang out as a challenge. Though tolerant of Thomas's need for proof, Jesus also called Thomas to task. He questioned the depth of Thomas's belief, wondering if he had become satisfied only because his doubting intellect had been assuaged. Note that John, once more, distinctly uses the verb "see." Jesus's last words in this account are "Blessed are those who have not seen and yet have come to believe." They are a deep caution and support for belief that honors the truth of the heart as well as the head—transcending the limitations of physical sight (recall Plato's cave) and the deceptions of the divided and divisive intellect. This was critical for the Ephesians—and for all Christians who would come after them, who would be generations removed from the historical events recounted by the gospel. Did their faith require physical evidence or intellectual proof? Or was the Christ alive for them in their lives and their hearts?

But Thomas (who was called the Twin), one of the twelve, was not
with them when Jesus came. So the other disciples told him, "We
have seen the Lord." But he said to them, "Unless I see the mark of
the nails in his hands, and put my finger in the mark of the nails and
my hand in his side, I will not believe." A week later his disciples
were again in the house, and Thomas was with them. Although the
doors were shut, Jesus came and stood among them and said, "Peace
be with you." Then he said to Thomas, "Put your finger here and see
my hands. Reach out your hand and put it in my side. Do not doubt
but believe." Thomas answered him, "My Lord and my God!" Jesus
said to him, "Have you believed because you have seen me? Blessed
are those who have not seen and yet have come to believe." Now Jesus
did many other signs in the presence of his disciples, which are not
written in this book. But these are written so that you may come to
believe that Jesus is the Messiah, the Son of God, and that through
believing you may have life in his name. (20:24–31)

THE THIRD APPEARANCE, with its story of Thomas, was the original ending of the Gospel of John. Many of us may find it the one to which we most
closely relate. Why? For one thing, like us, Thomas wasn't there. He wasn't
at the crucifixion, the burial, or the first two resurrection appearances. Furthermore, he is profoundly a man for our times. He's rational, a "show me"
guy, just like most of us are—like most of us have been *trained* to be. He is
the mirror of our human dilemma, and his struggle to live the principles of
the Prologue, of Jesus the Christ, is ours.

Since Thomas was a disciple, we have to assume that something in his
heart was touched by some words or evidence or actions of Jesus the Christ.
And despite Jesus's explicit promise that he would return ("I go and prepare a place for you[.] I will come again and will take you to myself, so
that where I am, there you may be also," 14:3), Thomas remained doubt-
ful enough to hamper his belief. He insisted on direct sensory experience.
He could not trust the truth of his own inner call, much less the words of
anyone else.

Thomas the Twin personified John's "world" of illusion in its most intimate guise. Thomas had initially opened his heart. He was neither a Phari-

see like Nicodemus, nor an outsider, but a genuine disciple. He longed for belief. In the house with the other disciples, he faced a door which, though not completely barred or "locked" by fear, was shut. Thomas, instinctually protective of the illusions so carefully crafted by his intellect—and unable to transcend them—kept it closed. This is a predicament many of us recognize all too well.

What does John tell us about Thomas, and what more can we intuit, and how is this of value to us in the third path? Presumably, Thomas overcame his self-protective doubt when he became a disciple. Yet his subsequent actions tell us that he likely neglected to build an inner practice to support his decision. Perhaps he lacked friends on whom he could rely, or failed to extend his trust to them. Rather, he indulged his questioning intellect, falling back into the comfortable, rational understanding with which he was familiar. He did not persist in and expand the ecstasy that had initially compelled him, and hence he was unprepared to accept the truth of the resurrection when it arrived. If we follow Thomas's path—and fail to take the more positive and expansive steps available to us—we, too, will find the door closed and the fresh air of transformation unavailable when it comes.

Faith requires real commitment. The eyes that read only words cannot see past the veil. Does this mean we should push all doubt aside? Absolutely not. Doubt is faith's true companion. Does this mean faith can, or should, be discovered only on the level of our feelings? Again, absolutely not. In the garden, the whole flower is treasured—root, stem, and blossom—with each part distinct, yet all necessary to nature's plan. Further, the separate elements of soil, light, air, and water are all needed if the blossom is to reach its greatest beauty and have the vigor to fend off its predators. Complexity is strength.

Our intellect needs the vitality of our emotions, and our vulnerable emotions require gentle guardianship by our intellect. Faith needs doubt to test itself. It raises the questions that fertilize faith, keeping it flexible and invigorated. We should ask, Which is the richest soil in which we can plant ourselves? What spiritual tradition or practice calls our heart to discipleship? Jesus's counsel to Thomas's doubt can give us perfect direction. When he entered, Jesus spoke, and then repeated, an instruction for balance and harmony: "Peace be with you." That should be our core instruction to ourselves, the daily condition for which we strive, as well as that toward which we journey—inner and outer peace.

Jesus offered the marks on his side and his hands to Thomas without hesitation. John's use of "marks" rather than "wounds" is as significant to us today as it was to the Ephesians. Each of us has been marked by our lives. We can choose to identify the signs of these profound passages as "wounds"—signs of our past (and sometimes present) suffering at the hands of others. We can use them to derive sympathy and attention and a sense of importance. Alternatively, we can choose to acknowledge them as the "marks" that identify our singular humanity—significant and necessary parts of our journey. We can hide our "marks," or we can offer them up to others, when appropriate, so that those pathfinders can use them as trail signs while making their own way through the wilderness.

There is a special lesson for us in the way Jesus offered Thomas the "proof" required by his demanding intellect. Jesus did so gently, without explanation, recrimination, or harangue. This is a very tough lesson for most of us, and its difficulty relates directly to how well we are "rooted" in our particular garden. Another vocabulary might refer to this as how well we are "centered." Can we merely be present to the need of another without extracting our own self-importance from the encounter? Are we able to give without needing to receive—esteem or attention or inner self-elevation—at the expense of another?

If we can answer yes, the further question is, Are we yet able to be as gentle with ourselves as we are with others? When we contemplate this example of Jesus, we may find we need to sit in the garden in seasons other than spring. We may require the darker days of autumn and winter, where the deepest self-honesty, pain, and even failure abide, before we gain the full measure of this lesson. Our love for ourselves is often the hardest to come by, yet the most necessary for our journey. Without it, we have no roots, and our garden will fail.

Toward the end of the gospel, and with great tenderness, Jesus asked Thomas his central question. He asked him to examine the source of his belief. Was its source faith or evidence? This question fills every aspect of our lives, no matter what tradition we are in—or even if we are in no spiritual tradition whatsoever. What "system" do we believe in, and how do we arrive at our belief?

What is the framework for our life on earth, our relationships with others, and our view of death? In the deepest places of ourselves that we can discover, do we feel isolated or accompanied? Are we able to hold a vision of unity that connects our inner aspects to each other, or (in other words) connects us to ourselves, and then to others, and finally to All? Are our steps taken in trust, even without understanding? Or do we fear life—and death? These questions are crystallized in the one question Jesus asked Thomas, "Have you believed because you have seen me?" And they are at the deepest core of our questioning and self-discovery in quadratos's third path.

The final words of Jesus in this gospel are the blessing, the challenge, and the promise of this third path. These original final words present a very personal affirmation, entreaty, and hope. They ask us to "see" with faith's eyes, to "come to believe" in Mystery and the promise of life. This is why our time in the garden must be sheltered. It takes time to know the fullness of the truths whose disclosure began with our ecstatic entry through the garden gate. Yet we must now leave so that we can garden alongside the one who appeared as a gardener.

John has scrupulously revealed the complex and wondrous nature of union to us. Through poetry, dialogue, and story, that revelation has expanded and deepened our feelings of epiphany. John has encouraged— even insisted—that we allow their full meanings to unfold in our lives and that we bring our full selves to the experience. Now, as we come to the end of this path, we begin to sense why we cannot stay here always, why we need to move on to the fourth path. The deep inner comprehension we have is clear to us only so long as we sit, unmoving, in the garden. But that immobility will inevitably lead only to stagnation or retreat. Therefore, we must continue on, despite the fact that our safety disappears the moment we step into our regular lives. We do not yet know how to walk the path of truth, but we will find our guide in the Gospel of Luke.

On the Beach: The Fourth, and Final, Appearance
of Jesus the Christ Resurrected

Most scholars believe that the account of the fourth appearance of Jesus the Christ resurrected was added later and is by a different author. Compared with the rest of John's gospel, the allusions and writing style of this account have an uncharacteristic awkwardness. It also introduces an entirely new metaphor—fishing. It is unlikely that just at the close of his inspired magnum opus, John would have abandoned the metaphors he spent so much effort building. It is much more logical that he closed his gospel with the blessing and entreaty to Ephesus (and future generations), found at the end of the third appearance. Regardless of its authorship, however, the fourth account is both interesting and useful to our discussion.

The fourth appearance has its own message, complete with a different vitality from the others. Unlike all the earlier parts of John, which transpired mainly in the city of Jerusalem, this account begins with the resurrected Jesus and seven of his disciples on the beach of the Sea of Tiberias (the Roman name for the Sea of Galilee). As in the first account with Mary of Magdala in the garden, the location is open and expansive, matching the message of its words. The setting also holds a subtler meaning: in Christianity, old superstitions have been dispelled by a greater power. Rather than the fearsome place of Jewish tradition that we read of in the Gospel of Mark, this sea is the backdrop for physical and spiritual nourishment.

Much of this account centers on a lengthy series of actions that revolve around fishing, and hold clearly metaphorical meanings, primarily reiterative of John's earlier themes. However, the end of the narrative is another matter. Not only is its theme consistent with the rest of John's gospel, but it also serves quadratos admirably and carries us forward into the Gospel of Luke very nicely. Therefore, we will happily examine its words without any concerns about their authorship.

As we have mentioned, the physical setting is spacious and unobstructed—as are the account's images. In the first appearance, Jesus showed himself to Mary as a simple gardener. Here, equally unadorned, he stood on the beach serving breakfast to his disciples. Repeating the earlier image of Annas's courtyard, mention was made that the meal was cooked over a charcoal fire. After the repast, there was a measured—almost ritual—

exchange between Jesus and Peter. Using his personal name, "Simon son of John," Jesus asked Peter three times, "Do you love me?" Three times—the equal number of times Peter had earlier denied Jesus in Annas's cold courtyard—Peter replied, "Yes , , , I love you."

Jesus responded to Peter twice with a direct instruction about humility and service: "Feed my lambs. . . . Tend my sheep." The third time, however, Jesus gave a lengthy teaching to Peter in a lyrical passage that is the primary message of this account.

Its wise and lovely words counseled that the presumptuous autonomy of youth passes, and is replaced in maturity by stretching "out your hands, [when] . . . someone else will fasten a belt around you and take you where you do not wish to go." When we read these words in this gospel's context of their direct juxtaposition to Peter's thrice-made denial, and then when we recall Peter's subsequent story, a kind of tragically glorious beauty opens for us.

After his experiences with the resurrected Jesus, Peter stayed awhile in Jerusalem and then moved on to Rome, only to encounter the slaughter of the Messiahnians. He hastily left the city, but received a vision of the Christ as he fled, which caused him to return to Rome and die a martyr's death. Peter was indeed taken by his faith "where he did not wish to go"—yet despite his clear fears and misgivings, he made the choice to follow.

The complexity of this passage is wonderful. The first image of outstretched hands—open, seeking, willing—describes a mature soul not closed and settled in its ways. The deeper implication of the story is twofold: first, without the element of "asking," of willingness, there is no maturity; second, unless one asks, nothing will come.

The next words of this chapter are the more commonly noted. They form a powerful picture, rich with meaning. "Someone else will fasten a belt around you," Jesus began in his words to Peter. In first-century Israel, all men wore a large belt—about four inches wide—that cinched the tunic, an undergarment, in at the waist. It also provided a way to tuck the tunic up, still covering the loins and protecting modesty (hence, "girding one's loins"), when needed for less encumbered movement. The image of "belt," therefore, brought Jesus's instruction directly and explicitly into daily life.

This "belt" that "will come" also refers directly to one of the best-known passages of the Hebrew scriptures. Found in the book of Isaiah, the lyrical

verse addresses the qualities of the Messiah and the positive transformations his coming will cause within the community. The specifically relevant
section of the lengthy and beautiful passage follows. Note how many of
John's other important words are also present.

> He shall not judge by what his eyes see, or decide by what his ears hear;
> but with righteousness he shall judge the poor, and decide with equity for
> the meek of the earth; he shall strike the earth with the rod of his mouth,
> and with the breath of his lips he shall kill the wicked. Righteousness
> shall be the belt around his waist, and faithfulness the belt around his
> loins. The wolf shall live with lamb, the leopard shall lie down with the
> kid, the calf and the lion and the fatling together, and a little child shall
> lead them. (Isaiah 11:3b–6)

Of course, most Christian Ephesians would have been familiar with
the entire passage. In reading John's gospel, they would have instantly connected various words—"see," "breath," "lamb," and "belt"—with that earlier, beloved text. They would have understood that the Jewish heritage
of their Christian faith was long and honored. They would have seen that
Jesus had come to earth to carry that heritage forward in a new way. And
with these final words of this gospel, both they and centuries of readers
after them would have known that the new Jerusalem was a living reality.

> When they had gone ashore, they saw a charcoal fire there, with fish
> on it, and bread. Jesus said to them, "Bring some of the fish that you
> have just caught." So Simon Peter went aboard and hauled the net
> ashore, full of large fish, a hundred fifty-three of them; and though
> there were so many, the net was not torn. Jesus said to them, "Come
> and have breakfast." Now none of the disciples dared to ask him,
> "Who are you?" because they knew it was the Lord. Jesus came and
> took the bread and gave it to them, and did the same with the fish.
> This was now the third time that Jesus appeared to the disciples after
> he was raised from the dead. When they had finished breakfast, Jesus
> said to Simon Peter, "Simon son of John, do you love me more than
> these?" He said to him, "Yes, Lord; you know that I love you." Jesus
> said to him, "Feed my lambs." A second time he said to him, "Simon

son of John, do you love me?" He said to him, "Yes, Lord; you know
that I love you." Jesus said to him, "Tend my sheep." He said to him
the third time, "Simon son of John, do you love me?" Peter felt hurt
because he said to him the third time, "Do you love me?" And he said
to him, "Lord, you know everything; you know that I love you." Jesus
said to him, "Feed my sheep. Very truly, I tell you, when you were
younger, you used to fasten your own belt and to go wherever you
wished. But when you grow old, you will stretch out your hands, and
someone else will fasten a belt around you and take you where you do
not wish to go." (21:9–18)

REGARDLESS OF ANY questions about authorship, this final teaching of
John's gospel is both timely and joyous. We are at the close of the third
path, and despite all of our work and revelation, at this point on our Journey of Quadratos we remain immature and uncertain. Our arms are filled
with young blossoms. We have a vision, some concepts, some ideas, even
some deeper, budding sensibilities—but no real practice or maturity. The
possibility of falling back into fear and division is still a strong and constant
threat.

We must remain open and allow ourselves to be guided, according to
John's verse, as if "by a belt," whether or not the places we are taken are
where we wish to go, or even if we feel we have outgrown them. As we move
from the third to the fourth path, it is the Gospel of Luke that first opens
to receive our fragrant bouquet and then unfolds to gird us in a sturdy
belt. Words of inspiration and experience will guide us surely as we walk
its roads, and wisdom greater than ours will take us where we need to go.
If we are patient and true, we will continue to deepen. Eventually, we will
come to a day of the greatest peace and truth we have ever known—and
on that day we will smile as we gather our provisions and herald the day of
beginning once again.

Prayer as We Leave the Third Path

PSALM 122
Joy drenched me when you said
Come inside my house
Now our feet stand within your gates, Jerusalem
Planted upon your wholeness

Jerusalem,
Place where each is welcome
All belong

For this is the place
Toward which people ascend
Giving thanks with their mouths
Singing the thousand names of the nameless
And here stand the upright chairs of David's justice

Pray for the peace of Jerusalem
Pray that all who love her will be well
May there be peace within her walls
Plenty in her palaces

For the sake of all that lives and is
Let me speak these heart words:
Peace, peace,
Peace for Jerusalem

And for your sake
From inside your house
I pledge myself to seek the good

translation by Norman Fischer

EXERCISES FOR THE THIRD PATH

As we noted earlier, the exercises for quadratos are cumulative, each path building upon the next. The first path asked us to practice the principles of *establishing temenos* and *welcoming the heyoeka*. In this way we could begin to create safety and listen to the voices we were not accustomed to hearing. The second path asked us to practice *holding opposites in tension* and *accepting that deepening often results from difficulty*. The exercises for the third path build on these, though they, like the earlier exercises, are very worthwhile standing on their own. They come to us as we leave behind our exhaustion from the strain of opposites and arrive in an epiphany.

Receive the Epiphany

For most of us, the epiphany of the third path comes as gift. The experience is so exalted—obviously much larger than our small selves—that we feel it cannot come from any source other than from beyond—from Spirit, from God. Even those who struggle with the gift due to a sense of inadequacy feel the power of its source.

Our practice now is that which all the contemplatives and mystics speak of as a practice of *being*. This is not an experience we can summon, although it requires our fullest intention, and we can certainly encourage it. And then our work is to relax and understand that this is not a goal-oriented quest. We need to melt and receive the blossoming awareness into our bodies, minds, and hearts. The "doing" is simple.

Go outside. (If that isn't possible, seat yourself facing a window.) Sit comfortably, and for a period of no less than fifteen minutes, calmly and quietly notice your surroundings. Put your attention to as many details as you are able. Do this daily. Vary the times of day you sit. Observe the changes, daily, weekly, by season—in the outside and in yourself.

Expand Awareness of *Dia-bol*

The gift arrives in us so that we may gradually grow into a wider, more paradoxical and whole interior vision (remember: symbol—*sumballein,* "to throw two or more things together"). But in order to accomplish this work, the energy of the gift must first help us to deconstruct and cleanse the vestiges of our former beliefs and attitudes. This can take time, and involves our participation in a great deal of inner scrutiny. This is, therefore, our "stage two" exercise.

As we observe the beauty of the divine whole, if we are honest and faithful, inevitably we will also be able to discern the many aspects and voices within ourselves that still move stiffly and speak with the judgmental divisions of black and white. Gradually, we will develop the capacity to identify our own Nicodemus voice that has unreflectively accepted a belief because mother or father or the government or a book or some other authority figure said it was so.

As we wend our way through the third path, our practice is to continue our discovery of exactly how pervasive dualism is in our life via the keeping of a "John's Journal." Maintain your journal in writing or, if it is easier for you, through an audio or video recording. In your journal, chronicle every time you "catch" yourself in dualistic thinking or preconception. Make an entry every day. If an actual experience hasn't occurred, try to imagine one—with a friend, a family member, in business matters, at church, in politics—anything at all in your life. Think of your "normal" response, and honestly assess its degree of dualism. If it lacks the fluidity of John's great vision, meditate until you are able to discern a more creative solution, and enter that into your journal. Consider this little book a spiritual training manual.

HOW DO WE RECEIVE JOY?
is the core question of the Gospel of John

The exalted language of the Prologue proclaims a vision of the Christ and creation beyond time and announces the unity of all in All. This is the base on which our faith rests.

Cana's wedding feast reminds us that our call in the third path is the full enjoyment of the wedding celebration. We are in an epiphany, after all. Yet we should not confuse this with the full work of the marriage itself. That portion of the journey will open, and soon.

The great teaching discourses—the stories of Nicodemus, the woman at the well, the man born blind, and the raising of Lazarus—tell us that our inner fears can easily put a stop to our journey. The third path requires us to learn how to use new voices and quell the power of old, if we are to throw off our bindings and move into more vital life.

Jerusalem is Jeru-Shalom, a metaphor for our spiritual home where opposites are joined and our infinitely complex natures can find an original expression in harmony with ourselves and others.

The ritual of footwashing and the discourse on intimacy and union bring us face to face with our deepest issues of unworthiness, challenging us to reflect on what is really required for a relationship of intimacy—for communion. They also bring our burgeoning sensuality to the fore and force our acknowledgment of its equal partnership with our emotional and spiritual nature.

The gatherings in the gardens and the meeting with Pilate give a prescription for how we may mediate the voices of old and new as they arise within us. We need to be particularly mindful of the ways in which we are still immature and attached to unproductive people and behaviors.

Jesus's calm embrace of his crucifixion teaches us that when we are on a genuine journey and allow things to unfold within a context of wholeness, pain can open into an experience of deep meaning and transcendence.

The first resurrection appearance of Jesus the Christ tells us to be alert for the sound of our true name when it is called. Will we hear it? And when we do, what charge or mission does it convey?

The second and third appearances of Jesus the Christ are lessons to us about maintaining our spiritual balance. Are we able to free our hearts from judgment and blame of others? Are we able to see and sustain a balance between matter and spirit? Between doubt and faith?

The fourth appearance of Jesus the Christ is about how we move forward into the fourth path, and beyond. Will we be able to stay open and remember that we will always need to receive appropriate guidance as we continue our journey?

6

. . .

Walking Luke's Road of Riches

COLEMAN'S BED*
Make a nesting now, a place to which
the birds can come, think of Kevin's
prayerful palm holding the blackbird's egg
and be the one, looking out from this place
who warms interior forms into light.
Feel the way the cliff at your back
gives shelter to your outward view
and then bring in from those horizons
all discordant elements that seek a home.

Be taught now, among the trees and rocks,
how the discarded is woven into shelter,
learn the way things hidden and unspoken
slowly proclaim their voice in the world.
Find that far inward symmetry
to all outward appearances, apprentice
yourself to yourself, begin to welcome back

---

* This poem references two sixth-century Irish saints. St. Coleman, a bishop, was known for his talent as bard and poet. St. Kevin, a charismatic teacher and animal lover, was so dedicated to his own spiritual growth that he, among others, inspired the Irish monastic movement.

all you sent away, be a new annunciation,
make yourself a door through which
to be hospitable, even to the stranger in you.

See with every turning day,
how each season makes a child
of you again, wants you to become
a seeker after rainfall and birdsong,
watch now, how it weathers you
to a testing in the tried and true,
admonishes you with each falling leaf,
to be courageous, to be something
that has come through, to be the last thing
you want to see before you leave the world.

Above all, be alone with it all,
a hiving off, a corner of silence
amidst the noise, refuse to talk,
even to yourself, and stay in this place
until the current of the story
is strong enough to float you out.

Ghost then, to where others
in this place have come before,
under the hazel, by the ruined chapel,
below the cave where Coleman slept,
become the source that makes
the river flow, and then the sea
beyond. Live in this place
as you were meant to and then,
surprised by your abilities,
become the ancestor of it all,
the quiet, robust and blessed Saint
that your future happiness
will always remember.

David Whyte

The Fourth Path:
How Do We Mature in Service?

The fourth path makes it possible for all our childhood dreams—and our adult hopes and aspirations—to become realities. Is your desire to find, give, and receive love? Know true friendship? Be a person of respect to yourself and others? Learn how to live with both strength and equanimity despite the travails that life gives you? Be at peace when you contemplate your life—and death? These are the riches promised—and delivered—by the fourth path of quadratos. One would think everyone on the planet would be lining up to walk down this road. Instead, the fourth path is largely neglected and often omitted as a formal part of most spiritual and psychological processes. Unsurprisingly, it is misunderstood by the very people who most need its wisdom.

There is a widespread belief among teachers of religion, spirituality, and psychology that, once revelation has been experienced, a transformed life will naturally follow. After all, once we have that precious epiphany, we *know* that God is Love, and God loves us, and All is One. Or, in psychology, we gain the insight that frees us of the burdens of unearned shame, and the larger pattern of our life is revealed. It is assumed that with such knowledge, a person's greatest trials are over and that, given a bit of gentle shepherding, everything will somehow proceed naturally in a positive direction. All it will take is simply thinking about our new understandings (with maybe a bit of reading and talking and some meditating), and we will become "self-aware," "self-actualized," "spirit-filled," a "true Christian," etc., etc. The vocabulary varies, but the unrealistic expectations at this juncture are consistent—and they are always wrong and very often tragic.

The problem is that no fundamental change actually occurred in the third path. We had a wonderful revelatory moment, but it has thus far served only one purpose. It has made us more conscious. We have become aware that it is possible for our feelings, our thoughts, and our attitudes—even our daily lives—to change. However, our egos are still in an immature state. They are struggling to evolve through fragile new understandings, but they are completely unequipped to help us deal successfully with our fourth-path challenges. Our old ego patterns are still controlling many of our core emotions and exerting powerful influences on our behavior.

Nonetheless, filled with new energy and excitement about our fresh insights, we confidently stride out of the safety of the third path's garden and into what we are certain will be our renewed and joyous life. However, the realities of the fourth path—real life—come charging straight at us the minute we take our first steps. If we are lucky, that onslaught will merely take the form of a minor crisis. More often, though, what we experience will be closer to some sort of crushing opposition in our lives. To meet this opposition constructively will require a mature, seasoned response and a practical application of the principles of paradoxical union that were revealed to us in the third path. Unfortunately, we haven't yet reached the level in our journey that will enable us to muster a response of that order.

Our still small ego-self has only *tasted* a new way; it hasn't yet transformed itself into maturity, or even had a chance to practice being mature. So what happens when our crisis hits? The ego-self tries to address the problem, to protect itself in the best way it knows how. Its first and most compelling instinct is to get rid of anxiety, as quickly as possible, because it assumes anxiety is a threat. And at this point, the ego knows how to accomplish this only by a return to its earlier, more accustomed pattern—that is, making a judgment, or taking action, through a selection of one of the available opposites presented. In our discussion of the third path, we called this *dia-bol,* choosing half of the union over the other—light over dark, up over down, left over right, masculine over feminine, rote over original, or vice versa. The most common model is our choice of whatever we perceive is right over wrong. If our "old ways" used to externalize our problems and point fingers at others, this will be what our ego will likely turn to now when it looks for solutions. If we used to abandon unity and our own self by internalizing our fear and going into depression, that same avoidance will call out to us again. *Dia-bol's* long list of possible ways to elude anxiety is almost endless.

This presents us with a new emotional dilemma. We learned in the third path that we need to resist these divisions, yet we have no real idea exactly how to do so. Most people give in to their confusion and discomfort at this point and retreat backward if they are not consciously on the Journey of Quadratos. The quandary proves too much for them, and they choose a familiar behavior from the second path—or even the first. And after their ego makes some choice of avoidance, it then covers the decision up with a denial system. Psychology calls this "rationalizing." The ensuing untruths created by the cover-ups and the denials proliferate. In fact, the reason many of us feel we live in an unsatisfactory world is largely a result of the number of people engaging in this avoidance and denial behavior over and over and over again. All those untruths add up. If, however, we make a decision to walk ahead on the fourth path, the crises we meet cannot be covered up. Why? Because transparency and learning to confront our dilemmas directly are part of the process of maturity.

As we stand in the courage of our journey—remaining steadfast in the times of our inner discomfort, praying, and using Luke's gospel—we begin to fully engage the fourth path. Although when we stepped ahead in faith, the path opened in crisis, we learn that that powerful onslaught may actually serve a purpose. Any overexaltation or arrogance we might have had needs to be tempered now, because "Go slowly" is the very first counsel we receive from Luke. We are asked to shelter our revelation, newly birthed, so that Spirit can nestle deeply, making her home in us comfortable and her course to our inner selves wide and unobstructed. In this way, the messages of Spirit can live side by side with those of the ever-chattering, control-driven intellect and receive equal attention. We discover that when Mystery is our inbreath, our ego-self will find it easier to quiet and be more patient.

The time does come, however, when Luke firmly instructs us to step out of shelter and grow active in the building of our new lives. This is how we find the answer to the fourth path's core question: How do we mature in service? As we move outward, our journey becomes a tumultuous and passionate adventure in discovering how to recognize and seize our strengths and navigate our relationships. At times, we undergo rigorous testing. Occasionally, this feels as perilous as crossing a deep chasm on a tightrope with no net beneath us. At other times, the gospel counsels us in a slower and more repetitious fashion. But the lessons are always available for us to use according to our unique needs and rhythms. We have setbacks, and our increased awareness causes these to be more painful than before; but at the same time, we are happily sensitized to surpassing bliss, thanks to our third-path epiphanies. Therefore, no matter what difficulties we encounter, we find many more times of joy than we have ever known to be possible.

Gradually, as we walk this path, we learn how to express our singular and completely original life in a way that serves us—and others. With the help of Matthew and Mark we kicked away the sharp rocks of our past. Now Luke suggests that we recover some of those "flaws"—reexamine them, understand and accept them as valuable and even beautiful foundational pieces of our history. We find ways in which we can build a place of homestead for our genuine life that shelters the full family of our inner self. The unruly child in us has a place to play, and the quiet child, a place to dream. The adult has space for joy, exercise, passion, action, thought, anger, challenge, and the expression of beauty. The sage of all seasons has space for prayer and making amends and service. Even the rebellious teenager is welcomed. As we honor and commit to protect the infinity of our richness, we recognize that this infinity is, indeed, the solid basis on which our inner peace is built.

Self-acceptance of our own originality, and our comfort with it, readily moves outward. We feel less overwhelmed and threatened by diversity of all kinds. We begin to discern previously unseen variances, and then we see the opportunities within them. The outside world becomes a kaleidoscope of flashing possibilities that open to us in ways we could not previously have imagined—in friendships, jobs, and varieties of networks at all levels.

The path of true service simultaneously begins to open in our lives. Having become more compassionate with ourselves, we naturally carry that into relationships with others. The ways in which we respect each other, take action, negotiate, join, separate, and perform service change dramatically. We help our neighbors whenever we can be of assistance and invite them to visit and help *us*—although many of us find that reciprocity very difficult. However, we have come to understand that genuine service, like real relationships, must move in two directions. Gradually, the practice of respect and compassion in our interactions fills our lives with the pragmatic truth that we cannot deprive others of even the smallest freedom and still insist on our own. It is these lessons that hold the seeds of real solutions to our present-day dilemmas—in communities and institutions (including our churches), in countries, and between nations.

Birthplace of the Gospel of Luke: Great Antioch and the Roman Empire, Mid-80s CE

The precise location of origin is not certain with this gospel, but it is highly likely that we find ourselves once again in the city of Great Antioch on the Orontes. Scholarship indicates that Luke probably wrote from the same city where Matthew had written his gospel a decade or so earlier.

In Matthew's time, remember, Messianic Jews were still part of Judaism, and his gospel concerned itself with the pain of these Jews whose center—the Great Temple and the priestly lineage—had been lost. Luke, believed to have been a companion of Paul and a seasoned follower, almost certainly knew Matthew's gospel well; indeed, he had likely preached from it. Matthew's gospel addressed a single community, as did those of Mark and John. Luke, however—writing later than Matthew and Mark (though before John), as Christianity was evolving and spreading—directed his message to multiple groups throughout the Mediterranean region. These communities, only beginning to call themselves Christians, had endured a series of dramatic events in the previous decade, and despite their deep faith and fervor, they found themselves troubled by high levels of pain and resentment.

To understand this fully, we need to briefly review some history. Nero had executed the Jewish Christus followers of Rome twenty years earlier, although persecution had not extended to Christus believers throughout the rest of the empire at that time. Then in 70 CE, Vespasian leveled the Great Temple of Jerusalem and massacred all its priests, throwing Judaism into total disarray. In the steps that religion took to survive, a process began that still resonates in the lives of Christians and Jews.

The slaughter resulted in a complete lack of religious authority. The Pharisees, educated teachers of Jewish religious law but not officially connected to the Temple, stepped into the vacuum. By the mid-80s CE, the time of Luke's gospel, their role had significantly increased. In many Jewish communities, their voices rose to roles of clear leadership. In others, they represented merely one of many voices struggling to advise how best to move forward in the face of great loss. Eventually, the Pharisees became the primary voice of the Jewish community, reunifying the people in the absence of the Temple and its priests—but not before Luke began to write.

When the Temple stood, all important rituals were hosted there, and only priests officiated at them. After the Temple fell, all rituals were forced to change dramatically. The Pharisees helped to rebuild a new Judaism that centered on home and synagogue life, with larger roles for the family and the rabbi. As one example, Seder—the Feast of Passover—had always been a family meal accompanied by an informal retelling of the Jews' coming out of Egypt. Indeed, it was this simple evening meal that Jesus shared with his disciples before the crucifixion. Now it became more formal. Special, symbolic ingredients were designated, as was the sequence of the service and the manner of the retelling. In the 80s, Jews started to write down and systematize these changes, making it certain that their faith would survive with its solemnity and resonance intact, despite the loss of its hierarchy.

The Pharisees took a further step. Their objective was surely the health and survival of their ancient faith and tribe, and we must assume they believed that wisdom and necessity guided their actions. Nonetheless, the results of the harsh decision they made are with us yet today.

The Pharisees advocated for the removal from Judaism of all variant sects who believed that the Messiah had already come. Chief among these were the "Followers of the Way" (the Christus sect), who maintained that the Messiah had arrived for the salvation of all people, not just Jews. Further, these Christus followers persisted in talking about their beliefs to anyone who would listen, complicating what the Pharisees were working so hard to rebuild. To the Pharisees, these upstarts presented a serious problem, for every convert to Christus belief represented a direct threat to their efforts to sustain traditional Judaism.

The Followers of the Way did not leave their religious home quietly or even voluntarily. The Pharisees reacted by arguing for forcible removal and shunning of the sect. Those communities with strong pharisaical influence followed these recommendations. Communities and families were confused and filled with pain by the debate, even if they didn't formally eject the group.

Worse still, the Pharisees wrote a formal curse—making the banishment unmistakably clear—and recommended that it be added to the close of every Shabbat service. Its words entreated God to bring his wrath down on anyone who believed that the Messiah had come. Anyone who failed to recite this curse aloud at the end of the service was deemed suspect, further fracturing all trust. The family of Abraham was rent asunder by these spiritually shattering events and filled with pain, anger, bitterness, resentment, and self-pity. Amidst this upheaval, the Gospel of Luke was born.

Luke's audience was reluctantly but surely coming to understand that they were being severed from Judaism. They proudly called themselves Followers of the Way, or of the Christus, but were relatively inexperienced as religious communities. They had faith and strength—and no small amount of zealotry. They carried pain, and some of them likely had a touch of arrogance attached to their lingering resentments. They had also migrated all over the Mediterranean basin, which presented them with persecution from another quarter. The Roman government was more than nervous about the Christus followers—it was terror-stricken.

The Roman Empire had skillfully used the ancient tribal antipathies of the Mediterranean world first to conquer, and then to maintain dominance. The mutual distrust of the people it ruled was the primary way in which the empire ensured the stability of its far-flung realms. However, as we discussed in our chapter on John, the egalitarian principle of Christianity overturned the tribal beliefs and customs that led to conflict—and, therefore, threatened the entire structure of the Roman Empire. Rome's fear of this message led to its oppression of the Christus communities—and the persecution increased steadily.

Although some scholars believe that the Gospel of Luke was written to a high Roman official in defense of Christianity, others think it was a teaching written in Antioch designed to be distributed among these burgeoning communities across the Mediterranean world. Because of its style and its content, the latter view seems more obvious—this gospel is a clear "how to" manual.

How were the nascent "Followers of the Way" to move forward in the face of being cursed by the Pharisees, abandoned by most of their Jewish friends, and oppressed by the Roman Empire? How could they deal with the hurt and resentments that threatened to poison their lives and divide their families? Should they verbally dispute and defend themselves against each hurt? Should they take up arms and fight? Should they hold to traditional practices? Did the Christ ask them to develop new and original ways? And if yes, what precisely were those new ways in actual practice in their lives?

The Gospel of Luke gives answers to these questions based on the teachings of Jesus, which were radical for their time. Luke draws a stark spiritual line, using his gospel to focus on spiritual maturation. He instructs the Followers of the Way to stringently challenge themselves, speak their truth boldly, yet maintain inner equanimity and avoid self-righteousness. Faced with opposition on all sides, the course Jesus taught in Luke's gospel was for the Christus believers to "be" peace, rather than taking up arms or trying to effect change through anger. This gospel is filled with instructions about growing into the capacity for mature relationships and compassion and generosity without boundaries. The transcendent and enduring parables of the Good Samaritan and the Prodigal Son are found only in the Gospel of Luke.

Luke knew these were the pragmatic lessons that would help the zealous new believers to not only survive, but to grow beyond their zealotry. Luke invites the emerging faith into a great adventure of Spirit—a journey of healing, examination, and transformation. He challenges Christianity to cross into unknown lands and thrive, despite social and communal bitterness and legal persecution.

Approaching Luke Today: Walking the Road

As we walk through the fourth path and the Gospel of Luke, we are moved in every direction. From the first huge setback most of us hit, to our time of quiet shelter, through our continuing trials—and errors—we are often unsure of our direction and only know that we are committed to carry on. Gradually, profoundly, and perhaps with a bit of surprise, we begin to realize that our struggles have not been just for our own sakes at all. The true questions appear: Whom does the grace we have received serve? How may we bring this grace to everyday life, relationships, and family? When our personal or communal values are challenged, what do we do? What is the proper use of our new strength and courage?

True answers to these questions do not come quickly or easily. Indeed, they will require us to enflesh the way of Jesus the Christ. We will have to be compassionate and fearless—perhaps even act unconventionally in the face of misunderstanding and direct opposition. Since the Journey of

Quadratos is about maturing into spiritual transformation, it now becomes very clear why the early church put the Gospel of Luke fourth in the reading sequence. This is a series of teachings specifically designed to expand on the basic truths of the other gospels and to establish a discipline that moves them into everyday life. It is also a much fuller story of Jesus's life, from his conception through his death and resurrection. Unlike any of the other gospels, it tells of Jesus's childhood, describing how he "grew in grace and truth." It is, in itself, an account of spiritual maturation.

If we are able to continue in this path—or, like the apostle Peter, recover and come back to the path—we discover new moral realizations and a shining courage. As we will learn as we study this gospel, Luke employs the word "heart" throughout as an integrated image of mind/body/spirit. We learn that we can act from our hearts in this expanded sense and, when we do, it frees us in a radical way. We experience the power that comes with speaking and acting from the divine in us joined to our inner truth. Not only do we discover that others receive us differently, but our fears diminish—even disappear. We no longer carry the fear of failure—of being thought badly of, or being shunned, or betrayed—or the fear of loss; nor are we burdened by the contrary fear of success.

Luke knows that epiphany is of no value in isolation; for that reason, teaching the myriad ways of mature service is his goal. He accomplishes this largely through the structure of his gospel. Almost every important event takes place "on the road," on the land between destinations. This is precisely the same way we mature in the process of our lives—in between experiences and places. Although Luke is supportive of his readers' fervent beliefs, he is well aware that no one bursts fully formed—wholly integrated—into a mature spiritual life. His use of "road" is, therefore, a precise metaphor for this lengthy, and often frustrating, time of inner exploration and outer practice.

Though the words seem paradoxical, as we become comfortable with an unceasing process of growth, the road eventually reaches its destination within us. We learn to relax and accept our place as part of the continuous process and pattern of Mystery—which will never cast us out—and absorb the strength that knowledge gives us. As we do, we increasingly act to accept our responsibilities as part of the Whole. In this way, we genuinely help transform the world, since most of the horrors created by humankind that happen on this planet occur only in the complicity of our silence or non-action. Our burdens therefore increase—but likewise our joys and our relationships, as well as our opportunities for action and empowerment and service.

Additionally, we can surmise, while reading the Gospel of Luke, that the author studied other gospels and texts and learned well from them. We believe, for example, that Luke was a disciple of Paul. We will see that their words often share a zealous, ardent style. This almost certainly suited the enthusiasm of Luke's readers. We can also find many places where Luke repeats large sections almost verbatim from the Gospel of Matthew; but, as we will see, the "almost" is significant, because Luke brings these accounts to different conclusions in every instance. Although Luke predates John (so he could not have read that gospel), he uses one similar technique, often reframing Jewish tradition, making Christianity, naturally, the more open and charitable option. Also similar to John, Luke's resentment against the Pharisees sometimes overwhelms him, and the resulting strident tones, such as a curse or berating text derived from Matthew, sit in odd contradiction to sublime teachings about openness and generosity. These inconsistencies, like those in John's gospel, serve as examples of human struggles in the midst of deep inspiration.

We will examine the gospel in three sections: its opening stories (including the angel Gabriel's appearance to Zechariah and Mary), the nativity, and the account of Jesus in the Temple as a young boy; the middle section, containing "the lessons"; and finally, the Passion and the resurrection accounts. As we read, observe how the straightforward language is perfectly suited to this pragmatic phase of our journey. Note how Luke's almost circuitous style of storytelling holds the rhythm of walking the path, footfall upon footfall, again and again. This is exactly how we will learn to put these lessons firmly into our lives—with practice and more practice, building habits upon which we can call even in crisis. The first three paths of quadratos are the (relatively) fast ones. Luke's road holds the greatest riches, but it is also the road of patience and persistence.

A Valuable Mirror: The Acts of the Apostles

The original second half of the Gospel of Luke is known as "The Acts of the Apostles," or what some contemporary authors refer to as "The Book of Mission." Originally, Luke and Acts were considered a single body of work—the lengthiest in the Christian Testament. Acts tells of the apostles Peter and Paul and their lives of service, and reflects many of the same themes found in Luke. It does not appear that Acts was read as a gospel text in any of the ancient Sunday cycles, nor is it found in the contemporary Sunday sequences. However, Acts does have a place of distinction. Some of its passages are read before the gospel text over the Sundays of the Easter Season.

Since it is not in the reading cycle, Acts has not been incorporated as a formal part of quadratos and is not included in this book. However, the original intent of both of these volumes—Luke and Acts—was that they work together seamlessly. They have a strikingly similar thematic sequence and development, and can be of great value to us. We suggest that you read the two volumes side by side if you wish to add additional richness to your journey. For example, read the first two chapters of Luke and then read the first two chapters of Acts. You will discover that they mirror each other, and that what happens with Jesus in Luke happens with Peter and Paul in Acts. By using the two volumes, we see a picture of maturation that moves back and forth from disciple to apostle—from learning to serving—the same roles that are true for all followers of the Way of the Christ.

The Gospel of Luke: The Opening Stories

The Salutation

Luke's opening salutation to "most excellent Theophilus" has caused great conjecture among scholars. Theophilus translates as "lover of God." However, the words "most excellent" suggest that Luke may have been addressing a wealthy, well-educated Roman official, inviting speculation that this gospel is an apologia for Christianity. In contrast, it has also been proposed that the intention was a generic salutation to *all* "lovers of God." Despite the controversy, the Gospel of Luke is not a letter at all. It is clearly a book—speaking to the challenges of the early Christians and the great opposition they were facing—and its style differs startlingly from the other gospels. This is no document of great pronouncements. Rather, though interspersed with zealotry, it is almost chatty. By recounting stories that hold contradictions—and particularly the contravening of convention—Luke encourages his readers to wrestle with ambiguity and to elevate their moral sense.

> Since many have undertaken to set down an orderly account of the
> events that have been fulfilled among us, just as they were handed
> on to us by those who from the beginning were eyewitnesses and
> servants of the word, I too decided, after investigating everything
> carefully from the very first, to write an orderly account for you, most
> excellent Theophilus, so that you may know the truth concerning the
> things about which you have been instructed. (1:1–4)

Willingness and Silence: Zechariah and Elizabeth and Mary

Immediately after saluting Theophilus, Luke tells the story of Zechariah and Elizabeth, descended from priestly and royal lineage, and thus "elevated" in Jewish society. Despite this status, however, their community assumed them to be sinners because they were childless—a clear indication of God's disfavor. In the Semitic culture of the day, Elizabeth's barrenness was certainly a matter of the deepest shame for the couple (and we can be certain that tongues wagged and gossip raged to discover their presumed sins); but in fact, Zechariah and Elizabeth were upright and blameless—merely childless.

One day, while Zechariah was serving at the Temple, the angel Gabriel came to him, promising that a child, a son, would finally be his, and that the boy would grow up to be very important in Jewish history. Zechariah, though he must have been delighted with the news, was terrified of the angel and reacted with doubt to the prophecy. Gabriel responded to Zechariah's lack of belief with immediate punishment. He rendered the new father mute and thus incapable of sharing the news of his great gift. Elizabeth, for her part, went into seclusion for five months as soon as she became aware of her conception.

The dearth of community support suffered by Zechariah and Elizabeth mirrored the predicament of the Christus communities. They, too, had been faithful followers of a holy journey and had received the announcement of a great birth—a grace to be made visible in their lives. But Judaism, their historical family, had been unable to understand or appreciate that experience. Instead, their faith family had responded with curses and shunning.

This is an extremely pointed story—particularly with which to open the gospel. Luke is telling his readers to temper their zeal. "Stop and think," he counsels. "No matter what joy is in your heart, be silent for a time. Gather wisdom before you speak." Both Zechariah and Elizabeth exemplify the virtues of husbanding an experience and allowing it to grow and mature before it is offered up publicly. Luke knows that euphoria needs time to settle. Resentment from others—which may fester and cannot quickly be overcome—is to be expected. The wise course requires patience.

In the days of King Herod of Judea, there was a priest named Zechariah, who belonged to the priestly order of Abijah. His wife was a descendant of Aaron, and her name was Elizabeth. Both of them were righteous before God, living blamelessly according to all the commandments and regulations of the Lord. But they had no children, because Elizabeth was barren, and both were getting on in years. Once when he was serving as priest before God and his section was on duty, he was chosen by lot, according to the custom of the priesthood, to enter the sanctuary of the Lord and offer incense. Now at the time of the incense offering, the whole assembly of the people was praying outside. Then there appeared to him an angel of the Lord, standing at the right side of the altar of incense. When Zechariah saw him, he was terrified; and fear overwhelmed him. But the angel said to him, "Do not be afraid, Zechariah, for your prayer has been heard. Your wife Elizabeth will bear you a son, and you will name him John. You will have joy and gladness, and many will rejoice at his birth, for he will be great in the sight of the Lord. He must never drink wine or strong drink; even before his birth he will be filled with the Holy Spirit. He will turn many of the people of Israel to the Lord their God. With the spirit and power of Elijah he will go before him, to turn the hearts of parents to their children, and the disobedient to the wisdom of the righteous, to make ready a people prepared for the Lord." Zechariah said to the angel, "How will I know that this is so? For I am an old man, and my wife is getting on in years." The angel replied, "I am Gabriel. I stand in the presence of God, and I have been sent to speak to you and to bring you this good news. But now, because you did not believe my words, which will be fulfilled in their time, you will become mute, unable to speak, until the day these things occur." Meanwhile the people were waiting for Zechariah, and wondered at his delay in the sanctuary. When he did come out, he could not speak to them, and they realized that he had seen a vision in the sanctuary. He kept motioning to them and remained unable to speak. When his time of service was ended, he went to his home. After those days his wife Elizabeth conceived, and for five months she remained in seclusion. She said, "This is what the Lord has done for me when he looked favorably on me and took away the disgrace I have endured among my people." (1:5–25)

The name of the angel Gabriel is extremely significant in Luke's gospel. Nowhere else in the four gospels is an angel identified by name. Gabriel means "God is my strength" in Hebrew, and derives from the traditional Jewish belief that there are four angels who always surround us. Rafael stands behind and represents healing; Oriel stands in front of us and represents knowledge; Michael is at our right hand and stands for mercy; and Gabriel—power and judgment—is at our left.

Therefore, when Luke invokes the name Gabriel in these deeply cautionary accounts, he emphasizes to the Christus community that the *power* of the Jewish faith has not abandoned them, even if the Jewish *community* seemingly has. They can rest assured that they carry God's strength with them into their new lives, and thus they will be protected.

In the same chapter, the angel Gabriel next appeared to Mary and told her that she would give birth to a son she should name Jesus. Mary did not understand how this could be true, because she remained a virgin. Though she questioned Gabriel, she was not frightened, and unlike Zechariah, she did not challenge the prophecy. Her response appears to have been more an expression of curiosity; she was completely accepting of the prediction, despite her lack of understanding. She wondered how events would unfold, but fully accepted their happening. Still, she chose not to speak of the impending birth. She joined Elizabeth in seclusion for three months, until her baby was viable, afterward returning home. Luke uses the opportunity to strongly reiterate his point: "Even for a gift as great as the birth of the Messiah," he seems to say, "my advice would be to stay silent and allow time for the seed to mature before you speak or act."

In Matthew's gospel, it was Joseph who received the prediction about Jesus's birth from an unnamed angel. In fact, the entire birth narrative revolved around Joseph and his predicament and his actions. In Luke's gospel, however, Joseph receives only a mention. Everything here—the announcement and, as we will see, the subsequent nativity story—focuses on Mary.

> In the sixth month the angel Gabriel was sent by God to a town in Galilee called Nazareth, to a virgin engaged to a man whose name was Joseph, of the house of David. The virgin's name was Mary. And he came to her and said, "Greetings, favored one! The Lord is with you." But she was much perplexed by his words and pondered what sort of greeting this might be. The angel said to her, "Do not be afraid, Mary, for you have found favor with God. And now, you will conceive in your womb and bear a son, and you will name him Jesus. He will be great, and will be called the Son of the Most High, and the Lord God will give to him the throne of his ancestor David. He will reign over the house of Jacob forever, and of his kingdom there will be no end." Mary said to the angel, "How can this be, since I am a virgin?" The angel said to her, "The Holy Spirit will come upon you, and the power of the Most High will overshadow you; therefore the child to be born will be holy; he will be called Son of God. And now, your relative Elizabeth in her old age has also conceived a son; and this is the sixth month for her who was said to be barren. For nothing will be impossible with God." Then Mary said, "Here am I, the servant of the Lord; let it be with me according to your word." Then the angel departed from her. (1:26–38)

Mary went to visit Elizabeth in her seclusion-place in Judea. When greeted, Mary responded to Elizabeth in verses that form a hymn of praise commonly called the Canticle of Mary. The words are lovely, but the most interesting part about them, spiritually and psychologically, is their grammatical tense. They speak of a future time, of circumstances that Mary hopes will come to pass—yet they are written in declarative present and past tense, as though the events they describe have already taken place, giving the beauteous prose the voice of one who walks in the equanimity of total faith, seeing the future as already inevitable and perfected. The way this hymn is written makes it the prayer and practice of one who holds a clear, positive vision of the future. Anyone who reads and prays these words is challenged to find an inner spiritual level that matches their serenity, which is clearly Luke's intention. Luke hopes that his audience will be able to use Mary and her prayer as a model from which to derive strength.

> In those days Mary set out and went with haste to a Judean town
> in the hill country, where she entered the house of Zechariah and
> greeted Elizabeth. (1:39–40)

> And Mary said,
> "My soul magnifies the Lord, and my spirit rejoices in God my Savior,
> For he has looked with favor on the lowliness of his servant.
> Surely, from now on all generations will call me blessed;
> For the Mighty One has done great things for me, and holy is his name.
> His mercy is for those who fear him from generation to generation.
> He has shown strength with his arm;
> He has scattered the proud in the thoughts of their hearts.
> He has brought down the powerful from their thrones,
> And lifted up the lowly;
> He has filled the hungry with good things,
> And sent the rich away empty.
> He has helped his servant Israel,
> In remembrance of his mercy,
> According to the promise he made to our ancestors,
> To Abraham and to his descendants forever." (1:46–55)

Welcome the Unfamiliar: The Nativity Account

The nativity story is distinctive in Luke's gospel. The author uses it to illustrate another profound spiritual practice. In Luke's account, Joseph and Mary lived in Nazareth in times that were both civilly and religiously oppressive. Authorities ordered them to Bethlehem for "census taking."

Unlike the nativity in Matthew's gospel, where a star announced Jesus's birth, and where the illustrious Magi followed that star and were adoring witnesses who paid homage, here we find no comfortable home birth. In Luke's account, Mary and Joseph were forced to leave home and travel when Mary was near to term. They didn't even have the shelter of an inn. Instead, Jesus was born in a stable, implying a rough, open building that housed animals. His tiny body rested in a manger, or feedbox. The environment could not have been more raw, instinctual, uncomfortable—or unconventional.

The stable as birthplace was an apt metaphor for Luke's readers. They, too, had been cast out of their original home, and hospitality in their new environment was meager. But Luke challenges them to transcend their bitterness and resentment. He asks them to see that their uncomfortable new circumstances are the perfect, powerful, and perhaps even *destined* way that the Christ can be born in them.

Luke tells of an angel that announced Jesus's birth to shepherds in the nighttime fields. But when he writes of shepherds, he certainly does not mean those passive fellows leaning on their crooks or carrying a lamb that we see in crèche scenes at Christmastime. In the first century, shepherds were outcasts, people who had few skills, no resources, and little family. Feared, they lived lives of near starvation, isolated from regular society. Our present equivalent might be the marginalized long-term homeless. Fairly or unfairly, they were considered to be an unstable element, potentially thieving and dangerous. In this scene they represent an extremely uncouth presence. Yet—in a detail recounted only in Luke's gospel—the angel who announced Jesus's birth came to these lowly and unwanted people, not just to accept them, but to honor them and rejoice with them. Notably, they were also the only witnesses of Jesus's birth. As for Mary, although she is clearly the central figure in the scene, she remained silent throughout, as she had during her pregnancy, holding her experience "in her heart."

Even though the births in the Gospels of Matthew and Luke differ so greatly, spiritually and psychologically, both are profoundly true. Matthew is writing to Messianic Jews, still in their "home" faith. Luke writes to Christus believers who felt as though they had been cast out onto a lonely road and were surrounded by predators. Matthew's charge is to hold trust and courage and to "begin anew" no matter what. Luke reminds his readers that their seeming exile offers the perfect conditions for the Christ's birth in them. He encourages them to be curious about the place in which they now find themselves—this rough home on the road—and to rejoice in their blessings, knowing that their future is bright.

In Luke, the baby Jesus is twice referred to as "wrapped in bands of cloth"—or swaddled—held secure, with strips of fabric binding his arms and legs. This is a great metaphor for the newly "birthed" communities, who are equally held securely by the divine truths of their faith. Luke is teaching about the need to focus on basics. It is not a time for wandering about or reckless speech. It is the time for protecting the infant Christians as they grow in faith, in effect "traveling away" from their original home. Once again, Luke's counsel is to ponder and move out slowly.

In those days a decree went out from Emperor Augustus that all the world should be registered. This was the first registration and was taken while Quirinius was governor of Syria. All went to their own towns to be registered. Joseph also went from the town of Nazareth in Galilee to Judea, to the city of David called Bethlehem, because he was descended from the house and family of David. He went to be registered with Mary, to whom he was engaged and who was expecting a child. While they were there, the time came for her to deliver her child. And she gave birth to her firstborn son and wrapped him in bands of cloth, and laid him in a manger, because there was no place for them in the inn. In that region there were shepherds living in the fields, keeping watch over their flock by night. Then an angel of the Lord stood before them, and the glory of the Lord shone around them, and they were terrified. But the angel said to them, "Do not be afraid; for see—I am bringing you good news of great joy for all the people: to you is born this day in the city of David a Savior, who is the Messiah, the Lord. This will be a sign for you: you will find a child wrapped in bands of cloth and lying in a manger." And suddenly there was with the angel a multitude of the heavenly host, praising God and saying, "Glory to God in the highest heaven, and on earth peace among those whom he favors!" When the angels had left them and gone into heaven, the shepherds said to one another, "Let us go now to Bethlehem and see this thing that has taken place, which the Lord has made known to us." So they went with haste and found Mary and Joseph, and the child lying in the manger. When they saw this, they made known what had been told them about this child; and all who heard it were amazed at what the shepherds told them. But Mary treasured all these words and pondered them in her heart. (2:1–19)

A Quality of Heart: The Boy Jesus in the Temple

The sole place in the entire gospels to tell of Jesus in his childhood follows. Luke recounts that in the year Jesus was twelve years old, Joseph and Mary, accompanied by many other faithful Jews, took him on their annual expedition to Jerusalem to celebrate Passover. On the return, Jesus somehow managed to stay behind. His parents, assuming he was with others in the crowd, were completely unaware he was missing. When they realized he was gone, they hurried back to the city to find him. They found Jesus in the Temple, intently questioning the teachers there.

This account is particularly fascinating as a demonstration of Luke's ability to delicately balance sensitive emotional realities, because Luke uses it as a metaphor for the young Christus community. We know this because a literal reading is clearly not fruitful—a twelve-year-old would have been deemed too young to converse in the Temple. In this story, Jesus referred to the Temple respectfully as his "Father's house." He was found there, on the cusp of adulthood, by his parents. He then left the Jewish Temple and, as Luke describes it, subsequently matured in age and spiritual understanding. Luke is saying that the Christus followers, who also began in Judaism, should honor their early foundation, but should realize that their genuine strength and maturity is found in the present—after having left their home faith.

When Luke refers to Mary watching her son's maturation, Luke is again counseling patience, noting that every stage is important and none can be skipped. This chapter reiterates Luke's earlier advice to ponder and reflect, still using Mary as the focus, saying that she "treasured these things in her heart."

Luke not only uses the word "heart" twice as many times in this gospel as do any of the other gospel writers, but he uses it differently. In Matthew and Mark, Jesus speaks about the quality of "heart" in those who follow or do not follow. John recognizes that strong emotion is necessary to balance intellect, but uses the word "grief" to express this principle. Luke prefers the word "heart," perhaps because of its well-established Jewish antecedents. However, Jesus—in Luke's account—does not speak the word "heart" himself. Luke uses it to exemplify the character and attitudes of Jesus's followers: twice with respect to Mary (here and at the nativity); with John at the river; in chapters six, eighteen, and twenty-one; and in the first resurrection appearance. What is the purpose of this frequent and singular metaphor?

"Heart," in Luke's usage, is certainly connected to the emphasis on Mary in the nativity, and very likely also references earlier Hebraic traditions. In Hebrew teachings, "heart" implies a unitive aspect of one's humanity that is greater than mere emotion—encompassing body, feelings, will, intuition, and thought—everything but soul. Consider these words from Deuteronomy: "You shall love the Lord your God with all your heart, and with all your soul, and with all your might. Keep these words that I am commanding you today in your heart" (6:5–6). These are part of the verses put in mezuzahs on the doorposts of Jewish houses and are also part of the daily liturgy.

Once again, Luke wants his audience to understand that the road to spiritual maturity winds through compassion—a path of the feminine, the intuitive, and the heart. The early appearance of the iconic angel Gabriel, and now the metaphor of heart, both resonate as Luke brings forth these well-understood Jewish truths to powerfully amplify his message.

When they had finished everything required by the law of the Lord,
they returned to Galilee, to their own town of Nazareth. The child
grew and became strong, filled with wisdom; and the favor of God

was upon him. Now every year his parents went to Jerusalem for the festival of the Passover. And when he was twelve years old, they went up as usual for the festival. When the festival was ended and they started to return, the boy Jesus stayed behind in Jerusalem, but his parents did not know it. Assuming that he was in the group of travelers, they went a day's journey. Then they started to look for him among their relatives and friends. When they did not find him, they returned to Jerusalem to search for him. After three days they found him in the temple, sitting among the teachers, listening to them and asking them questions. And all who heard him were amazed at his understanding and his answers. When his parents saw him they were astonished; and his mother said to him, "Child, why have you treated us like this? Look, your father and I have been searching for you in great anxiety." He said to them, "Why were you searching for me? Did you not know that I must be in my Father's house?" But they did not understand what he said to them. Then he went down with them and came to Nazareth, and was obedient to them. His mother treasured all these things in her heart.

And Jesus increased in wisdom and in years, and in divine and human favor. (2:39–52)

THE FOURTH PATH is one of maturing practice, and it is long, steady, and seemingly repetitive. The first lesson is, "Be silent!" and it is carried by the announcement stories of Zechariah, Elizabeth, and Mary. In varying ways, they tell us to welcome new experience, but to abide before we speak to others or act on that experience, so that the appropriate discernment can be developed. This appears similar to the practice of the third path, where we were told to sit in the garden and reflect on our revelation.

Yet this advice differs in its intention. In the third path, our waiting allowed us to become aware of the gifts we had received—revelation and the reality of union. Now the reason for our delay is so that we will have the time and opportunity to gradually develop an integrated response to events in our lives—particularly to crises. Studies have shown that a quick and instinctive first response is good when taking multiple-choice tests. It is almost certainly not a productive way to address almost any other problem, however—whether the problem is with children, a relationship, work, one's community, or the discernment of inner truth. Certainly there can be emergencies that overturn this rule; but generally, time should be taken to evaluate options. Meditation takes time, as does the discovery of a proper and loving course. Yet even if we do not devote ourselves to any deep discernment whatsoever, long human experience shows that the habit of keeping silent for a time before speaking will yield great benefits in our lives. "Hush!"

The stories in Luke go on to tell us that when we do contemplate and pray, we should trust what we discover in that inner process. Real transformations take place at a very basic inner level that is simultaneously extraordinarily delicate and intensely dynamic. Will we be able to coax our ego-self away from its determined role as the holder of rigid boundaries into a new future that is more flexible and more consonant with the divine reality of *sym-bol*? Our threatened ego-selves resisted change in the second path, but that was nothing compared to what happens now. Look at Zechariah. When change appeared wearing the face of the angel Gabriel, he was "terrified; and fear overwhelmed him." We have begun to comprehend that our new lives will have greater responsibilities, and thus greater trepidation.

When we feel increased anxieties, rigidity, or judgment, we can be certain these are all signals of our immature ego resisting transformation. Eventually, though, our fears will dissipate, especially if we begin our day with a time of contemplation. We can review the gifts in our life. We can be thoughtful about our dilemmas. We can ask for help from God in these challenges. In meditation, we can request a deeper bond with the frightened aspects of ourselves and "speak" with them, assuring them that they needn't fear—that greater safety and connection is the goal.

When our lives genuinely change, opposition will also come from without, even though most of us won't find ourselves in small, gossipy towns. Often the fiercest criticisms will be heard from our closest family and friends. We must not be surprised by this, or resentful. Every change we make forces them to make adjustments also, in their picture of us, in their expectations, and in their ways of relating to us. We need to be compassionate. We will find our new lives easier if we follow the example of Mary, who went to join Elizabeth, and seek out people who are likewise on a spiritual or transformative journey. Those with experiences similar to ours will be able to share with us and support us in our efforts. We are recommended to meet our own and others' resistance with a reflective—even playful— curiosity, holding our attitudes as lightly and flexibly as we can: "I wonder how all this will turn out—how unexpected circumstances will intervene to use this situation for the best?"

The Canticle of Mary expresses the future design of the Great Mystery as perfect and shows us that we are already a part of it. Many scientists of today have constructed mathematical formulas concluding that there is no such thing as linear time—that present, past, and future are mathematically one. Mary's Canticle held that exalted insight almost two millennia ago and still offers it to us today. Although, as we walk through our daily lives on the hard ground of what we call "reality," this may seem like the most arrant nonsense or some sort of silly crystal-gazing, many well-respected physicists and mathematicians with advanced degrees from major institutions would disagree. Before you mock too heartily, remember that there was a time when Galileo was imprisoned for expounding the theory of a round Earth when everyone else thought the world was flat. If we believe in the power of holding a positive vision of the future, and if we can hold Mary's insight as a clear mental picture on our journey, our belief cannot fail to help us.

Why? Because holding a positive system of belief is an extremely prag- matic approach, psychologically and spiritually. Since we tend to act in the direction of our expectations, a sincere faith that things will be well in- spires us to behave in a manner that creates positive effects in ourselves and others—and consequently, things do improve. Physiologically, many parts of our brains and our bodies still operate in survival mode and are outside our conscious control. But when we hold a belief that "things" are improv- ing, on a core level, our behavior will be more expansive and relaxed. We will tend to engage in activities that *invest* in a future that we feel is growing and beneficent. That behavior will lead, in turn, to responses from others that will generally tend to be positive and expansive. And with positive behavior that pattern continues. Conversely, if we believe that "things" are getting worse, then despite our best efforts to be benevolent, our core be- havior will tend to be contracted, because this is the appropriate survival response. Our unavoidable negativity will then generate corresponding negativity and encourage more contraction in others.

Holding a positive vision does not mean being unrealistic or denying our full personality in any way whatsoever, as is conveyed by the shepherds and the manger at Jesus's birth. These visitors to the divine event and its rough location stand for the rudest, crudest, most hidden and instinctual aspects we each carry within ourselves. In earlier paths, we made their acquaintance and identified their sources, but now we must actually invite them into our home and make a place for them at the birth of our new self and in our ensuing life—no matter how uncomfortable we may find that job. This is not a passive task, this welcome, for Luke shows that the angels went out to the shepherds. In the same way, the aspects of ourselves that we think of as our "highest" must seek out those we think of as our "lowest" or "ugliest," so that the two may come together in the fertile beginnings of what psychologists call "integration." This is difficult and gradual, and the work is far more than mere acceptance, for acceptance all too often becomes resignation. This task asks that we truly love and rejoice in those "lowly" aspects and fully join with them. Only in this way can we ensure that we have all the parts of us available when we need them for appropriate action—that no part of us has been cut off or repressed.

So how do we actually perform this joining? Some of us might find ourselves guided by a psychotherapist, a spiritual director, or a master teacher. But what if we don't have, or don't choose to make use of, these resources? What do we do? Probably the best basic process for self-remedy is described by the fourth step of twelve-step recovery programs: "Make a searching and fearless moral inventory." Take as long as is necessary to *write it all down.* Not only should both strengths and weaknesses be revealed, but they should be shared with a trusted friend or counselor. Though we suggested this in the second path, keep in mind that we have reached a different phase of growth, with new understandings and a different purpose. It is time to do this again. We need to find our angels and send them out to join our shepherds. The angels need the deep grounding bass of the instinctual self, and the shepherds need the soprano tones of hope. Together they can sound a holy chorus.

Luke used the account of the young Jesus in the Temple to "reframe" Jesus's early years in order to mirror and support the experience of his audience. We can likewise use this story to understand that our lives hold many elements. As we grow, much of our history will remain valuable—

even essential—while other parts will need to be discarded. Transformation will require some shedding, but of what? What do we need to preserve, and what do we need to leave behind in order to move forward—and what is the proper timing? We examined our history in the second path, and looked for the tentacles of division in the third, but now our chore is more complicated. We have to continue those tasks while learning to convert our discoveries into lasting, productive behaviors.

There are myriad dilemmas in this process of deciding on and implementing change. Many people have been raised in a particular faith and cherish their tradition as an unwavering and nourishing certainty throughout their lives, while others have an early experience of religion that is abusive and later decide to leave their tradition for a different faith or for none at all. Family is equally complicated: a family of birth can be wonderful and supportive—but it can also be terrible and hurtful. Marriages and partnerships offer continual testing, as do careers and employment. A mature life must make difficult decisions about change, regardless of society's expectations, and must do so on a fairly regular basis. Only discernments made from the most patient waiting, respectful dialogue, attentive prayer, and the considered work of our fullest selves can tell us whether, in a particular instance, we should stay where we are or cast a part of our lives aside.

Some of us resist any movement at all because it is too frightening, too foreign. Others of us find ourselves drawn to change merely for the sake of change—longing for an idyllic (and nonexistent) "other" person or place or condition. Another risk is the danger of moving to the rigidly opposite position of whatever wounded us (for example, children of alcoholics who, despite no problem of their own, become inflexible and unforgiving teetotalers), without understanding that this is only a new title for a wound that is still alive, well, and unaddressed.

Enormous change in things we value greatly requires enormous examination, and if we do decide to move in a different direction how do we take our leave and when? How do we prepare ourselves for the inevitable process of grief that always follows loss? What will our responsibilities be if our choices initiate grief or pain or damage within others?

All of these issues are closely tied to Luke's expansive use of the word "heart." When the angel Gabriel came to Mary with news of momentous change, she received his message with her *heart* and was not terrified, as

Zechariah had been. Luke's Hebraic "heart" calls us to experience the world not only from the rational and linear perspectives, but also from the nonrational and nonlinear—and count them as coequal. Throughout the gospel, Luke uses the word "heart" to mean mind, body, and feelings all together. The pulsing heart is also an apt metaphor for the movement of our lives in the fourth path of the quadratos journey—inward in contemplation, then outward in action. This is a pattern we will find in this gospel and that we need to put into place in our lives. Gradually, it will become our comfortable and natural practice. It is from the place of heart that we move deeper and further.

Truth-Telling, Perseverance, and Risk-Taking: The Lessons

Speak and Act in Truth: John the Witness, Not the Baptist

Luke begins chapter three with a recitation of names that would have evoked a sordid history of temporal and spiritual corruption to his contemporaries: Tiberius, Pontius Pilate, Herod, Philip, and the high priests Annas and Caiaphas. As he moves on into references from the book of Isaiah that plead for repentance and forgiveness, John enters the narrative. In this gospel, John is known simply by his first name, and is identified only as the son of Zechariah (and Elizabeth); he is the child of whose birth we read earlier. He is, however, the same John identified as John the Baptist in the Gospels of Matthew and Mark, and simply as "John" in the Gospel of John.

In each gospel, John performed baptisms at the River Jordan. In each, his appearance also announced the arrival of a particular spiritual practice. In Matthew, John urged the new journey, out from the place of the old Temple. In Mark, his call was to endure the trial of "repentance" in the wilderness, which we can now recognize as the second path of quadratos. In the Gospel of John, he pointed to, and proclaimed, the great visionary reality of Jesus the Christ, the glorious epiphany of the third path. In Luke, John called the assembled crowd to accountability for their actions, as they began the long walk to full maturity.

In all four gospels, John quoted from Isaiah, concluding his words in the other three with, "Prepare the way of the Lord, make his path straight." In Luke, however, John added five lyrical lines of joyous prophecy assuring all present that:

> *Every valley shall be filled,*
> *and every mountain and hill shall be made low,*
> *and the crooked shall be made straight,*
> *and the rough ways made smooth;*
> *and all flesh shall see the salvation of God. (3:5–6)*

John's next words addressed "the crowd," and this time, unlike in Matthew's gospel, there was no distinction made between the crowd and the Pharisees and Sadducees. No one escaped his scathing judgment. John railed against every last person present as part of the "brood of vipers," whom he challenged to "bear fruits worthy of repentance." What does this mean? Luke means, in these words he attributes to John, that the message of Jesus the Christ requires that *everyone* must make a genuine correction of their conscience and a change in their behavior or else they have not genuinely repented. Merely asking for forgiveness does not suffice.

When the crowd requested specific advice, John's response focused on actual practice rather than ideology. He called his listeners to lives of scrupulous honesty, moderation, and sharing and gave clear examples to each group present. He spoke with such maturity and strength that he prompted queries as to whether he himself was the Messiah, but he claimed no personal power, declaring himself merely a vessel for a higher divinity. This was a pointed lesson to teachers and evangelists of the new faith to maintain perspective and not misinterpret the adulation that inevitably arises in the relationships of teacher and student.

This instruction makes Luke's gospel very, very different from Matthew's. In that gospel, John separated out those he perceived as the historic villains, pointing his literary finger at them as the "vipers." Luke does not make that separation. His John gave a charge to every single person present at the River Jordan, and the overall message was not literary. Rather, his concern was the evidence of lives changed through the practice of charity and justice. As far as Luke is concerned, if one fails to "bear fruits" from one's faith—from grace received—then one is morally equiva-lent to a "viper" whose poison will kill that very grace. His moral judgment is directed to the practice of the person, rather than to that person's status or tradition. Luke attempts to encourage his audience to think of people as individuals rather than as categories. Additionally, he directs his words not only to the Christus believers, but also to the Jewish community, as a plea against the influence of the Pharisees.

> In the fifteenth year of the reign of Emperor Tiberius, when Pontius
> Pilate was governor of Judea, and Herod was ruler of Galilee, and
> his brother Philip ruler of the region of Ituraea and Trachonitis,
> and Lysanias ruler of Abilene, during the high priesthood of Annas
> and Caiaphas, the word of God came to John son of Zechariah
> in the wilderness. He went into all the region around the Jordan,
> proclaiming a baptism of repentance for the forgiveness of sins, as it is
> written in the book of the words of the prophet Isaiah,
>> *"The voice of one crying out in the wilderness:*
>> *'Prepare the way of the Lord, make his paths straight.*
>> *Every valley shall be filled,*
>> *and every mountain and hill shall be made low,*
>> *and the crooked shall be made straight,*
>> *and the rough ways made smooth;*
>> *and all flesh shall see the salvation of God.'"*
> John said to the crowds that came out to be baptized by him, "You
> brood of vipers! Who warned you to flee from the wrath to come? Bear
> fruits worthy of repentance. Do not begin to say to yourselves, 'We have
> Abraham as our ancestor'; for I tell you, God is able from these stones to
> raise up children to Abraham. Even now the ax is lying at the root of the
> trees; every tree therefore that does not bear good fruit is cut down and
> thrown into the fire." And the crowds asked him, "What then should we
> do?" In reply he said to them, "Whoever has two coats must share with
> anyone who has none; and whoever has food must do likewise." Even
> tax collectors came to be baptized, and they asked him, "Teacher, what
> should we do?" He said to them, "Collect no more than the amount
> prescribed for you." Soldiers also asked him, "And we, what should we
> do?" He said to them, "Do not extort money from anyone by threats

or false accusation, and be satisfied with your wages." As the people were filled with expectation, and all were questioning in their hearts concerning John, whether he might be the Messiah, John answered all of them by saying, "I baptize you with water; but one who is more powerful than I is coming; I am not worthy to untie the thong of his sandals. He will baptize you with the Holy Spirit and fire. His winnowing fork is in his hand, to clear his threshing floor and to gather the wheat into his granary; but the chaff he will burn with unquenchable fire." (3:1–17)

⸻

THE SCENES OF John at the river provide a prologue to the concrete actions offered up and reiterated throughout this gospel—the deeds that will call us out of our silence and contemplation. Using John as an example, one of the primary steps is our obligation to step out from the crowd and speak and act truthfully and compassionately despite our fear. John used the word "crowd" to emphasize the groupthink and moral paralysis that Luke scorns, and likewise John referred to the roots of the trees that bear the "good fruit." This is an important reminder to us that our actions in the fourth path must flow from whole and integrated attitudes, not just from our intellect, or our emotion. If they originate from our separated self, then our actions will likely be contaminated by fear, and will be a retreat from our journey. Although they may have the appearance of charity, false motives will inevitably lie just beneath their surface.

In the third path, we came to understand the nature of union. Now, in the fourth, it becomes our obligation to learn how to act on that truth—and to act against its opposite. What does this mean? The principle means that we will act and speak from our fullest individual truth, using as much of our integrated self as we can muster, and that we will not shrink from speaking and acting because we are fearful. But it also means that we will reject the pull of the group. We won't laugh at derogatory jokes, even when everyone else does; and when they are made, we might even choose to quietly say something that asserts our contrary truth. When we read media stories, we will think through *both* sides of issues and ask ourselves in what ways both sides are right and in what ways both sides are wrong. We will query ourselves about how each issue both affects and effects short-term and long-term values that matter to us. After this process, we will determine what our opinion is, and if we feel strongly, perhaps find a way to take effective action—action that goes beyond ego-based rhetoric and disparaging others.

Keep Your Path Straight: The Temptations

The devil's attempted seduction of Jesus by three temptations is found only in the Gospels of Matthew and Luke. A cursory reading might count them as the same stories, but they are actually subtly nuanced for the unique experience of the communities to whom they are directed.

Matthew's gospel was written in the aftermath of the annihilation of the Temple and the massacre of all its priests, so in his version Jesus spent forty days in the desert and the tempter appeared at the end of that period. Luke, however, depicts the tempter taunting Jesus continuously throughout his exile, and making the three climactic appearances at the end. This was the emotional experience of the late-first-century Christus followers to whom Luke was writing. They felt constantly bereft and, surely, intermittently angry as they struggled with Roman oppression and the process of being cast out of their Jewish home—conditions likely to continue for generations.

It is meaningful that Luke notes Jesus was "about thirty years old," had been baptized, and was "full of the Holy Spirit." The average life expectancy for a man in the Mediterranean at that time was in the thirties. In these stories, then, Jesus would have been considered well past the prime of his life—a seasoned elder teaching people much younger than he. The tempter was a metaphor for the short-term, expedient course, and it is noted that he left, temporarily, "until an opportune time." Due to his age, Jesus represented mortal as well as divine wisdom. He had actually experienced temptations and uncertainty and was therefore pragmatically credible as well as inspiring for first-century Christus followers.

In the first temptation, the devil taunted Jesus to show his power by making a loaf of bread out of stone. Significantly, Luke uses the singular, "stone," although in Matthew, the word is the plural, "stones." Luke refers to a single stone, thereby conjuring the image of a foundation's cornerstone newly laid, while Matthew, speaking to another audience, evokes the many stones of the former Temple and creates an image of them fallen, lost, and useless. Here the temptation lies in the insubstantiality of short-term gratification represented by bread to be consumed versus the rewards of long-term effort symbolized by the stone as part of a foundation of faith. "This is the first stone you are putting down," Luke is saying. "This is about your commitment to the work of faith. Spirit will sustain you."

Luke's depiction of the second temptation is also similar to that of Matthew, but there are two differences. This temptation is placed second by Luke, instead of Matthew's third, probably because Luke's readers would find it a greater temptation. In it, the devil showed Jesus "all the kingdoms" and offered power and "all this authority" over them, if he would only worship the tempter. This was a poignant message to the Christians, who would certainly have been strongly drawn by the opportunity to set themselves above their persecutors. By expanding the temptation with "all this authority"—meaning control over religious and temporal realms (words not in Matthew)—Luke heightens the message of enticement for the oppressed Christus believers. He understood that any form of self-righteousness, no matter how desirable it felt, would only have increased strife, ultimately leading to increased persecution of the heavily outnumbered group.

In the last temptation, placing Jesus on the pinnacle of the Temple and daring him to throw himself down, the tempter mocked Jesus with the words "[God] . . . will command his angels concerning you, to protect you." Luke quotes from Psalm 91, which is devoted entirely to words about rescue and safety. In contrast, the word "protect" does not appear anywhere in Matthew's text. Luke understood there was a deep longing for personal protection in the hearts of his readers, especially since the tempter challenged Jesus to doubt God's protection and act stupidly. This reference to Psalm 91, the word "protect," and the dramatic image of Jesus perched precariously atop the symbol of Judaism could scarcely be a more direct message. "Do not be rash in your actions," Luke counsels. "Your position feels frightening, but testing God is only arrogance—not a true path of faith. Faith is a steady journey of living and growing in truth. Do not be tempted. Do not let the frightened part of yourself determine the course you take."

Jesus, full of the Holy Spirit, returned from the Jordan and was led by the Spirit in the wilderness, where for forty days he was tempted by the devil. He ate nothing at all during those days, and when they were over, he was famished. The devil said to him, "If you are the Son of God, command this stone to become a loaf of bread." Jesus answered him, "It is written, 'One does not live by bread alone.' " Then the devil led him up and showed him in an instant all the kingdoms of the world. And the devil said to him, "To you I will give their glory and all this authority; for it has been given over to me, and I give it to anyone I please. If you, then, will worship me, it will all be yours." Jesus answered him, "It is written, 'Worship the Lord your God, and serve only him.' " Then the devil took him to Jerusalem, and placed him on the pinnacle of the temple, saying to him, "If you are the Son of God, throw yourself down from here, for it is written, 'He will command his angels concerning you, to protect you,' and 'On their hands they will bear you up, so that you will not dash your foot against a stone.' " Jesus answered him, "It is said, 'Do not put the Lord your God to the test.' " When the devil had finished every test, he departed from him until an opportune time. (4:1–13)

After Jesus struggled with the devil, he left the desert and returned to the region of Galilee, where he traveled from place to place preaching and performing miracles. In one notable story, Jesus went to a synagogue in Nazareth and, in the midst of his family and neighbors, read a scroll from Isaiah. The scroll's text proclaimed an anointing and brought good news to the poor, captive, blind, oppressed, and others. Those assembled congratulated Jesus, and he perceived their unspoken desire for him to perform miracles for them—"the things we have heard you did at Capernaum." Jesus not only demurred, but chided the crowd, recounting the ancient story of Elijah, who, though the land was filled with people in desperate need of miracles, had refused, granting only a single miracle—and that one for a gentile. Reproached, the Nazarene congregation became enraged and arose en masse, driving Jesus out of the town and toward a cliff over which they planned to hurl him. But, Luke recounts, "he passed through" their midst "and went on his way."

Through this wonderful story, Luke illustrates the resistance of the old social and religious frameworks to a new message that encourages the inclusion of all—even "gentiles." "Expect anger," Luke is saying, "and do not be surprised if it comes in groups that threaten your life. Remember this example of Jesus in Nazareth. He proclaimed his truth—a universal love that supplanted tribalism—and when people rose against him, he did not back down; nor did he argue or dispute. Filled with the power of the Spirit, he simply ignored the rage directed against him and walked away, going about his business."

> Then Jesus, filled with the power of the Spirit, returned to Galilee,
> and a report about him spread through all the surrounding country.
> He began to teach in their synagogues and was praised by everyone.
> When he came to Nazareth, where he had been brought up, he went
> to the synagogue on the sabbath day, as was his custom. He stood
> up to read, and the scroll of the prophet Isaiah was given to him. He
> unrolled the scroll and found the place where it was written:
>> *"The Spirit of the Lord is upon me,*
>> *because he has anointed me to bring good news to the poor.*
>> *He has sent me to proclaim release to the captives*
>> *and recovery of sight to the blind,*
>> *to let the oppressed go free,*
>> *to proclaim the year of the Lord's favor."*
> And he rolled up the scroll, gave it back to the attendant, and sat down.
> The eyes of all in the synagogue were fixed on him. Then he began to
> say to them, "Today this scripture has been fulfilled in your hearing."
> All spoke well of him and were amazed at the gracious words that came
> from his mouth. They said, "Is not this Joseph's son?" He said to them,
> "Doubtless you will quote to me this proverb, 'Doctor, cure yourself!'
> And you will say, 'Do here also in your hometown the things that we
> have heard you did at Capernaum.'" And he said, "Truly I tell you, no
> prophet is accepted in the prophet's hometown. But the truth is, there
> were many widows in Israel in the time of Elijah, when the heaven was
> shut up three years and six months, and there was a severe famine over
> all the land; yet Elijah was sent to none of them except to a widow at
> Zarephath in Sidon. There were also many lepers in Israel in the time
> of the prophet Elisha, and none of them was cleansed except Naaman
> the Syrian." When they heard this, all in the synagogue were filled with
> rage. They got up, drove him out of the town, and led him to the brow
> of the hill on which their town was built, so that they might hurl him off
> the cliff. But he passed through the midst of them and went on his way.
> (4:14–30)

Gifts of Response-ability: The Beatitudes

At every turn, in ways large and small, Luke's gospel cultivates the development of a mature practice of faith. In advance of every significant action, Luke shows Jesus departing to pray. In the sixth chapter, Jesus returned from his prayer and called all the disciples together. From the group, he designated twelve as apostles. For the remainder of the gospel, Luke uniquely distinguishes between the words "apostle" and "disciple," although both words are often applied to the same person. When "apostle" is used, it means "one who is sent out." "Disciple," however, is always applied in the context of "learner," and is always used when Jesus is teaching. The lesson Luke wishes to give to the emerging Christian communities is clear: the opportunity for apostleship comes with maturity, and yet discipleship—even for apostles—never ends. The spiritual journey will always require "continuing education" in how to offer wisdom appropriately and with compassion.

> Now during those days he went out to the mountain to pray; and he spent
> the night in prayer to God. And when day came, he called his disciples
> and chose twelve of them, whom he also named apostles: Simon, whom
> he named Peter, and his brother Andrew, and James, and John, and
> Philip, and Bartholomew, and Matthew, and Thomas, and James son of
> Alphaeus, and Simon, who was called the Zealot, and Judas son of James,
> and Judas Iscariot, who became a traitor. (6:12–16)

The Beatitudes of the Gospel of Luke could scarcely be more different than those in Matthew's gospel. In Matthew, Jesus appeared as the typical Jewish teacher, seated, while in Luke we find him standing. In Matthew, the Beatitudes were pronounced from high atop a mountain, while here we are "on a level place." Matthew speaks of an audience drawn from the provinces of Israel, so we may assume it was primarily Jewish. Luke's audience specifically includes people from outlying provinces—therefore, many gentiles. In Matthew, the sermon was designed as a profound teaching. In Luke, it was more: people came both to "hear him and to be healed." The most significant differences, however, are found in the tone of the Beatitudes themselves and the text that follows them.

Matthew's Beatitudes are solemn pronouncements that ring with the sound of a rich, deep bell. Luke's are personal promises. They are insistent, filled with active, colorful verbs, the personal pronoun "you," and the word "now"; and they do not hesitate to predict the direst calamity if one fails to meet the responsibilities of revelation.

After the recitation of the Beatitudes, there is a rhythmic, repetitive text similar to that found at the same point in Matthew. But Luke uses much more direct language and offers only two short stanzas. In the first, Jesus recited a code of conduct for his followers that commenced with "Love your enemies." In the second, he raised a higher challenge, demanding that the good conduct be extended to everyone, and be performed for its own sake: "If you love those who love you, what credit is that to you?"

Luke knew that if the communities could act on this new rule, they would be breaking the ancient proscriptions of tribe—and would also be strengthening all of their relationships and ensuring that they could withstand the challenges ahead of them. He knew that if they failed to do so, it was likely they would fall back into the old internecine tribal rivalries and eventually even warfare, which could weaken their ability to meet oppressors and might spell the end of the faith itself. Consequently, his Beatitudes were far more than an elevated code of niceties; they were practical rules for survival.

He came down with them and stood on a level place, with a great
crowd of his disciples and a great multitude of people from all Judea,
Jerusalem, and the coast of Tyre and Sidon. They had come to hear
him and to be healed of their diseases; and those who were troubled
with unclean spirits were cured. And all in the crowd were trying
to touch him, for power came out from him and healed all of them.
Then he looked up at his disciples and said:

"Blessed are you who are poor, for yours is the kingdom of God.
"Blessed are you who are hungry now, for you will be filled.
"Blessed are you who weep now, for you will laugh.
"Blessed are you when people hate you, and when they exclude you, revile
    you, and defame you on account of the Son of Man. Rejoice in that day
    and leap for joy, for surely your reward is great in heaven; for that is
    what their ancestors did to the prophets.

"But woe to you who are rich, for you have received your consolation.

"Woe to you who are full now, for you will be hungry.

"Woe to you who are laughing now, for you will mourn and weep.

"Woe to you when all speak well of you, for that is what their ancestors did
      to the false prophets.

"But I say to you that listen, Love your enemies, do good to those who hate you, bless those who curse you, pray for those who abuse you. If anyone strikes you on the cheek, offer the other also; and from anyone who takes away your coat do not withhold even your shirt. Give to everyone who begs from you; and if anyone takes away your goods, do not ask for them again. Do to others as you would have them do to you. If you love those who love you, what credit is that to you? For even sinners love those who love them. If you do good to those who do good to you, what credit is that to you? For even sinners do the same. If you lend to those from whom you hope to receive, what credit is that to you? Even sinners lend to sinners, to receive as much again. But love your enemies, do good, and lend, expecting nothing in return. Your reward will be great, and you will be children of the Most High; for he is kind to the ungrateful and the wicked. Be merciful, just as your Father is merciful." (6:17–36)

The concluding words of the sermon make reference to the same metaphor as the first temptation and liken faith to building a foundation from stone. More importantly, they constitute a forceful and direct challenge to Luke's readers regarding taking action. They ask why anyone would profess belief and then fail to follow the specific prescription that Jesus the Christ has laid down. Verging on the edge of contempt and scorn, Jesus delivered a rousing and emphatic finish to his Sermon on the Plain.

"Why do you call me 'Lord, Lord,' and do not do what I tell you?
I will show you what someone is like who comes to me, hears my
words, and acts on them. That one is like a man building a house,
who dug deeply and laid the foundation on rock; when a flood arose,
the river burst against that house but could not shake it, because it
had been well built. But the one who hears and does not act is like a
man who built a house on the ground without a foundation. When

the river burst against it, immediately it fell, and great was the ruin of that house." (6:46–49)

⟶

WHEN WE REFLECT on the temptations and what they signify for our travel through the fourth path, we see that the first temptation is unsparing. The devil taunts us with challenges such as, "Turn this stone into a loaf of bread," "Seize the sensation of the moment," "Forget the lengthy challenge," or "It's only once; what does it matter?" But our soul registers each bruise and wound to its self-respect and dignity—and our ego welcomes every opportunity to regress back to its former protective and self-centered ways. Yet, if we are truly on the spiritual Journey of Quadratos, the expedient course is not ours to take. When this temptation appears, it is time to call our steady friends into service: prayer, reflection, and counselors. Sometimes choices will seem unclear, in part because the world is complicated, and in part because the tricky ego-self is always on the lookout for ways to retreat back to safety. So we need to be vigilant and query whether the option we are being offered is genuine and congruent with our journey. The lesson of Jesus the Christ would have us reject anything on which we cannot build further, and in love.

The second temptation speaks to one of our most pernicious challenges. When we are either alight with new zeal or consumed with doubt, the devil offers us "all the kingdoms." This leads us into attempts to get others to join our point of view. We tell ourselves our intentions are only the best. As Luke says, our efforts at persuasion usually begin "in an instant." Our zeal takes many shapes—we find ourselves displaying hyper-enthusiasm, exploiting affinity, feigning friendship, withdrawing friendship, telling partial truths, sometimes even shaming people. If we prevail, the response we get gives us inner affirmation, confirming our position or reassuring our doubt. However, down deep, fear and a desire to control others lurks beneath our behavior. Why else would we need the confirmation or the reassurance? Giving in to this temptation leads us to denigrate a point of view that differs from ours and leads us into self-righteousness.

Quadratos calls us to identify our own intimate pattern of exerting control and then to be vigilant in resisting this temptation. Our mature course is to effect change by the example of our lives, rather than by overzealousness or by setting ourselves above others as "experts," no matter how well-intended we think we are.

The third temptation leads us to examine our deep desire to be protected from the consequences of our actions. The further we move into the fourth path, the more we are required to act in truth, with clarity and compassion. When we do this, no matter how compassionate we try to be, the repercussions of our change can run the gamut from uncomfortable to agonizing. We are tempted to avoid this discomfort. We can especially wish for protection from the consequences of truth-telling. Think of how difficult scrupulous veracity can be in a relationship. Think of how high the cost can be of telling political truth—of civil disobedience. As a result, we often remain silent, "dance around" the truth, or take action and then retreat into resentment or anger when the consequences arrive. We have watched these behaviors in friends, parents, ministers, political activists, and ourselves. We know we have fallen off the path by choosing avoidance of pain or its consequences, however small, instead of honesty.

All three lessons taught in the temptations coalesce in the story of Jesus speaking in Nazareth. Jesus was in his hometown being celebrated by family and neighbors until he perceived their desire for him to do "magic tricks" for them. He refused, reproaching them for their shallow attitude, and in return they tried to kill him. He left without comment. Toned down just a bit (but not all that much), this could be the story of innumerable family gatherings, corporate meetings, academic colloquia, and international assemblies throughout history. A noted person speaks wisdom which is not the common belief and is either not heard, or is misunderstood and rejected and/or reviled. At all levels, families and organizations are usually—and naturally—resistant to new insight. Should we, therefore, deny our wholeness and never say anything? Of course not. And if (and when) we are rejected, what should we do? As difficult as it may seem, we must bend every effort not to dispute or fight or allow the enmity of others to affect us, but rather simply go on our way.

Luke's definitions and flexible application of the terms "disciple" and "apostle" echo the unceasing cycles of the quadratos pattern. We are in a lifelong condition of inquiry—of trying to remain curious and flexible as we test ourselves in the world, and the world tests us back. We are always disciple and apostle, these roles bowing to each other in a perpetually challenging minuet of learning and service.

It often seems as though, just when we feel that we have achieved a bit of inner equanimity, a fresh obstacle arrives, sending us on a quick little side trip into arrogance or complacency or self-righteousness. In order to mend our lapse, self-honesty forces us right back into discipleship. We pray and ask for help once again, often feeling as though our knees can bend no lower and our nose is scraping dirt. Indeed, the condition of apostleship often *leads* us back to discipleship, which then *leads* on out to the apostle's field to share our experience, as the steps of God's dance lead us deeper into Spirit and service.

Another outgrowth of the synergistic association between disciple and apostle is the leveling out of the teacher-student relationship. The more we learn, the more we are able to discern both the strengths and the frailties of those we esteem. When this is understood and welcomed, it can result in growing collegiality and even friendship. If, however, the teacher or the student has an immature ego that requires either elevation or devaluation, then the relationship will likely falter and eventually be destroyed, often acrimoniously. If this occurs, it will be another opportunity for us to follow Jesus's example and go on our way compassionately, without resentment or rancor.

Luke's Beatitudes are startlingly different from those in Matthew's gospel, and our interpretation of them through the lens of quadratos is dramatically different from the common conception. Why? Because we view them as guides to living along the fourth path, flowing directly from the revelations of the third path. The epiphanies we received in John's garden came with increased responsibilities—with the need for more reflective responses to ourselves and to others. These are called out in the Beatitudes— one by one. The "blessed"/"woe" phrases state the overarching principles, and the text that follows is the amplification of those principles. In strictly psychological terms, the increased awareness of the third path brought new burdens to the maturing ego. The "blesseds" describe what the ego needs either to give or to let go of, while the "woes" speak about the psychological and spiritual poverty of the reverse course. If the "blesseds" and "woes" go out of balance, they inevitably surface and play out in our lives, resulting in corresponding spiritual consequences—both positive and negative.

Therefore, in quadratos, the Beatitudes are *not* pronouncements about our moods or socioeconomic status, as is commonly thought. They are messages about inner attitudes. Rereading them and reflecting on them from the perspective of quadratos is illuminating, and absorbing the deeper interpretation which follows is of critical importance.

In this radical and far-reaching understanding, being "poor" has nothing whatsoever to do with material goods. You are blessed if you can understand that the revelation you received in the third path came to you in your state of humble *spiritual* poverty and was not in any way from yourself. In this way you will remain a servant of what you have received. Accordingly, if you are "hungry," your hunger is to feed not only yourself, but others, from the grace and spirit you have received. You "weep" because the beauty and truth of epiphany have reached your heart, the essence of your being, and moved you deeply. Being "hated, excluded, reviled, and defamed" is a repetition of Luke's teaching that deep resistance is a natural reaction to new behaviors and we need to expect its arrival both within and without. It is not in any way a rationalization for being antisocial.

Corresponding to the positive promises offered in the Beatitudes are equal cautions, each preceded by "Woe to." If we are "rich," that means we have converted our revelation into a "feel-good" experience, into immediate gratification, and already "received [our] consolation." If we are "full," we have selfishly taken all the gratification of the experience for ourselves and not extended it to others in any way. If we are "laughing now," then our revelation stayed in the shallow realm of mere titillation and never reached the deeper, expanded realms of wholeness. And if "all speak well" of us, then we can be sure we have failed to speak out, or to speak our truth, and we are therefore not meeting the responsibilities of the gift we have been given.

Jesus's directives for loving action in the first stanza just after the verses of the Beatitudes are familiar to many of us. When we focus them on our inner lives, we see that they are asking us to review our behavior when we feel personally challenged—psychologically, emotionally, even spiritually. How can we respond to perceived threats from a more encompassing, gracious, and integrated position? At first, this will require us to pause and reflect—often for days. Practice will enable us to accomplish this more quickly and easily.

The second directive contains the well-known words, "Do to others as you would have them do to you." The actual practice of this instruction has a subtlety often overlooked. Most people assume this means we should extend to others the behavior that we think is best, whatever that is. Nothing could be further from the truth intended by these words. The words call for us to behave as we would have others *do to us.* And what each of us would most like is to be met on our own terms, in our own language, at our own present stage of understanding and development. None of us wants to be bullied or condescended to or lied to or shamed or shunned. We don't want assumptions made about us. So this was Jesus's directive to us. We are to meet others on *their own ground of being—not ours.* We are to grant them the same human dignity we would wish them to extend to us.

Each of the "blesseds" and the "woes" in Luke's Beatitudes are grounded in the soundest psychology. They are paired, and they quite clearly inform us that if we do not mature into the expanded understanding and practice offered by the fourth-path "blesseds," we will most certainly contract back into the misery of the "woes." If we want to think in terms of having a carrot and a stick for our journey, we may look forward to joy, and the "woes" surely qualify as the stick. Remember the horrors of the immature ego we knew in Matthew and Mark, when we felt as though we were the perpetual victims of an unfeeling, uncaring world where things were either tumbling down all around us, or were gray, mysterious, and unfathomable? Those are the woes. And we will return to them—all of us will, repeatedly—as we cycle back through the quadratos process, but we will probably never love them, and will always want to shorten our stay. It is well worth our energy to reach for the understanding of the "blesseds."

Even though Luke gives radical counsel for his time, he is no radical. His advice—based on history, experience, and, as we have noted, psychology—is always very practical. He deeply respects Jewish tradition, and constantly counsels self-reflection and a measured pace. Across millennia, he wants us to succeed in our journey. He asks us to pay attention and follow through—otherwise, "Why do you call me 'Lord'?" Spiritual transformation is tough. We face threat and challenge from within and without. We need a "well-built foundation," but we have already laid the first sturdy stones.

Compassion Without Boundaries: The Good Samaritan

Luke concludes this chapter with the famous and transcendent story of
the Good Samaritan, which appears in no other gospel. The parable opens
with a moving restatement of the core Judaic verses of Deuteronomy: "You
shall love the Lord your God with all your heart, and with all your soul,
and with all your strength, and with all your mind; and your neighbor as
yourself." (These are the same verses we referred to earlier as the spiritual
sense that underlies Luke's use of the word "heart" throughout this gospel.)
Queried, "Who is my neighbor?" Jesus answered with a story about a man
who had been beaten and left for dead on the road. Both a priest and a
Levite, a member of the priestly tribe, passed the injured man by without
tending to him. Jewish teachings held that if the priests had touched him,
they would have become "unclean" and would thus have been forbidden
to perform any ritual. Then a Samaritan, an outcast from Jewish society,
passed, saw the beaten man, and stopped. He bandaged the man's wounds
and, after taking him to an inn on the Samaritan's own donkey, paid the
innkeeper for his care.

This poignant story offered a revolutionary teaching. The behavior it
showed—and held up as expected of Christians—moved well beyond the
limitations of ritual or bureaucratic law to the benefit of all people. This was
not only timely for the burgeoning Christian communities, but essential. As
with the Beatitudes, Luke recognized that this principle of helping others
despite their background of birth had the potential to both spread and hold
Christianity together, because it superseded the centuries-old squabbles of
class and tribe. And if the fights could end, then larger and more powerful
social and economic groups could form, and greater strength would follow.
As always, Jesus's message was both divine and practical: act in love and
respond to those in need, regardless of origins. Luke writes every word of
his gospel accordingly.

> Just then a lawyer stood up to test Jesus. "Teacher," he said, "what must
> I do to inherit eternal life?" [Jesus] said to him, "What is written in the
> law? What do you read there?" He answered, "You shall love the Lord
> your God with all your heart, and with all your soul, and with all your
> strength, and with all your mind; and your neighbor as yourself." And

[Jesus] said to him, "You have given the right answer; do this, and you will live." But wanting to justify himself, he asked Jesus, "And who is my neighbor?" Jesus replied, "A man was going down from Jerusalem to Jericho, and fell into the hands of robbers, who stripped him, beat him, and went away, leaving him half dead. Now by chance a priest was going down that road; and when he saw him, he passed by on the other side. So likewise a Levite, when he came to the place and saw him, passed by on the other side. But a Samaritan while traveling came near him; and when he saw him, he was moved with pity. He went to him and bandaged his wounds, having poured oil and wine on them. Then he put him on his own animal, brought him to an inn, and took care of him. The next day he took out two denarii, gave them to the innkeeper, and said, 'Take care of him; and when I come back, I will repay you whatever more you spend.' Which of these three, do you think, was a neighbor to the man who fell into the hands of the robbers?" He said, "The one who showed him mercy." Jesus said to him, "Go and do likewise." (Luke 10:25–37)

Ask for What You Want: Bread at Midnight

After Jesus taught his disciples the words we know as the Lord's Prayer, he went on with a pointed and beautiful lesson unique to this gospel. He proposed to the disciples that if they were to go to a friend's home in the middle of the night asking for food to feed a newly arrived guest, the friend would help them, even if the friend was grumpy and only half awake. Why? Not from friendship, but from respect for the perseverance of the request. This teaching is then followed by the well-known words also found in Matthew's gospel that begin, "Ask, and it will be given you." Luke was taking the opportunity to insert an advanced principle about persistence that he knew his readers badly needed.

The teaching—dramatically set in the middle of the night, so no one would miss the point—emphasized the need to maintain inner stability and steadfastly ask for what one wants, though the moment or circumstances may not be opportune. Note that the request was for three loaves of bread—far above what would have been required until morning. The principle is to ask for what one *wants* rather than to ask based on need or subsistence. This parable illustrates the combined lessons of having a strong sense of self-worth, of persistence, and of holding a clear vision for the future—an invaluable combination for moving forward successfully.

> And [Jesus] said to them, "Suppose one of you has a friend, and you go to him at midnight and say to him, 'Friend, lend me three loaves of bread; for a friend of mine has arrived, and I have nothing to set before him.' And he answers from within, 'Do not bother me; the door has already been locked, and my children are with me in bed; I cannot get up and give you anything.' I tell you, even though he will not get up and give him anything because he is his friend, at least because of his persistence he will get up and give him whatever he needs. "So I say to you, Ask, and it will be given you; search, and you will find; knock, and the door will be opened for you. For everyone who asks receives, and everyone who searches finds, and for everyone who knocks, the door will be opened." (11:5–10)

Risk and Celebration: Two Stories and the Prodigal Son

Jesus told a series of three stories to challenge the thinking of the Pharisees and those whose hearts still followed the pharisaical teachings. At this point in the first century, the Pharisees were philosophically the people who promoted "holding on" and "gathering what is left," rather than moving ahead. Any story that teaches about seeking that which has wandered away is quite pointedly directed at challenging the Pharisees and their beliefs.

The first two stories tell of losing and then finding, first sheep and then coins. These accounts build to the third story, which is the well-known tale of the Prodigal Son. It, like that of the Good Samaritan, appears only in Luke's gospel. In this third parable, a father had two sons. The younger son left home and his traditional obligations, taking his share of the inheritance early in order to explore the larger world. After squandering everything on this quest, he returned home. Rejoicing at his homecoming, his father held a great reunion celebration for him. Highly resentful of this welcome, the elder brother referred to the younger as "your son" when he complained to the father about the injustice of honoring the wastrel—effectively disowning his filial relationship. The father refused to accept the older son's attitude, saying that he was "always with him," and reiterated the need to celebrate what "has come to life."

Through these parables, Luke provides differing ways to consider the cost of holding tightly to material things or to ideologies. He emphasizes the great value in putting material things at risk and going into a wilderness, into darkness or unfamiliar territory as the first-century Christus followers were doing. In the first two stories, the material possession—the sheep or the coin—was recovered. In the third, though the goods—or inheritance— disappeared, the much more valuable asset, the relationship of father and son, was regained. Unfortunately, the embittered older son, by disowning his brother, denied himself all the possibilities represented by the younger son and his relationship with the father—exploration, wholeness, and joy. In all three parables, Luke's point is that by focusing on what was genuinely important—on the element of heart—the end result was great happiness, rejoicing, and celebration.

> Now all the tax collectors and sinners were coming near to listen to
> him. And the Pharisees and the scribes were grumbling and saying,
> "This fellow welcomes sinners and eats with them." So he told them
> this parable: "Which one of you, having a hundred sheep and losing
> one of them, does not leave the ninety-nine in the wilderness and
> go after the one that is lost until he finds it? When he has found it,
> he lays it on his shoulders and rejoices. And when he comes home,
> he calls together his friends and neighbors, saying to them, 'Rejoice
> with me, for I have found my sheep that was lost.' Just so, I tell you,
> there will be more joy in heaven over one sinner who repents than
> over ninety-nine righteous persons who need no repentance. Or what
> woman having ten silver coins, if she loses one of them, does not light
> a lamp, sweep the house, and search carefully until she finds it? When
> she has found it, she calls together her friends and neighbors, saying,
> 'Rejoice with me, for I have found the coin that I had lost.' Just so,
> I tell you, there is joy in the presence of the angels of God over one
> sinner who repents." (15:1–10)

Then Jesus said, "There was a man who had two sons. The younger of them said to his father, 'Father, give me the share of the property that will belong to me.' So he divided his property between them. A few days later the younger son gathered all he had and traveled to a distant country, and there he squandered his property in dissolute living. When he had spent everything, a severe famine took place throughout that country, and he began to be in need. So he went and hired himself out to one of the citizens of that country, who sent him to his fields to feed the pigs. He would gladly have filled himself with the pods that the pigs were eating; and no one gave him anything. But when he came to himself he said, 'How many of my father's hired hands have bread enough and to spare, but here I am dying of hunger! I will get up and go to my father, and I will say to him, "Father, I have sinned against heaven and before you; I am no longer worthy to be called your son; treat me like one of your hired hands."' So he set off and went to his father. But while he was still far off, his father saw him and was filled with compassion; he ran and put his arms around him and kissed him. Then the son said to him, 'Father, I have sinned against heaven and before you; I am no longer worthy to be called your son.' But the father said to his slaves, 'Quickly, bring out a robe—the best one—and put it on him; put a ring on his finger and sandals on his feet. And get the fatted calf and kill it, and let us eat and celebrate; for this son of mine was dead and is alive again; he was lost and is found!' And they began to celebrate. Now his elder son was in the field; and when he came and approached the house, he heard music and dancing. He called one of the slaves and asked what was going on. He replied, 'Your brother has come, and your father has killed the fatted calf, because he has got him back safe and sound.' Then he became angry and refused to go in. His father came out and began to plead with him. But he answered his father, 'Listen! For all these years I have been working like a slave for you, and I have never disobeyed your command; yet you have never given me even a young goat so that I might celebrate with my friends. But when this son of yours came back, who has devoured your property with prostitutes, you killed the fatted calf for him!' Then the father said to him, 'Son, you are always with me, and all that is mine is yours. But we had to celebrate and rejoice, because this brother of yours was dead and has come to life; he was lost and has been found.' " (15:11–32)

Where Is Happiness? Jesus's Answer

Luke's readers were suffering difficult days. Oppression from Rome was increasing. This first meant the loss of good jobs, then the loss of *any* jobs, and eventually the loss of their homes—and all because they were Christians following a new way. Because these circumstances were not what the new believers had expected from the arrival of the Messiah, Luke crafts this answer to the Pharisees as a message to the Christians that the new kingdom is not a domain, but is instead found "among you"—in the ways individuals relate to each other in community. This would have substantial impact on the Christus group, helping them to find equanimity in their times together and in worship.

> Once Jesus was asked by the Pharisees when the kingdom of God
> was coming, and he answered, "The kingdom of God is not coming
> with things that can be observed; nor will they say, 'Look, here it
> is!' or 'There it is!' For, in fact, the kingdom of God is among you."
> (17:20–21)

LUKE USES THE story of the Good Samaritan to clearly explicate the responsibilities of Christian duty: love God as ourselves, and minister to our neighbor without hesitation or hierarchy. In the parable, both the priest and the Levite are unthinking, unreflective—blindly following rules passed on to them by their religion and caste. The Samaritan responds with a more engaged and flexible humanity. Daily, we are challenged in the same way. Outstretched hands and starving children greet us on the sidewalk and in our mailbox. Less dramatically, our friends ask us for time or assistance— even a loan. How do we respond?

The actions of the Samaritan present us with what may be our most difficult challenge to date. He did not hesitate to act. He did not suffer from a lack of compassion, nor did he act from inappropriate guilt or shame. So must we, in each instance, determine first whether to respond—and then how, based on specific circumstances and our abilities to either give or receive. If we act, we need to be certain that our motives derive from our inner wholeness; otherwise, our actions will come from the fractional self of the immature ego—from some outer "should," "have to," or groupthink— and the result will be self-aggrandizement rather than actual compassion.

Knocking at midnight aptly symbolizes the fourth path. Sometimes it seems that that is all we do. We knock on our stubborn habits. We knock on our recalcitrant and fearful egos. We knock at the hearts of those around us and hope for their patience as we make our slow progress. And it often seems that our requests are inconvenient and even embarrassing. We feel self-conscious and awkward with others. Sometimes our knocking needs to be done at the door of Spirit, and we are just too tired to pray—after all, it is midnight. But knock we must. We need to persevere, and it is important— for our dreams, for our good and whole lives—that we ask for all three loaves. Knocking and asking is the boring repetition from which the richness of our life emerges and rises.

The three stories, which include the Prodigal Son, encourage us to take the risks needed on the fourth path to test ourselves. Since we know we are at home with and within our God, we have at some level a deep surety and no risk at all. Yet there will always be parts of us that still feel frissons of fear now and again. A lot of what we are undergoing is new and unexplored, and we need a bit of help and some prodding. Our actions can seem wildly unwise or unnecessary to others who are outside the process, but this is precisely how we grow. We grasp in ever wider and deeper ways that our capacity for joy and celebration is in some measure directly linked to our corresponding willingness to expand ourselves. As we progress, the change is like the difference between seeing the night sky through a city window and experiencing it from the top of a high mountain. There is simply no comparison.

When we express our truths, others may find our opinions difficult to digest—may consider them unnecessary, even foolhardy. Therefore, truthtelling plays an important role not only in the story of the Prodigal Son, but throughout Luke's gospel. One of the most formidable demands of the fourth path, as reiterated by the third temptation (asking to be protected from consequences), requires speaking and acting truthfully. It is so much easier to remain silent, yet every justice we desire to see tomorrow is made from the injustice we refuse today, whether that takes place in our marriages, our jobs, our churches, or our countries. Recognizing the necessity to "speak up" is very simple, but doing so often generates conflict; therefore, opening our mouths can feel like a very weighty decision. Nonetheless, we are not relieved of our obligation to do so—and with practice, it does get easier.

Our ego's difficulty with conflict makes this fourth-path requirement of truth-telling very complicated. Psychologically, the initial impulse of our immature ego, the impulse we encountered in the first path, is to avoid conflict altogether. Our ego next comes into contact with conflict, gingerly, from behind the safety of a fence built of avoidance, as we generally discover in the second path. In the third path, we discover the truth of opposites, and our ego confrontation with conflict frequently escalates. We avoid engaging both inner and outer conflicts and instead focus on our conscious observation of them, struggling to keep the fence in place for the time being. Now, however, in the fourth path, we become able to engage conflict productively. Our egos likewise gain the ability to wait in the wings while truth-telling and truth-acting take center stage. It is a very long process, but probably one of the most worthwhile goals of the spiritual journey. To achieve the capacity to speak and act as our genuine selves with others in complete confidence—now *that* is a cause for rejoicing!

Finally, our delight all comes together—literally—in Jesus's definition of happiness. Community is the great tree that bears the fruit of all our work, and we shall know it by its fecundity and the harvest it offers to us, and to all generations. We dance around the sturdy trunk we have helped to grow and continue to feed. Happiness is, indeed, "among us."

Yearning, Acceptance, and Love: The Passion

Entering Jerusalem

Remember that each gospel has differing details of Jesus's final entry into Jerusalem. Luke employs a vivid allegory and has Jesus arriving on "a colt that has never been ridden." We can readily see how well the fresh, energy-filled Christians could relate to these words. By contrast, fulfilling other narrative purposes and sometimes prophecy, in Matthew Jesus entered on "a donkey and a colt that was its foal," in Mark he rode an "untamed colt," and in John a "donkey's colt."

As Jesus and his disciples entered the city in Luke's account, the disciples shouted praise to God as they announced Jesus's arrival, while the crowd threw their cloaks onto the road before him. The Pharisees objected, offended by the great tumult, but Jesus asserted that "the stones would shout out" if his followers did not. Only in this gospel do the disciples themselves raise their voices in joyful acclamation, rather than the surrounding crowd. With this description of Jesus's entry, Luke depicts the new truth, with full confidence and inspiration, directly confronting the old establishment. This is a portrait of that great day in history which shows the beginnings of an immensely vibrant and unstoppable movement—a picture still vivid centuries later.

In the midst of the celebration, Jesus, though hailed as "king," entered the city weeping—scarcely the demeanor of a traditional king—and lamented that Jerusalem had not understood "the things that make for peace." With this image, Luke characterizes the deeply revolutionary heart of the new faith and brings forward the major theme of peace. This scene and its words are found only in Luke. Jesus went on to predict that Jerusalem's blindness would create only tragedy, clearly foretelling the destruction of the Great Temple and the subsequent large-scale abandonment of the city by the Jews. Luke astutely seizes upon the reality that at the time he wrote—approximately fifteen years after the Temple's destruction—Jerusalem had never recovered and remained desolate.

> When he had come near Bethphage and Bethany, at the place called
> the Mount of Olives, he sent two of the disciples, saying, "Go into
> the village ahead of you, and as you enter it you will find tied there a
> colt that has never been ridden. Untie it and bring it here. If anyone
> asks you, 'Why are you untying it?' just say this, 'The Lord needs
> it.'" So those who were sent departed and found it as he had told
> them. As they were untying the colt, its owners asked them, "Why
> are you untying the colt?" They said, "The Lord needs it." Then they
> brought it to Jesus; and after throwing their cloaks on the colt, they

set Jesus on it. As he rode along, people kept spreading their cloaks on the road. As he was now approaching the path down from the Mount of Olives, the whole multitude of the disciples began to praise God joyfully with a loud voice for all the deeds of power that they had seen, saying, "Blessed is the king who comes in the name of the Lord! Peace in heaven, and glory in the highest heaven!" Some of the Pharisees in the crowd said to him, "Teacher, order your disciples to stop." He answered, "I tell you, if these were silent, the stones would shout out." As he came near and saw the city, he wept over it, saying, "If you, even you, had only recognized on this day the things that make for peace! But now they are hidden from your eyes. Indeed, the days will come upon you, when your enemies will set up ramparts around you and surround you, and hem you in on every side. They will crush you to the ground, you and your children within you, and they will not leave within you one stone upon another; because you did not recognize the time of your visitation from God." (19:29–44)

Leading as a Servant: The Last Supper

The Last Supper in this gospel is the Passover dinner. Despite the setting of a meal, Luke mentions only wine and bread, which Jesus directed to be divided among his followers, who are here identified as apostles. This designation sets the context of the meal as *service*. There are explicitly two cups of wine—one early on, and then another "after supper." Once the second glass had been drunk, Jesus announced that one of those present would betray him. Dismayed, the apostles began to discuss among themselves who the culprit might be, and then, in anger, they debated who would later come to be considered the "greatest" among them. Stepping in, Jesus excoriated the authority of the old ways and said that while all of them had gone through trials with him, the criterion for a true leader was not suffering, but service, citing himself as the exemplar. Luke's description of Jesus's reaction to the squabble is entirely different from other accounts, and by it he is clearly establishing a standard for Christian leadership.

If we again recall that each Passion account serves to sharpen the core question addressed by the individual gospel, then the telling of the Last

Supper here assumes even greater meaning. The question of Luke's gospel is, How do we mature in service? As the gospel moves through its lessons, the question crystallizes and becomes, How do we develop an original life that continues to grow and offers itself to the greater good? This is the context to which the entire Passion is devoted.

Luke even designs the sequence of the cups drunk at the supper to emphasize service. Although there are traditionally a series of cups drunk during the Passover ritual, the Gospels of Matthew and Mark mention only one cup at the meal. Luke's account differs, referring to two cups and naming, quite specifically, "the cup after supper." At the Passover meal, this is the final cup, also known as the Cup of Elijah, or the Cup of Compassion. It is named thus because Elijah was noted for feeding a Sidonian woman—that is, a non-Jew—during a major famine (1 Kings 17:8–16). Luke deliberately refers to that cup in order to evoke for the apostles someone of great faith who, like the Good Samaritan, broke the rules of tribe to act in service. This is the cup from which Jesus poured "the new covenant in my blood."

Luke's unique version of Jesus's words to Peter about his betrayal follows. Even though Jesus had prayed that Peter's faith would remain steadfast, Jesus informed Peter that he would still, inevitably, deny his Lord before the cock crowed. Jesus also knew that Peter would repent his action and specifically asked that, when he did so, he use his new understanding to "strengthen your brothers." Peter, shocked, at that moment still unaware of his capacity for perfidy, assured Jesus that he would never hurt him— that he would accompany him "to prison and to death." Both of these small variations, found only in this gospel, are directed to Luke's audience, communities who needed to strengthen each other, and who were possibly facing prison and even death.

Finally, the theme of lawlessness arose, as it does in several places in this gospel. This was a matter quite specific to Luke's audience, who were being unfairly persecuted for their "illegal" religious faith. Jesus instructed his disciples to go out as mendicants and spread his word. Then, in a clear reference to the branding of Christians as "lawless," Luke inserts an ironic exchange regarding the purchase of a sword to fulfill the prophecies of Jesus's rebellion. The zealous apostles offered "two swords," but Jesus calmly quelled their ardor. Luke wants to impress upon his audience that the world will always form its own opinions, often false. It is fruitless to fight against such false allegations, for fighting only amplifies them. Rather, the proper course—the course Jesus himself followed in Nazareth—is to simply continue calmly on one's own way.

When the hour came, he took his place at the table, and the apostles with him. He said to them, "I have eagerly desired to eat this Passover with you before I suffer; for I tell you, I will not eat it until it is fulfilled in the kingdom of God." Then he took a cup, and after giving thanks he said, "Take this and divide it among yourselves; for I tell you that from now on I will not drink of the fruit of the vine until the kingdom of God comes." Then he took a loaf of bread, and when he had given thanks, he broke it and gave it to them, saying, "This is my body, which is given for you. Do this in remembrance of me." And he did the same with the cup after supper, saying, "This cup that is poured out for you is the new covenant in my blood. But see, the one who betrays me is with me, and his hand is on the table. For the Son of Man is going as it has been determined, but woe to that one by whom he is betrayed!" Then they began to ask one another, which one of them it could be who would do this. A dispute also arose among them as to which one of them was to be regarded as the greatest. But [Jesus] said to them, "The kings of the Gentiles lord it over them; and those in authority over them are called benefactors. But not so with you; rather the greatest among you must become like the youngest, and the leader like one who serves. For who is greater, the one who is at the table or the one who serves? Is it not the one at the table? But I am among you as one who serves. You are those who have stood by me in my trials; and I confer on you, just as my Father has conferred on me, a kingdom, so that you may eat and drink at my table in my kingdom, and you will sit on thrones judging the twelve tribes of Israel. Simon, Simon, listen! Satan has demanded to sift all of you like wheat, but I have prayed for you that your own faith may not fail; and you, when once you have turned back, strengthen your brothers." And he said to him, "Lord, I am ready to go with you to prison and to death!" Jesus said, "I tell you, Peter, the cock will not crow this day, until you have denied three times that you know me." He said to them, "When I sent you out without a purse, bag, or sandals, did you lack anything?" They said, "No, not a thing." He said to them, "But now, the one who has a purse must take it, and likewise a bag. And the one who has no sword must sell his cloak and buy one. For I tell you, this scripture must be fulfilled in me, 'And he was counted among the lawless'; and indeed what is written about me is being fulfilled." They said, "Lord, look, here are two swords." He replied, "It is enough." (22:14–38)

Staying Present and in Truth: The Arrest

After the Passover meal, Jesus retired to the Mount of Olives, followed by everyone from the dinner, whom Luke at this point designates as disciples and, hence, learners. Jesus requested that all of them stay apart from him while he prayed, which he did once. By contrast, in the accounts of both Matthew and Mark, Jesus selected three disciples from the larger group, admonished them to stay awake, and withdrew three times. In John's gospel, the group left their final meal and went to an unnamed garden where—without prayer—Jesus was immediately arrested. Although it seems odd that Jesus the Christ would need succor while praying, Luke also provides an angel in the garden, who appeared to Jesus and gave him strength. This element, not found in many of the earliest documents, is presumed to have been added sometime later. The prayer was so earnest that Luke describes Jesus's sweat as being "like great drops of blood falling down on the ground." Once again we see Luke's emphasis on passion in the pursuit of Spirit.

Rejoining his disciples and finding them asleep, Jesus inquired why they had not also taken advantage of this opportunity for prayer. Suddenly, Judas arrived on the mountain with a crowd that included the chief priests, officers of the Temple police, and the elders. In this scene, Luke gives an image of the "old" Jerusalem arriving to snuff out the new. Judas approached to kiss Jesus, but before he could do so Jesus spoke. This is an allegory Luke's audience understood all too well. They, too, had no need to await the kiss of betrayal. They knew they needed to be prepared for the trials that awaited them.

Jesus was taken to the high priest's house, and a crowd, which included Peter, gathered outside. Contrasting with Jesus's acute receptivity to his fate, when Peter was questioned about knowing his teacher, he chose to lie—in effect, to be "asleep" to his spiritual path. Three times he denied knowing Jesus. When the Lord looked into his eyes, Peter—overcome with contrition—suddenly "remembered" and awakened to the responsibilities of his discipleship. Luke knew how easy it would be for his readers to also "fall asleep" to their faith—especially if the slumber maintained their place in the community, their jobs, or their homes.

He came out and went, as was his custom, to the Mount of Olives; and the disciples followed him. When he reached the place, he said to them, "Pray that you may not come into the time of trial." Then he withdrew from them about a stone's throw, knelt down, and prayed, "Father, if you are willing, remove this cup from me; yet, not my will but yours be done." Then an angel from heaven appeared to him and gave him strength. In his anguish he prayed more earnestly, and his sweat became like great drops of blood falling down on the ground. When he got up from prayer, he came to the disciples and found them sleeping because of grief, and he said to them, "Why are you sleeping? Get up and pray that you may not come into the time of trial." While he was still speaking, suddenly a crowd came, and the one called Judas, one of the twelve, was leading them. He approached Jesus to kiss him; but Jesus said to him, "Judas, is it with a kiss that you are betraying the Son of Man?" When those who were around him saw what was coming, they asked, "Lord, should we strike with the sword?" Then one of them struck the slave of the high priest and cut off his right ear. But Jesus said, "No more of this!" And he touched his ear and healed him. Then Jesus said to the chief priests, the officers of the temple police, and the elders who had come for him, "Have you come out with swords and clubs as if I were a bandit? When I was with you day after day in the temple, you did not lay hands on me. But this is your hour, and the power of darkness!" Then they seized him and led him away, bringing him into the high priest's house. But Peter was following at a distance. When they had kindled a fire in the middle of the courtyard and sat down together,

Peter sat among them. Then a servant-girl, seeing him in the firelight, stared at him and said, "This man also was with him." But he denied it, saying, "Woman, I do not know him." A little later someone else, on seeing him, said, "You also are one of them." But Peter said, "Man, I am not!" Then about an hour later still another kept insisting, "Surely this man also was with him; for he is a Galilean." But Peter said, "Man, I do not know what you are talking about!" At that moment, while he was still speaking, the cock crowed. The Lord turned and looked at Peter. Then Peter remembered the word of the Lord, how he had said to him, "Before the cock crows today, you will deny me three times." And he went out and wept bitterly. (22:39–62)

Arrested, Jesus was mocked and mistreated by the soldiers. Then he was taken to Pilate and charged as one "who stirs up the people by teaching throughout all Judea." Interestingly, this is very similar to the charges that were being brought against Christians in Luke's time. By elevating the role of women, caring for slaves, talking about equality between the educated and the uneducated, and making many other changes, they were threatening the status quo and those who derived power from it—most specifically, the hierarchy of the Roman Empire—just as Jesus had.

Pilate, not wanting to anger the populace, realized that he could shift any fury directed at him by sending Jesus to Herod, head of the Roman government in Galilee. Initially, this pleased Herod, who considered Jesus simply another magician who would perform tricks for him. When Jesus refused this role (even when mocked), Herod sent him right back to Pilate, draped in an "elegant robe." (The other gospels noted a variety of colors.) Luke reports that Herod and Pilate became friends afterward. We can assume they were unified in their desire to silence the obstreperous prophet; and, from a deeper perspective, we can see that they had joined forces in a battle to keep a threatening new reality at bay.

Now the men who were holding Jesus began to mock him and beat him; they also blindfolded him and kept asking him, "Prophesy! Who is it that struck you?" They kept heaping many other insults on him. When day came, the assembly of the elders of the people, both

chief priests and scribes, gathered together, and they brought him to
their council. They said, "If you are the Messiah, tell us." He replied,
"If I tell you, you will not believe; and if I question you, you will not
answer. But from now on the Son of Man will be seated at the right
hand of the power of God." All of them asked, "Are you, then, the
Son of God?" He said to them, "You say that I am." Then they said,
"What further testimony do we need? We have heard it ourselves
from his own lips!" (22:63–71)

Then the assembly rose as a body and brought Jesus before Pilate. They
began to accuse him, saying, "We found this man perverting our nation,
forbidding us to pay taxes to the emperor, and saying that he himself is
the Messiah, a king." Then Pilate asked him, "Are you the king of the
Jews?" He answered, "You say so." Then Pilate said to the chief priests
and the crowds, "I find no basis for an accusation against this man."
But they were insistent and said, "He stirs up the people by teaching
throughout all Judea, from Galilee where he began even to this place."
When Pilate heard this, he asked whether the man was a Galilean. And
when he learned that he was under Herod's jurisdiction, he sent him off
to Herod, who was himself in Jerusalem at that time. When Herod saw
Jesus, he was very glad, for he had been wanting to see him for a long
time, because he had heard about him and was hoping to see him perform
some sign. He questioned him at some length, but Jesus gave him no
answer. The chief priests and the scribes stood by, vehemently accusing
him. Even Herod with his soldiers treated him with contempt and
mocked him; then he put an elegant robe on him, and sent him back to
Pilate. That same day Herod and Pilate became friends with each other;
before this they had been enemies. (23:1–12)

The Green Wood Will Turn Dry: To Golgotha

Once more, Luke contains a significant passage not found in the other gospels. Dramatically depicting the journey to the crucifixion, Luke recounts
Jesus's address to the "daughters of Jerusalem," which spoke of frightening

times to come and referred to natural cycles. Many have considered this an apocalyptic message; however, natural cycles inevitably blossom into new life and hope, despite their times of dwindling into barrenness and the dark. Luke's message is therefore not one of despair at all. Instead, he is entreating, once again: "Don't be in denial. Prepare. Terrible adversity *is* coming. However, in God's good time, events will turn, as they always do, because we are all within a never-ending pattern." And indeed, in the ensuing generation, the bad times came, as the Romans set about hunting down Christians and massacring them whenever and wherever they found them. But ultimately, the circle did turn and the Roman Empire crumbled, while Christianity thrived.

> As they led him away, they seized a man, Simon of Cyrene, who was coming from the country, and they laid the cross on him, and made him carry it behind Jesus. A great number of the people followed him, and among them were women who were beating their breasts and wailing for him. But Jesus turned to them and said, "Daughters of Jerusalem, do not weep for me, but weep for yourselves and for your children. For the days are surely coming when they will say, 'Blessed are the barren, and the wombs that never bore, and the breasts that never nursed.' Then they will begin to say to the mountains, 'Fall on us'; and to the hills, 'Cover us.' For if they do this when the wood is green, what will happen when it is dry?" (23:26–31)

A Choice of Perspective: The Crucifixion

Jesus walked to Golgotha with two fellow prisoners Luke identifies as "criminals," a word that would resonate with his audience, many of whom were being charged with crimes against the Roman Empire. In Matthew and Mark the two are called "bandits." John simply states there were "two others, one on each side."

Then abruptly, in the midst of the crucifixion, we find Jesus's prayer: "Father, forgive them; for they do not know what they are doing." These words, though simple, are dramatic and radical, contravening the traditional tribal law which held that if there were injury, the proper response was injury in return, as in the adage, "An eye for an eye and a tooth for a tooth." This heartfelt prayer is not found in any of the earliest documents; therefore, it may have been added later. No matter when the prayer appeared in this gospel, however, its words are consonant with Luke's message. Presenting a new social doctrine, they offer a powerful challenge for Christians dying at the hands of the Romans.

As the three hung on their crosses, onlookers cast lots for Jesus's clothes and scoffed; and—in an echo of the third temptation—challenged Jesus to use his powers to save himself. The two criminals also spoke, and Luke clearly intends for them to represent two competing voices within the Christian community. The first was frightened and self-pitying, longing for a miracle-worker to rescue him. The other accepted the justice of his sentence, spoke of his faith in Jesus's kingdom to come, and rebuked the first criminal. And though the second criminal was scarcely equivalent in blamelessness, he does bring to mind the same kind of acceptance that Zechariah and Elizabeth displayed about their unexpected childbirth. This is the attitude that Luke seeks to engender in his audience, regardless of their station, circumstances, or tribulations. He implores them to be strong and faithful and, in turn, promises that for their efforts Paradise can be theirs.

> Two others also, who were criminals, were led away to be put to death with him. When they came to the place that is called The Skull, they crucified Jesus there with the criminals, one on his right and one on his left. Then Jesus said, "Father, forgive them; for they do not know what they are doing." And they cast lots to divide his clothing. And the people stood by, watching; but the leaders scoffed at him, saying, "He saved others; let him save himself if he is the Messiah of God, his chosen one!" The soldiers also mocked him, coming up and offering him sour wine, and saying, "If you are the King of the Jews, save yourself!" There was also an inscription over him, "This is the King of the Jews." One of the criminals who were hanged there kept deriding him and saying, "Are you not the Messiah? Save yourself and us!" But the other rebuked him, saying, "Do you not fear God, since you are under the same sentence of

condemnation? And we indeed have been condemned justly, for we are getting what we deserve for our deeds, but this man has done nothing wrong." Then he said, "Jesus, remember me when you come into your kingdom." He replied, "Truly I tell you, today you will be with me in Paradise." (23:32–43)

Jesus's death in Luke's gospel occurs at 3:00 p.m., after a period of darkness that lasted for three hours. Luke also tells us that the curtain of the Temple was torn in two. At the final moment, Jesus loudly and clearly commended his spirit into his Father's hands, and then he died. That is *all* Luke says. He provides no other emphasis or detail. There is no mention of Jesus's reciting Psalm 22. The watching centurion referred to Jesus simply as an innocent "man" rather than an innocent "Son of God." As a result, it is as though each spare, scant sentence has a deep breath between it, and every single word falls directly into our hearts, as though they were written about a beloved friend of ours who died horribly on a recent afternoon—a death in which God took a great interest. This surely must have been Luke's intention, having authored an entire gospel filled with this same closeness and intimacy. It is an extraordinary account, remarkable for its simplicity and power.

It was now about noon, and darkness came over the whole land until three in the afternoon, while the sun's light failed; and the curtain of the temple was torn in two. Then Jesus, crying with a loud voice, said, "Father, into your hands I commend my spirit." Having said this, he breathed his last. When the centurion saw what had taken place, he praised God and said, "Certainly this man was innocent." And when all the crowds who had gathered there for this spectacle saw what had taken place, they returned home, beating their breasts. But all his acquaintances, including the women who had followed him from Galilee, stood at a distance, watching these things. (23:44–49)

WE DO NOT exaggerate when we talk of the guide to mature spiritual practice that is held within the Gospel of Luke—and much of it is contained in the Passion account. As Jesus the Christ enters Jerusalem on the unridden colt, we are given an amazingly full metaphor of the new lives we are birthing as we leave John's garden. These lives are fresh and original. They are unique, challenging, young, and powerful. Because, like that colt, they have not yet been ridden, they are difficult to control.

We are becoming whole. Though we are still part of a larger human community, in our inner lives we have become our own community. We are laying down our covering cloaks, and we want to shout out our joy. We promise to honor the truth of Jeru-Shalom, where all the tribes can meet and honor their conflicts in peace. This is a reflection of our inner lives as well as the outer behavior we will strive for. We will speak our truth but will not demand that others do the same. We can only weep in compassion for those who still clutch their cloaks.

John's gospel showed us a Jesus who washed his disciples' feet at the final meal. Luke's Jesus made the simple statement that now carries that action forward and suffuses our lives: "I am among you as one who serves." Mandating service, he dismissed being merely "at the table." In other words, being a faithful follower is not enough. We gained a follower's understandings in the third path. Now we must be active in the performance of those principles.

Peter's actions are a good reflection for us. We can progress only through taking action, and we will inevitably make mistakes. We can readily get caught up in trying to do things the "right way"—whether those things are a role in our lives, a job, or a spiritual journey. The lesson here is that if we are able to stay in humble service to others, even if we get some details wrong, it is likely that we are still on the right track—or, like Peter, will be able to return to it.

Jesus also coupled his teaching with important comments about being perceived as lawless. This is a great truth. When we act in accordance with our new lives, at times we may—and probably will—be misunderstood. Some people will think we are acting for our own purposes, or for some unknown, sinister reason. Most people are not accustomed to those who act with genuine selflessness or real self-confidence. Both motivations can inspire suspicion and mistrust. Luke counsels us not to worry about it, but to stay in faith and proceed anyway. We will have "everything [we] need," by which Luke means everything we need *on the level of Spirit,* which is what sustains us.

As our awareness increases, so do our prayerful exertions, although they most likely will not cause us to sweat "like blood." Nonetheless, as we gain access to the fullness of our emotional lives, we will often find ourselves overwhelmed by the urge to shout out our joy. Furthermore, our greater levels of emotional sensitivity and self-awareness will enable us to anticipate Judas's proverbial kiss much sooner than we could previously—whether it arrives as danger, a gift, and/or possible solutions. Put simply, we will just "see things coming." This ability, if joined with courage and determination, can assist us to walk further on a proactive path toward the "good fruit" John the Witness asked of us.

We will begin to operate in a more capable, subtle, and confident manner as we practice and hone our fresh skills. The most powerful weapons in the universe are truth and love. Over time, no army, no power, can stand against these two. Yet the old and closed will always resist the new and open. We will each be judged and charged with inspiring people against the status quo, just as Jesus was charged by the chief priests. And what a wonderful charge that is! Though Herod meant the "elegant robe" as mockery, it became a badge of honor and beauty. We, too, can wear the badge of our journey with pride in the name of Jesus the Christ and our genuine lives.

Jesus's lack of response to the criminal who ridiculed him demonstrated a practice of deep compassion—what psychologists term "compassionate autonomy." He wasn't lured into the trap of entering the grievances and denial system that masked another's unaddressed, walled-off pain. He understood that there was no real relationship possible with that man. Instead, he met the criminal (and the others present who scoffed) with clarity and understanding. He asked that they be forgiven, because they "knew not."

In contrast, there was genuine relationship possible with the criminal who demonstrated greater understanding, and Jesus therefore reached out to him in what is known as "compassionate joining." These are precisely the skills we need to learn and put into practice on an everyday basis. We have to be able to distinguish which of the people we come into contact with have enough ego-maturity to sustain a real friendship, and which would simply pull us into their unfinished emotional problems (and should therefore be kept on a more casual level).

True compassion does not do for others what they are unwilling to do for themselves, because to do so robs the interaction of human dignity—it holds the implicit belief that another person is incapable, or is "less than" we are. Genuine compassion does not let us escape into a path of "easy forgiveness." Luke's profound wisdom is that when we are able to put these principles into effect in our lives, we will be filled with calm. We will not avoid pain—but pain will cease to be self-inflicted agony.

Jesus's words on the cross are the epitome of what is, for most of us, life's longest journey: the understanding of the practice of forgiveness. Jesus does not say, "I forgive them"; rather, he prays that forgiveness may come from God, the Source of All, moving through him and out to those who are breaking his body. The practice of forgiveness is a long road. We are responsible only to walk, step by step, breath by breath, removing the poison of hate and enmity toward another human from our own hearts. That is the forgiveness for which we strive—an inner cleansing of our own souls. It is not within our power, nor is it our right, to "forgive" or condone or make right any action performed by another. That is solely the prerogative of God. In the fourth path, there will be many instances that call us to inner cleansing, to forgiveness. Can we pray Jesus's words? Can we pray . . . to pray Jesus's words?

Jesus's final declaration is a reminder about perspective, and an invaluable frequent prayer: "Into your hands I commend my Spirit." It brings back to our consciousness the reality that, although we strive to do our piece, we are part of a whole, and it is truly not about us.

Expect the Unexpected: The Resurrected Jesus

Luke's resurrection accounts compare to those of Matthew and Mark like macaroni and cheese compares to *coq au vin*. As in the rest of his gospel, Luke is plain and simple in telling of the risen Christ, but that does not mean the food is any less nourishing—not at all. It is only a matter of style—and a very appropriate one, at that. A group of women that included the two Marys went to the tomb and found Jesus's body missing. "Suddenly two men in dazzling clothes stood beside them" and proceeded to announce the resurrection. The women rushed to tell the apostles the news. No one believed the women, although Peter did return to the tomb to check, and he verified that the winding cloths were indeed empty. That said, Luke sees no reason to elaborate further.

Instead, he switches the narrative away from the tomb and back to the most frequent location for all the lessons of this gospel—the road just between or just outside a place. This time, we are presented with two of Jesus's followers—not apostles—walking to a village named Emmaus, seven miles from Jerusalem. As they walked along, they were joined by the risen Jesus, but they were unable to recognize him. The two told the stranger how sorrowful they were about Jesus's death, and with wonder, they shared the story about the disappearance of his body. The stranger forcefully chided them, reminding them of the resurrection prophecies contained in Jewish scripture.

As they neared Emmaus, the two invited the stranger to stay with them, due to the lateness of the hour. He agreed. As they sat at table, the stranger blessed the bread, broke it, and handed it to the two, whereupon their true sight was restored and they recognized Jesus. After he abruptly vanished, the two recalled that earlier their "hearts [had] burned" strongly when the stranger had talked of scripture. They set out immediately to return to Jerusalem and share their story with the apostles. When they got back, they heard about another sighting of the risen Jesus. And though the gospel mentions that Simon witnessed an appearance, there are no details given.

While the group of apostles shared their experiences, the risen Jesus appeared among them a third time. Still forgoing fanfare, Luke describes a very ordinary scene complete with food—which Jesus consumed also, contributing to the proof of his corporeal rising. Once again, Jesus gave his followers a lesson in scripture and "opened their minds." Assuring those assembled that they were "witnesses," he told them to wait and "stay in the city" until they had "been clothed with power from on high," thereby echoing the opening words of the gospel.

Luke's resurrection accounts are completely antithetical to the traditional Messianic hope for a great, dramatic, and mighty warrior Messiah who would suddenly come and—in one climactic moment—rescue the Jews from all of their travails, smash their oppressors beneath his heel, and raise the Jews up forever and ever. In a sense, this gospel is a corrective for unrealistic expectations. Both appearances are very simple scenes where everything occurred in rhythms of ordinary life—at the normal pace of walking, eating, and talking. Jesus always appeared in human flesh, and he emphasized that fact. And yet, everything that happened was divine, extraordinary, and imbued with genuine complexity. Luke is instructing the Christians to expect the unexpected, but to watch for it *within their normal lives.* Additionally, in both accounts Jesus appeared to more than one person, clearly suggesting that the Christus followers search for their experience of the resurrection—the living reign of God— within community.

Luke has consistently advocated patience, particularly when allotting time for wisdom and strength to mature. He began the gospel with Mary's retreat into silence as she awaited Jesus's birth. Now, nearing the gospel's close, he instructs the apostles to resist evangelizing until they have gained more inner strength. In these two examples, Luke covers an immense territory. Addressing both the birth of a new spiritual life and the outward expressions of that life, he speaks equally to the female and the male aspects of his audience. He addresses the individual as well as the community. And in each of these, he continues to counsel, as he always has: "Abide, be patient; have realistic expectations. This is a process, not an overnight miracle."

But on the first day of the week, at early dawn, they came to the tomb, taking the spices that they had prepared. They found the stone rolled away from the tomb, but when they went in, they did not find the body. While they were perplexed about this, suddenly two men in dazzling clothes stood beside them. The women were terrified and bowed their faces to the ground, but the men said to them, "Why do you look for the living among the dead? He is not here, but has risen. Remember how he told you, while he was still in Galilee, that the Son of Man must be handed over to sinners, and be crucified, and on the third day rise again." Then they remembered his words, and returning from the tomb, they told all this to the eleven and to all the rest. Now it was Mary Magdalene, Joanna, Mary the mother of James, and the other women with them who told this to the apostles. But these words seemed to them an idle tale, and they did not believe them. But Peter got up and ran to the tomb; stooping and looking in, he saw the linen cloths by themselves; then he went home, amazed at what had happened. (24:1–12)

Now on that same day two of them were going to a village called Emmaus, about seven miles from Jerusalem, and talking with each other about all these things that had happened. While they were talking and discussing, Jesus himself came near and went with them, but their eyes were kept from recognizing him. And he said to them, "What are you discussing with each other while you walk along?" They stood still, looking sad. Then one of them, whose name was Cleopas, answered him, "Are you the only stranger in Jerusalem who does not know the things that have taken place there in these days?" He asked them, "What things?" They replied, "The things about Jesus of Nazareth, who was a prophet mighty in deed and word before God and all the people, and how our chief priests and leaders handed him over to be condemned to death and crucified him. But we had hoped that he was the one to redeem Israel. Yes, and besides all this, it is now the third day since these things took place. Moreover, some women of our group astounded us. They were at the tomb early this morning, and when they did not find his body there, they came back and told us that they had indeed seen a vision of angels who said that he was alive. Some of those who were with us went to the tomb and found it just as the women had said; but they did not see him." Then he said to them, "Oh, how foolish you are, and how slow of heart to believe all that the prophets have declared! Was it not necessary that the Messiah should suffer these things and then enter into his glory?" Then beginning with Moses and all the prophets, he interpreted to them the things about himself in all the scriptures. As they came near the village to which they were going, he walked ahead as if he were going on. But they urged him strongly, saying, "Stay with us, because it is almost evening and the day is now nearly over." So he went in to stay with them. When he was at the table with them, he took bread, blessed and broke it, and gave it to them. Then their eyes were opened, and they recognized him; and he vanished from their sight. They said to each other, "Were not our hearts burning within us while he was talking to us on the road, while he was opening the scriptures to us?" That same hour they got up and returned to Jerusalem; and they found the eleven and their companions gathered together. They were saying, "The Lord has risen indeed, and he has appeared to Simon!" Then they told what had happened on the road, and how he had been made known to them in the breaking of the bread. (24:13–35)

While they were talking about this, Jesus himself stood among them and said to them, "Peace be with you." They were startled and terrified, and thought that they were seeing a ghost. He said to them, "Why are you frightened, and why do doubts arise in your hearts? Look at my hands and my feet; see that it is I myself. Touch me and see; for a ghost does not have flesh and bones as you see that I have." And when he had said this, he showed them his hands and his feet. While in their joy they were disbelieving and still wondering, he said to them, "Have you anything here to eat?" They gave him a piece of broiled fish, and he took it and ate in their presence. Then he said to them, "These are my words that I spoke to you while I was still with you—that everything written about me in the law of Moses, the prophets, and the psalms must be fulfilled." Then he opened their minds to understand the scriptures, and he said to them, "Thus it is written, that the Messiah is to suffer and to rise from the dead on the third day, and that repentance and forgiveness of sins is to be proclaimed in his name to all nations, beginning from Jerusalem. You are witnesses of these things. And see, I am sending upon you what my Father promised; so stay here in the city until you have been clothed with power from on high." Then he led them out as far as Bethany, and, lifting up his hands, he blessed them. While he was blessing them, he withdrew from them and was carried up into heaven. And they worshiped him, and returned to Jerusalem with great joy; and they were continually in the temple blessing God. (24:36–53)

WE ARE NOT so different from the first-century Christians. There isn't one among us who hasn't longed for a quick solution or a flash of insight or some heavenly intercession that would solve our besetting problem or cure a crisis. That is one of the reasons the lessons of Luke are vitally important. Think of all the major careers in politics, in business, and—yes—in religion that have been won and lost by the precise manipulation of our feelings in this vulnerable area. How many times have we agreed to something or voted for someone because a quick answer was implied or promised? Or left them when they failed to give us the surety we longed for, no matter how facile? On a more intimate level, think of the daily relationships that have suffered because we spoke too quickly—or failed to speak when truth was needed.

The resurrection stories teach us about our ability to renew our vitality and stay present to the divine in our lives. When we find ourselves simply walking through our days, will we still feel the burning in our hearts? Will we come back together, break bread, and share our stories with others? Will we have eyes to be present to the miraculous throughout the day—to stay with wonder and curiosity and a positive attitude—to anticipate the unexpected ways that things can work out? And will we open ourselves to the new kindling of the first path when the beautiful home we have made in the fourth path turns once again to ashes?

In our personal relationships, will we understand that a genuine friend shares only when asked—and with mindfulness of the place where our companion is on his or her journey? We will continually meet others who are in different places of understanding than we are, and we should take this into account when we communicate, and when we consider how we think about their words and actions. We will need to suspend our judgment and condemnation. We may even need to meet them in a different path of worship or faith. It is both test and testament of our compassion and our commitment to the path of Jesus the Christ when we are able to greet all persons with the same degree of love and honor and respect with which we would meet our Lord himself. This is the lesson of the road to Emmaus.

When Luke speaks of not going out to share God's word until one is "clothed with the power from on high," it is this power—the power of love, compassion, and respectful understanding—to which he refers. It is a type of power that has been sadly misunderstood for a very long time in parts of the Christian church and which should endeavor to refashion Christian evangelism and speech throughout our lives and the world.

And then we can abide in Jeru-Shalom with great joy.

EXERCISES FOR THE FOURTH PATH

The exercises of quadratos are cumulative. By the time we have reached this point, we are ready to begin a series of activities that will, we hope, become lifetime practices rather than exercises. Like the lessons within the Gospel of Luke, they support us into discovery of the greatest riches of our revitalized life—and the longer we use them, the wealthier our spirits become. Because they are lengthy, we have detailed them in a separate chapter, which follows, titled "The Eight Essential and Continuing Practices of the Fourth Path."

Prayers for the Fourth Path

PSALM 131

You know that my heart is not haughty
Nor my eyes lofty
Neither have I reached for things
Too great and too wonderful for me

But I have calmed and settled my heart
And it is contented

Like a child surfeited on a mother's breast
Like a suckling child is my heart

Let those who question and struggle
Wait quiet like this for you
From this day forth
And always
                        translation by Norman Fischer

PSALM 133

How Good
How pleasant
When we abide intimate together
Like warm oil on the head
Trickling down the cheek
Aaron's cheek
And trickling down the neck onto the collar
Like the dew of Mount Hermon
The dew that runs down the mountains of Zion
Where you called forth the blessing
For life, life always
                        translation by Norman Fischer

HOW DO WE MATURE IN SERVICE?
is the core question of the Gospel of Luke

The Gospel of Luke is a map, guiding the maturation of the spiritual journey into a practice of genuine forgiveness and compassion. From this place of integration, we gain the ability to act from love despite tension and conflict.

Zechariah and Elizabeth and Mary teach us to receive the unexpected with equanimity and curiosity, remaining open to possibility. Then we have to be silent and ponder the changes that have come, allowing time for integration to find its way within us and take root.

The Canticle of Mary blesses us with the standard of holding a unified vision of the future. When we put the power of this positive expectation into our life, it will improve.

The nativity account likewise counsels patience and openness to the unexpected. As we walk the path of quadratos, our traditional "home" will often disappear. We, too, may need to seek a manger or build a fresh place for the birth of our "child," the new energy of our lives. And we must welcome and offer love to each and every part of ourselves—even the most unformed, awkward, fearful, and hidden aspects.

The story of the boy Jesus in the Temple reminds us that growth is a process of change. Some of our history is valuable, while some needs to be put aside; some new things are productive, while others are not. Patience and discernment of our motives are the focus of our reflection.

John at the River tells us to step up and out from the crowd and accept our responsibility for speaking and acting on our own truth, without concerns about whether our truth will be heard, accepted, or effective. John also cautions against the risk that our greater empowerment can turn into a need for adulation.

The temptations ask us to carefully discern whether we are acting truly or whether, when we speak and act, we are actually seeking power for ourselves, power over others, or protection from the consequences of our actions.

The Beatitudes sing out simultaneous promise and strong caution. First they offer the beauty and blessedness of the fourth path we are on.

Then they throw up dire warnings: they promise that if we fail to shelter our new life and act too soon, we *will* revert to immature behavior—and we *will* suffer terribly.

The parable of the Good Samaritan is a teaching about the importance of responding to human need with care and compassion and without regard to the strictures of societal boundaries or inner unworthiness.

When we are told to knock at the door, we are being counseled to be persistent and proactive in our lives—even if it is difficult or inconvenient. It is wise for us to keep a vision of what is self-worthy and appropriate for our future and ask for that vision to be fulfilled—to ask for "three loaves," not merely two slices for a sandwich.

The Prodigal Son and other stories of losing and finding remind us that lives lived without risk and exploration are not only dull; they are spiritually empty. The challenges of risk are a necessary tool for our growth. When we push ourselves toward change, regardless of the seeming result, we find inner growth and should celebrate.

Luke's Passion account speaks to us about the practice of compassion and genuine forgiveness. It does not let us escape into a path of "easy forgiveness," which deprives relationships of dignity. It tells us that genuine forgiveness removes the emotional pain that keeps us in bondage.

The resurrection accounts ask us to have fresh eyes and openness of spirit so that we may always recognize Mystery in our lives when it appears. They also ask us to have the patience to wait for maturity before we try to carry this message to others, so that when we finally speak, we will meet people at *their* place on the journey—and not where we might like them to be. Only in this way can we extend the respect, dignity, and freedom to others that we desire for ourselves.

7

. . .

The Eight Essential and Continuing
Practices of the Fourth Path

Rom the perspective of the fourth path, we ask for practical
approaches that help us continue our Journey of Quadratos. We
want to be deepened but are not always certain how to accomplish
this, particularly when our spiritual communities lag behind. This chapter offers eight essential practices, the basis for all of which can be found
within the gospels (particularly Luke). These practices, which have been
expanded somewhat and made specific for modern use, can be used both
by individuals and by groups. They are followed by suggested readings.

While the exercises appear to be focused mainly on individual practice,
all have much broader implications, which (in the fourth path) we realize is
true of every action we take. The last four exercises move well beyond our
personal sphere, and the final two are especially powerful in their potential
for far-reaching impact. In this chapter, we model ourselves after Luke,
moving from modest to lofty. Nonetheless, we consider all of these exercises essential, and believe that their practice will keep us at the heart of our
mature spiritual lives. As we flourish there, we will help to create a wiser
and more compassionate practice of Christianity, and therefore a safer and
more harmonious world.

Practice I: Speak Truth and Unity

*The deepest level of communication is not communication,
but communion. . . . We are already one, but we imagine that
we are not.*

Thomas Merton

The first path frequently brought us face to face with the consequences of untruth in our lives. In the second path we found ourselves caught between opposites. Then in the third path we received an experience of union that dispelled those illusions. Now, in the fourth path, we attempt to learn the behaviors of a new way of being, preparing ourselves to venture onto a new first path, and then another and another. If we wish to live maturely and consciously within the circle of the four paths, we must remain aware of every regressive force that might pull us backward. One of the greatest of these rests in the habits of our speech.

We are responsible for every word that issues forth from our mouths. And words have immense power. That is why, when addressing matters of importance, we should strive to bring forth those deeply reflected, long-held-in-the-belly truths (Elizabeth and Mary again, yes!) rather than the sentence that hurriedly pops out. We desire our speech to be genuine. We want the opinion we are expressing to be truly our own and not a rehashed version that actually belongs to some authority figure we have allowed to assume too much power in our lives. Spirit calls us to be accountable for our words, demanding the courageous expression of our truth, even at the risk of loss of esteem or liberty.

Yet, at the same time, we are called to compassion and unity. We are asked *never* to relinquish our truth, but simultaneously *never* to negate the truth of another—and to do our best to speak only in terms of ourselves and with kindness. Particularly in the early years of fourth-path practice, this can sometimes seem a difficult tightrope on which to balance. It often doesn't seem fair, or even possible, to meet all of these requirements.

However, this is one of our greatest challenges and the most important of all the eight practices. That is why we have placed it first. It is foundational. It is threaded throughout every aspect of our lives, particularly filling our families and our workplaces. It is habitual and relational, and change is extremely difficult. Although we can bring our awareness to the problem, we are likely to need help. One step is to patiently and carefully listen to those more adept than we are. Another is to enlist ourselves in a more formal practice, such as that of *contemplative dialogue* (for which we have listed the Web site below). However, this is such a vital and problematic issue that we believe it is also a completely appropriate matter for a buddy system. Two friends can commit to helping each other be mindful of compassionate and appropriate speech, as can a small group.

The third path taught us that the truth of reality is oneness. The human family, and every experience of that family, is part of a whole. This means that *no one and no thing* can ever truly be "other." Therefore, when we use absolutist language—language that is either/or or separatist in any way, we are expressing an untruth. This clearly has huge implications for our relationships, communities, and spiritual traditions—not to mention politics.

In practice, is this difficult? Of course it is! We not only struggle with ourselves, we struggle with the English language, which is built on categories and specificity. English has many more words than any other language on earth, and though it strives to find the perfect word for everything, it often lacks subtlety. For example, psychology tells us that every human emotion is a complex combination of feelings: joy contains sadness, for example, and laughter is poignant. Yet the English words carry no hint of the undertones—merely the single, dominant aspect. Correspondingly, light can have no dark within it, nor the converse, though in the twenty-four hours of the day, the variations are literally infinite.

We must work constantly to be mindful of our language and to creatively overcome its limitations, stretching to move away from words that separate and reaching for those that unite—even creating new metaphors when possible. In the paucity of our language, how can we continually describe the reality Merton refers to when he writes, "We are already one, and only imagine we are not"? How do we accomplish the circular reality of wholeness and communion in the linear limitation of our language?

The process must necessarily begin with monitoring our thoughts. This can be a challenge, because it is likely we have not been in the habit of giving them such careful scrutiny. The difficulty is increased by the fact that our culture has become so separated that even words heretofore perfectly innocent—left, right, liberal, conservative—have taken on absolutist and pejorative qualities. Even our hymnals and prayer books focus on "I" instead of "we." However, if we wish to walk a fourth path of love and compassion, we will be mindful and self-vigilant and refrain from terms such as these—even if we have to sing the song a little differently than everyone else.

Let us be clear. This is not about political correctness of any kind. Our aim is much deeper. There is no language that is free from a philosophy or worldview. English has millennia of accretions attached to it, plus some relatively recent distortions. Some of them are not a problem, but many of them are. When we take charge of our speech, we are taking individual responsibility for helping to heal the error of dualism in our world.

Let us therefore bend our every effort to speak in the language of "we," "us," and "our"—knowing that, eventually, the new Jeru-Shalom will be built upon the words of our honest and respectful wrestling with each other.

READINGS

Bernardo Olivera   *How Far to Follow? The Martyrs of Atlas*

Steven Wirth   *The Path of Contemplative Dialogue: Engaging the Collective Spirit,* available at www.contemplativedialogue.org

Practice II: Open and Engage the Truths of Beauty

I asked the earth, I asked the sea and the deeps, among the
living animals, the things that creep. I asked the winds that
blow, I asked the heavens, the sun, the moon, the stars,
and to all things that stand at the door of my flesh. . . . My
question was the gaze I turned to them. Their answer was
their beauty.

St. Augustine

Most of us are busy and distracted, with many demands on our time, energy, and emotions. Few of us are fortunate enough to live in the country, or to have a museum next door. Yet almost nothing integrates and refreshes and brings us more deeply into our soul-work than the experience of beauty. Beauty has three levels—the appreciative, the collaborative, and the creative. All are satisfying and important, and all will yield riches as fourth-path practices.

Regularly opening ourselves to the appreciation of beauty is invaluable. This does not mean we should trot down to the Modern Art Museum, unless that experience lifts our soul. Each of us is different. What this does mean is that we should regularly seek out the places that open us to wonder and awe, to a feeling of the holy, of being connected to All—and then revel in sight, touch, and smell: the entire sensory and tactile experience of beauty. It may be wiggling our toes in a white-sanded beach, being swarmed by a litter of kissing puppies, inhaling the fragrance of a perfect yellow rose—or, yes, contemplating a painting in a museum.

In order to expand our experience, we use our imagination. We select an episode or a feeling from our lives or our work or our relationships—something from our larger world. We bring that truth into our encounter with beauty in any way that seems appropriate to us. Then we combine the aspect of our life with the art, or the beach, or the puppies. We just hold it there for awhile. Do they relate in any way? Amplify each other? Diminish each other? Spark the thought of something or someone else? Then we try bringing in another aspect of our lives. We tend to think that comprehending wholeness is a part of the third path, but appreciating beauty can be a dynamic experience that enlarges our understanding of almost anything. It is able to bring a sense of rightness, wonder, and the holy to all parts of our journey.

The *collaborative* experience of beauty can be a bit more difficult to accomplish but is wonderfully rewarding. It is exactly as it sounds—the shared experience of beauty or, even better, of beauty-*making*. This might include making music, singing, dancing, working in a garden, or taking a nature walk with others. Some of us are fortunate or intentional enough to collaborate with others on a journey similar to our own, and then we can expand our experience through the sharing of its contemplative aspects, through chanting, or via other creative group projects. Collaborative efforts have the potential to combine all three forms of beauty: to create, to share, and to appreciate. When this is achieved, a special kind of richness opens, because the fourth-path gift of relationship and friendship based in equality that moves in both directions is added to the element of creativity.

The *creative* experience of beauty is, by far, one of the most valuable practices on our work of the fourth path. To create means to bring forth something that has not existed before. It is a birthing—by definition, a holy activity. It is unique and wonderfully mysterious.

In the arena of creative expression, we limit recommended practice to forms of expression that engage the body, because of their capacity to overcome the chatter of the ego-mind. This is particularly profound—and profoundly important—on the fourth path. There are many avenues to explore. It is critical, however, that we make a commitment to opening the deep well of the nonverbal aspect of ourselves and becoming accustomed to the reverberation of its sonorous echo in the other areas of our lives. Nonverbal creative work specifically engages the physical and the sensuous—and does so in a very direct way.

We can, of course, do this through drawing or painting, whether or not we have training. Without training, simple colored pencils, markers, or tempera paints are probably the most available and satisfying media to use. A *large* brush used on a *large* piece of paper or canvas can be especially gratifying, particularly with brilliantly pigmented tempera colors or broad-tipped markers. Graffiti artists might be on to something! And it is quite primal and centering to work with a big piece of clay. Many of the new varieties of clay are available in vivid colors and don't dry out quickly. A favorite of quadratos groups is collage—randomly choosing and cutting out images from magazines and gluing them to a large page, and later contemplating what can be seen in the pattern of the choices made. To these possibilities, we add the creativity of making gardens, and dances, and music.

Whatever the medium, the creative process is the same—and it replicates the process of quadratos. First, we begin—an admittedly difficult step. We do it anyway. We make the space, take the time, spend as many blank minutes just sitting as necessary. It is difficult to begin from nothing and go to something. There is typically time spent wrestling with the material. Then more time spent in what feels like vain efforts. (They are *not*. We should not stop.) Eventually, *something* comes. We just go with it until it ends. Then (or maybe next time, or eventually) a feeling emerges from some mysterious place that is akin to being lifted by wings. Time seems to stop, but our hands continue on. We have accessed a deep and holy region—and we have discovered why artists create. In our creative journey, we have progressed from Matthew, through Mark, to John.

Additionally, as we engage in *regular* creative work with image (or music or dance)—as we practice what we have learned and start to make it a part of our genuine and original new lives, our efforts move us further—into the fourth path. There, we reap other benefits. Imagery moves easily in all directions, through the full spectrum of human experience. Images can be emotional, physical, intellectual, and spiritual. They can attract, repel, uplift, and horrify. They can be filled with tension or calm, be erotic or mundane. If, in our creative work, we stretch to experience and appreciate all of the sides within and around us, our ability to understand and fluidly move through the paradoxical nature of Spirit will grow, as will our capacity to share it as it becomes more familiar.

Regardless of what type of creative practice we eventually choose (and maybe we will choose more than one), we should keep, photograph, or record our efforts. In this way, we can remain present to our entire quadratos journey. A periodic review will display all our paths before us. We will see the trepidation, the progress, and the joy. We will see Matthew and Mark and John and Luke displayed before us. We will see the great truths that have moved through us and led us forward.

READINGS

Seena B. Frost   *SoulCollage: An Intuitive Collage Process for Individuals and Groups*

Thomas Moore   *Original Self: Living with Paradox and Originality*

John O'Donohue   *Beauty: The Invisible Embrace*

Lindsay Whiting   *Living into Art: Journeys through Collage*

Practice III: Find the Quiet Center

The path to the center is never straight but always clear.
Gernot Candolini

Meditation and prayer have been strongly recommended throughout our entire Journey of Quadratos, and our need for them will never cease. In the fourth path, we come to understand their practice to be as regular and necessary as our breath. Historically, across spiritual traditions, there have been two major forms of meditation. These have grown out of two worship traditions—seen variously as both contradictory and complementary. In Christianity, they are called by Greek names. One is called "apophatic worship," which derives from the Greek word *aphonais,* meaning "to say no." Its underlying principle is that God is beyond all earthly symbols and human efforts at understanding; therefore, a meditator should attempt to transcend or remove all concepts and "empty oneself." When an image or thought arises, it is to be gently dismissed. The meditator's continuing effort is toward achieving what Buddhists call Nirvana—a completely serene, yet connected, awareness of the whole, of God.

The second form is called "kataphatic worship" (also spelled "cataphatic"), which comes from the Greek *kata,* which means "down into" or "down with," combined with *phasis,* which is Greek for an utterance which expresses feelings rather than propositions. Kataphatic worship affirms the knowledge of God, using expressions of wonder and glory. Its meditation form usually focuses on an image, although it can also use words or a story or even music. The practice is to focus on the image, move into it, then through it, and eventually find stillness. Some proponents of this type of meditation have claimed that it is more integrated with "real life" than apophatic meditation.

Apophatic meditation can be an active form of prayer employing a mantra and breathing, or it can be a silent contemplation such as that used in centering prayer, most notably espoused by Father Thomas Keating. This prayer is typically practiced as twenty to thirty minutes or more of quiet sitting. Another well-known apophatic form is a Society of Friends Meeting, which is one hour of silent contemplation. Yet it is possible for such a meeting to suddenly become kataphatic, because if Spirit so moves them, members may arise and speak aloud about any subject they wish, and the group will then respectfully meditate upon that subject. Likewise, centering prayer has expanded and developed a hybrid called "imaged centering prayer," introducing kataphatic elements.

Methods of kataphatic prayer range along a continuum from gazing upon an icon for an extended period (at the most traditional end) to modern dance. In between are practices such as labyrinth walks and pilgrimage, chanting, brush drawing, collage, working with paint or clay, and ritual. Sunday worship services are essentially kataphatic prayer forms that use image, senses, and body posture to engage participants and move them into a quiet center. This was more apparent with older rituals, which had greater use of music, incense, costume, and color than we are familiar with today. Nonetheless, present-day ritual in religious services is still intended to serve this purpose.

A kataphatic practice directly related to quadratos is *lectio divina,* which is found mentioned in documents dating from 220 CE. The words mean "sacred reading" and in its earliest form, *lectio divina* was practiced in monasteries. A monk would read a scripture passage aloud, and those assembled would meditate on the passage for an extended period. It likely grew from the ancient Jewish tradition of elders gathering in the Temple to hear, to chant, and then to verbally wrestle with each other about a text from the Torah. In the sixth century, St. Benedict strongly supported the practice in his writings, leading to its wider spread. In the twelfth century, a French Carthusian monk, Guigo II, set the simple reading into a formal four-step process he called a "ladder." This system was used extensively until the fifteenth century, when it all but disappeared, only reappearing again following the reforms of the Second Vatican Council in the 1960s.

Today, *lectio divina* is used far beyond monasteries. In his book *Sacred Reading,* Michael Casey describes *lectio divina* as "a means of descending to the level of the heart and of finding God." In its simplest form, this is done by a slow recitation of selected scripture, repeated and punctuated with periods of silence. A deep rhythm is developed—as much of silence as of the words—and the listeners are, without effort, moved beyond the questioning mind into a deeper, more peaceful space and, ultimately, closer to God.

In the formal, four-stage process, the beginning is *lectio* (reading), when the listener makes a concerted, repeated study of the words of the selected text. The second stage is *meditatio* (meditation), wherein one asks oneself how the passage affects one's life. *Oratio* (reflection/ prayer) flows from the text and the meditation, and may result in an inner question about what step to take, or a prayer of thanks or praise. The final step is *contemplatio* or *actio* (contemplation or action), when one fully enters the prayer experience in awareness, in gratitude, in praise, or perhaps in a discernment for change or action. These stages exactly match up with the quadratos sequence.

If we wish to consciously combine quadratos with *lectio divina,* we can use either the preceding or upcoming Sunday gospel reading from the three-year lectionary as our text. In this way, the entire four gospels, in the sequence of quadratos, are contemplated over a three-year time span. It is even better if this is done by a group. Then there is a community of support that will provide a fresh well of sustaining grace—regardless of which of the four paths is most present in our personal life. If we belong to a church community that doesn't follow the three-year Sunday cycle, we can still follow the quadratos *lectio* by praying the gospels of Matthew, Mark, and Luke in the sequence and stopping in Lent and Easter every year to pray the Gospel of John.

Another kataphatic method that mirrors the four paths is labyrinth walking meditation. As our feet cross the threshold, we are seeking growth and change (Matthew). Walking the circuitous path to the center, we note our many exhaustions and anxieties (Mark). As we rest in the center, contemplating the steps we have taken and those still to come, as they are displayed before us, we pray for communion (John). Retracing our path to the beginning, imbued with new understanding, we pray to carry out the truths of the blessings we have received (Luke). Labyrinths can now be found in many faith communities, and can readily be purchased in portable forms.

Regardless of how we choose to find the quiet center, time and experience have shown that both apophatic and kataphatic techniques are immensely valuable in leading us to our primary objective: a place where we can rest beneath our mind's chatter, gain perspective, and connect with Spirit. We may have an individual preference for one form over another based on what we were taught or what we personally find easiest. Because each form has virtues, it is good to experiment; even someone who is very knowledgeable in one form might benefit by stretching to learn the other; the less familiar style may render unexpected richness. It might even be worthwhile to combine the two styles. Increasingly, modern practice is showing us, and encouraging, a great deal of overlap. It may well be that the differences between the two styles are fairly illusory and arbitrary. In the end, the point of meditation is our experience of the reverent stillness, not how we get to it.

We need to add a note regarding both forms of meditation. Meditators typically speak of the "quiet" center (with quiet being more characteristic of apophatic meditation than kataphatic), and modern practice generally posits that meditation is done with the body held still. However, physical "quietness" is not at all consistent with ancient practice and we encourage people to free themselves from this conception. Wholeness is our objective, and wholeness is not a disembodied experience.

Historically, walking, rocking the body, and dance were completely acceptable expressions of prayer and meditation in both "methods." Many people use yoga practice as a form of meditation that incorporates bodily experience, and there are several other movement-based disciplines that provide deeply spiritual experiences to their practitioners. Remember our discussion in the Gospel of John: spirit is not superior to body, though, sadly, many religious and spiritual leaders seem to consider it so. *After* you have mastered the fundamental principles of the form you have chosen, please practice its expression in whatever way works best for you.

READINGS

Lauren Artress   *The Sacred Path Companion: A Guide to Walking the Labyrinth to Heal and Transform*

Lauren Artress   *Walking a Sacred Path: Rediscovering the Labyrinth as a Spiritual Practice*

Cynthia Bourgeault   *Chanting the Psalms: A Practical Guide with Instructional CD*

Michael Casey   *Sacred Reading: The Ancient Art of Lectio Divina*

Thelma Hall   *Too Deep for Words: Rediscovering Lectio Divina*

Ana Hernandez   *The Sacred Art of Chant: Preparing to Practice*

Thomas Keating   *Intimacy with God: An Introduction to Centering Prayer*

Alexander J. Shaia   "Sandplay and Spirit," *Presence* (June 2002), available at www.alexanderjshaia.com

Practice IV: Absorb the Deeper Rhythms

I go among trees and sit still. . . . As we sing, the day turns,
the trees move.

Wendell Berry

The four paths, the sequence of each day, and the order of the four seasons
are significantly connected. God breathes creation into these cycles, and they
are a daily resurrection, the ever-present mirror of the Christ in our lives. Our
common conversation reflects this. We talk of how we slept and how "our
day" is going. The weather is our most common topic. Our fourth-path practice is to behold this truth—the truth of our connection with the rhythms
of everyday life—with greater depth and mindfulness. The recommended
discipline is a simple one—like Luke's gospel. Go outside once a day, take a
deep breath, and reflect on our connections with the natural rhythms. (For
greater resonance with our ancestors, do this at sunset or sunrise.)

Ancient traditions celebrated the beginnings of days and years in times
of dark and quiet. We do not think this way today, but it used to be that
when the sun disappeared, it was the time to make ready. Sabbath begins
at dusk, and autumn was always considered the first season of the year, the
time when it was possible to see nature preparing for her long winter sleep.
This timing came more naturally to earlier, agrarian cultures, which viewed
everything in terms of the crop cycle. Thus the Jewish New Year begins in
autumn, followed closely by the harvest festival of Sukkot. Autumn marked
the ending of one crop's death, and the anticipation of the next one's life—
the year's turning.

It would help us if we could once again match ourselves to early evening
and autumn as natural expressions of the first path and the changing part
of a universal cycle. After all, in the evening our bodies decelerate (or try
to, in our busy lives). We review our day and make plans for the next. In
autumn, we watch the leaves lose their green and transition through color
into brown. Some plants begin to go dormant and others to die. Nonetheless, we realize that we will see many of them resurrect into new life come
spring, while others will decay into rich compost for future growth. The
turning of new life continues unceasingly. When we take a breath every
autumn day, we can ask what challenges face us and with what willingness

we face them. Are we attempting to cling to the green of the season past? Or are we willing to change—even if it means transformation?

Our nighttime slumber and the arrival of winter's cold reflect the second path to us. Both are intended to slow us and grow us. Our metabolism and our brain both require time to regroup. Long nights and winter snowfalls are our mirrors. They can be a picture of interminable suffering and restlessness when we are unable to feel at peace. The gasp of night and the breath of winter can feel difficult to take in, and a yearning for warmth and love may overtake us, trying to quell our lack of peace. Or, is it possible for us to see winter as a time of nothing stirring on the surface except the occasional storm, yet with tremendous work of growth being accomplished out of sight and underground? The second path holds pondering, and either terrible suffering or patient endurance. Quiescence is necessary for the life of an abundant spring to germinate and grow.

At last—or at least it seems so—our dark-accustomed eyes blink open and the first green shoots appear. The sun comes up, and the cycle releases spring! We breathe, stretch, wiggle our toes, enjoy, and notice anew. In spring, we exult in the bright colors of the flowers, in warmth and possibilities, yet there is tumult also. Sudden rainstorms pelt, air masses collide and bring tornadoes, and early heat creates flooding. Each day, as we awake, "it's always something," as the saying goes. This is the third path, when our awareness is continually stretched. Quadratos asks us to become sensitive and aware. Everything is part of the whole—the embrace of someone we love, the contempt of an embittered relative, the transcendent, exquisite sunrise, and the flood that devastates lives. When we take our daily breath in this third-path practice, we ask ourselves how to grow in understanding and acceptance of the complexities of this truth.

Almost without our notice, the freshness of the day turns, and spring becomes summer. The revelations of the third path become the attentive labor of the fourth. Equipped with more knowledge, yet a bit road-weary, we must allow wisdom to measure our pace and our actions. The sun is overhead and the summer days are long. When we take our summer breath, our questions have a different rhythm. They are more difficult. Sometimes they snag on the exhale of our good labor, or maybe the shallow inhale of our sanctimony. "Am I doing only for myself, and nothing for others?" or "Am I doing everything for others and nothing for myself?" or even "Does the life I am living match up with the beliefs I hold? Too much? Too little?" These are the questions of living and learning the balance and maturity of the fourth path, and we see them best reflected when the sun is high and the summer is hot.

Early evening, nighttime, morning, afternoon—autumn, winter, spring, and summer—these natural cycles of four bring the Journey of Quadratos into a fresh intimacy for us. The processes we witness outwardly we also see inwardly. Each day and every season holds both gift and challenge. The mindfulness of a daily breath will help remind us to ask where and who we are.

READINGS

Thomas Berry   *The Great Work: Our Way into the Future*
Nora Gallagher   *Things Seen and Unseen: A Year Lived in Faith*
China Galland   *Longing for Darkness: Tara and the Black Madonna*
J. Ruth Gendler   *Changing Light: The Eternal Cycle of Night and Day*
Joan Halifax   *The Fruitful Darkness: Reconnecting with the Body of the Earth*
Jan L. Richardson   *Night Visions: Searching the Shadows of Advent and Christmas*
————.   *In Wisdom's Path: Discovering the Sacred in Every Season*
Brian Swimme   *The Hidden Heart of the Cosmos: Humanity and the New Story*

Practice V: Expand into Risk

*And the day came when the risk to remain tight in a bud was
more painful than the risk it took to blossom.*
Anaïs Nin

Having made at least one turn of quadratos's fourfold cycle, we are certainly familiar with risk. We may not yet greet it as a friend, but we now recognize it as a necessary component of our journey. We have engaged in it, not once, but many times along our way. This fourth-path practice has a strong message: risk-taking is not over, now or ever. The paths of the quadratos cycle never end, any more than the recurring cycle itself does. We can enter into each new path and enjoy continuing growth, or we can attempt to ignore the call for change from this universal pattern and inevitably regress. Those are our simple choices. With the forward choice we gain vitality and joy, but at the price of continued vulnerability. When we "opt out" of our growth as individuals, the result is some variety of withering—we grow rigid, narrow, timid, fantastical, or depressed.

If we continue the journey, our major question becomes knowing *when* to risk, and finding ways to support our courage. Clarissa Pinkola Estés, author and psychologist, writes in *Women Who Run with the Wolves,* "Climb the highest tree. Walk out on its thinnest limb. Let it break." This is a terrific metaphor about maximizing human potential, but it could also be seen as a recommendation for recklessness. How do we discern the difference between an adventuresome spirit and downright stupidity? The quality of our daily lives is deeply affected by the answer to this question.

Furthermore, the consequences of our actions today—even of our words—are a great deal more far-reaching than they have ever been. We can travel literally with a virus by plane or train, or figuratively with one via the Internet; in either case, we can infect millions, and others can do the same to us. Words we speak and write and images we create arrive instantaneously in every corner of the planet. We can inflict great damage and are in physical and emotional jeopardy in ways we have never known and are not prepared for. We have no precedent for being so exposed, so known to each other, with such great responsibility for interdependence.

At the same time, on a personal level, many lack the support systems they used to find in families, neighborhoods, and social and fraternal organizations. Yet, in some ways, this is progress, as difficult as that may be to accept. A lot of the unwritten rules that undergirded those same families, neighborhoods, and organizations were precisely the ones that ruled ancient tribes. Strong support was provided to members, but it came in return for unquestioning allegiance—and the willingness to shun, hurt, fight, and even kill those outside of and rejected by the head of the group.

Some church groups have begun innovative programs to help fill the gaps in community, but most people languish with no connections. Internet organizations such as Facebook have had huge success, partially because they provide some sense of being a neighborhood, albeit in cyberspace; but by and large these are not real people on the ground putting their physical arms around each other for a hug. No substantial new ways or groups have yet been developed to fill these voids. As a result, many of us feel lonely and uncertain, particularly in the areas of relationships and discerning appropriate levels of responsibility.

In this tentative environment, when, how, and to whom do we risk saying the words, "I want," "I need," "I love"? Or go further and make the commitments of "I have" and "I do"? How do we foster the growth we desire—in ourselves and in the larger world? Is there a guidebook we can follow? The Journey of Quadratos is that guide, and the eight practices form a concrete and ongoing process we can use. Yet we acknowledge that it is very difficult to go it alone. In each of the practices, making the effort to join with others who also engage in the same activities will pay large dividends. It is likely that somewhere, when lifting a paintbrush or while in the parking lot of a labyrinth, we will encounter a kindred soul. That encounter can become the kernel of a friendship, which can lead to like-minded others, and even the formation of a quadratos group.

No matter what we do in this regard, however, moments of trial are still unavoidable. We will face something new, and we will feel that unmistakable, uncomfortable tightness in the chest or belly or cranium. That is the ego-mind letting us know it is frightened, digging its heels right into that particular body part—wailing, "I don't want to take a risk!" And that is our signal to pull out the tools we have placed in reserve for precisely this moment. This is when we talk with those trusted friends we have developed. And we pray, walk, grab some clay, or draw—and pray some more. We overcome our trepidation and move through our sense of peril.

Alternatively, our inner voice and counselors instead help us to discover that the signal to stop is—this time—accurate, wise, and protective, and we possibly *are* being foolhardy and misguided. If that is the case, then we either pause for more information, or stop our course completely. Regardless of the direction we move in, the decision is completely ours, and we are able to make it with serenity and finality. We have developed a fourth-path practice to deal with risk, and we are certain that our process is solid. We have no regrets, and we know we will find the next challenge a bit easier because of our experience.

READINGS

Joan D. Chittister   *Scarred by Struggle, Transformed by Hope*

Roger Housden   *Ten Poems to Set You Free*

Henri J. M. Nouwen   *The Inner Voice of Love: A Journey Through Anguish to Freedom*

Practice VI: Learn to Let Go

Your desire must be disciplined, and what you want to happen in time, sacrificed.

Rumi

Another way to state this practice, in more psychological terms, would be, "Don't be attached to results." It is possible that, next to truth-speaking, this principle affects an emotionally and spiritually mature life more substantially than all the other practices, yet no action or striving whatsoever is required. In fact, we are required to *not* strive or act. Luke gave a version of this practice when he assured his readers that *if* they lived a compassionate life and cared for each other, then despite every challenge, they would find passion and joy in their communal life, and their Christian beliefs would ultimately not only endure, but thrive. The modern version requires us to open ourselves to a realization having two parts.

First, we accept that positive results *will occur* provided we sincerely make our way through the universal spiritual paths of quadratos and then continue our fourth-path practices. Stated in another way: we grasp that it is completely outside our power to control how "life" changes, but completely up to us to use our best efforts to improve ourselves—and that "life" will tend to improve if we do.

Second, we accept that we are not in any way in charge of the greater processes of life or the universe. The great cycles move through us—in their own time and with their own vast and inexplicable wisdom. We won't always understand why things happen. We won't always get the results we want. Good people unaccountably suffer, and bad people mysteriously thrive. At the same time, it is possible for us to become so attuned to the visible face of the Christ in our lives that we discover miracles as ever-present and literally uncountable. We know deeply that we are a significant part of the whole. We also comprehend that every person and every living thing shares our significance equally—that we are part of the All that is animated by the creative, intelligent force of Spirit, of God, which is Love—and which will ultimately prevail.

However, understanding these matters intellectually does not make letting go or learning to detach simple or easy. In fact, letting go can be extremely difficult, because we largely proceed through the same steps as if we were going to remain attached. We focus intensely, make decisions and plans, and take action—everything we would normally do, especially all of us who are really doers. It differs only at the end—but then it *really* differs. At the very end, no matter what plans, projects, prayers, or endeavors we are engaged in, small or large, we give up.

We examine everything we have done. We make sure we have been rigorous. We make certain we have been faithful in our process of quadratos: setting out, enduring a time of meaningful struggle, coming to understanding, evaluating, allowing things to unfold and find maturity, praying frequently and going into silence, taking risks as we walk our truth, finding and using our true voice and our creativity, and breathing many times with the whole world to be certain our intentions are in service. Then we stop, abruptly. The time has come for us to take the final step. It is time for one last prayer—the words of letting go, the same prayer we recognize as Jesus's in Gethsemane (Matthew, Mark, and Luke): and so we pray, "Yet, not my will but yours be done" (Luke 22:42).

At this moment, we release all of our efforts, our hopes, our doubts, and our fears—every single one of them—to the power we know is greater than ours. Perhaps our efforts will bear the fruit we desire. That depends on complexity and intelligence greater than ours. Quite often, something entirely unexpected opens from our exertions and we get a pleasant surprise. Sometimes we are disappointed, or left patiently waiting—as Nelson Mandela waited in prison for twenty-seven years. Yet our inability to control the ending cannot change our actions. The course of our heart and conscience is unequivocal. We are asked to act and speak in the same way that Mary pronounced her transcendent canticle in Luke's gospel—as if we are completely certain everything that Jesus the Christ spoke as truth has already come to pass on this earth.

Readings

Beatrice Bruteau   *Radical Optimism: Practical Spirituality in an Uncertain World*

Kathleen Dowling Singh   *The Grace in Dying: How We Are Transformed Spiritually As We Die*

Practice VII: Build the New Jeru-Shalom

Through our scientific and technological genius, we have made of this world a neighborhood and yet we have not had the ethical commitment to make of it a brotherhood. But somehow, and in some way, we have got to do this. We must all learn to live together as brothers or we will all perish together as fools. We are tied together in the single garment of destiny, caught in an inescapable network of mutuality. And whatever affects one directly affects all indirectly. For some strange reason I can never be what I ought to be until you are what you ought to be. And you can never be what you ought to be until I am what I ought to be. This is the way God's universe is made; this is the way it is structured.

Martin Luther King Jr.

This seventh practice doesn't seem, on its face, to require too much of us. It requests that we not isolate ourselves from others when we become fearful. Yet there are times when not holding ourselves separate can be very difficult indeed; when the mere asking for help from another human being is the hardest task we can set ourselves. Yet, as Luke says, we will be greatly rewarded if we bring ourselves to "knock at midnight." Conversely, there are many occasions when extending our hand and heart in compassion to some surly, ungrateful opponent is the very last thing we want to do. Yet it is through these apparently simple tasks that peace will ultimately be born.

The participants in any relationship or association that endures over a long period take precisely these simple actions, over and over and over again, whether it is a marriage, a community, a church synod, or the Congress of the United States. We are sometimes able to observe such associations from a distance and assess whether or not people manage them with as much skill and success as they could. When the answer is no, we respectfully suggest that if they included the principles of quadratos in their equation, they could improve matters substantially.

Why might that help? Because quadratos provides awareness of three things: the real nature of "shalom," the stages of the universal cycle of change and growth, and the absolute necessity of carrying that growth outward into service. Grounded in quadratos, we enter all relationships with the comprehension that Jeru-Shalom is a place that invites, mediates, and discovers the dynamic yet peaceful tension of opposites. As we move through difficulty and challenge, we remain conscious of what is actually happening in the *process* of relationship at all times. This helps us to not overreact. Furthermore, if we are practicing our journey, when our tendencies to move away from others overwhelm us (or when we try to control things or to move too close), we have a countervailing impulse. We are able to stop, make an assessment, and take appropriate and compassionate action—whether toward others or ourselves.

Spirit seen through the perspective of quadratos reminds us that the whole is composed of All. We are held in love and significance, but not as *more* significant than others. We are not entitled to special treatment, to have our views heard over those of others, nor do we have a right to "win" over others. It is our great human challenge to creatively discover ways to accommodate all voices, all perspectives, and all needs in single communities, single countries, and on one globe. We *all* belong. This is precisely why the gospel map of transformation was given to us originally, and is now revealed again, supported by advances in psychology, sociology, and other sciences.

Jesus the Christ said, "Let anyone with ears to hear listen!" (Mark 4:9). The Gospels of Matthew and Mark led us up the mountain and through the sea to the epiphany in John. Then we walked through the lessons that taught us how to complete the process in Luke. If we wish to build the new Jeru-Shalom, we must, without fail, walk Luke's roads. Genuine empathy arises through the activity of service. When we see through another's eyes, our separations disappear as the largely illusory divisions they actually are. From this place of new understanding, we can join together and find the creative solutions that allow us to become authentic communities, sitting together in the mutual respect of Jeru-Shalom, the place of peace.

READINGS

Peter Block   *Community: The Structure of Belonging*
M. Scott Peck   *The Different Drum: Community Making and Peace*

Practice VIII: Make the Great Leap of Trust

But all shall be well, and all shall be well, and all manner of thing shall be well.

Julian of Norwich

In each of the early Christian communities, faced with the rigid strictures of tribe and the dramatic crises of history, trust between individuals and groups was a grave issue. And it could easily be said that one of the practical results we most need from the Journey of Quadratos is a capacity for the appropriate discernment of trust, which is a deepening and expansion of Practice V, the ability to risk. Trust may well be *the* issue of our time. We often think fondly of the past, and when we do, most of us are yearning for two things: trust and simplicity. We remember when bookies and steroids did not crop up in reports of our sports heroes, when police officers and politicians ostensibly protected our interests, and when the word "pedophilia" was unthinkable in the same sentence as "church." We could rely on what the doctor told us, walk into a store and buy something without comparison shopping, and a handy person could repair their own car without an advanced degree. We have the sense that we used to have fewer decisions to make and that those decisions were somehow easier. We feel that, formerly, we were more able to rely on things, on institutions, and on people in some greater or stronger way than we do today, whether or not that is actually true. We are filled with apprehension and mistrust.

Fear lurks beneath the lack of trust we feel today. What do we fear? Is it pain, loneliness, loss of position, loss of respect? Is it possible that underneath all of these fears, real as they are, lies one core dread: the fear of not having love? If we dig deeply enough, will we discover that our deepest question is, What will I do if no one loves me? We believe it is, and we believe further that it is the most powerful and painful fear we have. Why? Because it is our very first feeling. It is the primordial cry of the helpless infant who cannot feed itself and knows it will die without the parent who loves it. It is why a baby smiles—with every gurgle begging, "Love me, feed me, and don't let me die." This fear is the terrible, painful truth with which we begin our lives, and we carry it with us to our graves—a gaping, psychological wound that no other human being ever fills for us, though we keep asking them to, over and over.

How, then, is it possible for us to find trust? Only with great difficulty. We learn at very young ages how physically vulnerable we are, and other children teach us the ease of betrayal. Sadly, our families, none of them trained as parents, are also frequently culpable in the lessons that breed our wariness. If the entire question of trust were left up to our egocentric, logical brains, focused on self-protection, by adulthood we would believe only that the entire world is intrinsically unsafe. But in that eventuality, our lives would be barren and bitter. Therefore, logically, trust is a great conundrum. Fortunately for the emotional and spiritual quality of our existence, the signals of doubt are not an intellectual matter. They are carried by the body and its complex animal warning chemistries. We *feel* when someone or something is safe—or not. Our bodies and emotions are, therefore, what give us most of our options, and they generally get the deciding vote in choices about trust—which describe most of the significant choices in our lives.

However, because the brain's safeguards still need to be overridden, the act of trust requires courage. "Courage" derives from the French word for heart, *coeur;* it means to be heart-filled. The dilemma is, How do we fill ourselves with heart and gain the capacity to trust and overcome our fear without being just plain foolhardy? The eight practices of quadratos's fourth path are precisely designed to complete the epiphany of the third path and make it into a permanent reality. Over time, the truth discovered through these practices fills the body and emotions and forges a spiritual connection powerful enough to overcome the natural anxieties that reside in most people; and that connection allows trust to form and find a home. It is then possible for the intellect to develop a belief system of faith and engage the trust that has been established—to make a "leap of faith," as the saying goes (even though there has been a whole process and no sudden leap at all).

This is the heart—and truly the soul—of the fourth path. Once the intellect is able to cross that chasm of terror, everything is changed forever. The infant's deep fear, which we have carried all our lives—a fear that felt like the fire of some terrible inner apocalypse—was stoked by the fuel of our own intellectual despair. Now that fear is entirely replaced by faith, which fills us, *body, mind, and soul*—a luminous certainty that we are loved and accompanied from beyond our beginning; that we are in Union forever, and will never be abandoned. In this wholly embodied vision of the Christ, there are no outsiders, and the idea of us versus them becomes unnecessary, even a bit silly.

READINGS

Phil Cousineau   *The Art of Sacred Pilgrimage: The Seeker's Guide to Making Travel Sacred*

T. S. Eliot   *Four Quartets*

Pierre Teilhard de Chardin   *Hymn of the Universe*

8

. . .

Paradigms and Promises

NOW THAT WE HAVE made our way through the Journey of Quadratos and its reflection in the four gospels, it is time to return to the beginning, where many promises were made. There, we stated that quadratos shows a way in which we can absolutely trust the four Christian gospels as revelations of divine truth. We pledged that the four gospels, read together, form the experience of a universal guide to spiritual transformation. Furthermore, we vowed that if you chose this experience, the vision and practice of your Christian faith would be renewed. Never again would the discovery of a new bit of information about Jesus's life or the history of the early Christian church cause you a moment of anxiety or dismay.

Our promises did not stop with matters of faith. We went much further. We said that if you followed this journey in a serious and committed manner, your life would change. It would become better—incredibly better—although we did not promise an overnight metamorphosis. It *would* take some time, and some spiritual elbow grease as well. But eventually, equanimity would replace anxiety, compassion would supplant resentment—and instead of loneliness, curiosity, community, and joy would be the blessings of your life.

Now that you have taken those first tentative steps up Matthew's mountain, endured the bleak time in Mark's stormy sea, luxuriated in John's garden, and steadily marched along Luke's road, it is time for us to ask the big question. Have these promises been kept?

A New Paradigm

You know our core premise—that the four gospels were selected *together* to be used as a process for inner transformation. This is quite different from Christianity's prevailing view. Quadratos makes the assumption that the four gospels were initially selected because they held a pattern incorporating wisdom already known to be powerful—and therefore certain to move a great and glorious new faith forward. The more common view—that the gospels were four separate stories of Jesus's life and teachings—seems unlikely to accomplish this purpose as successfully. Since there were dozens of gospels available to pick from, the "separate stories" view deems a matter as important as the choosing of the gospels to be less like making a serious plan and more like a committee squabbling and then settling on "the best of the bunch."

If, however, we instead choose to comprehend the four gospels as one continuous story of renewal divided into four chapters—as an integrated and sequential account of transformation through Jesus the Christ—then we have an entirely different picture. We can readily see the logical, serious, inspired blueprint for a great text that accompanies a great purpose. We have an approach that provides a more logical and satisfying answer to the struggles of our heads, and a deeper and more lyrical song for the rhythm of our hearts. It is this new and more fulfilling paradigm—the paradigm of quadratos—that we offer to you. It is the story of Jesus the Christ, who lives *eternally* within time.

Quadratos also provides a base for spiritual renewal on a larger scale, because it moves Christianity away from its current focus on dogma and historicity into practice. It is through spiritual practices that advance us toward spiritual maturity that we will discover new lives in community and as religious bodies. The dilemmas of our faith will not be solved through continually looking for answers using the same principles we currently follow. New pieces of papyri, new translations, or new pronouncements from our various denominations are not going to solve the significant problems we face. Our only answers lie in a different precept altogether. As Einstein said, "No problem can be solved from the same consciousness that created it."

We understand that certainty of this new paradigm—indicated rather than explicit in early Christian writings—may feel difficult. We know that formal church support always lags behind. And quadratos is *not* a reworking of the gospels as we have known them. It *is* a paradigm shift, and its philosophical basis is discontinuous from that of many current writers and scholars. Therefore, how do we—more importantly, how do *you*—assess whether this is wishful thinking or a sound new frontier?

Anytime we see a pattern—whether we're looking at clouds or at masses of statistics—the easy criticism suggests that we are discerning a nonexistent design or making some negligible linkage larger because we have an emotional longing for connection. Could that be the case with quadratos? We think not. We have shown you a great deal of historical evidence, and we have searched for the deep patterns revealed by its details, rather than focusing on the details for their own sake. Unlike many biblical historians, we see no sense in using only the narrow strictures of historical and theological documents that have so often been abridged and edited for political, abusive, and self-serving purposes. We have demonstrated to you that quadratos is based solidly on spiritual, psychological, anthropological, and sociological patterns that have shown us their faces over time. That patterning is bolstered by like patterns in nature, hard science, and art. This great rhythm revealed in quadratos is universal. To quote Albert Einstein once again, "I shall never believe that God plays dice with the world."

Therefore, the words of Genesis 2:10—"A river flows out of Eden to water the garden, and from there it divides and becomes four branches"—do not surprise us. Our diverse sources of corroboration prove that quadratos is a valid, newly recovered foundation of Christianity and is simultaneously a fresh paradigm that makes the ancient heart of faith conscious within us. The designs of four-ness that we have shown are solid and human-based. They have appeared and demonstrated their worth over significant periods of time. Most of them are universal. Many of them are permanent and match up with the patterns of our bodies and our very planet. Taken together, they provide compelling evidence that a pattern in Christianity based on four-ness is far more logical than one that is not.

We of quadratos, therefore, unequivocally state that Christianity made a right choice in choosing exactly four gospel texts. Furthermore, of all the available choices, we logically believe—and faithfully trust—that these specific four texts were precisely the correct texts to choose, and that the ancient reading cycle was the purposeful plan for spiritual growth. Our certainty is based not on "accurate" biographies of Jesus, but on an eternal truth found throughout the millennia of human history—the universal journey of transformation.

Keeping Promises

And what of the personal promises we made in the first chapter—promises that go well beyond the questions of theology? If you are reading this book for the first time, there is obviously no real way to know if your faith has, indeed, been rejuvenated. It takes awhile to discover the improvement in a life. Here is what we do know. We know that the message of quadratos has been communicated to thousands upon thousands of people through lectures, workshops, and retreats every year for many years now. We know that its influence has spread sufficiently that quadratos is used in the training of clergy, spiritual directors from diverse Christian denominations, and psychotherapists using various modalities. There are also multiple programs and study groups at work within churches and outside of them, nationally and internationally, including grief and loss support groups, death and dying seminars, and art creativity training. Quadratos is being used as essential reading for those in spiritual direction, psychotherapy, and sermon, worship, and baptism preparation, as well as for parents wishing to understand the cycle of attachment with adoptive children. Legions of people in these areas and others have successfully incorporated this process into their lives.

We would like to offer a suggestion to you now. Make the fourfold journey and its practices a part of your life and see what happens. We have complete confidence that, when you seriously engage this process, you will find your life in faith and your life in general revitalized. Why? Because the gospel cycle is based on sound psychological and spiritual principles, and provides a true opening to Jesus the Christ. We at Quadratos have experienced deep transformation ourselves and continue to do so, as the four gospel paths form the spiritual and creative home for our lives, and we have watched as the same process unfolds in the lives of many others.

Because it offers tools and answers we need now, the Journey of Quadratos is critically relevant to this time in history. Therefore, we believe that its advance from individuals to the general population will continue to follow the same pattern as it has been doing—which is the same as that of any other timely shift in perspective, including its predecessors, the gospels themselves. Change occurs from the bottom up. Each person whose life has improved tells another person, or probably several people. Some of them try the program, and it works for them; then *they* share it—and the word spreads again and again and again and again. It doesn't take as long as one might suspect. These days, it is called "viral networking," and the mainstream is closer than we often think. Once the new perspective has been widely absorbed, we will look back and wonder why anyone ever thought the gospels had become irrelevant or out of date, and why they were presented only as four separate and profound stories of Jesus's life.

Your Journey

So if all the promises are either clearly met or likely so, the question now becomes this: How will you, as an individual, respond to the revelation of this profound new journey? When your belly begins to fill up with truth, or an angel's voice comes announcing visions to your innermost self, is it Zechariah's fear that will answer the swelling, or Elizabeth's and Mary's willing acceptance? Will you be able to quiet your uncertainties and discern the greater pattern—even when your friends or communities are not yet aware?

Because, regardless of what happens broadly or in any church or in any other person's words or experience, each and every individual still has to find his or her own way. Although some people try to use what they read in books—or hear in worship—as a shield *against* the world and their genuine feelings, quadratos does not work that way. We are in the transformation business here, which is certainly no quick fix. Reading this book is just the beginning. Deep understanding takes a serious commitment of time and a Bible close at hand, not to mention the help of others. And each path still has to be lived out in the real world by each individual seeker, exploring and experiencing myriad trials and errors as we slowly learn how to put all of this into practice in our lives.

For quadratos to work in your life, it must have the qualities of the resurrection story in the Gospel of Luke. It must operate in the real stuff of our day-to-day experience, where we arise and eat and work and struggle. In Luke, Jesus explicitly did *not* reappear as a ghost, and he made sure all the apostles touched him and watched him eat. This was a message to the early Christians, and it is a message to us today: Jesus the Christ is alive, and alive in a very specific way. We are not striving for a life that we "spiritual-ize," as though it is a layer we somehow add to ourselves. We are striving to recognize that our lives and our spirit are *already together,* and attempting to live out that truth. This is what the Journey of Quadratos brings to us.

In addition to our hoped-for changes, we also reap an unexpected bo-nus from quadratos. It turns out that the periods of intense anxiety and chaos we undergo along the way, as well as the times of sweet calm, are clear and identifiable parts of the journey's pattern. Hence the names of the paths become our everyday "shorthand" for this remarkable plan of Spirit and its perpetual cycle of testing and improvement. We hit an extended tough time, and we know that it is a "Mark moment," yet we also know that it will pass—and that prayer is our succor. A call to render service arrives, and we yield to it as a loving message from Luke that yanks us out of our self-absorption. The journey falls into our practice, our thought—and our language.

Inevitably, this book has focused on our individual spiritual journey. We are bringing the Journey of Quadratos to you for the first time. How-ever, our personal journey in the Christ means little if it does not result in greater emphasis on how we belong to each other in the Christ, and how we form and live in communities that announce the truths of Jeru-Shalom. From that long-ago moment after the fire when Sitto pronounced the words "No hate" around the big family table, that has been our primary objective, and it continues to be. Yet this is only one volume; and though we have said much about community, there is a great deal more to be written on that topic than we have been able to cover in this book. Even defining *community* from the new paradigm would take many chapters.

After all, when we honor the reality of the Christ, we are talking about eliminating the boundaries between our bodies and our minds and our hearts. When we fully absorb the epiphany we received in John's gospel and act on it, we abolish dualism and accept complexity and paradox. The application of this principle sharpens discernment and we discover new unities, such as the fact that dark holds light and female holds male and life holds death. Walls of every kind come down: those between biology and mathematics and anthropology and music and physics and art and language and theology and many more.

However, all of the many specific ways in which we think and hope that quadratos can be applied to community are going to have to wait for our future books. Our intention is to follow this book with guides on quadratos-centered ritual and prayer and community development. To be apprised of new work, go to the "Connect with Quadratos" page at the end of this book.

We have redefined and reproposed the ways in which we see and talk and move through our lives. We reiterate: quadratos is a complete shift. It will require an unflinching decision on our part to live our lives through its lens. As the great theologian Paul Tillich wrote in *Systematic Theology,* "Decision is a risk rooted in the courage of being free." Quadratos frees us, individually and collectively, to be closer to our greater purpose, closer to God.

Last Thoughts

Compared to our lives today, first-century Christians lived a simple, uncomplicated life. However, they faced terrific challenges, and they had to use every bit of strength and determination they could muster to live their new, radical faith in the face of fierce oppression by the Roman Empire. In the twenty-first century, insofar as externals go, our daily lives are infinitely more complex than those of the early Christians, yet our inner challenges haven't changed an iota. As we have discussed, trust is very, very hard for us, and we are just as beset by fear and anxiety and challenge—sometimes oppression—as they were. This entire book has asked the question, How did they manage? And how can we?

They used the gospels. They read them. They prayed them. And the gospels spread from person to person, gradually covering the world, because when people applied the words in the texts, their lives were changed. The approach provided by quadratos refreshes those eternal words of inspiration and returns them to their original role as agents of transformation.

Nothing on earth is needed more today than transformation. As a species, humanity has made genuine progress in many ways. We are physically healthier, and in some respects we are psychologically and emotionally healthier also. Despite all the appalling and brutal things we still perpetrate on each other, we have had an authentic increase in self-awareness. It is difficult for us to realize that less than one hundred years ago, in the United States of America, women could not vote, small children worked in factories, and families packed a picnic and went on outings to hangings. Today, many of us are willing to acknowledge our shortcomings, and when the most egregious sins are discovered, cries of "For shame!" echo worldwide.

Yet too many of our emotional, moral, and spiritual paths are still murky and tenuous. In 1945, *within weeks of each other,* two immense and public proclamations of power were made, though of very different kinds: atomic bombs were dropped on Hiroshima and Nagasaki, and the Nuremberg trials were opened. We announced the capacity to annihilate ourselves and simultaneously asserted that the individual has an unambiguous moral responsibility for all of humankind. In retrospect, the timing of those two events seems an almost surreal conjunction. But it sharply points to the kind of moral quandaries with which we are increasingly faced. These are precisely the deep and heavy burdens for which spiritual transformation is an absolute necessity.

Our world is complicated and dangerous. It dazzles us with its beauty and tantalizes with the immensity of possibility it holds out to us. Yet we could well incinerate ourselves at any second, or set in motion the ingredients of irreversible, lingering planetary suicide. We *are* growing up as a species, but so far most of our progress has been focused on the externals—on science and technology—through using our intellectual skills. By comparison with the strides in the technological world, our psychological and spiritual progress has lagged far behind. Each day, we experience constant un-expected intimacies, intrusions, demands, and confusions, without any real guidance or inner wisdom. This maelstrom with a void at the center brings us daily and frighteningly closer to virtual—or even real—Armageddon.

In the great arc of our humanity, it is as though we are in those impossible, painful teenage years. Before us stretches every potential: glory, love, thousands of poignant moments, success—as well as mediocrity, failure, and utter destruction. Rationalism has stripped us of our parental, squabbling gods way up on Mount Olympus or in Valhalla. In a sense we feel orphaned, parentless. We have a relationship with one God who tells us that we have free will. We must find our own way, and the way must be to our greater purpose.

We hope that, by now, we have persuaded you that your life will be improved by the Journey of Quadratos. And perhaps that is reason enough for you to thoroughly study and engage in its practices. But we would like to present you with another motive. This one is both critical and timeless. It has been around for a couple of millennia now, and it has not changed. It has to do with our greater purpose—that mysterious part of us that we all refer to, search for, but never quite seem to find. We too often end up settling for putting its responsibility on our children, donating money to causes in return for plaques with our names inscribed on them, or making myriad other futile efforts. Each of these is an attempt to make us feel as though we are somehow increasing the impact of our small humanity on the earth and decreasing the force of our inevitable physical death. But is that what our greater purpose is truly about?

Our answer is both yes and no. Two millennia ago, Jesus the Christ taught through his words and life that much of what the world accepts is only illusion. Among the truths he gave us were the understandings that all are One and there is no death. He also gave us the solemn charge to humbly share the experience of our transformation and the example of our lives with others, so that eventually the entire world might be freed of illusion and become one with God.

Therefore, yes—through sharing, we do expand our small humanity, and toward that end, our work takes many forms. It tells stories, dances, and paints paintings. It shepherds groups, both small and large, in worship and in song. It brings matter and spirit together and helps to guard the health of our mother, the living planet. It speaks up against injustice and runs for office. It leads without waiting for a leader to arise. It doesn't place responsibility on anyone else, and never expects a plaque on a wall. These labors are never lonely, because God's Advocate is by our side at every precious moment.

But no, we do not work to decrease the impact of our physical death. Not at all. Time and death are of little or no concern. We know with certainty that life is eternal and God's time is the only one worth marking. We have our greater purpose and it is very clear. We are focused on the noble work with which Christians were charged two thousand years ago, and it hasn't changed: follow the journey, understand and know God, follow the journey, grow and live with God, follow the journey, pass it on and serve God—and do this with the utter devotion of our heart and soul and mind. So that All may be One.

> [Jesus prayed to the Father,] "I ask not only on behalf of these, but also on behalf of those who will believe in me through their word, that they may all be one. As you, Father, are in me and I am in you, may they also be in us, so that the world may believe that you have sent me. The glory that you have given me, I have given them, so that they may be one, as we are one, I in them and you in me, that they may become completely one, so that the world may know that you have sent me and have loved them even as you have loved me." (John 17:20–23)

Connect with Quadratos

Visit our Web site,
www.quadratos.com,
where you will find . . .

A free discussion guide for *The Hidden Power of the Gospels: Four Questions, Four Paths, One Journey.* The guide, which can be downloaded, contains study questions for individual or group use. You will also find tips on how to form and sustain a quadratos study group with your circle of friends, psychological group, spiritual organization, or church.

Our Web site is the central meeting place for the Quadratos Community, which grows daily. On it, you can sign up for our e-newsletter; discover exclusive excerpts of new works; read reflections on the four paths, gospel passages, and thoughts on rituals; find out about online courses and upcoming seminars, retreats, and workshops; obtain materials such as books, DVDs, and CDs; and access links to other helpful sites.

Complete information on the Revised Common Lectionary (RCL) and the Roman Catholic Sunday Lectionary is also available on the Web site.

If you are interested in having Dr. Shaia speak, all booking information can be found at alexanderjshaia.com and quadratos.com.

Acknowledgments

To my jiddo and sitto, parents, family, and friends—my deepest gratitude to you for maintaining a big table and always keeping my place at it open. Thanks to my clients, colleagues, formative professors at the University of Notre Dame, and the many other teachers and authors who pointed the way.

To my collaborator, Michelle Gaugy, there are no words to express the honor of working with you and my gratitude for your contributions to quadratos—its ideas, logic, and beautiful prose and your faithful wrestling with the material in times we could not see a way forward.

My profound thanks and recognition to Connie Cox, who has always been the faithful, untiring angel of this work, doing whatever was requested, without question or demur.

Immense thanks (and praise) to the remarkable group at Harper-One: Mickey Maudlin, Mark Tauber, Claudia Boutote, and Laina Adler. You "got it" from the very first. And thanks to Melissa Weiner, publicist; Peter Honsberger, CEO, Coldtree Publishing; Gail Ross, agent; and Nicole Reinecker, Web designer—who all went the distance.

The larger Quadratos family are too numerous to mention by name, but know that you are honored and held in sincere appreciation. Without you, the journey could not have become visible.

To each, it is my prayer that the grace with which you continually envelop this work be returned to your heart and to the world in even greater measure, so that we "may all be One."

Bibliography

Armstrong, Karen. *A History of God: The 4000-Year Quest of Judaism, Christianity and Islam.* New York: Alfred A. Knopf, 1993.

Arnold, Patrick M. *Wildmen, Warriors, and Kings: Masculine Spirituality and the Bible.* New York: Crossroad, 1992.

Arrien, Angeles. *The Four-Fold Way: Walking the Paths of the Warrior, Teacher, Healer, and Visionary.* San Francisco: HarperSanFrancisco, 1993.

Artress, Lauren. *Walking a Sacred Path: Rediscovering the Labyrinth as a Spiritual Practice.* New York: Riverhead Trade, 2006.

———. *The Sacred Path Companion: A Guide to Walking the Labyrinth to Heal and Transform.* New York: Riverhead Trade, 2006.

Athanasius. *The Life of Anthony and The Letter to Marcellinus.* Translated by Robert C. Gregg. New York: Paulist, 1980.

Augustine of Hippo. *Selected Writings.* Translated by Mary T. Clark. New York: Paulist, 1984.

Bass, Diana Butler, and Joseph Stewart-Sicking. *From Nomads to Pilgrims: Stories from Practicing Congregations.* Herndon, VA: Alban Institute, 2006.

Bass, Diana Butler. *Christianity for the Rest of Us: How the Neighborhood Church Is Transforming the Faith.* San Francisco: HarperSanFrancisco, 2006.

————. *A People's History of Christianity: The Other Side of the Story.* San Francisco: HarperOne, 2009.

Bass, Dorothy C., ed. *Practicing Our Faith: A Way of Life for a Searching People.* San Francisco: Jossey-Bass, 1997.

Benedict, St. *The Rule of St. Benedict.* Edited by Timothy Fry. New York: Vintage Press, 1998.

Berry, Thomas. *The Great Work: Our Way into the Future.* New York: Three Rivers, 2000.

Berry, Wendell. *A Timbered Choir: The Sabbath Poems, 1979–1997.* New York: Counterpoint, 1998.

Block, Peter. *Community: The Structure of Belonging.* San Francisco: Berrett-Koehler, 2008.

Bolen, Jean Shinoda. *Crossing to Avalon: A Woman's Midlife Pilgrimage.* San Francisco: HarperSanFrancisco, 1994.

Bonneau, Normand. *The Sunday Lectionary: Ritual Word, Paschal Shape.* Collegeville, MN: Liturgical, 1998.

Boorstein, Sylvia. *It's Easier Than You Think: The Buddhist Way to Happiness.* San Francisco: HarperSanFrancisco, 1995.

Borg, Marcus J. *Meeting Jesus Again for the First Time: The Historical Jesus and the Heart of Contemporary Faith.* San Francisco: HarperSanFrancisco, 1995.

————. *The Heart of Christianity: Rediscovering a Life of Faith.* San Francisco: HarperSanFrancisco, 2003.

Borg, Marcus J., and John Dominic Crossan. *The Last Week: A Day-by-Day Account of Jesus's Final Week in Jerusalem.* San Francisco: HarperSanFrancisco, 2006.

Bosnak, Robert. *Tracks in the Wilderness of Dreaming: Exploring Interior Landscape Through Practical Dreamwork.* New York: Delacorte, 1996.

Bourgeault, Cynthia. *Chanting the Psalms: A Practical Guide with Instructional CD.* Boston: New Seeds, 2006.

Bradshaw, Paul F. *The Search for the Origins of Christian Worship: Sources and Methods for the Study of Early Liturgy.* New York: Oxford University Press, 1992.

Bradshaw, Paul F., and Lawrence A. Hoffman, eds. *Passover and Easter: Origin and History to Modern Times.* Notre Dame, IN: University of Notre Dame Press, 1999.

Brown, Raymond E. *Jesus God and Man*. New York: Macmillan, 1967.

———. "Symposium on the Gospel of John"—course notes. Birmingham, Alabama, 1977.

Brown, Raymond E., and Francis J. Moloney. *An Introduction to the Gospel of John*. New Haven, CT: Anchor Yale Bible Reference Library, 2003.

Bruteau, Beatrice. *Radical Optimism: Practical Spirituality in an Uncertain World*. Boulder, CO: Sentient, 1997.

Campbell, Joseph. *The Masks of God: Creative Mythology*. New York: Viking Compass, 1970.

———. *The Masks of God: Occidental Mythology*. New York: Viking Compass, 1970.

———. *The Masks of God: Oriental Mythology*. New York: Viking Compass, 1970.

———. *The Masks of God: Primitive Mythology*. New York: Viking Compass, 1970.

———. *Thou Art That: Transforming Religious Metaphor*. Edited by Eugene Kennedy. Novato, CA: New World Library, 2001.

Candolini, Gernot. *Labyrinths: Walking Toward the Center*. Munich, Germany: Claudius Verlag, 2004.

Caprio, Betsy. *Star Trek: Good News in Modern Images*. Kansas City: Sheed Andrews McMeel, 1978.

Casey, Michael. *Sacred Reading: The Ancient Art of Lectio Divina*. Liguori, MO: Liguori, 1996.

Catholic Encyclopedia. Digital version compiled and © Catholic Online. *Catholic Encyclopedia* © Catholic Encyclopedia. New York: Robert Appleton Company—vol. 1: 1907; vol. 2: 1907; vol. 3: 1908; vol. 4: 1908; vol. 5: 1909; vol. 6: 1909; vol. 7: 1910; vol. 8: 1910; vol. 9: 1910; vol. 10: 1911; vol. 11: 1911; vol. 12: 1911; vol. 13: 1912; vol. 14: 1912; vol. 15: 1912.

Chittister, Joan D. *Scarred by Struggle, Transformed by Hope*. Grand Rapids, MI: Eerdmans, 2005.

Clément, Olivier. *The Roots of Christian Mysticism*. London: New City, 1993.

Clift, Jean Dalby, and Wallace B. Clift. *Symbols of Transformation in Dreams*. New York: Crossroad, 1984.

Cooper, David A. *God Is a Verb: Kabbalah and the Practice of Mystical Judaism*. New York: Riverhead Books, 1997.

Cousineau, Phil. *The Art of Sacred Pilgrimage: The Seeker's Guide to Making Travel Sacred.* Berkeley, CA: Conari, 2000.

———. *Once and Future Myths: The Power of Ancient Stories in Modern Times.* Berkeley: Conari, 2001.

Crossan, John Dominic. *The Historical Jesus: The Life of a Mediterranean Jewish Peasant.* New York: HarperCollins, 1992.

Dalai Lama, His Holiness the. *Buddha Heart, Buddha Mind: Living the Four Noble Truths.* Chestnut Ridge, NY: Crossroad, 2000.

Daniélou, Alain. *The Myths and Gods of India: The Classic Work on Hindu Polytheism.* Rochester, VT: Inner Traditions International, 1991.

Daniélou, Jean, S.J. *The Bible and the Liturgy.* Ann Arbor, MI: Servant Books, 1956.

Donovan, Vincent J. *Christianity Rediscovered.* Maryknoll, NY: Orbis Books, 1982.

Doty, William G. *Mythography: The Study of Myths and Rituals.* Tuscaloosa: University of Alabama Press, 1986.

Douglas-Klotz, Neil. *Prayers of the Cosmos: Meditations on the Aramaic Words of Jesus.* San Francisco: HarperSanFrancisco, 1990.

———. *The Hidden Gospel: Decoding the Spiritual Message of the Aramaic Jesus.* Wheaton, IL: Quest Books, 1999.

Driver, Tom F. *Liberating Rites: Understanding the Transformative Power of Ritual.* Boulder, CO: Westview, 1998.

Duggan, Robert, ed. *Conversion and the Catechumenate.* New York: Paulist, 1984.

Dujarier, Michel. *A History of the Catechumenate: The First Six Centuries.* New York: William H. Sadlier, 1979.

———. *The Rites of Christian Initiation: Historical and Pastoral Reflections.* New York: William H. Sadlier, 1979.

Dunne, John S. *The Way of All the Earth: Experiments in Truth and Religion.* New York: Macmillan, 1972.

———. *Time and Myth: Meditations on Storytelling as an Exploration of Life and Death.* New York: Doubleday, 1973.

———. *A Search for God in Time and Memory.* Notre Dame, IN: University of Notre Dame Press, 1977.

———. *The Reasons of the Heart: A Journey into Solitude and Back Again into the Human Circle.* New York: Macmillan, 1978.

Edinger, Edward F. *The Bible and the Psyche: Individuation Symbolism in the Old Testament.* Toronto: Inner City Books, 1986.

———. *The Christian Archetype: A Jungian Commentary on the Life of Christ.* Toronto: Inner City Books, 1987.

———. *Archetype of the Apocalypse: A Jungian Study of the Book of Revelation.* Peru, IL: Open Court, 1999.

Ehrenreich, Barbara. *Blood Rites: Origins and History of the Passions of War.* New York: Henry Holt, 1997.

Ehrman, Bart D. *Misquoting Jesus.* San Francisco: HarperSanFrancisco, 2005.

———. *Jesus Interrupted.* San Francisco: HarperOne, 2009.

Eliade, Mircea. *Rites and Symbols of Initiation: The Mysteries of Birth and Rebirth.* New York: Harper & Row, 1958.

Eliot, T. S. *Four Quartets.* New York: Harvest Books, 1968.

Ephrem the Syrian. *Hymns.* Translated by Kathleen E. McVey. New York: Paulist, 1989.

Estés, Clara Pinkola. *Women Who Run with the Wolves.* New York: Ballantine Books, 1996.

Eusebius. *Ecclesiastical History.* Books I–V and 6–10; vols. 153 and 265 in Loeb Classical Library. Cambridge, MA: Harvard University Press, 1926.

Fischer, Norman. *Opening to You: Zen-Inspired Translations of the Psalms.* New York: Viking, 2002.

Fowler, James W. *Stages of Faith: The Psychology of Human Development and the Quest for Meaning.* San Francisco: Harper & Row, 1981.

Fox, Matthew. *Breakthrough: Meister Eckhart's Creation Spirituality in New Translation.* New York: Image Books, 1980.

———. *Original Blessing: A Primer in Creation Spirituality.* Santa Fe, NM: Bear & Company, 1983.

Francis, St., and St. Clare. *The Complete Works.* Translated by Regis J. Armstrong and Ignatius C. Brady. New York: Paulist, 1982.

Frost, Seena B. *SoulCollage: An Intuitive Collage Process for Individuals and Groups.* Santa Cruz, CA: Hanford Mead, 2001.

Gallagher, Nora. *Things Seen and Unseen: A Year Lived in Faith.* New York: Alfred A. Knopf, 1998.

———. *Practicing Resurrection: A Memoir of Work, Doubt, Discernment, and Moments of Grace.* New York: Alfred A. Knopf, 2003.

Galland, China. *Longing for Darkness: Tara and the Black Madonna.* New York: Penguin Compass, 1990.

Gendler, J. Ruth. *Changing Light: The Eternal Cycle of Night and Day.* New York: Perennial, 1993.

Gold, Peter. *Navajo and Tibetan Sacred Wisdom: The Circle of the Spirit.* Rochester, VT: Inner Traditions, 1994.

Gregory of Nyssa. *The Life of Moses.* Translated by Everett Ferguson and Abraham J. Malerbe. New York: Paulist, 1978.

Griffith-Jones, Robin. *The Four Witnesses: The Rebel, The Rabbi, The Chronicler, and The Mystic.* San Francisco: HarperSanFrancisco, 2000.

Grimes, Ronald L. *Deeply into the Bone: Re-Inventing Rites of Passage.* Berkeley: University of California Press, 2000.

Groves, Richard F., and Henriette Anne Klauser. *The American Book of Dying: Lessons in Healing Spiritual Pain.* Berkeley: Ten Speed, 2005.

Halifax, Joan. *The Fruitful Darkness: Reconnecting with the Body of the Earth.* New York: HarperCollins, 1994.

Hall, Thelma. *Too Deep for Words: Rediscovering Lectio Divina.* New York: Paulist, 1988.

Harris, Bud. *The Father Quest: Rediscovering an Elemental Psychic Force.* Alexander, NC: Alexander Books, 1996.

Harris, Massimilla, and Bud Harris. *Like Gold through Fire: Understanding the Transforming Power of Suffering.* Alexander, NC: Alexander Books, 1996.

Henderson, Joseph L. *Thresholds of Initiation.* Middleton, CT: Wesleyan University Press, 1967.

Hernandez, Ana. *The Sacred Art of Chant: Preparing to Practice.* Woodstock, VT: Skylight Paths, 2004.

Hildegarde of Bingen. *Hildegarde of Bingen's Book of Divine Works.* Santa Fe, NM: Bear & Company, 1987.

Housden, Roger. *Ten Poems to Set You Free.* New York: Harmony Books, 2003.

http://www.blueletterbible.org lexicon/concordance KJV translation/concordance.

http://www.perseus.tufts.edu/ Greek language references and translation, Tufts University, Boston, MA.

Ibn ʿAbbād of Ronda. *Letters on the Sufi Path.* Translated by John Renard. New York: Paulist, 1986.

Ibn Al'Arabi. *The Bezels of Wisdom.* Translated by R.W.J. Austin. New York: Paulist, 1980.

Ignatius, St. *The Spiritual Exercises of St. Ignatius of Loyola.* Whitefish, MT: Kessinger, 2007.

Irenaeus of Lyons, St. *Against Heresies.* Whitefish, MT: Kessinger, 2004.

Jaskolski, Helmut. *The Labyrinth: Symbol of Fear, Rebirth, and Liberation.* Boston: Shambhala, 1997.

John of the Cross. *Dark Night of the Soul.* Translated by Mirabai Starr. New York: Riverhead Books, 2002.

Johnson, Maxwell E. *The Rites of Christian Initiation: Their Evolution and Interpretation.* Collegeville, MN: Liturgical, 1999.

Johnson, Robert A. *Owning Your Own Shadow: Understanding the Dark Side of the Psyche.* San Francisco: HarperSanFrancisco, 1991.

——. *Balancing Heaven and Earth.* San Francisco: HarperSanFrancisco, 1998.

Jones, Alan. *Soul Making: The Desert Way of Spirituality.* London: SCM, 1986.

——. *Reimagining Christianity: Reconnect Your Spirit without Disconnecting Your Mind.* Hoboken, NJ: Wiley, 2005.

Julian of Norwich. *Revelations of Divine Love.* St. Meinrad, IN: Abbey, 1975.

Jung, C. G. *Symbols of Transformation: An Analysis of the Prelude to a Case of Schizophrenia.* Vol. 5 in *Collected Works.* Princeton, NJ: Princeton University Press, 1956.

——. *Memories, Dreams, Reflections.* New York: Vintage Books, 1963.

——. *Alchemical Studies.* Vol. 13 in *Collected Works.* Princeton, NJ: Princeton University Press, 1967.

——. *Psychology and Alchemy.* Vol. 12 in *Collected Works.* Princeton, NJ: Princeton University Press, 1968.

——. *The Symbolic Life: Miscellaneous Writings.* Vol. 18 in *Collected Works.* Princeton, NJ: Princeton University Press, 1989.

Kalff, Dora M. *Sandplay: A Psychotherapeutic Approach to the Psyche.* Santa Monica, CA: Sigo, 1980.

Kalsched, Donald. *The Inner World of Trauma: Archetypal Defenses of the Personal Spirit.* New York: Routledge, 1996.

Kavanagh, Aidan. *The Shape of Baptism: The Rite of Christian Initiation.* New York: Pueblo, 1978.

———. *On Liturgical Theology.* Collegeville, MN: Liturgical, 1981.

Kawai, Hayao. *Buddhism and the Art of Psychotherapy.* College Station, TX: Texas A&M University Press, 1996.

Keating, Thomas. *Intimacy with God: An Introduction to Centering Prayer.* New York: Crossroad, 1994.

———. *The Human Condition.* New York: Paulist, 1999.

———. *Open Mind, Open Heart: The Contemplative Dimension of the Gospel.* New York: Continuum, 2006.

Kelly, Henry Ansgar. *The Devil at Baptism: Ritual, Theology and Drama.* Ithaca, NY: Cornell University Press, 1985.

Kelsey, Morton T. *Encounter with God.* Minneapolis, MN: Bethany Fellowship, 1972.

———. *The Other Side of Silence: A Guide to Christian Meditation.* New York: Paulist, 1976.

———. *Christo-Psychology.* New York: Crossroad, 1982.

———. *Companions on the Inner Way: The Art of Spiritual Guidance.* New York: Crossroad, 1983.

Kornfield, Jack. *A Path with Heart: A Guide through the Perils and Promises of Spiritual Life.* New York: Bantam Books, 1993.

Lamott, Anne. *Bird by Bird: Some Instructions on Writing and Life.* New York: Anchor Books, 1995.

Lane, Belden C. *The Solace of Fierce Landscapes: Exploring Desert and Mountain Spirituality.* New York: Oxford University Press, 1998.

Levine, Peter A. *Waking the Tiger: Healing Trauma—The Innate Capacity to Transform Overwhelming Experiences.* Berkeley, CA: North Atlantic Books, 1997.

Lew, Alan. *This Is Real and You Are Completely Unprepared: The Days of Awe as a Journey of Transformation.* New York: Little, Brown, 2003.

Luke, Helen M. *Dark Wood to White Rose: Journey and Transformation in Dante's Divine Comedy.* New York: Parabola Books, 1989.

Mahdi, Louise, Steven Foster Carus, and Meredith Little, eds. *Betwixt and Between: Patterns of Masculine and Feminine Initiation.* La Salle, IL: Open Court, 1987.

McCann, I. Lisa, and Laurie Anne Pearlman. *Psychological Trauma and the Adult Survivor: Theory, Therapy and Transformation.* New York: Brunner/Mazel, 1990.

McLaren, Brian D. *Finding Our Way Again: The Return of the Ancient Practices.* Nashville, TN: Thomas Nelson, 2008.

————. *The Secret Message of Jesus: Uncovering the Truth That Could Change Everything.* Nashville, TN: Thomas Nelson, 2006.

Meador, Betty DeShong. *Uncursing the Dark: Treasures from the Underworld.* Wilmette, IL: Chiron, 1992.

Merrill, Nan C. *Psalms for Praying: An Invitation to Wholeness.* New York: Continuum, 2007.

Merton, Thomas. *Seven Storey Mountain.* Ft. Washington, PA: Harvest Books, [1948] 1999.

————. *No Man Is an Island.* New York: Harcourt, Brace, 1955.

————. *The Hidden Ground of Love: The Letters of Thomas Merton on Religious Experience And Social Concerns.* New York: Farrar, Straus and Giroux, 1985.

Moore, Robert, and Douglas Gillette. *King Warrior Magician Lover: Rediscovering the Archetypes of the Mature Masculine.* San Francisco: HarperSanFrancisco, 1990.

Moore, Thomas. *Original Self: Living with Paradox and Originality.* New York: Harper Perennial, 2001.

Murphy Center for Liturgical Research. *Made, Not Born: New Perspectives on Christian Initiation and the Catechumenate.* Notre Dame, IN: University of Notre Dame Press, 1976.

Neville, Gwen Kennedy, and John H. Westerhoff III. *Learning through Liturgy.* New York: Seabury, 1978

Nouwen, Henri J. M. *Reaching Out: The Three Movements of the Spiritual Life.* New York: Doubleday, 1975.

————. *The Inner Voice of Love: A Journey through Anguish to Freedom.* New York: Image Books, 1999.

O'Donohue, John. *Beauty: The Invisible Embrace.* New York: Harper Perennial, 2005.

Olivera, Bernardo. *How Far to Follow? The Martyrs of Atlas.* Petersham, MA: St. Bede's Publications, 1997.

Origen. *On First Principles.* Book IV, translated by Rowan A. Greer. New York: Paulist, 1979.

Osborn, Eric. *Irenaeus of Lyons.* New York: Cambridge University Press, 2005.

Pagels, Elaine. *Beyond Belief: The Secret Gospel of Thomas*. New York: Vintage Books, 2003.

Palmer, Parker J. *The Courage to Teach: Exploring the Inner Landscape of a Teacher's Life*. San Francisco: Jossey-Bass, 1998.

Peat, David F. *The Blackwinged Night: Creativity in Nature and Mind*. Cambridge, MA: Perseus, 2000.

Peck, M. Scott. *The Road Less Traveled: A New Psychology of Love, Traditional Values and Spiritual Growth*. New York: Simon & Schuster, 1978.

———. *The Different Drum: Community Making and Peace*. New York: Simon & Schuster, 1987.

Pennington, Basil M. *Lectio Divina: Renewing the Ancient Practice of Praying the Scriptures*. New York: Crossroad, 1998.

Perera, Sylvia Brinton. *Descent to the Goddess: A Way of Initiation for Women*. Toronto: Inner City Books, 1981.

Perry, John Weir. *Lord of the Four Quarters: The Mythology of Kingship*. New York: Paulist, 1991.

Pfatteicher, Philip H. *Liturgical Spirituality*. Valley Forge, PA: Trinity, 1997.

Pope Benedict XVI. *Jesus of Nazareth: From the Baptism in the Jordan to the Transfiguration*. Translated by Adrian J. Walker. New York: Doubleday, 2007.

Pope John XXIII. *Journal of a Soul*. Translated by Dorothy White. New York: McGraw-Hill, 1965.

Richardson, Jan L. *Night Vision: Searching the Shadows of Advent and Christmas*. Cleveland, OH: Pilgrim, 1998.

———. *In Wisdom's Path: Discovering the Sacred in Every Season*. Cleveland, OH: Pilgrim, 2000.

Rohr, Richard. *Quest for the Grail*. New York: Crossroad, 1997.

———. *Everything Belongs: The Gift of Contemplative Prayer*. Chestnut Ridge, NY: Crossroad, 2003.

Rosen, David H. *Transforming Depression: Healing the Soul Through Creativity*. New York: Penguin, 1993.

Rumi, Jalal al-Din. *The Soul of Rumi: A New Collection of Ecstatic Poems*. Translated by Coleman Barks. San Francisco: HarperSanFrancisco, 2001.

Safed Spirituality: Rules of Mystical Piety and the Beginning of Wisdom. Translated by Lawrence Fine. New York: Paulist, 1984.

Sandner, Donald. *Navaho Symbols of Healing.* New York: Harvest Books, 1979.

Sanford, John A. *The Kingdom Within: A Study of the Inner Meaning of Jesus' Sayings.* New York: Lippincott, 1970.

———. *Mystical Christianity: A Psychological Commentary on the Gospel of John.* New York: Crossroad, 1993.

Schachter-Shalomi, Zalman. *Paradigm Shift: From the Jewish Renewal Teachings of Reb Zalman Schachter-Shalomi.* Northvale, NJ: Jason Aronson, 1993.

Schmemann, Alexander. *Great Lent: Journey to Pascha.* Crestwood, NY: St. Vladimir's Seminary Press, 1969.

———. *Of Water and the Spirit.* Crestwood, NY: St. Vladimir's Seminary Press, 1974.

Searle, Mark. *Christening: The Making of Christians.* Collegeville, MN: Liturgical, 1980.

———, ed. *Sunday Morning: A Time for Worship.* Collegeville, MN: Liturgical, 1982.

Shaia, Alexander J. "Sandplay and Spirit." *Presence* (June 2002). Available on the quadratos Web site: www.quadratos.com.

Shea, John. *Stories of God: An Unauthorized Biography.* Chicago: Thomas More, 1978.

Singh, Kathleen Dowling. *The Grace in Dying: How We Are Transformed Spiritually As We Die.* San Francisco: HarperSanFrancisco, 1998.

Somé, Malidoma Patrice. *Ritual: Power, Healing and Community.* Portland, OR: Swan/Raven, 1993.

Spong, John Shelby. *Liberating the Gospels: Reading the Bible with Jewish Eyes.* San Francisco: HarperSanFrancisco, 1996.

Stein, Murray. *Transformation: Emergence of the Self.* College Station, TX: Texas A&M University Press, 1998.

Storm, Hyemeyohsts. *Song of Heyoehkah.* San Francisco: Harper & Row, 1981.

Swimme, Brian, and Thomas Berry. *The Universe Story: From the Primordial Flaring Forth to the Ecozoic Era: A Celebration of the Unfolding of the Cosmos.* San Francisco: HarperSanFrancisco, 1992.

Swimme, Brian. *The Hidden Heart of the Cosmos: Humanity and the New Story.* Maryknoll, NY: Orbis Books, 1999.

Symposium on Christian Initiation. *Becoming a Catholic Christian*. New York: William H. Sadlier, 1978.

Talley, Thomas J. *The Origins of the Liturgical Year*. Collegeville, MN: Liturgical, 1991.

Teilhard de Chardin, Pierre. *Hymn of the Universe*. New York: Harper Perennial, 1972.

Teresa of Avila. *The Interior Castle*. Translated by Mirabai Starr. New York: Riverhead Books, 2003.

Tickle, Phyllis. *The Great Emergence: How Christianity Is Changing and Why*. Grand Rapids, MI: Baker Books, 2008.

Turner, Victor. *The Ritual Process: Structure and Anti-Structure*. Ithaca, NY: Cornell University Press, 1969.

Twenty-Four Hours a Day. Center City, MN: Hazelden, nd.

Ulman, Richard B., and Doris Brothers. *The Shattered Self: A Psychoanalytic Study of Trauma*. Hillsdale, NJ: Analytic, 1988.

van der Kolk, Bessel A. *Psychological Trauma*. Washington, DC: American Psychiatric Press, 1987.

van Gennep, Arnold. *The Rites of Passage*. Chicago: University of Chicago Press, 1960.

Warren, Rick. *The Purpose Driven Life*. Grand Rapids, MI: Zondervan, 2002.

Weinrib, Estelle L. *Images of the Self: The Sandplay Therapy Process*. Boston: Sigo, 1983.

West, Fritz. *Scripture and Memory: The Ecumenical Hermeneutic of the Three-Year Lectionaries*. Collegeville, MN: Liturgical, 1997.

West, Geoffrey B. "The Scale of the Tree of Life from Molecules and Cells to Whales and Ecosystems." Stanley Ulam Memorial Lectures, Santa Fe Institute, Santa Fe, NM, 2001.

West, Geoffrey B., and James H. Brown. "Life's Universal Scaling Laws." *Physics Today*. September 2004.

Whitaker, E. C. *Documents of the Baptismal Liturgy*. London: Hollen Street, 1970.

Whiting, Lindsay. *Living into Art: Journeys through Collage*. Montclair, NJ: Paper Lantern, 2008.

Whyte, David. *River Flow: New and Selected Poems.* Langley, WA: Many Rivers, 2007.

Williamson, John. *The Oak King, the Holy King, and the Unicorn: The Myths and Symbolism of the Unicorn Tapestries.* New York: Harper & Row, 1986.

Wills, Garry. *What Jesus Meant.* New York: Viking, 2006.

Wirth, Steven. *The Path of Contemplative Dialogue: Engaging the Collective Spirit.* Open Source, www.contemplativedialogue.org.

Wuthnow, Robert. *Creative Spirituality: The Way of the Artist.* Berkeley: University of California Press, 2001.

Yarnold, Edward. *The Awe Inspiring Rites of Initiation: Baptismal Homilies of the Fourth Century.* Slough, UK: St. Paul Publications, 1972.

Zoja, Luigi. *Drugs, Addiction and Initiation: The Modern Search for Ritual.* Boston: Sigo, 1989.

Zolbrod, Paul G. *Diné Bahané: The Navajo Creation Story.* Albuquerque: University of New Mexico Press, 1984.